THE WTO AND GLOBAL CONVERGENCE IN TELECOMMUNICATIONS AND AUDIO-VISUAL SERVICES

This edited collection consolidates research on the current and future perspectives of international trade law applicable to telecommunications services and audio-visual services in a context of convergence. It is divided into three main parts. The first part analyses the current regulatory framework applicable to telecommunications services in the context of the WTO, including the controversial issues of accounting rates and international competition rules. The second part discusses and analyses the current regulatory framework applicable to audio-visual services. Particular focus is given to the impact of content regulation and network convergence on international trade rules. The status of negotiations on safeguards, subsidies and public procurement is also discussed. The final part analyses convergence from different angles. One chapter explains what convergence means in technical terms. Other contributors review the legal and economic consequences of convergence for trade in telecommunications and audio-visual services. This research leads the editors to summarize the findings made in the chapters and to draw up a tentative set of issues to be discussed in the context of the Doha Round of negotiations.

DAMIEN GERADIN is a Professor of Law and Director of the Institute for European Legal Studies at the University of Liège, and a Professor and Director of the Global Competition Law Centre of the College of Europe, Bruges. He is the author of numerous publications in the area of competition, telecommunications and trade law. He is the co-editor-in-chief of the *Journal of Network Industries.*

DAVID LUFF is a partner in a Brussels law firm and a researcher and assistant professor at the Universities of Liège and Brussels. He has specialized in WTO law and has been practising international trade law at both EC and WTO levels for more than ten years.

THE WTO AND GLOBAL CONVERGENCE IN TELECOMMUNICATIONS AND AUDIO-VISUAL SERVICES

edited by

DAMIEN GERADIN

and

DAVID LUFF

CAMBRIDGE
UNIVERSITY PRESS

PUBLISHED BY THE PRESS SYNDICATE OF THE UNIVERSITY OF CAMBRIDGE
The Pitt Building, Trumpington Street, Cambridge, United Kingdom

CAMBRIDGE UNIVERSITY PRESS
The Edinburgh Building, Cambridge, CB2 2RU, UK
40 West 20th Street, New York, NY 10011–4211, USA
477 Williamstown Road, Port Melbourne, VIC 3207, Australia
Ruiz de Alarcón 13, 28014 Madrid, Spain
Dock House, The Waterfront, Cape Town 8001, South Africa

http://www.cambridge.org

First published 2004

Printed in the United Kingdom at the University Press, Cambridge

Typeface Minion 10.75/12.75 pt. *System* LaTeX 2ε [TB]

A catalogue record for this book is available from the British Library

Library of Congress Cataloguing in Publication data
International Conference 'Telecommunications and Audio-Visual Services in the Context of the WTO: Today and Tomorrow' (2001 : Geneva, Switzerland)
The WTO and global convergence in telecommunications and audio-visual services / edited by Damien Geradin, David Luff.
p. cm.
Consists of papers presented at the International Conference entitled 'Telecommunications and Audio-Visual Services in the Context of the WTO: Today and Tomorrow', held in Geneva in November 2001.
Includes bibliographical references and index.
ISBN 0 521 83611 5 (hardbound)
1. Telecommunication – Law and legislation – Congresses. 2. Data transmission systems – Law and legislation. 3. World Trade Organization – Congresses. I. Geradin, Damien, II. Luff, David, 1968– III. Title.
K4304.8.I58 2004
343.09′94 – dc22 2003060537

ISBN 0 521 83611 5 hardback

CONTENTS

PART III International regulation of audio-visual services

PART IV Towards convergence?

CONTRIBUTORS

Jean-François Bellis, Senior Partner, Van Bael & Bellis, Brussels, and Professor of Competition Law, University of Brussels

Ivan Bernier, Professor of Law, University of Laval

Kelly Cameron, Partner, Powell Goldstein Frazer and Murphy, Washington, DC

Peter Cowhey, Dean, Graduate School of International Relations and Pacific, Studies, and Director, Institute on Global Conflict and Cooperation, University of California, San Diego

Robert Frieden, Professor of Telecommunications, College of Telecommunications, Penn State University

Damien Geradin, Professor of Law and Director, Institute for European Legal Studies, University of Liège and Professor of Law, College of Europe, Bruges

Christoph Beat Graber, Professor of International Communications and Art Law, University of Lucerne

Boutheina Guermazi, PhD candidate, McGill University

Michel Kerf, Policy Infrastructure Advisor, East Asia, World Bank

Pierre Larouche, Professor of Competition Law, Tilburg University, and Director, Tilburg Law and Economics Centre (TILEC), Tilburg University

David Luff, Partner, O'Connor & Company, European lawyers, Brussels, and Assistant Professor at the University of Brussels

Milton Mueller, Associate Professor, School of Information Studies, Syracuse University

Paul Nihoul, Professor of Law, Catholic University of Louvain

Eli Noam, Professor of Finance and Economics, Columbia Business School, and Director, Columbia University Center for Tele-Information

FOREWORD

The very recent dispute between Mexico and the United States concerning access pricing in telecoms by the former was, for most trade insiders, another dispute in the ever growing WTO docket. A deconstruction of this mundane phrase, however, should help raise a few eyebrows: telecoms, access pricing, compulsory third (WTO) party adjudication. Surely all of this seemed to be a distant future in the aftermath of the Tokyo Round. So what happened these last twenty-five years?

Essentially, domestic policies became more and more rational under the influence of exogenous parameters (technology) which greatly helped mobility of production factors around the world to reach unprecedented levels. Rationalisation of domestic policies meant, *inter alia*, rethinking the extent of the state along more or less economics-friendly lines.

Now, it is true that rationalisation did not occur everywhere and, even where it did, it evidenced different speeds. Regulatory diversity continues to be very much the case in most state expressions of societal-revealed preferences. This observation notwithstanding, however, it is this process of rationalisation that made it possible to discuss within and across national borders issues which remained 'untouchables' over the years.

Telecoms is one of the areas where the prevailing orthodoxy (general service means only state carriers can undertake such operations, natural monopoly, etc.) was put emphatically into question. Some states started a de-monopolisation process which, although looked at with suspicion by less than innocent bystanders, found imitators around the globe in record time.

There was, it is true, a growing discomfort with the fact that, in many democracies (there is not much room for public discomfort in non-democracies), monopolies like telecoms were often used as outlets for dumping unemployed people. Beneficiaries would return the favour by voting for those who placed them in the job market. The result was ever growing phone bills since at the end of the day someone had to pay for those initiatives.

Traditional tools, like price caps, were used in an effort to calm down consumers. Occasionally, as the British experience shows, they worked, in the sense that price caps led to rationalisation of the administration of operations by the state telecoms actor. Unfortunately, there is not much empirical evidence that this is a safe way to go.

Hence, sooner or later, something more dramatic was about to happen. The break-up of AT&T in 1982 and the emergence of the 'baby bells' dropped the cost of phone calls drastically in the US and sensitised policy-makers about the merits of competition. The positive externalities of the AT&T break-up has been, first, the acknowledgment that we can live in a world where more than one carrier will compete in the telecoms market, and, secondly, the effective implementation, in other parts of the world, of policies designed to do away with monopolies in the telecoms market.

It was only a matter of time before the trade authorities would be brought to the table of international negotiations: de-monopolisation (privatisation) of telecoms services was soon followed by a discussion on liberalisation (and, sometimes, liberalisation was used as the tool to incite de-monopolisation). This is what happened in the Uruguay Round. The resulting agreement is the first multilateral effort to liberalise trade in telecoms.

The Telecoms Agreement and its Annexes are an incomplete contract: subsequent case law is necessary to shed light on notions like 'reasonable interconnection rates'. It is this angle of the Agreement that has managed to attract most of the criticism, at least in the literature. There are other angles as well: for example, eventually, that is when more and more states join the current sixty-nine signatories of the Agreement and more 'daring' liberalisation commitments have been made, negotiators will inevitably have to discuss to what extent the Agreement, as we now know it, can happily live and produce the expected results within the current context of regulatory diversity in the field of competition law. This is not an issue for tomorrow, but is an issue which will become more and more relevant as liberalisation progresses. And the list of questions can go and on.

The discussion on audio-visual services has followed a different trend so far. At the domestic level, one can witness a series of initiatives aiming to undo the state monopoly on broadcasting services. There is still some debate as to the wisdom of such approaches: for example, competition authorities are struggling with the idea of the quality of intervention in the audio-visual market (the term as such not being acceptable to all) and the ensuing issues of imposing some harmonised content on private carriers;

information can be a positive or a negative externality in itself and there is still an often-voiced anxiety in trusting it outside 'official' channels.

Then there is the international trade angle of the issue: should we treat audio-visual products like any other product? Should we treat them as services? There are widespread differences among the various actors in the international scene as to the approach to be taken on this issue. Proponents of the 'cultural exception' point to the uniqueness of audio-visual services as 'carriers' of civilisation and national tradition. On the other side, there are those who believe that nothing in principle distinguishes such products (services) from other products and that, for democratic reasons as well, the public should be offered the widest possible choice. This debate is still very much alive: as a consequence, there is no progress when it comes to liberalising services. But the item is very much on the WTO agenda and hence the interest in discussing it.

In this remarkable book, the editors (Damien Geradin and David Luff) achieve two targets: they provide us with an excellent discussion of the Telecoms Agreement and a clarification of the issues blocking progress in the context of trade in audio-visual services; and they sensitise us to what we should expect in this field in the years to come. Choosing a star selection of authors, of course, greatly helped their endeavour. But the editors should be credited with this achievement as well.

The discussion on the Telecoms Agreement is far from being a mere analysis of the most relevant provisions. It is placed in the wider policy context and it thus brings to the reader information valuable in understanding what was really at stake when negotiating and concluding the Agreement. At the same time, all technical aspects of the Agreement are presented in a series of careful and detailed contributions.

This book is one of the many that focus on this subject-matter. It is, though, probably the first that discusses from an authentically interdisciplinary angle one of the most important achievements of the Uruguay Round. And, as I mentioned above, the book, because of the quality of the contributions, is also an inventory of future issues.

I have left for last what I consider to be the most important achievement of the editors: they manage to make a coherent 'whole' out of a series of individual 'parts'. The reader, having finished the book, will be left with the impression that he or she has read one piece on the present and the future of the Telecoms Agreement.

On the other hand, the editors and the contributors managed to provide us with a very comprehensive inventory of the preliminary questions that need to be addressed in order for progress in the field of audio-visual services to occur: from purely technical issues, such as the question of whether such services should be covered by the GATT or the GATS (a question the resolution of which has not been helped by the WTO jurisprudence so far), to more 'loaded' concerns such as the uniqueness of this particular field. This is the first book that examines together the two issues and the ensuing interplay between them.

The inescapable compromise between the legitimate optimism derived from the fact that we now have a Telecoms Agreement and a series of holes and loopholes in the Agreement constitutes the appropriate recipe to distinguish between optimists and pessimists. Works like this one will help us avoid the mistakes of the past and move into the future armed with knowledge. On the other hand, trade practitioners and negotiators will greatly benefit from the groundwork done here on audio-visual services: this book explains in very detailed terms the current disagreements and provides thoughtful ideas as to what should be done for progress to be achieved.

Petros C. Mavroidis
University of Columbia Law School and
University of Neuchâtel (CEPR)

ACKNOWLEDGMENTS

This book constitutes the final outcome of a research project undertaken at the Institute of European Studies of the University of Liège with the financial support of the Interuniversity Poles of Attraction Programme P4/04, Belgian State, Prime Minister's Office, Federal Office for Scientific, Technical and Cultural Affairs.

This financing enabled the organisation of an international conference entitled 'Telecommunications and Audio-visual Services in the Context of the WTO: Today and Tomorrow', held on the premises of the World Trade Organization in November 2001. We would like to thank here all speakers and panels' chairs for their active participation. Clearly, their presence, the quality of their presentations and their questions were key to the success of the event and constituted an invaluable input in the ensuing written contributions. In particular, we would like to mention here H. E. Sergio Marchi, Professor Paul Demaret, Andy Stoler, Roberto Blois, Michael A. Wagner, Lee Tuthill, Marco Bronckers, Sergio Dos Santos, Tilman Kupfer and all the contributors to this book.

The conference would not have been possible without the additional support of the World Trade Organization which offered its infrastructure to accommodate the conference in Geneva. We are particularly thankful to Patrick Low and Hamid Mamdouh. Logistic support and essential help was also provided by Jolita Butkevicienne, Claudia Locatelli, Lora Borissova, Mercedes Candela and Dominique Coquelet who find here the expression of our gratitude.

Finally, concerning the book itself, we would like to thank Petros Mavroidis for his foreword, as well as the authors of the various chapters of the book for their outstanding contributions and for their patience: Kelly Cameron, Peter Cowhey, Boutheina Guermazi, Michel Kerf, Christoph Beat Graber, Ivan Bernier, Eli Noam, Milton L. Mueller, Jean-François Bellis, Robert Frieden, Paul Nihoul and Pierre Larouche. Ellen Bradford also deserves here to be congratulated for her work.

Clearly, research like this, in a field which is by nature multidisciplinary, and which promotes speedy adaptation of the law to technical and societal evolution, is most successful when handled internationally and collectively.

Damien Geradin and David Luff
October 2003

PART I

Introduction

1

Introduction

DAMIEN GERADIN AND DAVID LUFF

The broad picture

The subject of this edited book is the interface between four major trends in the global economy, which have become apparent during the last two decades.

The first of these trends is the large expansion in trade between nations. International trade has been growing since the adoption of the GATT in 1947, but it has significantly accelerated over the last two decades. During the period 1980–2000, global trade grew very significantly. In addition, a number of new nations (e.g. China) have joined the WTO in recent years, thereby expanding the scope of application of WTO trade rules. It is widely believed today that participation in international trade is a key factor in economic development, and that increased global trade contributes to the prosperity of nations.

The second of these trends is the revolution that took place in the telecommunications sector. The first aspect of this revolution relates to market-opening reforms. For much of the twentieth century, telecommunications were organised in many countries around a monopolistic operator. The performance of these operators proved, however, to be disappointing and, in the 1980s, some countries decided to liberalise their telecommunications sector. These countries believed that competition in telecommunications would provide for lower prices, greater innovation, and a greater degree of consumer satisfaction. Such reforms have now extended to a large number of countries. While less than twenty countries had opened the provision of any fixed basic telecommunications services by the mid-1990s, 40 per cent of all countries had done so by the year 2000, including about seventy countries which have allowed competition in basic local services. In addition, a very large number of countries – 80 per cent or more – have allowed competition in the provision of wireless and Internet services.

The second aspect of this revolution relates to technological progress. Until recently, much of the telecommunications traffic was dominated by voice telephony. Technological evolution has, however, stimulated the development of new services, such as wireless telephony and the Internet. In many countries, wireless telephony is now more significant in terms of traffic than wireline telephony and it has become the primary means of communication among individuals. Over the last decade, the growth of the Internet has also been astonishing. It is, for instance, estimated that in 2002 the United States had 186 million Internet users, while the global Internet population amounted to 550 million. The large number of Internet users has stimulated the development of an increasingly large number of applications, which have in turn stimulated the demand for broadband.

The combination of these first two trends was reflected in the adoption of the WTO Agreement on Basic Telecommunications Services. This Agreement is of considerable significance since its sixty-nine contracting parties represent over 90 per cent of the world's basic telecommunications revenues. While several parties had already liberalised their telecommunications market before the adoption of this agreement, there is little doubt that it triggered significant market-opening reforms in many other nations. It is expected that the new Doha Round will seek to push liberalisation further by encouraging Members that are already part of the Agreement on Basic Telecommunications to make further commitments, as well as by inducing Members that are not party to the Agreement to join it and commit themselves to telecommunications liberalisation.

The third trend is the growing tensions between WTO Members in the area of audio-visual services. Unlike in the telecommunications sector, little progress has been made in this area in the context of the WTO. A number of WTO Members have engaged in domestic market-opening reforms in audio-visual services, for instance by allowing the development of new commercial TV channels. The broad wave of reforms that has been witnessed in the area of telecommunications finds, however, no equivalent in audio-visual services as many Members continue to maintain measures designed to protect public broadcasters, as well as locally produced content. In recent years, these measures have led to growing conflicts between Members, such as the United States, which consider that audio-visual products do not differ from other goods and services and should therefore be subject to market access, and other Members, such as the European Union, which argue in favour of a cultural exception. In this context, one of the central objectives of the Doha negotiations will be to find a common ground between these two positions so as to allow a greater degree of market opening in the sector of audio-visual services while allowing certain Members to ensure the protection of cultural diversity within their frontiers.

The fourth and final trend discussed in this book relates to the process of convergence between the telecommunications and audio-visual sectors. Although these two sectors have generally been treated as separate industries subject to different legal regimes, they increasingly converge into a single communications sector. Convergence first takes place at the network level as, thanks to digitalisation, both telecommunications and cable networks are no longer dedicated to one type of service. Convergence also takes place at the service level as new 'hybrid' services, such as video-on-demand, are placed on the market. Finally, convergence has also a business component as telecommunications companies have entered the audio-visual market, whereas audio-visual companies are now active in the telecommunications market. As will be seen throughout this book, convergence will have significant regulatory implications as current classifications are becoming rapidly outdated and lead to distortions.

Summary of the content of the book

The chapters comprised in this book are grouped into four Parts: Part I (this Introduction) and Parts II, III and IV (the substantive chapters).

Part II analyses the current regulatory framework applicable to telecommunications services in the context of the WTO. The first two chapters of Part II provide a general discussion of the WTO Basic Telecommunications Agreement, as well as other WTO agreements that may be relevant to the telecommunications sector. Chapter 2, by Kelly Cameron, provides an historical overview of the WTO Basic Telecommunications Agreement. The author explains why the negotiations of this Agreement took several years. Contentious issues included foreign investments in telecommunications, licensing and the use of electromagnetic spectrum, and international services. The author also explains why the negotiations of an agreement on audio-visual services in the context of the Doha Round are likely to be difficult. He analyses, however, some factors that could make the achievement of an agreement for market access for audio-visual services possible. Chapter 3, by David Luff, provides a broad discussion of current rules concerning telecommunications services. This includes an explanation of the structure of the GATS, the Annex on Telecommunications and the Reference Paper. Many references are made to these texts in the subsequent chapters of the book and, without these clarifications, the book may be incomprehensible to those who are not tuned into WTO law.

The next two chapters address one of the most complex issues of international trade in telecommunications services: the issue of accounting rates (i.e. the price for interconnecting calls between countries). In Chapter 4, Peter Cowhey argues that accounting rates create considerable distortions in the market for international telephone services. Despite such distortions, the WTO Basic Agreement on Telecommunications does not require changes to the accounting rates system. In response, the United States took a unilateral regulatory action outside the WTO to cut inflated international accounting rates. In addition, market access commitments made in the context of the WTO Basic Agreement on Telecommunications over international simple resale put additional pressure on international accounting rates. These factors led to a reduction of accounting rates among industrialised countries. The author then analyses the trade issues posed by new services and technologies, such as Internet Protocol (IP) telephony, international access to Internet Traffic Exchange (ITE), and mobile services and international networking. The author concludes that the development of these new services, and the trade issues they generate, may require either the clarification of prior WTO obligations or a consideration of new market access commitments.

In Chapter 5, Boutheina Guermazi analyses accounting rates from a developing country perspective. The author observes that the accounting rates issue has raised a North/South controversy. On the one hand, developed countries suffering from deficit payments are eager to reform the accounting rates regime and align it with cost. On the other hand, developing countries are reluctant to consider any change to the system. The reason for this is that developing countries largely benefit from the current system. Due to traffic imbalances, the total amount of settlement payments received from developed countries is around US$10 billion per annum. The author admits that the regime as it operates today is unsustainable and that efforts should be made at the international level to bring the system into conformity with the trade principles contained in the WTO. She calls, however, for a differentiation between developed countries and developing countries. While it is not acceptable that the accounting rates system continues to subsidise the telecommunications sector in countries with well-developed infrastructure, it is both necessary and justifiable under the WTO Basic Agreement on Telecommunications that the accounting rates system continues to fund telecommunications development in developing countries. In this context, accounting rates could be singled out as a prime means for telecommunications development under the liberalised environment for telecommunications services.

In Chapter 6, Damien Geradin and Michel Kerf analyse the mechanisms provided by the WTO to prevent anti-competitive practices in telecommunications. The authors observe that the removal of barriers to entry in the telecommunications markets following the adoption of the WTO Basic Agreement on Telecommunications is a major step forward, but it might not be sufficient to create thriving competition in such markets. This is because the telecommunications sector has certain features that allow the incumbents to retain a substantial degree of market power. Controlling market power in telecommunications is usually achieved through a combination of competition rules and sector-specific rules. The theme of this paper is to analyse whether these instruments can be found in the WTO. The authors observe that WTO Members have so far failed to adopt competition rules. By contrast, the Members that are party to the WTO Basic Agreement on Telecommunications managed to agree on a set of specific regulatory principles designed to ensure that the commitments made by participating countries would not be compromised by anti-competitive practices. These principles, which are comprised in the so-called 'Reference Paper', complement the general principles that are included in the GATS which also apply to the telecommunications sector. Though the Reference Paper is a truly exceptional document, the authors argue that it contains several weaknesses. They also make suggestions as to how the Reference Paper could be improved. The authors also argue that, even if the Reference Paper could be strengthened, two factors suggest there would still be a need for horizontal competition rules. First, competition rules are needed to deal with a range of anti-competitive practices that are not necessarily addressed by sector-specific rules. Secondly, one considerable limitation of the Reference Paper is that it only applies to basic telecommunications services. It does not apply to other services, such as audio-visual services, therefore leaving such services without any form of protection against anti-competitive practices. Finally, the authors offer a proposed model for the elaboration of horizontal competition rules at the WTO level.

Part III discusses and analyses the current regulatory framework applicable to audio-visual services. The first two chapters of Part III provide an analysis of the tension between trade liberalisation and audio-visual policy. In Chapter 7, Christoph Beat Graber provides an overview of the various WTO agreements that are currently relevant to audio-visual services. He then offers a typology of the governmental measures designed to sustain audio-visual and cultural policy. These measures include subsidies, restrictions on market access and national treatment, special licensing requirements, as well as taxes. As these measures often create barriers to trade, the author analyses their actual or potential points of conflict with the WTO. Furthermore, the author reviews the various provisions of theWTO regime providing for flexibility towards measures of national cultural policy. Finally, he concludes with various observations concerning some open questions.

In Chapter 8, Ivan Bernier focuses on content regulation in the audio-visual sector. The author draws a distinction between 'content requirement' (which refers to regulations that usually prescribe a given percentage of local content in film and television programmes or a given percentage of television and radio programmes in one or more national language or languages), 'content restriction' (which refers to regulations that exclude certain types of content or allows them subject to certain conditions) and 'content production' (which refers to interventions that are intended to stimulate the development of local content). He then examines the compatibility of these various types of content regulation with WTO rules.

In Chapter 9, David Luff focuses on the means used to convey and receive audio-visual products (whether content or services). He examines how current WTO rules enable a certain degree of liberalisation of those means, what the remaining limitations are, and to what extent culture is an issue in this area. He first addresses the current application of WTO rules to the provision of networks. He then discusses the current principles and regulations concerning the allocation of scarce resources, such as frequencies and satellite orbits and the rules applicable to terminal equipment. He also examines the impact of convergence, particularly the rise of broadband networks, which enable the transmission of both telecommunications and audio-visual services, on the application of WTO rules. He highlights the irrelevance of certain classifications in this context and the difficulties that are likely to appear. He concludes by arguing that technological development will inevitably orient the manner in which audio-visual policy will be pursued and that future commitments should be crafted accordingly.

In Chapter 10, Jean-François Bellis analyses whether the GATS contains rules that address the right of Members to take emergency measures to safeguard their interests, as well as the issues of government procurement and subsidies. The presence or absence of such rules has a significant impact on suppliers of telecommunications and audio-visual services. The author observes that the GATS does not contain rules on these issues. However, the GATS contains mandates inviting Members to enter into negotiations for the adoption of such rules, and negotiations have begun in this regard. These negotiations are at various stages, but none have been concluded yet. The author notes that Members must attach great importance to the negotiations of GATS rules on the above issues. The lack of such rules is partly a cause of the reluctance of Members to make new commitments. These negotiations, however, raise systemic difficulties, and the core issues of the desirability and feasibility of such rules is still being questioned by a number of Members. For all these reasons, it appears very unlikely that the negotiations, which began over six years ago, will soon be concluded.

Part IV comprises chapters analysing convergence under different angles. One chapter explains what convergence means in technical terms. Other chapters review the legal and economic consequences of convergence for trade in telecommunications and audio-visual services.

In Chapter 11, Milton Mueller describes the technological and economic forces that support convergence, and then considers some of the consequences for trade in communication industries. The author observes that convergence means the digitisation of all media forms and the adoption of compatible digital formats by all networks and information appliances. Convergence means an enormous reduction in the cost of interconnecting and interoperating various forms of communication and information technology. The author argues that this cost reduction will have a particularly significant effect in the audio-visual sector. The quantity of audio-visual services supplied will grow enormously as the production costs decline, and as this happens new media forms with market structures and business models quite different from the norms of broadcasting and cinema will evolve. As convergence progresses, broadcasting and cinema will be forced to operate in an entertainment and culture economy in which the Internet and other new distribution channels account for an ever larger share of the relevant markets and play an increasingly prominent role in defining the content choices of the public. As a result, subsidised programming and national origin quotas will affect only a diminishing slice of the average household's content alternatives.

In Chapter 12, Robert Frieden explains how regulatory dichotomies in converging markets may lead to opportunistic behaviour, which may undermine the effectiveness of existing regulation. He first presents what he calls the 'integrated information communications and entertainment

(ICE) market place' in which not only traditional service providers operate, but also new ventures that may escape current regulatory models. He then explains the concept of regulatory opportunism, i.e. where an undertaking organises its activities so as to fall under classifications which entail the least regulatory constraints, in order to acquire competitive advantage. Several examples are provided, illustrating how Internet service providers (ISPs) have proven skilful in both the US markets and internationally to provide services functionally equivalent to those of regulated carriers, while avoiding the duties imposed on the latter. Other examples are drawn from the experience of the US Telecommunications Act of 1996 and from tariff imbalances due to traffic origin or destination. Disparities created by accounting rates and how these have been used by operators to avoid their settlement are discussed in this context. The GATT v. GATS debate is also relevant since in the absence of commitments annexed to the GATS in a specific sector, there might be opposing interests in classifying a delivery as a good or as a service. Robert Frieden also examines regulatory opportunism generated by IP voice telephony. He concludes by warning that regulatory asymmetry in a converged environment, such as that of the ICE, where technological differences are not sufficient to distinguish between functionally equivalent services, may unduly favour the less regulated providers, while jeopardising further technological innovations and regulations such as those promoting universal service or cultural identities. The author therefore stresses the need for a new regulation that would avoid such dichotomies and be technology-neutral, i.e. examining 'the nature of a service without regard to the medium or the mode of delivery'.

In Chapter 13, Paul Nihoul analyses the impact of convergence on the regulatory classifications used in the WTO context. He first provides a detailed review of the definitions given to telecommunications services and audio-visual services, in light mainly of the classification contained in the W/120 list, on the basis of which commitments were made. Since, however, WTO rules do not define these services, definitions are drawn from the UN Provisional Central Product Classification List (CPC), market practice, the views and legislative experience of Members and documents produced by delegations. While distinctions between basic and value-added telecommunications services and definitions of each individual service can easily be grasped, difficulties arise in relation to borderline differences between audio-visual and broadcasting services and between audio-visual and telecommunications services. Not only is there no clear international guidance in this regard, but also pragmatic criteria traditionally used in practice to justify them are no longer relevant in a converged environment. The author then explains why the new regulatory framework adopted by the European Communities, which abandons old distinctions and focuses on horizontal policy-making, the outline of which is provided, could inspire the evolution of international trade law in this respect.

In Chapter 14, Pierre Larouche recalls that, while convergence is not taking place to the extent expected, it is a reality that challenges the current regulatory framework. He underlines the key issues surrounding the regulation of convergence, i.e. classifications, technological neutrality, the role of competition law, content regulation and institutional issues. He analyses the EC and the US responses for each one of them. From a structural point of view, while the EC created a new framework based on the distinction between content and networks, the US maintained pragmatic divisions based on current industry realities and technological features. Both approaches are criticised: the distinction proposed by the EC may seem artificial in a number of cases and not necessarily in accordance with industry reality, while in the US regulatory imbalances due to technical features may impair the development of a competitive playing field. Both models also seem unsatisfactory from an institutional point of view, as they enable useless duplications. The author then assesses the relevance of these two approaches in the international trade arena. He underlines the inappropriateness of the structure of the GATS, which relies on commitments that are themselves based on classifications that are too constrained. He also argues that technological neutrality is currently not sufficiently reflected in GATS, and examines ways to do so. Finally, he notes that the emergence of common competition principles beyond those of the Reference Paper, as well as a common regulatory framework for universal service and for control on content are unlikely. After examining how these regulations could fit into the current GATS, he concludes that they might become unenforceable without their reorientation and a reclassification of services within the WTO.

Finally, in Chapter 15, Eli Noam argues that convergence will bring many benefits, but that these will not be distributed equally between developed and developing nations. In this context, the author analyses the problem of the 'digital divide', and identifies three kinds of gaps that need to be addressed by developing countries. The first gap is that of telecommunications connectivity. This gap is being closed by investment in infrastructure and by liberalising policy reform. The second gap is that of Internet access. Internet usage is more expensive in developing countries.

Facilitating Internet access is partly dependent on an improvement of the telecommunications infrastructure. The third gap is e-commerce. At present, developing countries account for a very small share of the world's commercial websites and Internet commerce revenues. This may create a large divide between developed nations, which will dominate the field of Internet transactions, and developing countries, which will remain secondary players in this field. Noam therefore urges the governments of developing countries to take measures to stimulate the development of e-commerce. A policy of free entry and investment based on market forces and competition could contribute to this development. Other reforms will, however, be needed, including the development of e-government applications, the reform of the legal system in order to make e-transactions possible, a strengthening of physical delivery infrastructures, and the support of technological education.

The main findings made in the book and an agenda for Doha

The chapters contained in this book, and which are summarised in the preceding section, offer an extremely rich and interdisciplinary analysis of telecommunications and audio-visual services in the WTO context. We may now underline some of the main findings that may be drawn from a reading of these chapters.

Telecommunications services

Current WTO rules concerning telecommunications services are among the most elaborate rules in the international trade in services arena. As we have seen, these rules have proven effective in fostering domestic liberalisation in more than 90 per cent of the markets in telecommunications services.[1] The rules also encourage the development of advanced telecommunications systems and appear to be sufficiently flexible to accommodate non-trade objectives, such as the need to ensure a universal service, the integrity of the public network and the maintenance of essential public services (emergency lines, security, etc.).[2] Yet, a number of important issues concerning trade in telecommunications services are unresolved, due either to a lack of rules or to their imprecision.

[1] See Kelly Cameron, Chapter 2 below.
[2] See David Luff, Chapter 3 below.

The first difficulty concerns the magnitude of and variations in international settlement rates. A 'peace clause' resulting from a gentleman's agreement, according to which Members agreed not to challenge settlement rates at the WTO, is still in force,[3] but this is not a satisfactory long-term solution for most Members. It merely maintains the *status quo*, while in fact the progressive dismantling of excessive settlement rates would be desirable.[4] Conversely, financing the development of a decent telecommunications infrastructure in developing countries may still be necessary and politically unavoidable.[5]

The second difficulty concerns the link between non-trade concerns (universal and public service, safety of networks, etc.) and the principles of free trade. Currently, such a link is addressed in most cases by the necessity test.[6] In other words, restrictions on trade liberalisation and access to networks for non-trade purposes are permitted, where commitments are taken, if they are 'necessary' or 'not more burdensome than necessary' to achieve a legitimate objective.[7] While it is generally admitted that the definition of such an objective and the level of protection sought are a sovereign choice of states,[8] without any further clarification of the notion of 'necessity', the selection of the right measure might be problematic.

The third difficulty, which is more controversial, concerns the lack of precision of the Reference Paper. While this document appears to be a good first step to prevent abuses of market power from incumbents, it is subject to the question, however, of whether it should not be extended to other fields subject to WTO commitments. A further question is to what extent additional competition rules are necessary to ensure the effectiveness of market access commitments, regardless of the social and economic conditions of WTO Members and, if so, what should be the content of such rules. While several issues, such as interconnection prices and the

3 See WTO, 'Report of the Group on Basic Telecommunications to the Council for Trade in Services', S/GBT/4, 15 February 1997, para. 5.

4 See Peter Cowhey, Chapter 4 and Boutheina Guermasi, Chapter 5 below.

5 *Ibid.*

6 See Articles VI:4 and VI:5 of the GATS (applicable to domestic regulation that is more restrictive to trade than regulation existing at the time of commitments), Article XIV(a) and (c) of the GATS, Article (d) and (e) of the Annex on Telecommunications, and Section 3 of the Reference Paper.

7 This is without prejudice to the capacity of Members to limit the scope of their commitments in accordance with Articles XVI and XVII of GATS.

8 This covers for instance the scope of universal service required. See, by analogy, Article 2.2 of the Agreement on Technical Barriers to Trade and Articles 3.3 and 5.5 of the Agreement on Sanitary and Phytosanitary Measures.

level of required unbundling, arguably should not be further regulated, other key issues deserve specific international attention, such as obvious cartels, abuses of dominant positions, cross-subsidisation, number portability and carrier selection.[9]

Audio-visual services

Not much progress was realised in liberalising trade in audio-visual services during the last round of negotiations. This was due mainly to conceptual misunderstandings between those Members believing that audio-visual services are of a commercial nature like any other service and those believing that cultural concerns justify a form of cultural exception for these services. Further efforts will have to be made in Doha to reconcile both views. Yet, it is now generally admitted that WTO rules should not affect the capacity of Members to regulate their audio-visual market and to foster cultural policies within them.[10] The GATS appears in this regard to be characterised by its exceptional flexibility: Members have the right not to schedule commitments in audio-visual services. When they do so, they may insert limitations in order to give effect to their domestic policies.[11] They may also enact non-discriminatory regulations that pursue the 'quality' of the services[12] and even, in certain circumstances, derogate from basic GATS rules.[13]

Current WTO rules, however, are incomplete. They maintain a number of uncertainties that still jeopardise efforts to further liberalise trade in the audio-visual sector.

First, as systematically complained about by all authors dealing with this issue, a definitive clarification of the applicability of GATT v. GATS appears to be necessary.[14] Indeed, cultural goods supplied using telecommunications networks (such as books or films) have an ambivalent nature. Are they goods or services? The issue is important. Indeed, while trade restrictive audio-visual policies may be compatible with few commitments taken under the GATS, they might be undermined if the traded 'content'

[9] See Damien Geradin and Michel Kerf, Chapter 6 below.
[10] See Preamble to the GATS, para. 4.
[11] Articles XVI, XVII, XIX:2 and XX:2 of the GATS.
[12] Article VI:5 of the GATS, read in conjunction with Article VI:4 of the GATS.
[13] Articles II:2 and XIV of the GATS.
[14] See Christoph Beat Graber, Chapter 7, Ivan Bernier, Chapter 8 and Robert Frieden, Chapter 12 below. See also UNCTAD Secretariat, 'Audio-visual Services: Improving Participation of Developing Countries', TD/B/COM.1/EM.20/2, 30 September 2002, p. 14.

is eventually to be considered as a good subject to the GATT. The latter is indeed a less flexible instrument, and all its provisions apply equally to all non-agricultural goods. Thus, formal clarification would be welcome here.

Secondly, current definitions of audio-visual services under the GATS may be confusing. They do not distinguish between the services themselves and the networks used to supply them. Thus, it is not always clear whether liberalisation of a specific audio-visual service entails the right of its provider to operate its own network. Furthermore, current classifications arguably do not take into account the complexities of the audio-visual sector. No distinction is made between music and multimedia applications, nor is account taken of the variety of the latter.[15] Also, there is no distinction between the many different services that can be provided in the production phase of audio-visual content, such as casting, studio services, dubbing, etc. Arguably, distinguishing these services would enable better tailored commitments under the GATS without jeopardising cultural policies.

Thirdly, the Annex on Telecommunications, which recognises the right of providers of scheduled services to use basic domestic telecommunications transport networks and services, does not provide similar rights to broadcasters or cable distributors of TV and radio programmes.[16] This runs counter to the basic philosophy of the Annex. It is also unclear whether the Annex covers access to cable networks which may be used for other audio-visual services. In this respect, although the principle of technological neutrality seems to be promoted by WTO Members, it may not be sufficiently reflected in the Annex.[17]

Fourthly, certain important notions require more precision in the GATS. Currently, in sectors for which commitments were made, domestic regulations that are more restrictive to trade than regulations existing at the time of commitments may be adopted under the GATS only if they are not discriminatory and not 'more burdensome than necessary' to achieve 'the quality of the service'.[18] Obviously the application of these principles to cultural policies would require that the notions of 'necessity' and 'quality of the service' be further defined. One may wonder, indeed, what would be the aptitude of panels to do so.

[15] See Paul Nihoul, Chapter 13 below.
[16] Article 2(b) of the Annex on Telecommunications.
[17] See David Luff, Chapter 9 below.
[18] Articles VI:4 and VI:5 of the GATS read together.

Fifthly, additional rules may be needed to address domestic support programmes. Currently, subsidies are authorised under the GATS, provided they are not discriminatory and comply with commitments taken. In other words, should unlimited commitments be taken for a specific service, subsidies are possible but cannot be granted to domestic operators only. The GATT appears to be more tolerant in this respect. Indeed, pursuant to Article III:8(b) of GATT, discriminatory subsidies are authorised, provided they take the form of an actual expense for the government and not of tax cuts that are arguably less transparent.[19] Perhaps consideration should be given to this aspect.

Conversely, it must be recognised that, under certain circumstances, subsidies can unduly harm importing countries' industries, thus undermining local production. Corrective measures are not yet regulated under the GATS. Only certain countries included exemptions to their MFN obligations to authorise the adoption of such measures against injurious 'imports' of foreign services.[20] This confirms the need for specific disciplines, as mandated by Article XV of the GATS. The challenge of negotiators in this context is to draft provisions that, while enabling domestic support programmes, avoid abusive subsidies which would confer illegitimate advantages in international markets. The question would thus be, among others, what level of support is acceptable. Would subsidy programmes only be possible to 'create an environment to nurture local culture'[21] (i.e. support to art schools, local facilities, advertisement, etc.), or could they specifically organise transfers to local production companies?

Finally, considering the existing pressures for market opening in the audio-visual sector, the question then arises: of what kind of regulation can be adopted to address specific market imbalances. It is indeed generally admitted that these might result from excessive market power of US producers.[22] Imbalances may also result from mergers between global operators in search of economies of scale and competitive advantage. While imbalances, when they are due to comparative advantages, may be acceptable in the context of trade in goods, they appear to be problematic

[19] See Appellate Body Report, 'Canada – Certain Measures Concerning Periodicals', WT/DS31/AB/R, 30 June 1997, Section VII.

[20] See the Schedule of Commitments of the European Communities, Doc. GATS EL/31, 15 April 1994.

[21] See WTO, Council for Trade in Services, Communication from the United States, 'Audio-visual and Related Services', S/CSS/W/21, 18 December 2000, para. 10(iii).

[22] For an analysis of the international audio-visual markets, see UNCTAD Secretariat, 'Audio-visual Services: Improving Participation of Developing Countries', TD/B/COM.1/EM.20/2, 30 September 2002, pp. 3–5.

in the audio-visual sector. Indeed, they would impair cultural diversity[23] and aggravate the digital divide between developed and developing countries.[24] The question is therefore whether current GATS rules enable domestic policies that are sufficient to address such imbalances or whether specific trade protectionist instruments, such as a safeguard or a form of 'antidumping' agreements, are required. These alternatives, however, raise a number of systemic difficulties. For instance, notions like 'increase of imports', the 'origin' of services, 'domestic industry', 'injury', 'normal value', etc. must be defined, and mutual understanding concerning them is still not in sight.[25]

Convergence

WTO law does not address convergence between telecommunications and audio-visual services. The lack of consideration of this phenomenon by the WTO, mainly due to outdated classifications in the GATS, may entail unexpected regulatory consequences, possibly jeopardising certain cultural policies.

First, the inadequacy of current classifications is now generally admitted.[26] Indeed, undue distinctions are made between services that are becoming interchangeable in the markets. This is the case in particular of TV and radio broadcasting services and TV and radio supplied by the Internet. Clearly, different commitments for arguably like services may give rise to odd regulatory dichotomies, entailing the kind of opportunism that could circumvent restrictive audio-visual policies.[27] The question is thus whether a regulatory framework distinguishing between network services and the supply of content should be devised.[28] Although occasionally this division may not be obvious, such as in the case of TV

[23] Indeed, when productions of one country are cheap, unless quotas are implemented, they may acquire too important a place in the distribution channels (movie theatres, TV channels etc.). As to market concentration, clearly the number of suppliers of cultural goods would be reduced, thereby affecting cultural diversity.

[24] See Eli Noam, Chapter 15 below.

[25] See Jean-François Bellis, Chapter 10 below.

[26] See, among others, Christoph Beat Graber, Chapter 7, David Luff, Chapter 9, Robert Frieden, Chapter 12, Paul Nihoul, Chapter 13 and Pierre Larouche, Chapter 14 below.

[27] See Robert Frieden, Chapter 12 below.

[28] See EC Commission, Green Paper, 'The Convergence of the Telecommunications, Media and Information Technology Sectors, and the Implications for Regulation', COM(97)623, 3 December 1997.

broadcasting or voice telephony,[29] it is not to be excluded that, in a converged environment, separate businesses will emerge for different kinds of services. Classifications should, in any event, take into account the reality of current and upcoming competitive relations.

Another question could arise: considering that broadband networks enable the transmission of large amounts of data, is content regulation still necessary?[30] Scarcity arguments may no longer warrant content requirements, as virtually unlimited amounts of data are now available on the Internet. However, bottlenecks may still be possible, and access to them is important for small local productions. There are indeed intermediaries that are much more effective than others at distributing content. Clearly, access to a TV channel or to movie theatres, or even to well-known Internet search tools, more significantly improves the visibility of a programme or of a film than does their simple availability on the web. Scarcity concerns may therefore be relevant in this context, and both content regulation and competitive safeguards appear to be indispensable.

Clearly, much work still needs to be done, in the context of convergence, to accommodate trade liberalisation with the kind of domestic policies addressed in the audio-visual and telecommunications sectors. It would be surprising if Doha negotiations were more than a first step in this regard. It is the objective of the authors of this book to contribute to this effort.

[29] See Pierre Larouche, Chapter 14 below.
[30] See Milton Mueller, Chapter 11 below.

PART II

International regulation of telecommunications services

2

Telecommunications and audio-visual services in the context of the WTO: today and tomorrow

KELLY CAMERON

I have been asked to discuss the negotiating history of the WTO Basic Telecommunications Agreement. As interesting as that topic is, it seems more useful to try to put it in the context of the prospects for a similar agreement for audio-visual services.

At the end of the Uruguay Round in 1993, the conclusion of the General Agreement on Trade in Services was surely one of the new World Trade Organization's greatest achievements. After all, services account for more than 50 per cent of developed economies and so bringing services within the international trading system was an important step forward. That achievement was diminished, however, by the failure of Members to agree to market access commitments in basic telecommunications services and several other important services sectors (most notably financial services). Out of more than 120 Members at the time, only one had made significant market access commitments for basic telecommunications services and it later turned out this was an accident. In contrast, in the field of value-added telecommunications services, fifty-seven Members had made commitments to provide market access for a wide range of services with relatively few market access limitations.

Why was there such a difference in the treatment of value-added and basic services? Value-added services were a small percentage of the overall telecommunications industry at the time and, in perhaps all of the fifty-seven countries that made market access commitments, the provision of these services had already been liberalised. Thus, the value-added telecom commitments essentially constituted a *status quo* agreement.[1]

[1] Although the value-added telecommunications commitments did not, generally, further liberalise services, the Uruguay Round produced one very important document that benefits providers of value-added telecommunications services as well as other services for which market access commitments have been scheduled. That document is the GATS Annex on

In contrast, liberalisation of basic telecommunications was still a fairly novel and somewhat radical idea. Only a handful of countries – the United States, the United Kingdom, Canada, Japan, Australia and New Zealand – had agreed to permit competition in any sector of the telecom industry. None of these countries – including the United States – had yet fully opened the basic telecom market to full competition, even from domestic suppliers, much less from foreigners. In the vast majority of countries, basic telecom remained a monopoly and, in most of these countries, a state-owned monopoly as well. Even in those few countries that had liberalised, governments imposed strict limits on foreign ownership. Thus, an agreement to provide meaningful market access for basic telecommunications would require significant changes in most countries' laws, either in advance of an agreement or as a condition of its implementation.

The resistance to making such changes was not due only to bureaucratic inertia, although that surely played a role. The consequences of liberalising telecommunications were certain to be far-reaching and posed great risks for established stakeholders. Consider, for example, that, where the telephone company had been privatised, it was very often the most valuable company on that country's stock exchange and accounted in many cases for a substantial percentage of the stock exchange's overall market capitalisation. In addition, the telephone company was in many countries one of the largest single employers in the nation. Further, the global telecom industry was then approximately a US$500-billion-a-year business with projections of astronomical future growth. To open one's market to global competition meant putting your domestic industry's share of that market at risk without guaranteeing any benefit to the domestic industry.

Under the circumstances, then, it may have seemed either an act of faith or a futile gesture when nineteen Members of the WTO formed the Negotiating Group on Basic Telecommunications (NGBT) at the Marrakech

Telecommunications, which ensures that suppliers of scheduled services (whether value-added telecommunications or legal services, for example) have a right to use the public telecommunications network on reasonable and non-discriminatory terms. While it is important for these reasons, the Annex on Telecommunications explicitly does not provide market access for basic telecommunications services and therefore is outside the scope of this paper.

Ministerial Conference in 1994.[2] The mandate of the NGBT was to enter into negotiations

> with a view to the progressive liberalization of trade in telecommunications transport networks and services (hereinafter referred to as 'basic telecommunications') within the framework of the General Agreement on Trade in Services. Without prejudice to their outcome, the negotiations shall be comprehensive in scope, with no basic telecommunications excluded *a priori*.[3]

The Decision that created the NGBT also established a 'standstill agreement', that is, a provision under which members agreed not to take actions during the negotiations that would improve their leverage in the negotiations. The Decision set a deadline of 30 April 1996, or just over two years from the date of the Decision, for the completion of the group's work.

The first task undertaken by the NGBT was the completion of a questionnaire that outlined each Member's regulation of basic telecommunications. The first question it posed was how each country defined basic telecommunications. It seemed a bad omen that, even on this point, there was no consensus among the members of the negotiating group.[4] In general, the responses demonstrated that, while many governments were considering liberalising their telecom markets, very few had actually done so and under the circumstances the prospects for an agreement were not necessarily bright. This seemed especially true because the basic telecom negotiation, like other services negotiations that took place at the same time, were sector-specific negotiations. It was therefore impossible

[2] The nineteen original members of the NGBT (counting the European Communities and their then twelve Member States as one) were Australia, Austria, Canada, Chile, Cyprus, the European Communities and their Member States, Finland, Hong Kong, Hungary, Japan, Mexico, New Zealand, Norway, the Slovak Republic, South Korea, Sweden, Switzerland, Turkey and the United States. Austria, Finland and Sweden subsequently joined the European Union and ceased to be members of the NGBT in an independent capacity.

[3] Decision on Negotiations on Basic Telecommunications, The Results of the Uruguay Round of Multilateral Trade Negotiations: The Legal Texts (GATT Secretariat, 1994).

[4] Although there was no formally agreed definition of 'basic telecommunications', either within the context of the negotiations or otherwise, a term that was used both in the Decision on Negotiations on Basic Telecommunications as well as in the GATS Annex on Telecommunications provided guidance. That term, 'public telecommunications transport services', is defined in the GATS Annex on Telecommunications to mean 'any telecommunications transport service required, explicitly or in effect, by a Member to be offered to the public generally. Such services may include, *inter alia*, telegraph, telephone, telex, and data transmission typically involving the real-time transmission of customer-supplied information between two or more points without any end-to-end change in the form or content of the customer's information.'

to trade greater liberalisation in telecom for concessions in other service or goods sectors.

The negotiations proceeded through the bilateral presentation of requests for market access and offers of market access. While I cannot speak for other delegations, the US delegation took the mandate of the Decision that no sector be excluded *a priori* very much to heart. Beginning in April 1995, the United States presented an identical market access request to each of its negotiating partners. In essence, the US request was for full market access for all basic telecom services with no market access limitations – such as restrictions on foreign investment – as of 1 January 1998. In addition, the United States specifically identified those measures that we believed would need to be either eliminated or adopted in order to implement the broad market access that we sought.

In turn, the US delegation received comparable requests for market access from many of our negotiating partners. Like our own request to other Members, these requests specifically sought elimination of all restrictions on foreign ownership, notably the provisions of section 310(b) of the US Communications Act of 1934.[5] For many years, the Federal Communications Commission (FCC) had interpreted section 310(b) as prohibiting any foreign company from controlling a company that holds a radio licence. The FCC maintained this position despite the fact that the language of the Act very clearly gives the FCC authority to allow any amount of foreign ownership – even 100 per cent – unless it finds that this would not serve the public interest.

Likewise, other delegations requested elimination of rules that the FCC adopted in 1995 that governed the terms under which it would grant licences to foreign telecom companies in the absence of WTO market access commitments. These rules, commonly known as the Effective Competitive Opportunities (ECO) test, were intended to ensure that entry by foreign carriers with market power into the US market would not harm competition. The FCC reasoned that, if the foreign carrier's market were open to competition from US carriers, it could not abuse its market power to distort competition in the US market. Other Members took a different view of the ECO test, because the FCC's determination that a foreign carrier would not harm competition in the US market was based on an analysis of market access and regulatory conditions in the foreign carrier's home market. Thus, while the FCC justified its rules as a legitimate competition policy measure, others considered it a reciprocity test – if the

[5] 47 USC section 310(b).

foreign government allowed US carriers into its market, the FCC would let the foreign carrier into the US market.

In truth, both sides were right. The FCC's ECO test was a measure designed to promote competition because it applied only to dominant carriers seeking to provide service between the United States and their home country. US carriers and the FCC legitimately feared that dominant foreign carriers would be able to use their market power in their home markets to discriminate against or compete unfairly with US carriers unless the foreign market was fully open to competition. The FCC's rules, by these terms, would not have applied to a non-dominant foreign carrier providing service between the United States and its home market. Nor would they have applied to any foreign carrier providing service between the United States and a third country.

Of course, as a practical matter, the ECO test did amount to a reciprocity test because typically only dominant foreign carriers applied to the FCC for entry into the US market, and they quite naturally were mainly interested in providing service between the United States and their home markets. Few dominant foreign carriers could have demonstrated in 1995 that their markets offered the same opportunities to US carriers or that they had in place rules that would ensure fair competition. These facts, of course, illustrate precisely what the FCC was worried about – foreign markets were not open, by and large, and dominant foreign carriers had the incentive and the ability to use their market power at home to compete unfairly in the US market. In any event, the US delegation consistently promised to eliminate the ECO test if an agreement were reached, which, ultimately, the FCC did.

Much of the debate over the ECO test focused on whether a Member could maintain an *ex ante* competition test in deciding to grant a licence. The United States took the position that *ex ante* regulation was consistent with the GATS. Other Members contended that such regulation amounted to a denial of Most-Favoured Nation (MFN) treatment and could not be maintained. Rather, they argued, the United States and other Members must await actual harm to competition before taking measures to address the situation. This issue was never definitively resolved. The United States, like many other countries, continues to maintain *ex ante* licensing rules. The European Union has threatened to bring a WTO dispute based on US *ex ante* regulations but has not done so, perhaps because the United States has not denied European carriers' applications.

Both the United States and other Members used some creativity to address the foreign investment issue. For its part, the United States offered to allow foreign suppliers to own up to 100 per cent of any US telecommunications supplier indirectly, that is, through US subsidiaries. In substance, this is no different from the FCC granting licences directly to the foreign company. In form, however, it meets the requirements of US law. Other Members also scheduled market access limitations that provide that only indirect foreign ownership is permitted. Ultimately, most of the developed nations, with the exception of Canada, agreed to permit up to 100 per cent foreign investment in basic telecom suppliers. In addition, most Members of the NGBT, again with the exception of Canada, agreed to permit foreign control of basic telecom suppliers, even if they permit less than 100 per cent foreign ownership.

Issues related to the licensing and use of the electromagnetic spectrum also presented problems in the negotiation. Under US law, the question of foreign ownership only arises in the context of companies that hold radio licences. Ironically, many other Members, particularly among the developing countries, were entirely willing to commit to market access for wireless companies. The electromagnetic spectrum is a finite resource, however, and is used for a variety of purposes in addition to basic telecommunications services, such as broadcasting and public safety. Many Members were concerned, therefore, that, if they made market access commitments for wireless services, they might find themselves obligated to grant licences to foreign suppliers even if there was no available spectrum. Many Members, therefore, included in their draft market access schedules a limitation that market access for wireless services was subject to spectrum availability. Ultimately, most Members removed these limitations because the NGBT concluded that they were not necessary to preserve a Member's right to undertake legitimate measures to regulate and license use of the electromagnetic spectrum.

In contrast, relatively few Members made clear in the first two years of the negotiation that they were prepared to commit to market access for satellite services. In part, this is because satellite operators did not become involved in the negotiations until relatively late in the process. In part, the lack of explicit market access commitments for satellites was a result of the negotiators' evolving understanding that commitments should be technologically neutral. That is, if a Member made a commitment for the provision of a basic telecommunications service, service suppliers of other Members could supply the service by any technical means – by wire, radio or satellite – unless the Member limited market access by means of particular technologies.

By far the most controversial area of the market access negotiations was international service. Although international service constituted only approximately 10 per cent of global telecom service revenues, international service was extremely profitable. In addition, it was particularly easy for a dominant carrier in one market to exploit its market power to the detriment of its competitors and it was correspondingly difficult for even the most well-intentioned regulator to do anything about it. In large part, this was due to the international accounting rate system under which telecommunications operators traditionally exchanged international traffic. Under the accounting rate system, international operators would negotiate a rate for the provision of international service that bore no relation to cost. When every country had a monopoly provider of international service, and when incoming and outgoing traffic was fairly well in balance, this situation was not considered a problem. When incoming and outgoing traffic are unequal, however, the result is that the carrier that originates more traffic has to pay very high prices to the carrier that terminates traffic for every additional minute of traffic it sends. The carriers receiving these payments had every incentive to find ways to maintain or even increase them. In contrast, the carriers that made these payments, notably US carriers, were eager to find ways to prevent this from happening and instead to reduce the amount they had to pay out.

This situation led to extensive discussion of the international accounting rate system in the NGBT. Members debated, for example, whether accounting rates, although negotiated commercial agreements, were nevertheless government measures, particularly in view of the fact that most carriers were still state-owned at the time. The Australian delegation, in particular, explored ways of subjecting accounting rates to GATS disciplines. Australia suggested, in informal papers distributed within the NGBT, that the termination of international traffic was a basic telecommunications service that should be scheduled and that the rates for termination services would then have to be transparent and non-discriminatory.

As with some other issues, the negotiators never reached a final conclusion on whether accounting rates were measures, and this left Members free to seek their own solutions to the problem of accounting rates. The FCC, for example, adopted new rules that limited the level of payments that US-licensed international carriers could pay to their foreign partners. The FCC has also retained rules that allow it to deny a foreign service supplier a licence to provide international service if the FCC believes that the foreign carrier can use the accounting rate system to distort competition in the US market. Many Members condemned these *ex ante* measures as inconsistent with the market access the United States was offering and insisted that the United States must grant a licence and act only if a foreign service supplier actually engaged in anti-competitive conduct. Other Members, fearful of attempts to use the WTO dispute settlement process as a tool to force down high accounting rates, scheduled MFN exemptions for accounting rates, ensuring themselves the ability to discriminate between foreign carriers if accounting rates were deemed to be measures.

Despite the many difficult issues that arose during the course of the negotiations, an enormous amount of progress was made between April 1994 and April 1996. By the scheduled conclusion of the negotiations, forty-seven Members had made market access commitments and most of these were also willing to sign on to regulatory commitments as well. The offers were far from perfect. Many were subject to lengthy phase-in periods and quite a few contained limitations, including restrictions on foreign ownership and control. Many important Members of the NGBT, particularly in Asia, but also in Latin America and other regions as well, had made no meaningful offers. And, as I have noted, a number of issues remained unresolved, including whether market access commitments applied to satellite operators. For this reason, US industry and the US Government concluded that the deal on the table in April 1996 was not adequate to justify concluding an agreement. Rather than rejecting the deal, however, the negotiators agreed to extend negotiations until 15 February 1997.

As the foregoing discussion demonstrates, there was obviously much work to be done in negotiating market access commitments. It became apparent both to the industry and to the negotiators at the outset of the negotiations that simply committing to provide market access would not be good enough. This is because, unlike probably any other industry within the framework of the GATS, basic telecom had been a monopoly for over a century. Indeed, telecom had been universally regarded as a 'natural monopoly', an industry whose economic characteristics made competition impossible. While it is now universally agreed that telecommunications is not a natural monopoly, the former monopolist, or incumbent supplier, has huge advantages, both commercial and political, that new entrants – especially foreign entrants – cannot match. Therefore, in parallel with discussions of market access, some members of the NGBT began to discuss a set of regulatory principles that would be necessary to ensure that market access commitments were valuable. The two basic objectives for these regulatory principles were to prevent the incumbent from abusing its dominant position in the market and to ensure that governments treated foreign service suppliers fairly.

Even as negotiators were discussing the substance of such regulatory commitments, there were also debates over what form they would take and whether existing GATS disciplines might reasonably be interpreted to provide the necessary protections for new entrants. Some participants in the negotiations suggested initially that in fact no new disciplines were needed. After all, Article III guarantees transparency, and Article VI establishes rules for domestic regulation, and particularly for licensing. In addition, the GATS Annex on Telecommunications guarantees reasonable and non-discriminatory access to and use of the public telecommunications network. Some suggested that, taken together, these provisions were sufficient to ensure fair and robust competition in the telecom industry.

Generally, however, it was agreed that existing disciplines were not adequate to protect competition. For example, while the Annex on Telecommunications ensures reasonable and non-discriminatory access to and use of the public telecom network, it does not prevent the incumbent from charging unreasonable prices for that use. Moreover, Article VI only provided interim licensing disciplines, and Article III did not specify how disputes between operators would be resolved.

Thus, while it was agreed that additional rules were needed, the question became how to make them binding.

Additional, legally binding disciplines could have been adopted by amending the text of the GATS, for example by adding a new Annex on Basic Telecommunications. This approach, however, would have required the consensus of the WTO membership as a whole and was, therefore, entirely impractical. Other approaches, such as attaching headnotes or footnotes to the individual schedules, were of uncertain legal effect.

For these reasons, the negotiators concluded that the best way of incorporating specific disciplines for basic telecom was by making additional commitments pursuant to Article XVIII of the GATS. There was, however, some debate as to whether the additional commitments column, like the market access and national treatment limitations columns, should be restricted to limitations or could be used to schedule positive commitments as well. The consensus view was that Article XVIII should not be read as a provision for the scheduling of additional limitations, but rather as a device to enhance the market access commitments contained in the schedule.[6]

[6] Negotiators could not rely on precedent because, before the Basic Telecom Agreement was concluded, no Member had scheduled Article XVIII additional commitments in any sector.

These additional commitments, which were negotiated over a period of more than a year, had their genesis in a paper first tabled by the US delegation. That paper argued that it was

> Essential that, for purposes of progressive liberalisation of trade in basic telecommunications services, market access commitments must be accompanied by commitments to:
> - set disciplines for interconnection of competing basic telecommunications suppliers;
> - provide competition safeguards on dominant carriers;
> - ensure transparency of regulatory processes; and
> - guarantee the independence of regulators.

These principles form the core of the regulatory commitments that ultimately were agreed to, which have come to be known as the WTO Reference Paper. Other elements were added, notably provisions relating to allocation of scarce resources, such as spectrum. Some other provisions were proposed by one or more Members but not agreed to, such as a US proposal that Members require international carriers to publish their accounting rates and require dominant carriers to justify any accounting rate that differs significantly from domestic interconnection rates. In summary, however, the regulatory commitments negotiated by Members were designed to prevent dominant carriers from abusing their market power and to ensure that new entrants, particularly foreign entrants, would be treated fairly by the regulator. Ultimately, fifty-five Members scheduled the Reference Paper in its entirety while another ten included portions of the Reference Paper in their schedules. As with any rules, the precise meaning of the Reference Paper obligations is subject to interpretation. The negotiators fully anticipated that these rules would be interpreted in the context of WTO dispute settlement. It should be noted that, so far, only one dispute under the Basic Telecom Agreement has been brought to a panel.[7]

The WTO Basic Telecom Agreement opened markets that account for more than 90 per cent of global telecom service revenues to competition from service suppliers from all over the world and promised the enforcement of fair rules of competition. It is doubtful anyone with knowledge of the industry and the lack of progress made in the Uruguay Round would have predicted such a positive outcome when the telecom negotiations began in 1994.

[7] See 'Mexico – Measures Affecting Telecommunications Services', Request for the Establishment of a Panel by the United States, WT/DS204/3, 18 February 2002.

The situation with respect to audio-visual services today is in many ways similar to the situation with respect to telecom in 1994. In fact, there are a number of important parallels between the two industries. Obviously, both involve communications – the dissemination of content between and among users. Increasingly, too, the lines between different communications technologies are blurring and it is technologically feasible to use the same network – whether it is a telephone network, a cable television network, a wireless network, or a satellite network – for the provision of either telecommunications or audio-visual services.

The similarities are not only technological. Some of the legal and political circumstances surrounding liberalisation of audio-visual services today are much the same as the issues surrounding telecom services seven years ago. This, of course, is because national regulatory regimes for broadcasting and similar services are based on the need to license and regulate the use of the scarce resource of the electromagnetic spectrum. But it is also because governments have long recognised the enormous power of mass communications and are reluctant to lose control of that power. In the basic telecommunications negotiations, Members were able to reconcile themselves to such changes and perhaps they can do the same in discussing audio-visual services.

The negotiating dynamic is likely to be similar as well. Obviously, both telecom and audio-visual services are concentrated in developed countries, especially the United States. US industry would undoubtedly like greater access to foreign markets but most other countries are unlikely to have global ambitions, although they may have regional market access objectives. Under these circumstances, there is likely to be relatively little interest in opening the global market to competition and running the risk of being further inundated by American culture.

These facts will undoubtedly make it difficult to negotiate further liberalisation of audio-visual services. Still, there are at least three factors that could facilitate the achievement of an agreement for market access for audio-visual services.

First, unlike the basic telecom negotiations, discussions of audio-visual services will take place in the context of a comprehensive round of trade negotiations. While this is certainly no guarantee of success, it does at a minimum create an opportunity to trade market access in the audio-visual sector for concessions in equally controversial sectors like agriculture or textiles.

Secondly, there is already a degree of liberalisation in the audio-visual sector. For example, rules prohibiting foreign ownership of broadcasters often do not apply to cable television networks. Similarly, some countries permit the reception of foreign satellite television programming, which, like cable television, is typically provided on a subscription basis to consumers. Ironically, at the end of the basic telecom negotiations, the United States announced that it would not provide market access for direct broadcast satellite services, which the United States considers to be telecom services, rather than audio-visual, and that it would take an MFN exemption for such services. This might be an example of an area in which greater liberalisation of audio-visual services could lead to US market access commitments in another sector, telecommunications.[8]

Finally, and most importantly, a trade agreement on audio-visual services may happen now because liberalisation may be inevitable. Although our laws still largely reflect an era of scarcity in the audio-visual industry, we now live in an era of plenty. Nowhere is this more evident than on the Internet where a vast amount of audio-visual material is available to anyone in the world. Certainly, the Internet is not currently a perfect substitute for broadcasting. Obviously, even in the most developed countries, personal computer penetration rates remain well below the penetration rates for television and radio. Similarly, broadband access to the Internet, which is critical to making the Internet a substitute for broadcasting, is in its infancy. Nevertheless, consumers increasingly have access to dozens if not hundreds of video and audio programmes, by cable, satellite and the Internet, often from all over the world. Under these circumstances, why should national broadcasters continue to be protected from the outside world? As telecom, audio-visual services and the Internet continue to converge, further liberalisation – and even market access commitments – may become inevitable. This, in turn, may make a trade agreement easier to achieve.

I believe this is why the basic telecom agreement succeeded when it did and not before. In 1994, few countries were prepared to open their telecom markets to competition, even from their own citizens. By 1997, the number of countries that had irreversibly committed to opening their

[8] It is particularly ironic today that the United States has resisted granting access to foreign direct broadcast satellite (DBS) providers. Echostar, the second largest US DBS provider, attempted in 2002 to acquire DirecTV, its larger nationwide DBS rival. Echostar and DirecTV contended that the merger was necessary to make them a more effective competitor to cable. The US Government (both the FCC and the Department of Justice) immediately rejected the merger because the video marketplace was already concentrated and the merger would have made matters worse. The situation might be remedied by opening the market to foreign competition.

markets had exploded and telecom liberalisation became inevitable. If liberalisation of audio-visual services continues to advance, thanks to the Internet and other forces, an audio-visual agreement may also become inevitable, or at least possible.

There will certainly be difficult issues to resolve along the way, notably those related to intellectual property rights and the desire of some countries to protect their unique cultural heritage. Still, if the basic telecom agreement demonstrated anything, it is that the WTO is an extremely creative and flexible body when its Members have the will to achieve something. In audio-visual, as in telecom, if there is a will, there will be a way.

3

Current international trade rules relevant to telecommunications services

DAVID LUFF

Introduction

This paper describes current WTO rules concerning telecommunications services. It includes an explanation of the structure of the GATS, its Annex on Telecommunications, and the Agreement on Basic Telecommunication Services. As discussed in the previous chapter, the latter reflects the commitments of sixty-nine countries that agreed to open their markets to foreign basic telecommunication services and to foreign suppliers of these services. It also contains additional rules which are linked to these commitments and are assembled under the so-called 'Reference Paper'.

The GATT is relevant in relation to equipment and terminals used to convey and receive telecommunications signals. This, however, constitutes a different line of trade, which is discussed in Chapter 9 of this book.

The GATS

The GATS, similarly to the GATT, aims at protecting equality of competitive opportunities for companies in domestic markets regardless of their origin and the origin of their services. It aims at facilitating progressive liberalisation of services while enabling WTO Members to regulate them "in order to meet national policy objectives".[1] The GATS thus constitutes the framework agreement relevant to all services and particularly those that, like telecommunication services, have been or are being liberalised.

In contrast with the GATT, the GATS contains a mix of horizontal commitments applicable to all services and service suppliers and sector-based commitments only applicable to those sectors which have been explicitly open to trade by WTO Members.

[1] GATS, Preamble, third paragraph.

Horizontal disciplines that concern all services and service suppliers

Horizontal rules apply to all measures by Members affecting trade in services.[2] There are no limits in the scope of services except those supplied on a non-commercial basis or outside any form of competition, such as national security or justice.[3] Thus, horizontal rules of the GATS would apply to all existing and new telecommunication services, as well as to audio-visual services. The only exception in this last respect could be some form of public broadcasting which is reserved to a governmental entity (or an entity delegated by the government) supplying TV or radio programmes at non-commercial rates.

The contents of the horizontal rules are as follows.

Most favoured nation treatment

Article II of the GATS contains the obligation to grant the most-favoured nation (MFN) treatment to all services and service suppliers of any WTO Member. This implies the prohibition of *de facto* as well as *de jure* discriminations between foreign services and service suppliers.[4] However, a Member may exempt itself from this obligation. Several WTO Members listed detailed exemptions in the sector of communications services. The most elaborate ones are those of the European Communities on audio-visual services.[5] Exemptions on telecommunications services often concern the ability of countries to maintain their regime of accounting rates (see chapters 4 and 5 below).[6]

Obligation of transparency

Article III of the GATS contains an obligation of transparency that obliges all WTO Members to publish promptly all laws, regulations or administrative guidelines that significantly affect trade in services. Arguably, this

[2] Article I.1 of the GATS. In accordance with Article I:3, GATS rules apply to central, regional or local public authorities, and non-governmental bodies in the exercise of powers delegated by the above public authorities.

[3] Article I.3(b) and (c) of the GATS.

[4] See Appellate Body Report, 'European Communities – Regime for the Importation, Sale and Distribution of Bananas', 9 September 1997, WT/DS27/AB/R, para. 234.

[5] Doc. GATS EL/31, 15 April 1994.

[6] Exemptions concerning telecommunications services, on accounting rates and/or other issues, have been made, among others, by Antigua and Barbuda (Doc. GATS EL/2), Argentina (Doc. GATS EL/4), Bangladesh (Doc. GATS EL/8), Brazil (Doc. GATS EL/13/Suppl.1), India (Doc. GATS EL/42/Suppl.1), Pakistan (Doc GATS EL/67/Suppl.1), Sri Lanka (Doc GATS EL/79), Turkey (Doc. GATS EL/88/Suppl.2) and the United States (Doc. GATS EL/90/Suppl.2).

would concern all significant sector-based regulation concerning not only the provision of services themselves, but also other public concerns such as consumer protection or the protection of the environment that might have an impact on the provision of the services considered.

Monopoly suppliers

Pursuant to Article VIII of the GATS, the above rules, particularly the most-favoured nation obligation, apply to monopoly suppliers, i.e. enterprises that have been granted special or exclusive rights[7] (see below). Therefore, discrimination by one of these enterprises, such as a provider of a national network, between entrants of different nationalities, amounts to a violation by the state in which it operates of its own most-favoured nation obligation.

Subsidies

In contrast to trade in goods, trade in services is not directly subject to disciplines relating to subsidies and cannot in principle be subject to countervailing measures (Article XV of the GATS).[8] Therefore, public subsidisation originating from public resources (or resources of public operators) is in principle shielded from the scope of the GATS, with the exception that, in such cases, governments are supposed to enter into consultations and accord each other 'sympathetic consideration'. This is all the more surprising as, in sectors subject to specific commitments, cross-subsidisation by independent entities may well fall within the scope of prohibited behaviours under the GATS (see 'Activities of public monopolies' below).

Disciplines that apply to sectors open to international trade

The specific sector-based commitments are the most important ones and condition the entire effectiveness of the GATS. Generally speaking, they address the same issues as those accompanying liberalisation of services in domestic markets, albeit in a much less detailed fashion. Indeed, as previously indicated, the rules of the GATS do not have the objective of

[7] See Article VIII:5 of the GATS. The notion of monopoly suppliers does not include *de facto* monopolies, i.e. those which benefit from an exclusive sale capacity by the mere operation of market forces (see Article XXVIII(h) of the GATS).

[8] The European Community, however, reserved the possibility to impose corrective measures against injurious prices in the audio-visual services sector, in their MFN Exemption List.

regulating conditions of competition, but are merely intended to ensure that these conditions are not regulated at a national level in such a manner as to constitute an undue obstacle to trade.

Schedules of Commitments

For the more stringent rules under the GATS to apply to a sector of the service industry, it must be specifically included in the Schedule of Commitments of a WTO Member. Under GATS, commitments are made according to a classification of services prepared by the Secretariat during the Uruguay Round, on the basis of the United Nations Central Product Classification list (CPC list).[9]

Telecommunications services are listed as sub-sectors of communications services, like audio-visual services.[10] Distinctions between telecommunications services and audio-visual services are further specified in certain Schedules. For instance, the EC's Schedule makes the following clarification:

> Telecommunications services are the transport of electro-magnetic signals – sound, data, image and any combinations thereof, excluding broadcasting . . . Broadcasting is defined as the uninterrupted chain of transmission required for the distribution of TV and radio programme signals to the general public, but does not cover contribution links between operators.[11]

Furthermore, the EC distinguishes telecommunication services from content provision:

[9] See WTO Doc. MTN.GNS/W/120.

[10] They are classified as follows:

- Telecommunications services: voice telephone services; telegraph services; circuit-switched data transmission services; packet-switched data transmission services; private leased circuit services; voice mail; electronic data interchange (EDI); code and protocol conversion; telex services; facsimile services; electronic mail; online information and database retrieval; enhanced/value-added facsimile services; online information and/or data processing; and other telecommunication services, including analog/digital cellular/mobile telephone services, mobile data services, paging, personal communications services, satellite-based mobile services (including e.g. telephony, data, paging, and/or PCS), fixed satellite services, VSAT services, gateway earth station services, teleconferencing, video transport, trunked radio system services and call-back services.
- Audio-visual services: motion picture and videotape production and distribution; motion picture projection service; radio and television services; radio and television transmission services; sound recording; and other services, such as dubbing services (translation of the sound-track of motion pictures and videotapes from one language to another).

[11] WTO Doc. GATS/SC/31/Suppl.3.

> [C]ommitments in this schedule do not cover the economic activity consisting of content provision which require telecommunications services for its transport. The provision of that content, transported via a telecommunications service, is subject to the specific commitments undertaken by the European Communities and their Member States in other relevant sectors.[12]

However, not all Schedules are the same and the additional distinctions brought by the EC are not included in most of WTO Members' Schedules.

The following question could arise: to what extent do the CPC classification and Members' Schedules of Commitments reflect technological developments and market reality? For instance, e-mail services are classified as telecommunication services, and commitments might be taken with respect to them. But what about TV or radio programmes transmitted through the Internet? Considering these are not supplied through an uninterrupted chain of transmission, as they require switching nodes, they are not, in the EC at least, considered as broadcasting services. They could qualify as packet- or circuit-switched data transmission services.

The CPC classification also apparently mixes services and networks. It seems to assume that the provision of a service is inseparable from the network required to provide it. Taking the example of voice telephony or data transmission services, it is unclear whether a commitment for these services also entails a commitment in the provision of networks over which they can be provided. The Chairman of the Group on Basic Telecommunications Services indicated that services listed in the Schedules 'may be provided through any means of technology (e.g., cable, wireless, satellites)'.[13] Yet, certain services contained in the CPC list actually constitute separate network elements (the so-called mobile or satellite services) and no specific category seems to have been defined for cable. The latter has indeed been traditionally used for audio-visual services. Cable communication could nevertheless qualify as a telecommunication service, as it enables the transmission of electromagnetic signals. Thus, some confusion is possible and additional clarity in the definitions would be welcome, especially considering that, in a converged environment, increased competition between networks is likely.

In summary, in applying GATS, it is important to examine and interpret each relevant Schedule of Commitments as these differ from Member to Member and no general presentation can be made of them. It is only when

[12] *Ibid.*

[13] WTO Doc. S/GBT/W/2/Rev.1, 16 January 1997.

a service has been included in a Member's Schedule of Commitments that it can be considered open to international trade in the market of that Member, to the extent described in the Schedule.

The rules that apply in sectors open to international trade are the following.

Market access

Subject to commitments taken in individual Schedules, Article XVI of the GATS (Market Access) requires Members not to maintain national measures limiting the number of service suppliers in a domestic market, or the value or the quantity of services supplied or the number of persons authorised to supply a service.[14] It also requires them not to maintain limitations as to the participation of foreign capital or restrictions as to the legal entity in which a service supplier is authorised to provide a service. Capital movements that are an essential part of the service must be authorised.[15]

When fully applicable, Article XVI thus indirectly obliges WTO Members to dismantle special or exclusive rights granted to service providers for the supply of services.[16] It applies to all aspects of the supply of a service, i.e. 'the production, distribution, marketing, sale and delivery of a service'.[17] Limitations are possible to the extent described in the Schedules of Commitments. In telecommunications services, these concern, for instance, the possibility of countries to reserve to themselves the provision of a universal service.[18]

[14] Article XVI applies to market access through the modes of supply identified in Article I. These are the supply of a service (a) from the territory of one Member into the territory of any other Member (cross-border mode); (b) in the territory of one Member to the service consumer of any other Member (consumption abroad mode); (c) by a service supplier of one Member through commercial presence in the territory of any other Member (commercial presence mode); and (d) by a service supplier of one Member, through presence of natural persons of a Member in the territory of any other Member (physical presence mode).

[15] See note 8 to para. 1 of Article XVI and Article XI of the GATS.

[16] See, however, Article XVIII, paras. 4 and 5, of the GATS, which provide for an obligation of notification of monopoly rights regarding the supply of a service covered by a specific commitment established after the date of entry into force of the WTO Agreement. This provision should not mean, however, that these new monopolies are authorised.

[17] Article XXVIIIb of the GATS.

[18] In the EC's Schedule of Commitments, for instance, there is a specific limitation on market access commitments, which applies to all services listed in the Schedule and which reads as follows: '[I]n all EC Member States services considered as public utilities at a national or local level may be subject to public monopolies or to exclusive rights granted to private operators... Public utilities exist in sectors such as related scientific and technical

National treatment

Article XVII of the GATS contains the national treatment obligation that has the same meaning as Article III of the GATT.[19] This implies the prohibition of *de jure* as well as *de facto* discriminations between domestic and foreign services and service suppliers. The national treatment obligation, as the market access one, may nevertheless be limited by the contents of WTO Members' Schedules of Commitments.

Reasonableness, objectivity and impartiality of domestic regulation

Article VI:1 of the GATS imposes on governments a general obligation of reasonableness, objectivity and impartiality in the administration of domestic regulations affecting trade in services. It means in particular that the manner in which domestic regulation is administered cannot have a negative effect on the competitive position of the undertakings affected in a manner that is not necessary to achieve the intended objective. Impartiality and objectivity in the administration of domestic regulation also require that the interests of regulators do not conflict, and thus strongly encourage, in an implicit manner, WTO Members to separate regulators from operators.

Article VI:3 of GATS imposes disciplines in the provision of authorisations and licences. Service suppliers applying for authorisations must be informed without delay on the status of their application and of the decision on their application.

Article VI:5 of the GATS, read in conjunction with Article VI:4, requires measures relating to qualification requirements and procedures, technical standards and licensing requirements, that nullify or impair commitments of Members, to be based on objective and transparent criteria. They cannot be more burdensome than necessary to achieve the quality of the service and must also have been reasonably expected at the time commitments on the service concerned were made. Articles VI:4 and VI:5 of the GATS do not further specify these rules, but arguably, concerning telecommunication services, they apply to universal service obligations, frequency allocation, licensing, ownership restrictions, lines of business restrictions and general competition law. Only regulation that is new or

consulting services, R&D services on social sciences and humanities, technical testing and analysis services, environmental services, health services, transport services and services auxiliary to all modes of transport.'

[19] See Appellate Body Report, 'European Communities – Regime for the Importation, Sale and Distribution of Bananas', 9 September 1997, WT/DS27/AB/R, p. 101, para. 241.

more restrictive to trade than that existing at the time the commitments were taken seems to be concerned.

Activities of public monopolies

The rules above may also apply to service supply activities of monopolies and exclusive service suppliers, in addition to governments, in accordance with Article VIII:1 of the GATS. The notion of monopoly suppliers covers all enterprises that have been granted special or exclusive rights. In telecommunication services, this could concern national satellite operators, cable companies or telecommunications companies providing services which have not yet been liberalised.

Article VIII:3 also requires WTO Members to ensure that these monopolies do not abuse their dominant position in the reserved markets in relation to those activities subject to specific commitments in which they operate in competition and which are outside the scope of their monopoly rights. For example, if voice telephony is still subject to monopoly rights, but not data transmission services, the national telecommunications operator cannot use its dominant position in voice telephony to unduly confer an advantage to its data transmission activities.

The notion of 'abuse of dominant position' is not explained in the GATS, which thus leaves a wide margin of discretion to the legal interpreter. It is unclear whether such discretion will belong exclusively to national authorities and, therefore, only their inaction against such monopolies would be subject to a WTO violation claim, or if a WTO panel would exercise control over the manner in which states assess and combat abuses of dominant position. In theory, WTO rules do not prevent a panel from interpreting for itself the notion of abuse of dominant position and to make an objective assessment in accordance with the standard of review contained in Article 11 of the WTO Dispute Settlement Understanding.

Article VIII of the GATS may thus cover certain types of anti-competitive practices by private operators that are not otherwise prohibited by GATS, such as private cross-subsidisation or abusive control on bottlenecks, excessive interconnection prices etc. It may also lead to a WTO version of the 'essential facilities' doctrine entailing a general obligation on the part of incumbent operators to grant access to their networks for the operation of scheduled services.[20]

[20] See Commission Decision No. 94/119 of 21 December 1993, Port of Rôdby, OJ 1994 L55/22.

Article VIII of GATS, however, would not by itself mandate positive regulation by governments such as unbundling of the local loop, accounts separation or vertical divestiture.

Restrictive business practices of private operators

With regard to the activities of service suppliers that are not granted special or exclusive rights, WTO Members recognise that certain business practices of such service suppliers may restrain competition and thereby restrict trade in services (Article IX of the GATS). Even though, strictly speaking, states are not obliged to combat such practices, at least they must, at the request of any other member, enter into consultations with a view to eliminating these anti-competitive practices. Article IX of the GATS might be useful in those countries where communication services have been recently liberalised, but where an incumbent operator remains *de facto* dominant in the market.

Also, in accordance with the 'administrative guidance' doctrine developed under the GATT by the 'Japan – Trade in Semiconductors' Panel, the practices of private operators which are 'guided' by public authorities and which nullify or impair benefits granted under the GATS should be included within the scope of the GATS.[21] However, in light of this doctrine, strategic alliances between independent companies, which are not encouraged by governments, would not be covered by the GATS and not be prohibited by international trade law although they might be contrary to competition rules.

Additional commitments

The principles above may be complemented by additional commitments regarding, among others, competition rules, qualifications, standards and licensing matters. These additional commitments may be inscribed in WTO Members' Schedules of Commitments for specific sectors, in accordance with Article XVIII of the GATS. Such additional commitments are contained in the Reference Paper relating to basic telecommunication services (see below).

[21] See GATT 1947 Panel Report, 'Japan – Trade in Semiconductors', Adopted on 4 May 1988, BISD 35S/116, paras. 106–9. See also Panel Report, 'Japan – Measures Affecting Consumer Photographic Film and Paper', WT/DS44/R, paras. 10.49 and 10.376.

The Annex on Telecommunications

The GATS Annex on Telecommunications does not mandate specific liberalisation of telecommunications services or networks.[22] It complements the GATS by adding general commitments applicable to WTO Members with respect to all services that have been inscribed in their Schedules of Commitments. It is based on the assumption that use of, and access to, public transport telecommunication networks and services is an essential element for the proper provision of these services.[23] Thus, to the extent international trade in a service is authorised in a domestic market, the Annex on Telecommunications requires the competent national government to grant access to its public networks and services to whoever supplies it.

Scope of the Annex: public telecommunications transport networks and services

The Annex mandates access to and use of *public telecommunications transport network and services.* 'Telecommunications' is defined as 'the transmission and reception of signals by any electromagnetic means'.[24] Thus signals transmitted and received through networks using at some point the electromagnetic spectrum appear to be covered by this definition. Arguably, this also includes cable distribution of signals.[25] However, explicit clarification would be appreciated here.

'Public telecommunications transport *service*' is defined as

> any telecommunications transport service required, explicitly or in effect, by a Member to be offered to the public generally. Such services may include, 'inter alia', telegraph, telephone, telex, and data transmission typically involving real-time transmission of customer-supplied information between two or more points without any end-to-end change in the form or content of the customer's information.[26]

[22] Article 2c1(x) of the Annex on Telecommunications.
[23] *Ibid.*, Article 1.
[24] *Ibid.*, Article 3(a).
[25] Cables transmit electromagnetic signals (whether digital or analogue) and themselves use the electromagnetic spectrum.
[26] Article 3(b) of the Annex on Telecommunications.

This definition thus covers 'telecommunications services' according to the degree of their public availability in the domestic market of the WTO Member taking the commitment.

'Public telecommunications transport *network*' is defined as

> the public telecommunications infrastructure which permits telecommunications between and among defined termination points.[27]

It is unclear whether such a definition would cover all infrastructure required for the supply of 'public telecommunications transport services'. In particular, the status of cable networks should be clarified. Their full inclusion would make sense. Indeed, to the extent a service falling under the scope of the Annex requires broadband technology, arguably, access to this kind of technology, whether through cable or through the radio-electric spectrum should be guaranteed in accordance with the principles set out in the Annex.

It should be noted that cable or broadcast distribution of radio or television programming are explicitly excluded from the scope of the Annex (for further comments, see Chapter 9 below).[28]

Access to and use of public telecommunications transport network and services

The Annex on Telecommunications obliges Members to provide all suppliers of a scheduled service access to their public telecommunications infrastructure and to let them use all 'public' telecommunication services (i.e. those to be offered to the public generally), on reasonable and non-discriminatory terms and conditions.[29] Service suppliers must also have the right to purchase or lease terminal equipment or to interconnect private leased lines or privately owned circuits within the public network. They must be given the possibility to use their own operating protocols and to have access to international communications and to information contained in databases.[30] This means that service suppliers can choose how to supply their services, including via the Internet.

[27] *Ibid.*, Article 3(c).
[28] *Ibid.*, Article 2(b).
[29] *Ibid.*, Article 5(a).
[30] *Ibid.*, Article 5(b) and (c).

Exceptions to these obligations are allowed to the extent that they are necessary: to ensure the security or confidentiality of messages;[31] to safeguard the public responsibilities of suppliers of public telecommunications transport network and services; to protect the technical integrity of the network; or to ensure that services that are not being opened to international trade are nevertheless supplied.[32] Authorised limitations are listed in the Annex (for further details, see Chapter 9 below).[33]

Transparency, technical cooperation and international standards

The Annex on Telecommunications requires that all information relating to the conditions of use and access to public telecommunications transport networks and services is made publicly available, including technical interfaces, bodies responsible for the preparation and adoption of standards, and any kind of registration or licensing requirements.[34] The Annex thus complements Article III of GATS in this regard.

The Annex also encourages international cooperation in the development of the most efficient and advanced telecommunications infrastructure,[35] and supports the transfer of technology and the adoption of international standards. The latter are indeed considered as an important means to ensure the compatibility and interoperability of telecommunications networks. In this connection, the role of the International Telecommunications Union (ITU) and of the International Organization of Standardization (IOS) is officially recognised in the Annex.[36]

The Agreement on Basic Telecommunication Services

As previously indicated, GATS rules may be completed by additional commitments on specific scheduled sectors, in accordance with Article XVIII of the GATS. A good example is the Agreement on Basic Telecommunications Services (ABTS), between sixty-nine countries, which entered into force on 5 February 1998. The ABTS first obliges its parties to include

[31] *Ibid.*, Article 5(d).
[32] *Ibid.*, Article 5(e).
[33] *Ibid.*, Article 5(f).
[34] *Ibid.*, Article 4.
[35] *Ibid.*, Articles 6 and 7.
[36] *Ibid.*, Article 7.

basic telecommunication services in their Schedules of Commitments.[37] The ABTS then specifies additional rules to be observed in relation to these services, in order to ensure the effectiveness of national commitments taken on them. These additional rules are included in the so-called Reference Paper, which is so named because these rules are integrated into the GATS by reference made to them in the Schedules of Commitments of parties to the ABTS.

The additional principles contained in the Reference Paper are the following.

Competitive safeguards

Section 1 of the Reference Paper requires parties to the ABTS to maintain 'appropriate measures . . . for the purpose of preventing suppliers who, alone or together, are a major supplier from engaging in or continuing anti-competitive practices'.

Anti-competitive practices are defined as:

- engaging in anti-competitive *cross-subsidisation*;
- *using information* obtained from competition with anti-competitive results; and
- *not making available* to other service suppliers on a timely basis *technical information* about essential facilities and commercially relevant information which are necessary for them to provide services.

Such limitation of private anti-competitive practices is an exceptional feature in the WTO that usually does not regulate competition within the domestic markets of its Members. However, competitive safeguard rules of the Reference Paper are only intended to ensure that market access commitments are not impaired by the most obvious and damaging violations of competition principles. They do not aim to establish a full competitive environment within the countries that are parties to the ABTS.

Indeed, obligations contained in Section 1 of the Reference Paper only concern undertakings which, alone or together, are qualified as 'major suppliers'. These are defined as those which

[37] For a description of the services concerned, see the Background Note of the Secretariat of the WTO, 'Telecommunications Services', Doc. S/C/W/74, 8 December 1998.

> have the ability to materially affect the terms of participation (having regard to price and supply) in the relevant market for basic telecommunications services as a result of
> – control over essential facilities or
> – use of its position in the market.

Essential facilities are themselves defined as

> a public telecommunications transport network and service that
> – are exclusively or predominantly provided by a single or limited number of suppliers; and
> – cannot feasibly be economically or technically substituted in order to provide a service.

Thus, the competitive safeguard rules of the Reference Paper mainly prevent abusive restrictions on bottleneck facilities that may result in *a de facto* limitation on market access of basic telecommunications services. They also prevent abusive conduct of dominant suppliers of such basic telecommunications services, even if they do not control essential facilities, but may obstruct entry of foreign competitors.

Interconnection

Section 2 of the Reference Paper imposes an obligation on major suppliers of public telecommunications transport networks or services to enable interconnection with their networks and services. Such interconnection must be granted on non-discriminatory, transparent and reasonable terms and conditions, on a timely basis and at chosen network termination points. There is also a requirement of transparency of rates and of their relation to costs. Additionally, interconnection must be 'sufficiently unbundled so that the supplier need not pay for network components or facilities that it does not require for the service to be provided'.

There is no indication as to the level of unbundling required, the methodology for defining interconnection prices and the kind of regulation to be adopted in this regard (*ex ante* vertical rules or *ex post* competition law). Section 2 of the Reference Paper only requires that interconnection procedures as well as reference interconnection offers and/or agreements reached must be made publicly available.[38]

[38] One could question whether publicising offers and agreements would constitute an infringement of domestic competition laws.

Finally, Section 2 of the Reference Paper requires parties to the ABTS to organise independent dispute resolution procedures between operators with respect to interconnection disputes.

Universal service

Section 3 of the Reference Paper clearly stipulates that commitments on basic telecommunication services should not impede the adoption of universal service requirements. It provides that these requirements must be 'administered in a transparent, non-discriminatory and competitively neutral manner and are not more burdensome than necessary for the kind of universal service defined'. Article VI:1 of the GATS, requiring that all measures affecting trade in scheduled services be administered in a reasonable, objective and impartial manner, is also relevant here. Consistently with its soft approach, the Reference Paper does not give any indication of the kind of universal service that could be mandated by the Members.

Licensing criteria

Section 4 of the Reference Paper stipulates an obligation of transparency and publication of licensing criteria and conditions similar to the one contained in Articles III and VI:3 of the GATS. It requires in addition that the terms and conditions of individual licences also be made public.

Independent regulators

Section 5 of the Reference Paper requires the regulator to be independent of the suppliers of basic telecommunications services and to take impartial decisions. This section thus specifies, with regard to basic telecommunications services, the rule of impartiality and objectivity contained in Article VI:1 of the GATS.

Allocation and use of scarce resources

Section 6 of the Reference Paper specifies that the procedures for the allocation of scarce resources must be carried out in 'an objective, timely, transparent and non-discriminatory manner'. Scarce resources include frequencies, numbers and rights of way. Section 6 also provides that the current state of allocated bands must be made publicly available. In practice, this could favour any supplier of a network over which a basic telecommunications service can be supplied, even if such network is also used for an unscheduled service (see Chapter 9 below).

Summary

For services for which no specific commitments were made, probably the most important obligation under the GATS is that relating to the most-favoured nation clause. This entails some important consequences for service suppliers which traditionally benefit from special or exclusive rights. Indeed, pursuant to Article VIII:1 of the GATS, they must treat all their trade partners in a non-discriminatory manner. This means, for instance, that the effects of preferential bilateral agreements between an undertaking which has been granted exclusive rights for the operation of a network and other service suppliers which would require access to such network must in principle[39] be extended to service suppliers of all WTO Members.[40]

For those services for which commitments were made, subject to possible limitations in individual Schedules, the GATS provides for the elimination of special or exclusive rights in national markets. It prohibits discriminatory conditions of competition within these markets and prevents, in broadly defined terms, anti-competitive practices of dominant suppliers. It also requires that all national regulation governing the provision of the service concerned or which has an impact on such provision be administered in a reasonable, objective and impartial manner, and defines general principles governing the issuance of licences.

Furthermore, telecommunications services and networks, for which commitments were made, may benefit from the rules of the Annex on Telecommunications, to the extent domestic laws (or *de facto* practices) of the countries taking commitments require them to be offered to the public generally. Finally, pursuant to the Agreement on Basic Telecommunications Services, these services may benefit from the rules contained in the Reference Paper.

It is important to stress that, in the absence of commitments, the GATS and its Annexes do not provide a very useful tool to entrants or new users

[39] Account must be taken of exemptions listed by Members pursuant to Article II:2 of the GATS.

[40] As indicated below, the Annex on Telecommunications could also be relevant, but the latter only applies to scheduled services. This is not the case of Article VIII:1 of the GATS, read in combination with Article II of the GATS.

in a specific market. Consequently, service liberalisation, and in particular the development of converged communication services and broadband networks, depend on specific commitments made sector by sector. They thus heavily rely on the classifications and definitions made.

When commitments are made, existing rules address typical concerns that are inherent to the liberalisation processes in a network industry. They prevent the most obvious anti-competitive practices of dominant operators resulting in restrictions to trade, such as abusive control of bottleneck facilities, abusive cross-subsidisation and unfair conditions of interconnection. They also prohibit, for the same reason, restrictive licensing procedures and the presence of joined regulators and operators. However, their provisions remain general and are limited to broad obligations necessary to eliminate barriers to trade within domestic markets. Clearly, they do not extend to rules whose objective would be to harmonise conditions of competition between markets, as this would clearly unduly expand the scope of international trade law.

The GATS and the Reference Paper are not highly regulatory *per se.* They leave a wide margin of discretion to states as to how they wish to conduct liberalisation in their territory. They thus enable states to pursue a policy fostering a network-based competition rather than a service-based competition or *vice versa.* There is also no mandate as to whether regulation should be a symmetric or an asymmetric one.[41] The only requirement is that those who control essential facilities do not behave in an abusive manner.

Finally, existing rules do not prevent states from pursuing social policy objectives and offering universal services. However, they do not define these objectives or services. Such policy-making is adequately left to the discretion of national governments, which are only under a duty to administer their rules in a non-discriminatory and reasonable manner.

The subsequent chapters of this book discuss audio-visual policies and content regulation in the context of the WTO.

[41] A symmetric regulation is one which imposes the same competition rules on all operators. An asymmetric regulation is one which imposes more obligations on incumbent operators.

4

Accounting rates, cross-border services and the next WTO round on basic telecommunications services

PETER F. COWHEY

Introduction

One of the most contentious issues in the negotiations on basic telecommunications services in 1997 was the treatment of 'accounting rates' for switched international services (these switched services are primarily cross-border telephone and fax services). This arcane pricing system for interconnection between national carriers nearly sank the negotiation because it masked major issues involving financial flows and competition in international services.

The negotiation cobbled together a package that allowed a trade agreement in 1997 even though there was no general consensus about accounting rates. This package included a tacit understanding between the United States and the European Union that the European Union would be silent while the United States used unilateral regulatory measures to change prevailing practices about accounting rates. In return, the United States would have to risk a possible WTO challenge and the possibility of a diplomatic brouhaha about its actions.

Conflict and protest persist over accounting rates and their Internet descendant, international charging arrangements for Internet traffic exchange. Cross-border service disputes may also spill over into the world of wireless networking. The second part of this chapter briefly explains why it is so politically difficult to get good policy and practice on these issues. The third part of this chapter explains the underlying economic significance of the accounting rate debate. The fourth part of this chapter examines changes in the market for traditional international switched services and the issues for the WTO. And the final part of this chapter examines new forms of market distortion and the policy options for regulatory and trade authorities.

Why international services are hard to reform

Issues concerning the reform of the market for international services have been very hard for regulators and trade authorities to confront. The underlying reason is simple and clearly shows that trade agreements are an exercise in *political* economy. Countries too often try to maintain large flows of rents in the international services marketplace to compensate carriers for lower margins on domestic services as competition in the domestic market increases. This politically expeditious approach might not be excessively troubling because the WTO agreement of 1997 (and accompanying national policy measures) unlocked enough market change to erode the rents on traditional switched international services strongly over time. There are still significant risks, however. The issues regarding new services are far more important than lingering disputes about international switched services.

The third part of this chapter examines the economics of the market in detail. This part focuses on the political economy of protecting market incumbents through regulatory action or inaction. The underlying political and economic problem – a propensity to cushion market risks for major companies in the market – could harm such new cross-border services as Internet protocol and wireless services. This could weaken the technological foundation for the creation of seamless global networking over wired and wireless networks that will intersect with scalable distributed computing (over a variety of information devices). The market must be efficient enough to encourage such innovations.

Why is rent seeking so difficult to curb? Large flows of rents have befuddled the implementation of many economic policy reforms. The international services market reflects six classic problems of political economy.

1. *It is hard to provide collective goods.* Those who bear large losses from improving market efficiency (a collective good) are more motivated to act politically than those who will receive smaller, diffuse benefits. This complicates reform.
2. *Reform coalitions are not angels.* Supporters of regulatory change also want concentrated benefits from reform. This means that reform packages have their own flaws.
3. *Political entrepreneurs make reform possible, but politicians like concentrated, visible, political benefits from reform.* This introduces distortions of reform.

4. *Compromises built around the timing of benefits are vital.* Deferred losses are less painful. Classic compensation mechanisms for market-change policy measures allow losers to lose more slowly. Winners get policy skewed to assure selective up-front benefits but defer their biggest gains until later.
5. *All stakeholders are not created equal.* Foreigners are not as vital to political success, so deals at their expense are attractive.
6. *Inaction is an easier way to distribute economic rents than action.* Monitoring and enforcement problems for regulators in complex specialised markets make it easy for regulators to act slowly.

A major axiom of modern political economy flows from the work of Mancur Olson.[1] Collective goods, like efficient markets, produce diffuse benefits and concentrated costs. Therefore, it is easier to mobilise those who will lose from reform than those who will benefit. This strongly influences the politics of reform. In the case of telecom carriers there was an entrenched coalition of the carrier, its labour force (usually extremely well paid and highly unionised) and the equipment suppliers for the carrier (who shared in rents earned by the carrier).[2] Although this coalition lost the war over general telecommunications competition globally, it remains to try to slow specific forms of competition that threaten the most lucrative remaining sources of market rents.

Change came in the telecom market, as in others, because a counter-coalition was established among those who could receive concentrated benefits from reform. (This is completely consistent with Olson's logic.) In telecoms this coalition consisted of large corporate users (who constituted a large percentage of total long-distance traffic), equipment suppliers outside of the traditional vendors to the telephone monopolies, and carriers who had identified potentially profitable market entry strategies.[3] This coalition did not support reform simply to get market efficiency. Members were interested in particular reforms in specific sequences as their

[1] Mancur Olson, *The Logic of Collective Action: Public Goods and the Theory of Groups* (Cambridge, MA: Harvard University Press, 1971). The Stigler-Peltzman interest group theory of government (capture theory) goes back to George Stigler, 'The Theory of Economic Regulation', *Bell Journal of Economics and Management Science* 2 (Spring 1971): 3–21; and Sam Peltzman, 'Towards a More General Theory of Regulation', *Journal of Law and Economics* 19 (1976): 211–40.

[2] Eli Noam, *Telecommunications in Europe* (New York: Oxford University Press, 1993).

[3] Peter F. Cowhey, 'The International Telecommunications Regime: The Political Roots of High Technology Regimes', *International Organization* 44 (Spring 1990): 169–99.

business needs demanded them. Thus, reform coalitions also sought special benefits from the particular shape of the reform package.

Political entrepreneurs serve as the catalyst for forging a combination of the reform coalition's concerns with the political gains of supporting general reform.[4] Entrepreneurs are looking to advance their individual careers and the welfare of their political parties (assuming the existence of a democracy) by reforming markets in ways that win credit from voters. This dynamic adds its own spin to the particular path of reform. For example, reforms in the United States are often justified on the basis of creating 'good jobs', or in other countries on the basis of spurring investment and network construction projects. In developing countries privatisation of the former monopoly and the introduction of competition often boosts the local stock market dramatically.[5] Politicians like to point to such visible benefits of reforms to counter complaints by losers. As a result, once competition is introduced initially, political leaders often trade some diffuse benefits, such as price reductions (especially less visible and transparent prices), for 'success' on these grounds. This leads to a temptation to create competition that is friendly not to more vigorous market performance, but to large competitors instead. Thus, when carriers run into trouble there is a temptation to find ways to ease their troubles. The carriers most likely to be assisted are those with the country's most ubiquitous business and workforce deployment and those who seem essential to the provision of services visible to voters on a daily basis. Thus, it is one thing to see some new entrants in fibre optic networking stumble; it is another to see France Telecom or Telmex in trouble.

Maintaining margins on international services is a convenient way of bolstering these carriers. Moreover, as conventional switched services experience declining margins due to more competition, governments may let new forms of international rent seeking go unchallenged. This is especially tempting because the traditional organisation of international services makes high margins easy to reap unless regulators intervene

[4] On the incentives for political entrepreneurship, see, for example, Gary Cox and Matthew D. McCubbins, *Legislative Leviathan* (Berkeley: University of California Press, 1993).

[5] For example, finance ministries in developing countries had mixed incentives about the treatment of the dominant national carrier. On the one hand, telecommunications competition policy was a prominent part of economic reform packages. On the other hand, government often had a substantial equity stake in the carrier (which usually had been a state-owned monopoly prior to privatisation and competition). Moreover, the newly privatised carriers were frequently a large percentage of the total value of the local stock exchange. Finance ministries often tried to deflect financial shocks to these carriers in order to stabilise the market.

vigorously to stimulate competition (see the fourth part of this chapter, below).

A technologically dynamic market with diverse demands can upset any effort to manage rent sharing once some competition emerges. Thus, the time value of money plays out in balancing gains and losses. Political leadership often follows this strategy: competition can let major players lose, but market tinkering can make it possible to let them lose more slowly. (Think of the slowly declining farm or steel industries.) The same is true in telecommunications. A dollar lost tomorrow is less painful than one lost today. So, a company that sees that it cannot win in the long run will bargain for more market protection today in return for a bigger market reform in the future. The winners will accept a slower transition to secure the ultimate reform. Of course, the most concerned stakeholders will get special deals up front. For example, massive discounts to large corporate customers may thrive at an early date even though policy defers general competition for several years.

Not all stakeholders with concentrated interests are politically equal. As a rule of thumb, most countries value the interests of domestic consumers and producers more than those of foreign consumers and producers. Foreigners don't vote.[6] In politically difficult market transitions, then, governments may redistribute rents from foreign consumers and producers to their domestic counterparts. International services were classic sources of substantial rents. Governments are thus more likely to tackle problems concerning bolstering competition in domestic markets than those influencing competition in cross-border services.[7]

Finally, as regulatory processes become more transparent in competitive markets, it is harder (but not impossible) to take affirmative action to give financial assistance to particular market stakeholders. It is easier for a regulator to help a company that is profiting from market inefficiency by doing nothing, proceeding slowly, or acting weakly, even if there is a

[6] Political scientists have demonstrated that the structure of government institutions, such as the nature of electoral systems or the form of executive power (for example, parliamentary or presidential) will influence how these strategies play out in a particular country. For the purposes of a review of global markets I have omitted analysis of these factors. See George Tsebelis, 'Decision Making in Political Systems: Veto Players in Presidentialism, Parliamentarism, Multicameralism, and Multipartyism', *British Journal of Political Science* 25 (1995): 291–325; and Fiona McGillivray, 'Government Hand-Outs, Political Institutions, Stock Price Dispersion', unpublished manuscript, Yale University, 2001.

[7] There are joint costs involved in international services, so cost-sharing is logical (assuming that a single carrier does not provide end-to-end service). If traffic flows are totally symmetric there will be no net transfer of monies between two carriers.

clear lack of competition. This tactic is particularly attractive in markets where monitoring and enforcing competition rules is hard. Specialised and complex market segments with fewer participants often fit this category. International markets are especially prone to these problems.

In summary, many countries introduce reforms to create competition in telecommunications markets. These reforms usually introduce a major change in the market structure and substantially improve market performance. These reforms are usually Pareto superior, but not Pareto optimal. As political leaders seek to ease the risks for larger competitors of a market transition to more competition, international service markets can emerge as a politically convenient source of rents.

The significance of accounting rates

To understand how the WTO agreement influenced the economics of cross-border services, it is useful to imagine two rivers intersecting and then branching off in a new direction. One river was the flow of rents created by the traditional provision of cross-border services under the accounting rate (or, more properly, settlement rate) system. The other river was the interest in market liberalisation that drove the WTO negotiation. A new branch is emerging from the intersection of these two flows.

Accounting rates are an obscure product of the traditional way of organising the cross-border telecommunications market in the age of monopolies. They continue to plague the market now that competition has become the general rule in the largest market centres. Thus, the debate about accounting rates is only a subset of the problems of how to create an efficient competitive market for cross-border transport and end services that will benefit consumers.

The old market structure for international telecommunications services was built around the 'joint supply' of international telephone services using accounting rates. Under this system each carrier theoretically contributed half of the international phone or fax services (so-called 'switched' international services) – for example, taking the international call from a hypothetical midpoint in the ocean and terminating the call to a local household in its country. Presumably, the supply of an international call depended on each national carrier providing half of the facilities for the call.[8] Jointly provided services allowed one party to block production

[8] See note 7 above.

and/or control the total cost of production through unilateral decisions about the pricing of its services. The price for interconnecting calls between the two countries, the accounting rate, was negotiated between the two national carriers and was computed on the basis of a price for one minute of a traditional circuit-switched call.[9] While trade negotiators traditionally talked about accounting rates, the economically relevant concept was the *settlement rate* (typically one-half of the accounting rate). The settlement rate was really the interconnection fee paid to a country for terminating a call from another country.[10]

Most developing countries traditionally priced phone services in ways that had little relation to costs, so there was enormous pressure to cover shortfalls on local services by inflating rates for international services. All countries suffered from inflated rates for international services, but the situation was especially bad in developing countries.[11] Moreover, since demand is elastic, the inflated prices effectively turned communications into a lower-volume luxury good in these countries.

At the same time, the developing countries found it particularly attractive to extract rents from carriers in industrial countries by inflating settlement rates.[12] Under a settlement rate system, the national carriers of the United States and, say, Mexico periodically settled up on the cost of settlement. If the settlement rate was fifty cents per minute and the United States sent a million minutes more of switched traffic to Mexico than it received (that is, more people called for longer periods from the

[9] Carriers conduct the negotiations and conclude a commercial contract to establish the accounting/settlement rate. The settlement rate is not the end price to consumers. National carriers mark up the price still further for originating an international call. However, the costs created by settlement rates influence the minimum price for the service. The key cost for a national carrier is the net settlement payment (the settlement rate multiplied by its net surplus or deficit of minutes of traffic with another country). Large traffic imbalances and high settlement rates soon inflate the size of net settlement payments.

[10] It bundled under one price the service of providing one-half of the international circuit, the termination in the cable station, the short-haul transport from the cable station to the national long-distance station, and the termination of the call to the local customer.

[11] For example, international services in Asia were typically 30–60 per cent of total revenues, even though international traffic was a small percentage of total traffic. Craig Irvine, 'International Telephony and Asian Network Expansion,' in Gregory Staple, ed., *Telegeography 1998* (Washington, DC: Telegeography, 1998), pp. 41–3. In larger South American countries, prices for international services in 1998 were still typically four to six times higher than for domestic long distance. Myles Davis, Luiz Carvalho and Josh Milberg, 'International Long Distance in Latin America' in ibid., pp. 44–6.

[12] It was so attractive that finance ministries routinely diverted the monies to cover other budgetary needs.

United States to Mexico than *vice versa*), then the US carriers would owe a US$500,000 settlement payment to Mexico.

US carriers paid over US$5 billion in net settlement payments to foreign carriers in 1996, mostly to developing countries. (This was a remarkable sum. In 1996, the United States accounted for US$12 billion of a US$50 billion world market for international telecommunications services.) The Federal Communications Commission (FCC) estimated that at least 80 per cent of this total constituted an economic rent.[13] And, as this was rent collected from foreigners, not local citizens and businesses, it was particularly attractive politically.

The stream of rents from cross-border services was one powerful 'river' in the global market. The fall-out from domestic liberalisation of a few key markets was the other river.[14] It led to the WTO negotiation because the OECD countries were impatient to secure their mutual rights to market access in basic telecommunications services, including telephony, and the WTO was a convenient forum for achieving this goal.

The Annex on Basic Telecommunications of the GATS outlined a legal framework for extending WTO negotiations on basic telecom services after the general conclusion of the Uruguay Round.[15] However, the multilateral features of the WTO (particularly the most-favoured nation (MFN) and national treatment obligations) meant that mutual opening among OECD countries automatically conferred benefits on the telephone carriers of developing countries. The industrial countries feared a two-tier market would emerge – general competition in industrial countries and a blend of privatisation and very limited competition in developing

[13] Peter Cowhey, 'FCC Benchmarks and the Reform of the International Telecommunications Market', *Telecommunications Policy* 22 (1999): 899–911. In the era of state-owned monopolies, companies relied primarily on public financing to build the network. While profits from settlement rates contributed to the convertible currency needed to buy foreign telecommunications equipment, higher settlement rates did not induce more network build-out. Rent collection predominated over strategic investment. Scott J. Wallsten, 'International Telecommunications Accounting Rate Reforms: The Effects of Reduced Rates on Telecom Traffic and Investments in Developing Countries', Stanford Institute for Economic Policy Research, June 2000.

[14] For a review of these developments, see Peter Cowhey and John E. Richards, 'Dialing for Dollars: Institutional Designs for the Globalization of the Market for Basic Telecommunications Services', in Aseem Prakash and Jeffrey Hart, eds., *Coping with Globalization* (New York: Routledge, 1999), pp. 148–69.

[15] This section draws materially on: Peter Cowhey and Mikhail M. Klimenko, 'The WTO Agreement and Telecommunications Policy Reform', Policy Research Working Paper 2601, Washington, DC: World Bank, May 2001); and Cowhey and Richards, 'Dialing for Dollars'.

countries. This mix would sabotage hopes of creating truly global competitive networks.

After a rocky negotiation, the WTO agreement on basic telecom services featured specific commitments on market access from an impressive number of signatories: sixty-seven of sixty-nine participating governments made significant liberalisation commitments. The poorest participation was by African countries and the smallest developing countries. Participation by the newly industrialised countries was strong.

The WTO obligations came into effect on 1 January 1998. (The date deliberately coincided with the introduction of competition in the European Union.) Commitments on market access typically included all forms of basic communications services (from cellular through land-line), were technology-neutral (and this made no distinction, for example, between satellite and wired services), and included the right to ownership by foreign investment.[16] A critical feature of the commitments of industrial countries was *international simple resale* (ISR). ISR permits a foreign carrier to lease a transmission circuit between countries and then send switched voice and data traffic over the circuit. Because the carrier is providing the service on its own (it is not 'jointly provided'), it is exempt from the settlement rate.[17] This opened the way to moving traffic between countries at the cost of competitively provided transmission facilities, a radically lower cost than one set by settlement rates.

About 85 per cent of the world market, measured by revenues, was covered by strong market-access commitments in the final agreement. With a few specific exceptions on particular issues or market segments, all the OECD nations were bound to unconditional market access on 1 January 1998. Some developing countries used the 1997 agreement to accelerate policy reforms and others to bind intended future liberalisation of basic telecommunications. Other governments bound only the existing policy regimes or even made WTO commitments that were below existing

[16] Countries also scheduled limits on market access. These included limits on total foreign ownership of a common carrier, limits on the total number of phone companies in the market, or a phase-in schedule for obligations on market access.

[17] ISR is better understood as the logical alternative of being able to create a cross-border transport network under the control of a single carrier. A carrier could own a complete transmission network of its own in addition to leasing circuits from another country's carrier. The key point is that regulation permits the carrier to make this choice on a business-like basis and does not impose the cost and service structure of settlement rates on international services. It should also be noted that the ability to transport traffic across borders does not resolve the issue of the ability to terminate the traffic into the building of a local customer. This last-mile transport remains an issue for global networks.

levels of competition.[18] In general, the major industrialising countries made significant commitments on market access that increased rapidly over a period of a few years (typically after transition periods ranging from two to five years).[19]

The changes embodied in the WTO pact were thus likely to accelerate even if there was no future trade round simply because changes in the core of the world market influence the market environment of all other nations. A combination of market changes and new expectations about the industry enshrined in international agreements created a shift in the 'international regime'. The concept of a 'regime' captures the principles, norms and rules expected of participants in major fields of governance in the world economy. In other words, it encapsulates expectations about how the market and governments will interact that go beyond strict legal agreements.[20]

This regime change had numerous implications. For example, it raised the bar for market access commitments on telecommunications services for China and other new members of the WTO. More critically, the agreement changed the expectations of all economic agents, including governments. The newly industrialising countries' binding commitments on introducing general market competition provided credible and easily summarised evidence (the opposite of 'cheap talk') to all other developing countries that competition was coming. Since the 1997 WTO agreement, key industrialising countries have quickened the pace of introducing competition. For example, in 1999, Argentina, Peru and Brazil introduced competition in long-distance services that went beyond their WTO commitments. So, too, has India, a major sceptic about the 1997 liberalisation.

[18] Several features of the WTO can lead these countries with weaker commitments to ratchet up their market opening to all countries faster than they would have otherwise without WTO commitments. Patrick Lowe and A. Mattoo, 'Reform in Basic Telecommunications and the WTO Negotiations: The Asian Experience', Staff Working Paper, Research and Analysis Division, Geneva, World Trade Organization, 1997.

[19] The US government scoring system on market-access commitments for Asia, for example, rated the South Korean, Singaporean and Hong Kong offers as strong; the Philippine and Malaysian offers as good; and the offers of India, Indonesia and Thailand as ranging from poor to fair.

[20] A close analogy in economic theory would be a bargaining game's 'focal point' – a point in the continuum of options that comes to dominate expectations and thus shapes the initial strategies of actors, including specialised interest coalitions. Robert Keohane, *After Hegemony: Cooperation and Discord in the International System* (Princeton, NJ: Princeton University Press, 1984); Cowhey, 'International Telecommunications Regime'.

The continuing struggle over market rents

There is a very large caveat to the regime change story. More competition meant painful industrial restructuring by the dominant incumbent. Given inefficient domestic pricing structures that kept prices below costs (often enshrined in regulatory mandates) the difficulty of this adjustment became greater if the previous large rents on international services declined significantly. Meanwhile, incumbent operators had a powerful political weapon against introducing extensive competition: the argument that new entrants would choose to serve only urban areas and global markets (thus 'skimming the cream' from the market).[21] This argument had special political strength in regard to international services.

Unsurprisingly, in 1997, developing countries planned to create less competition in international services than domestic services.[22] The WTO agreement did not automatically require radical changes in the settlement rate system even by countries introducing competition.[23] Many countries thus allowed some or substantial domestic competition but withheld the opening of their market for cross-border switched services either entirely or until a much later date. Countries could still insist that newly authorised carriers operate under the framework of jointly provided services and settlement rates. For example, Mexico licensed new international carriers but insisted on their use of settlement rates for all phone and fax traffic. It further insisted that the dominant incumbent carrier, Telmex, have sole authority to negotiate the settlement rate for all carriers. Moreover, with only a few exceptions (such as Hong Kong and South Korea) most developing countries drafted their WTO obligations so that they could avoid ISR.[24] In short, developing countries, even with more competition,

[21] A geographically averaged rate, which inflates prices for urban areas, makes entry into urban areas quite profitable. Cowhey and Klimenko, 'The WTO Agreement', p. 51, outline remedies.

[22] For a review of the commitments at the WTO, see Background Note by the WTO Secretariat, Telecommunications Services, presented to the Council for Trade in Services (S/C/W/74), 8 December 1998.

[23] To assure the legality of accounting/settlement rates at the WTO, at least for a time, the Chairman's Note on Accounting Rates at the conclusion of the WTO negotiations made it doubtful that any country could bring a WTO challenge before 1 January 2000 (Alex Arena, 'The WTO Telecommunications Agreement: Some Personal Reflections', in *TeleGeography* (Washington, DC: TeleGeography, 1997). Therefore, no one could force the abandonment of the benchmarks through a WTO challenge until late 2002.

[24] For an analysis of how countries in the Americas limited ISR in their WTO commitments, see the presentation of Maria Cruz Alonso Antolin to the World Services Congress, Atlanta, Georgia, November 1999, which is available at www.ahciet.es.

desired a slower decline in settlement rates than industrial countries, all the while acknowledging that settlement rates would decline steeply and likely disappear in the long term.

Nonetheless, switched international services are being brought closer to the costs found in a competitive market. Perhaps the most dramatic political event around this change came because the United States was not content to let the settlement-rate system stand. MFN and national treatment rules meant that other countries could have access to the US market for international services without making a similar commitment on market access. For example, India could obtain a licence for ISR service out of the United States and essentially make all the incoming switched traffic from India to the United States disappear. At the same time, US carriers could not use ISR to deliver traffic, so their net settlement payments to India's then-monopoly carrier, VSNL, would skyrocket. The United States FCC estimated that these tactics could, in the worst case, inflate US net settlement payments by about US$5 billion in 1998, a huge cost increase in a US$10–12 billion market for US international services.

In response, the United States took unilateral regulatory action outside the WTO to cut inflated international settlement rates. It set 'benchmarks', or price caps (that is, legal limits on the maximum price), on the level of settlement rates that US carriers may pay to terminate their international traffic in other countries. If benchmarks worked, they would remove the bulk of the economic rents that fuel anti-competitive behaviour in the market. (The details of the original benchmarks are set forth in Appendix 1 to this chapter.) The US government did not seek to negotiate this regulatory measure at the WTO. It simply declared that the new US policy would meet the WTO obligations that required competition regulations to honour the principles of MFN and non-discrimination.

Needless to say, benchmarks attracted fierce criticism from many countries and carriers. But the US government believed that benchmarks were fully compatible with MFN and other WTO obligations.[25] In addition, for several reasons, the United States believed that no WTO dispute settlement liability would materialise before 2004, two years after the moratorium on settlement rate challenges. By that time, benchmarks would have reduced

[25] MFN requires a country to offer the same level of benefits to all Members of the World Trade Organization. MFN does not forbid countries to undertake competition policy measures the practical impact of which may vary from carrier to carrier. The regulatory principles embraced by most countries do require the least burdensome response to a competition problem. The FCC argued that benchmarks were less burdensome than other alternatives.

rents. As subsequent research has confirmed, lower settlement rates have stimulated international traffic (thus easing the impact of lower rates).[26]

Even as benchmarks eroded rents, the WTO agreement's global scope facilitated new cross-border services. For example, new entrants with innovative business models and new technological approaches, such as Level Three and Global Crossing, built fibre-optic networks that covered the United States and large parts of Europe and Asia. The networks included a wholesale business division that supplied other carriers, not retail customers.[27] By 2000, the new entrants controlled significant world capacity and offered it on cheaper and more flexible terms than anything existing in 1997. This capacity lowered barriers to entry for international retail services. Over time, lower entry barriers and more flexible transport spurred lower prices.[28] The crash in the market valuations of these new carriers in 2000 simply accelerated the plunge in capacity prices and the flexibility of deals for providing transport circuits.

Carriers in competitive industrial markets who wanted to move traffic under the traditional system of jointly provided services soon lowered settlement rates to levels in line with the costs of owning and running a global network. As a result, settlement rates among industrial countries have plummeted since the WTO agreement. The decline in US settlement rates with the rest of the world increased from about 6 per cent per year before 1997 to 16 per cent per year from 1997 to 2000.[29] No industrial country with full commitments had a settlement rate with the United States above fifteen cents in 1998, and many were around eight cents. This was the bulk of the world's traffic.[30] This rate of decline is understated because a modification of FCC rules in 1999 meant that many of the

[26] The same analysis also indicated that settlement rate payments do not determine national investment levels in developing-country telecom infrastructures. Settlement payment revenues were largely a rent used to satisfy distribution claims by various stakeholders. Wallsten, 'International Telecommunications.'

[27] The United States believed that the WTO agreement created the political opportunity (and competition policy necessity) to further speed the change. Whether or not the FCC ever drops its 'benchmarks', the initiative contributed mightily to the expectation that the settlement rate system will change fundamentally (Cowhey, 'FCC Benchmarks'). In addition, the agreed-upon delay in WTO challenges to settlement rates (discussed earlier) meant that benchmarks could not be overturned by a WTO challenge until late 2002.

[28] There can be barriers to entry in the provision of international transmission capacity. On the largest routes, however, they have been receding significantly, starting in 1997, and even much more so since 2000.

[29] Cowhey and Klimenko, 'The WTO Agreement'.

[30] Settlement rates are available on the website of the International Bureau of the FCC, www.fcc.gev/ib/

lower settlement rates were not published.[31] While numerous market imperfections linger, ISR, the growth of new international transmission facilities, and the flood of new entrants have greatly improved the market's performance.[32] Even outside the OECD, no newly industrialised country had a settlement rate above nineteen cents by the end of 2000, and some were matching the rates of industrial countries. For example, a number of Eastern European countries with aspirations to join the EU (such as Croatia, Estonia and Lithuania) managed to reach very low settlement rates even without the WTO commitments.

The rapid changes in the settlement rates (and the tradition of keeping them secret) also opened up numerous opportunities for arbitrage in delivering traffic to developing countries.[33] In addition, many carriers secretly offered volume discounts to discourage arbitrage.[34] Larger flows

[31] Plunging settlement rates and the introduction of ISR with industrial countries led the FCC to modify its benchmark policy. In FCC Order 99-73, the FCC abolished the benchmark policy (and other competition safeguards) on all routes where the foreign carriers either lacked market power or terminated US traffic at rates 25 per cent below the benchmark rates. The exempt countries are nearly all from the OECD: Canada, Denmark, France, Germany, Hong Kong, Ireland, Italy, the Netherlands, Norway, Sweden and the United Kingdom (Wallsten, 'International Telecommunications' FCC, 'List of International Routes that Satisfy Criteria for Relief from the International Settlements Policy and Associated Filing Requirements', Public Notice, DA 99-1510, 29 July 1999). The FCC presumes that a foreign carrier does not possess market power on the foreign end of a US international route if it possesses less than 50 per cent market share in each of three relevant foreign product markets: international transport facilities, including cable landing station access and backhaul facilities; intercity facilities and services; and local access facilities and services on the foreign end.

[32] Many dominant incumbents tried to keep margins up on international voice and data traffic by maintaining high prices for international leased circuits. This tactic has the added advantage of raising margins on Internet traffic, which now dominates international routes but is priced much more cheaply than voice traffic. Although an explosion in backbone long-haul infrastructure will undermine high rates for ISR, the WTO round negotiation should explore regulatory barriers to translating capacity into better market performance.

[33] Callback services are the most familiar version of this arbitrage. Rerouting international traffic to 'cheat' on settlement rates is even more important. A move to general competition in a region's major international traffic centre undermines the high profits earned on international services in less competitive markets in the region. For example, the settlement rate to Hong Kong from the United States is very low. Hong Kong may then be used to reroute traffic from the United States in order to reach other Asian countries where Hong Kong enjoys a favourable settlement rate. The United States typically has had the lowest settlement rates in the world and the most complete disclosure of its rates.

[34] Some think that worries about settlement rates are obsolete because data traffic is now larger than voice traffic globally, and is growing more rapidly. There is much to be said for this view over the long run, but it is myopic in the medium term because voice traffic still constitutes the majority of international service revenues.

of traffic outside of traditional settlement rates made it harder to enforce bilateral pricing and route arrangements designed to reinforce high rates. Moreover, the gradual integration of all forms of services over the Internet, a packet-switched network whose transmission is not even measured in minutes of use, is just beginning to limit prices on many international services. (Internet services can substitute for faxes readily, and for voice at some reduction in quality.) Using the surge in transmission capacity, new entrants fuel the growth of hybrid, Internet Protocol – network mixtures of voice, fax and data services that defy traditional market categorisations and pricing.

Altogether, unconventional traffic (including IP telephony) was probably equivalent to 6 per cent of world switched traffic in 1999, and IP telephony could soar to as high as 20 per cent of the traffic on a route with very high settlement rates, like the US–China route.[35] As a result, investors began to discount their expectations about the profitability of telecom monopolies, and former monopolists became interested in expanding new services and entering the markets of neighbouring countries.[36] As prices began to drop for international services in some countries, and quality of service improved, political leaders in other countries in the region felt pressure to match the improvements. In a manner unimaginable in 1997, the International Telecommunications Union's World Policy Telecommunications Forum in 2001 was cautiously supportive of IP telephony as a positive force for developing countries.[37]

On balance, the WTO created a regime where market expectations are that change (much lower margins and prices on international services) is inevitable in the medium term, and players are beginning to adjust in anticipation of that predicted equilibrium. Nonetheless, settlement rates remain high and end prices for international services higher yet. There are still numerous attempts to tinker with the market to slow the decline in rents.

There are several issues regarding settlement rates that may emerge in the upcoming WTO round. To begin, suppose a country maintains different settlement rates for different countries. Does this violate the WTO's fundamental premise of non-discrimination (embodied in the MFN and national treatment rules)? Different settlement rates might

35 TeleGeography, *TeleGeography, 2001* (Washington, DC: TeleGeography, 2001), p. 123.
36 Embratel, the former long-distance monopoly in Brazil, for example, is both entering into local service markets in Brazil and expanding into other South American countries.
37 See www.itu.int/itunews/isse/2001/02/ip_telephony.html, accessed 2 March 2002.

arguably be equivalent to different tariff rates on a good depending on its country of origin. The answer may depend on how we understand settlement rates. Settlement rates may, arguably, be outside the control of the WTO if they are deemed to be a commercial contract between carriers (even state-owned carriers). Accordingly, as many countries argued in the 1997 negotiation, they are not a 'measure' by governments that can be subject to a WTO challenge.

Even if settlement rates are not a government measure, one might argue that the settlement rates of a dominant carrier (for example, Telmex in Mexico) fall under the interconnection obligations set out in the WTO regulatory principles if the carrier's country has market access commitments under the regulatory principles.[38] If the settlement rates are not transparent, are not related to costs, and do not provide equal treatment of carriers of WTO Members, there may be a failure by the government to live up to its WTO regulatory commitments.

This second approach emphasises interconnection obligations and must take into account two sets of market considerations. First, does a carrier have market power? The United States believes that no US international service carrier has market power. Furthermore, it has published a list of countries also lacking carriers with market power over international services.[39] If no carrier has the power to exercise market power, then there is no breach of regulatory obligations at the WTO. In general, only industrial countries and a few newly industrialising countries have markets with enough competitive features to be in this position. Secondly, do countries permit ways of terminating international voice and fax traffic other than settlement rate services? Practically speaking, the one major alternative is to permit international simple resale. (Countries allowing ISR tend to have blunted the market power of their most powerful carrier, but this is not necessarily the case.) ISR means that the practical effect of any differences in settlement rates among countries is limited because a carrier can obtain the transport and termination services to a country without using a settlement rate.

The moral for WTO negotiators is simple. The settlement rate system is unlikely to be overhauled by general agreement among governments whether at the WTO or at the International Telecommunications Union

[38] The Mexico–US dispute shows that the precise schedule of market access commitments (and scheduled limitations to the WTO commitments) is important in understanding the extent of the obligation.

[39] Wallsten, 'International Telecommunications'.

(ITU).[40] A new round could yield a Secretariat's note on the interpretation of market access commitments, and this could spell out how interconnection commitments apply to international services. This will be politically difficult. In contrast, adding more countries with market access commitments on international services, especially permitting ISR, would promote competition and consumer welfare globally. This is feasible in the course of the normal WTO round. In the meantime, the dispute settlement mechanism will have to cope with disputes over past commitments. The market has permanently changed, however, as a result of the last round.

Protection of incumbents and issues posed by new services and technologies

Declining margins on international services force major incumbents into rate rebalancing (because domestic services must cover more of their own costs) and an expansion of new services (to create new revenue streams). These shifts favour more competition because a major deterrent to competition in the past was the protection of cross-subsidies and high margins on some services. This section focuses on high-growth services that define key features of the network of the future. The last WTO round focused on the world of traditional switched services, predominantly over the wired network. The political efforts of countries wishing to improve the productivity and consumer welfare benefits of the global network should focus on the services discussed in this section because they are central to the network of the future.

Internet Protocol (IP) telephony

Although Internet Protocol (IP) telephony is important in itself, its treatment also quickly becomes entangled with the politics of regulating the Internet. In the United States, where worries about excessive government intrusion in regard to the Internet cut across conventional political lines,

40 The ITU has proposed the idea of a global agreement on benchmarks. This would establish a transparent, non-discriminatory termination fee for each country that would be available to all countries. Unfortunately, the cost calculations of the ITU produce rates that are unlikely to be acceptable to industrial countries and do not address the issues raised by the FCC. There is unlikely to be an international agreement on this matter. See Cowhey, 'FCC Benchmarks'; Eli M. Noam, *Interconnecting the Network of Networks* (Cambridge, MA: MIT Press 2001), pp. 124–8.

this is dangerous ground. In the European Union, there are similar worries, but there is a countervailing political desire by some governments (such as France) to support some regulatory intervention. The motivation for regulation in this case is concern about the cross-over of media into Internet services (cultural protection issues). Moreover, the European Union is harmonising its regulatory framework around the idea of technology neutrality in respect to end services to consumers. Such an approach eliminates senseless regulatory distinctions between different types of network technologies, but it is also a wedge for allowing the regulation of Internet-delivered services that are 'broadcast-like'.[41] The United States has not bought into this approach.

All discussions of IP telephony are complicated by the indecisive intent of the major Atlantic trading partners.[42] However, three issues will dominate trade policy for IP telephony.

First, does IP telephony constitute a fully, or almost fully, substitutable alternative to wired voice services? The answer is not yet. Quality of service (QOS) is still erratic compared to the switched network. The solution to QOS problems requires complicated network arrangements. Not all consumers care about top QOS for all calls, however. IP telephony is thus a partial substitute for conventional telephone and fax traffic, and is especially attractive if settlement rates are high. Crucially, for international regulatory purposes the distinction between IP and switched telephony is irrelevant if countries permit competitive international transmission networks and/or international simple resale.

Secondly, does IP telephony endanger the funding of universal service measures by removing telephone traffic from the pool used to subsidise universal service? Restrictions on IP telephony to subsidise universal service would become an issue at the WTO if the measure proved to be fundamentally anti-competitive.[43] More fundamentally, IP telephony does not correspond to the logic of a system based on the per minute, per second or per pulse measurements found in switched systems. Thus, if one does want to include IP telephony revenues as part of a scheme to fund

[41] European Commission, 'The Results of the Public Consultation on the 1999 Communications Review and Orientations for the New Regulatory Framework', COM(2000)239, Brussels, 26 April 2000.

[42] Scott Blake Harris, 'The WTO and the Internet', Inernational Communications Committee Newsletter, American Bar Association, Fall 1999. Text available at www.harriswiltshire.com.

[43] Countries bound by the Reference Paper on regulatory principles have an obligation to make provision of universal service subsidies transparent, competitively neutral, and as least burdensome as possible.

universal service subsidies, one needs an appropriate and competitively neutral way to do so. The ITU's proposal that countries adopt a simple tax on total service revenues is one approximation of such an alternative.

Thirdly, is IP telephony (or other Internet services) covered under WTO market access commitments? It is fair to say that many negotiators did not think about the matter seriously during the last round. The text of the Uruguay Round gives clear guidance, however. The negotiation that closed in 1994 (set forward in the Telecom Annex to the Round) largely covered value-added services (for example, the computer networks of the day). Paragraph 5 of the 1994 Telecom Annex called explicitly for freedom of protocol selection by users of the public network's transport capacity. (This was often called the 'IBM clause' because it was associated with lobbying by companies running large global data networks on proprietary architectures such as IBM's Systems Network Architecture.) Countries agreed to lease circuits in market access commitments for data and value-added service transmission and to allow freedom of choice of protocol.

The Internet is a network of networks that is made available by using a particular protocol. Thus, at a minimum, market access commitments on data cover the Internet's data-centric services. The basic telecommunications agreement further reinforces this by including market access commitments on packet switched services (the core of Internet services). Moreover, the basic telecom agreement was explicitly 'technology-neutral' in respect to the delivery of services covered by market access commitments. A country is arguably bound to allow market access for IP telephony unless it took reservations on market access commitments that explicitly limited the ability to deliver voice services other than by settlement rates. This assumes that IP telephony should be treated as fully substitutable for switched voice service. If it is not fully substitutable, then it is a value-added service covered by market access commitments on data.

During the US and China negotiations on WTO accession, the Chinese government eventually conceded that the Internet is simply a technology for delivering services. Its compromise with the United States (which believes that Internet services are covered in its own WTO commitments) was as follows. China would respect the technology neutrality of delivery of services. As China's market access commitments for various end services become effective, Internet service delivery of those services would be agreed to automatically.[44] This means that China will have a powerful constraint on the level of its settlement rates in the long term.

[44] Author interview with US trade negotiator, 2001.

International access to Internet traffic exchange (ITE)

Web traffic between countries requires networks taking traffic from one country to the other. In mid-1996, for example, it was common that a user in one country would want something from a web-hosting server in another country and then (after getting information from the server) need the information sent back to her home computer. Given the early US dominance of the web and its content, far more traffic seeking access to websites came into the United States than went out to the rest of the world. Reinforcing the balance of demand for US content was the pricing and capacity structure for data transport internationally. Earlier competition and higher capacity demands led the United States to become the hub of international data networking. Internet traffic between two points within Europe or within Asia frequently transited through the United States in order to move at higher speed and lower costs.[45] The traffic flow of the Internet was the opposite of switched international services (that is, the United States received more traffic than it sent out), especially through the end of the 1990s.

A few major backbone data networks, called Tier I carriers, dominated long-haul Internet traffic in the mid-1990s. They agreed to 'peer', or exchange traffic, with other Tier I carriers without charge. Typically, these networks charged smaller, regional and local networks for long-haul traffic transport. When US carriers signed contracts with many foreign networks they treated them as something more than a regional network but less than a true peer. For example, a US backbone carrier might insist that an Asian carrier agree to be responsible for transporting all of the traffic of the US carrier and the Asian carrier between the two countries. In return, the US carrier would agree that, once the Asian carrier's traffic arrived in Los Angeles, the US carrier would transport it anywhere in the continental United States and bring the reply back to Los Angeles, where the Asian carrier would transport it back to its home country.

This is a rough description but it gets to the heart of the two issues that have made Internet traffic exchange (ITE) at the global level both sensitive and hard to grasp. First, unlike settlement rates, the international exchange described above did not require the United States to share the cost of international transport. The foreign carrier provided all of the international transport capacity. The US carrier only provided transport

[45] TeleGeography, *Hubs and Spokes: A TeleGeography Internet Reader* (Washington, DC: TeleGeography, 2000), pp. 15–26.

around the United States, a service that used to be bundled with provision of half of the international transport capacity under the settlement rate system. This revision took place just as the United States was undermining the traditional settlement rate and jointly supplied service system that required carriers to share international transport costs. Many countries concluded that the United States intended to use its market power to force foreign carriers to shoulder a disproportionate share of international network costs.[46] Discontent was so strong that the ITU's 2000 World Telecommunications Standardisation Assembly passed a resolution that endorsed governments making bilateral arrangements for Internet traffic exchange to ensure fair cost-sharing. The United States dissented from this resolution.[47]

Secondly, the primary alternative to the settlement rate system is to assemble networks through complex 'make or buy' decisions. For example, a carrier can build its own dedicated network to all the major world websites and pay no one else for transport (assuming that all the markets are open to competition and foreign entry), or it can rent transport from another carrier (ISR is one example of renting capacity). If it rents, it can use a variety of methods. Backbone capacity is exploding internationally and domestically for long-haul traffic, and control of that capacity is finally diversifying significantly. This means that a more competitive market is emerging. It may require some time to reach an efficient equilibrium but the ingredients are there.[48] In some regions of the world, government

[46] The early peering agreements did not distinguish between incoming and outgoing traffic. That is, once a Japanese request for a reply from a US web server in Chicago arrived in the United States, the US backbone carrier agreed to take the Japanese traffic to the server in Chicago and take the server's response back to Los Angeles to be handed back to the Japanese carrier. Thus, in this model there was no true international traffic balancing, and even local termination (going to Chicago) and origination (returning from Chicago) services were co-mingled. Whether this worked in favour or against the interests of the Japanese carrier financially is arguable. But, in the late 1990s, it was a less transparent market where US carriers had the trump card (transport access to US web servers and their content).

[47] 'US Plays Role of Dissenter at ITU's World Standards Meeting', *Telecommunications Reports International*, 13 October 2000, pp. 116–17. Compliance with such resolutions is voluntary under international law.

[48] Many other developments, such as the practice of mirroring for websites (whereby US websites are set up in Asia to reduce service-time delays) and the decline of the dominance of US content and the English language on the web have also changed the original contracting problem. Report on OECD Workshop 'Internet Traffic Exchange', 7–8 June 2001, available on the OECD website at http://oecd.org/EN/home. On this issue, see also TeleGeography, Telegeography, 2001 (Washington, 2001), pp. 58–9. As the Internet continues to grow and becomes more sophisticated, the peering/settlement system will also

policy may hinder this development but certainly not in the United States or the North Atlantic region. At least in major traffic markets, including the United States (on which most of the complaints about ITE have focused), the long-haul transport market is becoming efficient.[49] Further reducing the magnitude of the problem is the growing diversification of web content and web servers globally. A greater proportion web content and traffic is now created outside the United States than was the case in the late 1990s.

The favourable competitive trend on long haul does not fully clear up the issue. The control of the last mile or so of transport for terminating or originating services to websites is very similar to two familiar problems in local interconnection arrangements. First, do the companies that control local networks have the ability and incentive to discriminate against other carriers in a way that harms consumers? Inter-exchange carriers (such as Internet backbone providers) constitute a significant share of the data traffic revenues of US operating companies like Bell South. Arguably, discouraging this profitable wholesale market is not in the local carrier's interest. However, this is one area where regulation has been reasonably effective (as opposed to detailed unbundling of the local network), especially for well-entrenched data networks that have established long-term contracts for capacity supplemented by direct ownership of facilities to the largest customer sites. There have been complaints that newer entrants do less well in obtaining this access. Secondly, if there is any question of market power, have regulators taken measures to improve the transparency of the market? Some complaints have focused more on the need to improve information about peering arrangements for market participants than on demands for specific regulation of financial arrangements.[50]

raise questions about how to manage pricing while dealing with quality of service issues. Richard Cawley, 'Policies to Support the Scaling and Extensibility of the Internet: Principles to Guide Settlements Policy Consistent with Technical and Pricing Development of Internet', available at www.ksg.harvard.edu/iip/cai/cawley.htm, accessed 15 November 2001.

49 Another problem is the possibility of a backbone carrier market where the major carrier(s) have the ability and incentive to maintain prices over efficient competitive levels. The US Department of Justice and the European Commission competition authorities worried about this risk if they permitted a merger of Worldcom and Sprint (which, at the time of the proposed merger, controlled 53 per cent of the US backbone network). Eventually, they required a divestiture of MCI's transmission capacity to Cable & Wireless. The risk was one well understood in competition policy. The explosive growth of the backbone network in the United States and Europe reduces the risk, but the question is subject to empirical investigation using the tools of competition analysis.

50 TeleGeography, *Hubs and Spokes: A TeleGeography Internet Reader* (Washington, DC: TeleGeography, 2000), p. 28.

In short, ITE may pose competition policy issues simply because interconnection arrangements frequently do. Regulators need to be vigilant. More importantly, any traffic exchange system also has to ask how the Internet will manage other, far more complex pricing issues. For example, quality of service goals, often required by commercial customers, may require different pricing based on assured service levels (higher quality requires a method of giving priority access to the network to the traffic in question). A whole set of specialised market entrants, such as InterNAP, facilitates greater consumer choice over selection of carrier capacity and priority access to networks for corporate web traffic by serving as sophisticated intermediaries between users and carriers. These intermediaries undercut the exercise of market power by making it practical for customers to access multiple backbone networks quickly and easily.

To the extent that the controversy over traffic exchange is fundamentally a question of interconnection policy (in terms of the obligations of governments at the WTO), the current WTO commitments of the OECD countries (and a number of industrialising countries) seem sufficient to cover the problem. A trade obligation to regulate in a pro-competitive manner, however, does not specify the best way of charging for traffic flows on the Internet. National communications regulators and competition authorities, in consultation with industry and outside analysts, should discuss best policy practices, but this does not require new WTO agreements. The alternative approach, having governments attempt to create something akin to the settlement rate system for Internet traffic exchange, simply invites the type of rent creation that was central to the settlement rate system, as discussed in the earlier parts of this chapter. This would be a very undesirable outcome.

Mobile services and international networking

Scalable distributed computing (for example, supercomputing capacity created by running linked desktop computers as a virtual single machine) enabled by giant fibre network backbones (operating with far larger traffic flows than anything existing today) is now on the close technology horizon. Such networks will be fuelled by gigabit streams of data delivered by wireless networks from ubiquitous inexpensive sensors, whether in the human body or on highway bridges, and its applications will frequently be delivered on wireless information appliances (see Appendix 2 to this chapter). The challenge for policy is to be sufficiently pro-competitive (and thus favourable to efficient pricing) and technologically neutral (and thus friendly to technological innovation) to allow such possibilities to emerge. Therefore, it is important to address initial practices that work against the development of ubiquitous global wireless traffic.

There are three issues of special concern regarding mobile services and global networking. All reflect the tendency of regulators to act slowly when faced by complex, politically sensitive markets where some incumbents have found new ways to extract rents. First, incumbent operators look to develop rents in new cross-border markets. Mobile services are at the top of their list. The cost of terminating calls originating on the terrestrial network onto the mobile network is very high in many countries, including most of Europe (but not the United States). This is a source of considerable profit to mobile operators and takes on interesting dimensions in the international realm. Secondly, there are issues tied to lingering industrial policy. All of the world's major technology centres have some temptation to promote technology companies with new wireless communications technologies. Since governments license the spectrum, the major players habitually consider lobbying for favourable government policies in regard to spectrum allocation and licensing to be a significant part of their competitive corporate strategies. Some of these spectrum decisions pose fundamental challenges for the creation of efficient global networks and markets. Thirdly, there is a significant tension between carrier control of network architecture, and thus the terms on which the service applications are created, and the user control over these networks.

Let us examine the case of manipulating the charging system for international mobile services. To understand the issue requires a short review of the charging system for a wireline (or rival wireless) network operator to connect a call to a customer on a mobile network. 'Calling party pays' – the caller pays the cost of the call to the mobile customer receiving the call – is the most common approach to billing. Its opposite, 'receiving party pays', the US model, tends to discourage the growth of wireless traffic because it does not efficiently reflect the incentives of calling (the calling party wants to connect to the receiver). Unfortunately, 'calling party pays' also gives an incentive for domestic mobile wireless networks to charge high fees to callers from domestic wireline networks.[51] This is an issue being debated among European regulators; in the meantime it keeps up

[51] *Ibid.*

margins for wireless operators. In Japan, the manipulation of these fees by NTT's DoCoMo has been the subject of trade complaints.[52]

Now consider the case of a mobile user who roams to another country where it is possible to use the same technical standard as in the user's home country. In general, OECD countries apply a 'receiving party pays' approach to international roaming even in countries where 'calling party pays'. According to an OECD study, if a UK user logs into an Australian network and makes a call inside Australia, the charges range between US$0.42 and US$0.56 per minute.[53] The UK roamer can receive a call from the United Kingdom at a cost of US$1.50 per minute. If the UK roamer made a call from Australia back to the United Kingdom, rates vary from US$1.43 per minute to US$1.64 per minute at peak times. (The cost to the United States would be about the same.) Compare this fee to the cost of an international call using the settlement rate system. Settlement rates from Australia to the United States since the introduction of competition have declined to US$0.10 per minute. Even if one paid the full roaming charge for calling within Australia (US$0.56 per minute), the cost for the call would be no more than US$0.66 per minute to the carrier. Margins on roaming are obviously inflated.[54] In addition, because roaming arrangements are largely treated as commercial agreements, the way is opened for domestic operators to use them as barriers to entry to foreign operators.[55]

52 'USTR Report Targets Japan, China, Mexico', *Telecommunications Reports International*, 3 April 2001, pp. 2–3.

53 This example is taken from the excellent report of the OECD, *Cellular Mobile Pricing Structures and Trends* (Paris: OECD, 2000). The OECD report used Vodafone data from June 1999. On 7 November 2001, the UK regulator OFTEL issued a public notice questioning the rates for international roaming by UK consumers. OFTEL suggested that the primary problem was poor information for consumers. See 'Oftel Warns of the High Cost Using Your Mobile Abroad', Press Office releases, available on the OFTEL web site at www.oftel.gov.uk/press/releases/2001/pr74_01.htm, accessed 16 November 2001.

54 Data on European Union roaming rates are reported in Teligen, *Report on Telecoms Tariff Data as of December 2000*, produced for European Commission, DG Information Society, May 2001. Arbitrage specialists who provide the service of switching a mobile roaming call in a foreign country onto their own network and terminating it for a far cheaper rate are springing up.

55 The European Commission is also investigating the possibility that control of the spectrum is used in such a way as to restrict new entrants into Europe from other regions by denying them access to roaming agreements. The new European Union telecommunications legislation authorises the Commission to create standardised fees for terrestrial-to-mobile network connections on cross-border and roaming calls. Philip Shishkin, 'Why Mobile-Phone Firms Find It So Hard to Roam Europe', *Wall Street Journal*, 19 July 2001, p. A19; Michael Romanello, 'EU Telecom Package Passes with Last-Minute Compromise',

The same OECD study also notes a growing tension between terrestrial and mobile operators in Europe over the cost of terminating international calls. (In 2000, up to 30 per cent of all international calls in Europe terminated on mobile phones.)[56] Suppose a call from Italy went to a wireless user in France. France Telecom, for example, may receive a payment of US$0.08 per minute for terminating the Italian call in France. France Telecom then gives US$0.05 per minute to the customer's French mobile operator for terminating the international call. If the same mobile call originated in, say, Paris, and was delivered to a mobile user in Lyons, France Telecom would have to pay US$0.33 per minute to the mobile operator. This gives France Telecom a strong incentive to reroute wire network calls destined to terminate on a rival's domestic mobile network via a third country. For example, France Telecom could route the call from Paris to Munich, and then re-originate in Munich to Lyon to terminate on a mobile network there.

The quarrelling between terrestrial and mobile operators in industrial countries with quite competitive markets may erode margins on roaming and termination onto mobile networks through the forces of arbitrage and judicious regulatory prodding. This is not self-evident, however. The financial fall-out from third-generation service problems tempts governments to assist the mobile industry in a variety of ways. One alternative is to encourage a cross-subsidy from terrestrial to mobile networks while deciding that it is permissible to have an inefficiently priced market for international mobile services. Other methods are also emerging. They include allowing a *de facto* forgiveness of part of the sum bid at the licence auctions. Another is to permit shared build-out of the network among licensees, an approach that may facilitate horizontal collusion on pricing and service plans.

A more troubling alternative involves developing countries. Many of these countries have call volumes on wireless networks that rival or exceed the wireline network. Suppose that the effort to protect the largest incumbents from unduly difficult financial waters led to the proposition that settlement rates should not fall so deeply as to undercut the termination rates from wired to wireless networks? This would be, as with IP telephony, an effort to save the old by hindering the new. While the crudest form of

Telecommunications Report International, 17 January 2002, pp. 1–2; Patrick Xavier, 'Licensing of Third Generation (3G) Mobile Briefing Paper', 42–6, prepared for the ITU Workshop on Licensing 3G Mobile, 19–21 September 2001, Geneva.

[56] Data posted on website of TeleGeography at www.telegeography.com, accessed 2 March 2002.

this alternative might be rejected, one could easily imagine tacit support for keeping settlement rates higher in order to protect the margins on termination rates for wireless carriers.

The general point is that cross-border services (wireline and wireless) have raised numerous issues about how to interpret WTO commitments on market access. A technology-neutral approach to interpreting the commitments may mean that we are simply stuck with disputes about both wired and wireless services when they cross borders. But the WTO process is ultimately more political than legal. It is a vehicle for getting countries to agree to goals and then finding ways to achieve those goals through international agreement. Of course, countries make painful tradeoffs among goals as they bargain. But, ultimately, there is no telecom agreement unless a significant core of countries wants to achieve what the countries bind legally. The 1997 round did not seriously discuss the competition and trade impact of how wireless and wired networks intersect, except for the narrow case of satellite services. The next round needs such a discussion to see if either a note of the WTO Secretariat can interpret how past commitments apply to this case or if additional commitments would be an improvement.[57]

Another major difficulty in cross-border mobile services arises from significant discrepancies in the spectrum allocation plans of each country. These discrepancies mean, for example, that phones on the same standard often have to be dual band. The most exciting developments involving wireless data networking involve the 'wireless local area network', and the major industrial regions have different spectrum set aside for these systems. This reduces economies of scale in equipment. Just as importantly, government is involved in micromanaging the selection of standards in many countries (but hardly all) and restricts the market from developing flexibly once the government has licensed the spectrum. The United States, for example, is now considering much greater freedom of spectrum resale after it is initially assigned through auctions. The United Kingdom and, more cautiously, the European Commission are also looking to change the system substantially.[58] The point here is simple. The last round had to deal with finding some common ground for more flexible entry and competition in the building of wired networks. Part of the challenge of the

[57] Alternatively, countries may agree that nothing needs to be done after a discussion of the issues. The point is that mobile services deserve a careful collective discussion and review in the same way that wireline international services and satellite services were dissected in the last round. A mutual education process is necessary.

[58] Xavier 'Licensing of 3G Systems', pp. 30–3.

next round will be finding ways to encourage more efficient build-out of global wireless networks. A careful examination of spectrum policy practices may suggest additional market access or regulatory commitments that might promote this goal. One such option is an additional market commitment regarding resale of spectrum rights. Aside from questions of political will, this would require significant thought about scheduling language.

Finally, competition in wireless services has evolved in a very different regulatory tradition than that for wired networks. Regulators have nearly universally agreed that the major incumbents at the time of competition had the capacity and motivation to exercise market power. Thus, these carriers had obligations to interconnect with the other carriers, and those interconnection obligations included making parts of their network's elements and functions available for other carriers' use on terms overseen by regulators.[59] In contrast, regulators declared that the only interconnection obligation of wireless carriers (even in the days of duopoly) was simply to allow a reciprocal exchange of traffic. The rationale for this decision was that no carrier had market power.

The decision to exempt the largest wireless carriers from any form of unbundling rules had an important implication. The industry has remained much more vertically integrated in the provision of services than in the wired network world. Large wireless carriers expect to license the spectrum, own the network infrastructure, and significantly control the packages of specialised services provided over their networks. This is very different from the wired world of, for example, Bell South, Worldcom, Earthlink and Yahoo sharing in the provisioning of different layers of services to consumers.

There is nothing inherently wrong with vertical integration for market efficiency and consumer welfare. But an important lesson from the Internet experience was that the vertical disintegration of information services was a driving force for innovation and unexpected consumer welfare gains. The reason was simple. Users and innovative third-party providers gained a very influential role in the design of the network and its application services. While all governments prize innovation, they have not considered that innovation done by vertically integrated carriers is

[59] François Bar, Stephen Cohen, Peter Cowhey, Brad DeLong, Michael Kleeman and John Zysman, 'The Next-Generation Internet: Promoting Innovation and User-Experimentation', in BRIE-IGCC E-conomy Project Task Force on the Internet, eds., *Tracking a Transformation: E-commerce and the Terms of Competition in Industries* (Washington, DC: Brookings Institution Press, 2001), pp. 435–73.

likely to look quite different than the types found in the wired Internet world. However, this approach to wired networks tended to drive margins down for telephone carriers, and this is a concern to political leaders trying to assure the success of the highly publicised investments in wireless networks.

Discussions about the practices of wireless network carriers in regard to opening their network to third-party services and technologies are in the early stages. The new phrase to cover this category of suppliers is Mobile Virtual Network Operators (MVNOs).[60] Two immediate regulatory questions raised by this innovation are pricing for network access and the degree of unbundling. Regulators could mandate something like a non-discrimination clause – a wholesale resale rate made available to one MVNO would be available to all, for example.[61] Unbundling of network elements is yet another issue, one on which little work has been done. Some governments, like Japan, have explicitly set up a licensing system for value-added mobile services, but they do not require unbundling.[62] Hong Kong has required that 3G (third generation) operators set aside 30 per cent of their network capacity for unaffiliated third parties to provide specialised virtual network and content applications, but the implications for unbundling are murky.[63]

These issues may not require new WTO commitments. The trade negotiation process should, just as it did in the negotiations leading to the 1997 pact, feature extensive regulatory consultations to clarify the utility of the Reference Paper for addressing key features of the emerging global market. This process might lead negotiators to think about scheduling additional commitments in regard to opening up mobile networks to third-party services.

Conclusion

This paper has reviewed the evolution of cross-border services in light of the WTO agreement. The market has changed significantly for the better,

[60] Xavier, 'Licensing of 3G Systems', pp. 35–40; European Commission, 'Results of the Public Consultation', Section 3.1.

[61] Xavier, 'Licensing of 3G Systems', p. 40. Given the presence of several mobile operators in major markets, it might be possible to adopt the 'third party neutrality' approach to interconnection of Noam, *Interconnection*, pp. 110–12.

[62] See the ITU report on 3G licensing at www.itu.int/itunenews/issue/2001/08/licensing3g.html, accessed 2 March 2002.

[63] 'Hong Kong Sets Rules for 3G License Auction', *Telecommunications Reports International*, 3 August 2001, p. 6.

judged by the standards of market efficiency and consumer welfare, but problems remain because international services are a lucrative source of rents. WTO commitments were weaker in this market segment, and regulatory implementation has been less vigorous. This is predictable given the political economy of reform.

A review of most current issues in regard to traditional international services suggests more of a need for regulatory consultations and an improvement of national market access commitments, but they do not require a major set of innovations in the current WTO telecom agreement. However, several network pricing and regulatory practices in regard to Internet traffic and global wireless networking may require either clarification of prior WTO obligations or consideration of new market access commitments. These issues in regard to new services are critical to the creation of more powerful and efficient global networks.

Appendix 1: FCC benchmark levels and transition periods

The FCC Benchmark Order grants additional transition time for countries whose loss of US settlement income in a given year would exceed 20 per cent of national telecom revenues. Given the timing of the effect of benchmarks (the order took effect on 1 January 1998; the first 'milestone' is 1 January 1999), the first critical point for a developing country is probably at the end of the first quarter of 1999.

The benchmarks were tied directly to the WTO agreement by a simple rule. A foreign carrier will not have a transition period if its affiliate receives a US licence to provide international facilities-based switched from the United States to its home market. A condition for the use of the licence

National income level (GDP)	Benchmark rate	Transition period
High income	15 cents/minute	1 year
Upper middle income	19 cents/minute	2 years
Lower middle income	19 cents/minute	3 years
Low income	23 cents/minute	4 years
Low teledensity/low income*	23 cents/minute	5 years

Source: FCC Benchmark Order, paras. 111 and 165.
*Less than 1 line per 100 people.

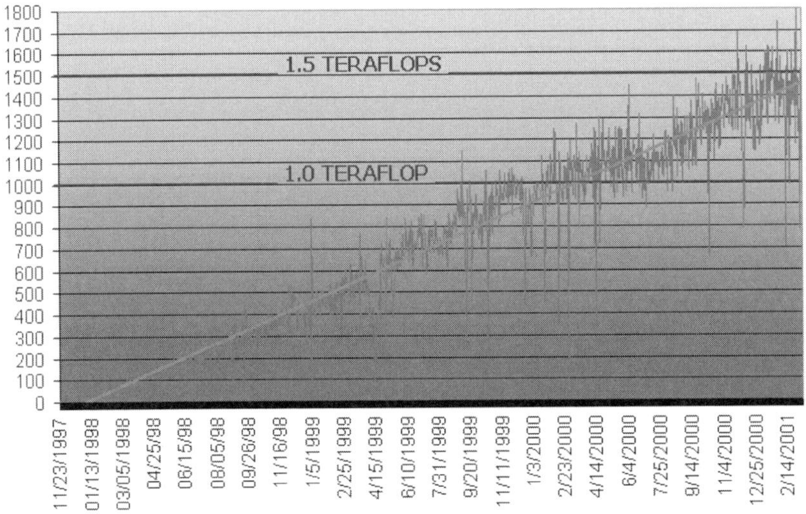

Source: California Institute on Telecommunications and Information Technology Scalable Computer Grids: Entropia achieved 1 teraflop capacity in nineteen months while searching for the one-million-digit prime number.

for such traffic would be immediate compliance with the final benchmark rate (that is, immediate movement to nineteen cents for a carrier from an upper-middle-income country). If carriers were later determined to be acting anti-competitively (in ways defined by the Order), the FCC would have the option of lowering the settlement rate to one consistent with best international practices (defined as eight cents per minute in the Order). The purpose of lowering settlement rates as a licensing condition is to remove the ability to use high profits from settlement rates to permit anti-competitive tactics.

Appendix 2: the big terabit optical Internet core: the emergence of a distributed (networked) planetary computer

1. Storage of data everywhere (Napster is peer-to-peer storage).
2. Scalable computing power (Entropia and SETI@home as peer-to-peer computing):
   (a) fed by by gigabit wireless streams;
   (b) vast sensor nets in wireless streams:
      (i) small pervasive self-powered sensor 'motes' – erosion, medical, anthrax;

(ii) embedded processors – highways and autos;
(iii) cheap one-cent radios.

The all optical fibersphere in the centre finds its complement in the wireless ethersphere on the edge of the network.

George Gilder

5

Reforming international accounting rates: a developing country perspective

BOUTHEINA GUERMAZI*

Introduction

In the last few years, international accounting rates, the century-old revenue-sharing mechanism for the joint provision of international switched telecommunications services,[1] has come under tremendous pressure. Long considered the cornerstone of international telecommunications, the international accounting rates regime is at odds with the new telecommunications environment brought about by the liberalisation of international trade in telecommunications services under the WTO.[2]

International accounting rates were discussed during the Uruguay Round[3] and more specifically during the negotiations of the Agreement

* This chapter is an updated and expanded version of an earlier paper published in 1999. Boutheina Guermazi, 'International Accounting Rates, Developing Countries and the WTO: The Dilemma and a Possible Solution', *International Journal of Communications Law and Policy* (1999), www.ijclp.org/3_1999/ijclp-webdoc_1_3_1999.html.

[1] The international accounting rates system will be described in detail below. At present, it suffices to mention that, under this mechanism, carriers in the originating countries compensate carriers in the country of destination for matching the international circuits and providing switching capabilities and domestic routing to deliver the call to the recipient. Where there is an imbalance in the volume of incoming and outgoing traffic, the operator which originates more traffic will pay a settlement rate (usually half the accounting rate) to compensate the terminating operator.

[2] The GATS is the first multilateral agreement to take into account trade in telecommunications services. Liberalisation started gradually with the enhanced telecommunications services under the GATS Annex before embarking on the liberalisation of basic telecommunications service. Enhanced services, also called value-added services, are services that involve the application of computer processing capabilities over the basic telephone network. Value-added telecommunications services are so named because they add value to basic telecommunications services. By contrast, basic telecommunications include all the services that consist in transmitting electronic signals from one point to another without modifying the signal.

[3] The issue of accounting rates came up during the drafting of the telecommunications Annex under the GATS. The Annex applies to access to and use of public telecommunications

on Basic Telecommunications.[4] The debate revealed a disagreement on the need and feasibility to include the issue of accounting rates in a new agreement. The contentiousness of the issue revolved mainly around a North/South controversy.[5] On the one hand, developed countries suffering from deficit payments are eager to reform the accounting rates regime and align it with cost.[6] For example, the United States alone paid out US$5 billion more than it received in international settlement (almost 5 per cent of its trade deficit). On the other hand, developing countries are reluctant to consider any change to the current regime. The total amount of settlement payments received from developed countries is around US$10 billion per annum. According to the Secretary General of the International Telecommunications Union (ITU), the revenue generated by the settlement payment in developing countries for one year exceeds by far

transport networks and services by service providers. The first draft of the telecommunications Annex contained a provision that access to and use of PTTNS (public telecommunications transport network and services) should be cost-oriented. This provision triggered a controversy between those who argue that above cost access is a barrier to trade and others who consider that pricing is a commercial matter and should not be subject to GATS rules. The pricing clause was completely deleted from the final version of the Annex. See B. K. Zutshi, 'GATS – Impact on Developing Countries and Telecom Services', *Transnational Data and Communications Report*, July–August 1994, p. 24.

[4] The Agreement on Basic Telecommunications Services is the fourth protocol to the GATS. The protocol contains specific commitments in the field of basic telecommunications from sixty-nine countries, representing over 90 per cent of the world's basic telecommunications revenues. In addition to market access and national treatment commitments, the Agreement on Basic Telecommunications contains a negotiated set of pro-competitive regulatory principles contained in the Reference Paper. The WTO agreement covers basic telecommunications services whether local, long-distance or international for public and non-public use provided on an infrastructure basis as well as through resale. It covers telecommunications services provided by any means of technology including cable, wireless and satellite. Market access commitments cover cross-border supply of services as well as those provided through commercial presence. The protocol is reprinted in ILM 36 (1997): 366.

[5] It should be emphasised that the problem with accounting rates is not exclusively a North/South problem. In many cases, traffic imbalances and difference in rates lead to important flows of payments between developed countries, but, as we shall see below, the North/South controversy is central to the problems facing the reform of accounting rates.

[6] Countries with liberalised markets which have implemented price cuts in their international services suffer from deficits in settlement payments. Those countries are the US, the UK, New Zealand, Sweden, Australia and Japan. However, those economies do not publish data systematically. The example of the US will be present throughout this paper for the availability and detailed data published by the FCC. The FCC has also published a comparison between accounting rates with the US, the UK and New Zealand. The table is available at the FCC International Bureau website, www.fcc.org/ib/.

the cumulative sum of the lending programmes in telecommunications of all development banks around the world for the first half of the 1990s.[7]

The conflict in attitudes was resolved during the basic telecommunications negotiations by an agreement to defer the debate over accounting rates until the next round of negotiations on trade in services. The contracting parties concluded a gentleman's agreement waiving their rights to recourse to dispute settlement procedures under the WTO. However, the compromise is very fragile as it conceals a critical discrepancy and anomaly in the new liberalised regime for international telecommunications services.

The regime as it operates today is indubitably an 'unacceptable inheritance'[8] of the old era of telecommunications regime. Efforts should be deployed at the international level to bring the system into conformity with the trade principles extended to the telecommunications sector under the fourth protocol to the GATS. However, focusing mainly on the position of developing countries and pleading for arranging a 'soft landing' for developing countries in the new liberalised environment,[9] the paper calls for a differentiation between relations involving developed countries and those involving developing countries. While it is not acceptable that the accounting rates system continues to subsidise the telecommunications sector in countries with well-developed infrastructure, it is both necessary and justifiable under the Agreement on Basic Telecommunications that the accounting rates system continues to fund telecommunications development in developing countries.[10] In this context, international accounting rates could be singled out as a prime means for telecommunications development under the liberalised environment for telecommunications services.

This paper employs a clinical approach to the accounting rate problem. After a diagnosis of the malaise of the regime, the paper will propose a remedy for the system. The paper is organised in three sections.

[7] P. Tarjanne, 'Reforming the International Accounting Rates System', *ITU News* 2 (1998).

[8] The expression is inspired by the title of an article written by H. Ergas and P. Paterson, 'International Telecommunications Settlement Arrangements: An Unsustainable Inheritance', (1991) 15:2 *Telecommunications Policy* 15(2) (1991): 29.

[9] The concept of a soft landing for developing countries in the new liberalised environment for telecommunications services was conceived by the ITU Secretary General in his paper on accounting rates of November 1996. www.itu.int/intset/ITUpap/sg_com3.htm.

[10] An important proportion of settlement payments goes to OECD countries. In 1997, the ITU reported that countries such as Canada, Japan and South Korea received settlement payments in excess of US$100 million. ITU, *World Telecommunications Development Report: International Trade in Telecommunications* (Geneva: ITU, 1996–7).

The first section focuses on the difference in attitudes between developed and developing countries *vis-à-vis* accounting rates. The second section demonstrates how the conflict in attitudes led to a peculiar cohabitation between the accounting rate regime and the new liberalised environment for telecommunications services under GATS and the telecommunications Protocol. The last section demonstrates how to accommodate developing countries' concerns through a development-inspired interpretation of preferential provisions appearing in GATS. The solution aims to alleviate the conflict in attitudes and avoid the institutional contradiction in the new regime for international telecommunications services.

International accounting rates at the heart of a North/South controversy

To understand the magnitude of the conflict between developed and developing countries over accounting rates reform, this section will start by describing how the system is engineered to favour developing countries with high accounting rates and low outbound traffic.

Overview of the regime and the roots of the problem

The revenue-sharing mechanism for international telecommunications resulted from the way international telecommunications were conducted. From the beginning, international telecommunications have been treated as jointly provided services between monopolistic telecommunications operators in two countries. Under this regime of joint provision, the telecommunications operator in the country where the call originated conducts the call over its own facilities to a certain point in the international gateway. The telecommunications operator from the country of destination takes the call over from the middle point and delivers it to its destination using its own facilities.

The accounting rate is the rate per unit of traffic agreed upon between two countries for the joint provision of service. In case of traffic imbalance, the carrier with more outbound traffic transfers funds to the carrier terminating those calls. The payment is called a settlement payment. It usually equals half the accounting rates. The settlement payment compensates the terminating carrier for the service of delivering the call to its final destination. The accounting rates regime has thus two important constituents: the applicable rate per unit of traffic and the splitting formula according to which accounting rates are divided between operators.

Both elements are at the heart of the developed/developing country controversy over accounting rates.

Different reasons were presented by commentators for the near collapse of the accounting rates system. It is easy to discern distant causes and immediate ones. Distant causes are related to the fact that both technological developments in telecommunications and the unleashing of market forces have tremendously altered the traditional bilateral mode of international telecommunications. The Agreement on Basic Telecommunications is precisely accelerating the move towards a multilateral framework. The Agreement on Basic Telecommunications is likely to have a threefold impact on the accounting rate regime.[11] First, with the Agreement on Basic Telecommunications, more than three-quarters of international traffic is now submitted to competitive supply. Increased competition will drop accounting rates to closer to cost. Analysis of the impact of competition on the level of accounting rates between the United States and a selection of countries before and after the introduction of competition in international services shows that the decrease in accounting rates as a result of competition can be very significant. In the case of Hong Kong, accounting rates with the US fell from 79 cents per minute before 1998 to 13 cents per minute after the introduction of competition, an 84 per cent reduction. Other examples include accounting rates in US/Israel routes and US/Malaysia routes with a decline of 50 per cent and 39 per cent respectively.[12] Secondly, with an open trade framework, carriers do not necessarily have to go through the half circuit regime to deliver international services. It is increasingly possible for carriers to offer end-to-end services, either by establishing a foreign presence under mode 3 of supply or by leasing lines from foreign carriers. Finally, it is important to stress the impact of telecommunications alliances on accounting rates. With alliances becoming increasingly global, an important proportion of international traffic will be based on the internal transfer of funds between partners rather than on traditional accounting rates.[13]

The most immediate causes for the shock to the accounting rates system are principally the discrepancy between accounting rates and cost as well as the growing imbalance in traffic.

[11] ITU and TeleGeography, *Direction of Traffic: Trading Telecom Minutes* (Geneva: ITU, 1999).

[12] See *ibid.*, p. 23, Table 2.4 (impact of competition on accounting rate levels).

[13] *Ibid.*

Discrepancy between accounting rates and cost

From the inception of the practice of using accounting rates as revenue-sharing mechanism in international telecommunications, the applicable rate per unit of traffic has never been directly related to cost. The discrepancy between accounting rates and the costs of conducting international telecommunication has grown extremely wide in recent years. Studies show that accounting rates are sometimes ten times higher than the actual cost of delivering international service.[14] In the last few years, the cost of international links has been dropping by 30 per cent per year[15]due to the decline of the cost of infrastructure as well as the increase in transmission capacity.[16] This decline has not been mirrored by a similar decrease in accounting rates. It is the dissociation between international accounting rates and the cost of terminating international services that caused the dissatisfaction of developed countries led by the United States. According to the US Federal Communications Commission (FCC), settlement payments flying from the US to other countries to compensate for above cost termination services constitute a subsidy paid by US consumers to foreign operators. The campaign against accounting rates led by the US aims at bringing accounting rates closer to cost and abolishing the regime of subsidy embodied in above cost accounting rates.

Growing imbalance in traffic between developed and developing countries

The relationship between traffic and wealth has been established in some studies. According to the Secretary General of the ITU, for the majority of countries, the general rule is that an increase of GDP per capita of US$1,000 will generate around six minutes of extra traffic per inhabitant

[14] In the Benchmark Order, the FCC estimates the actual cost of terminating a call to be not higher than eight cents per minute (settlement rate). Many developing countries charge as much as 80 cents per minute.

[15] P. Tarjanne, 'The 1998 Telecommunications Revolution', Study Group 3, Meeting of 27 May 1997, p. 6.

[16] Note, for example, that TAT-14, an undersea cable owned by a consortium of fifty international operators and connecting many European cities to the US allows simultaneous transmission of 15 million phone calls. See TeleGeography, *International Bandwidth* (2001). In 1982, TAT-7 had a much more limited capacity of 4,000 simultaneous calls. For an overview of cost trends in the telecommunications industry, see ITU and TeleGeography, *Direction of Traffic: Trading Telecom Minutes* (Geneva: ITU, 1999), Chapter 4, 'Cost and Price Trends'.

per year.[17] Cheong and Mullins went even further to ascertain that US traffic imbalances are strongly correlated with differences between foreign and US per capita incomes. The authors' estimate is that a 1 per cent increase in foreign per capita income translates into a 0.55 per cent decrease in the US bilateral deficit.[18]

The study of the pattern of international outgoing traffic per inhabitant reveals once again the relation between telecommunications traffic and wealth. The basic telecommunications Indicators database of the ITU reports that, while inhabitants of low-income countries spend only 0.9 minutes on average for international calls, inhabitants of high-income countries spend up to 71 minutes.[19]

The imbalance between outgoing and incoming traffic has been growing over the years. The 1999 telecommunications indicators show that global outgoing telephone traffic is almost 84 billion minutes. The United States alone accounts for one quarter of the world's total outgoing traffic. At the other end of the spectrum, many countries have a total outgoing traffic of less than one million minutes.[20] In 1999, the total outgoing telephone traffic of low-income countries (a total of sixty-one economies) was 1.7 billion minutes, down from 2.5 billion minutes in 1995. The group accounts for only 2 per cent of global outgoing traffic. High-income countries, originated 80 per cent of global outgoing traffic, a total of 66.2 billion minutes, up from 49.4 billion minutes in 1995.[21]

Two reasons explain the difference in the pattern of traffic between developed and developing countries: the difference in collection charges and the development of alternative calling procedures.

The difference in collection charges is an important element in the determination of the level of demand. Different economic studies demonstrate that demand for international telecommunications services is

[17] P. Tarjanne, 'ITU, Trade in Telecommunications: Towards a New World of Telecommunications Development', keynote address by ITU Secretary General, tenth anniversary and eleventh annual conference and trade exhibition, Caribbean Association of National Telecommunications Organizations (CANTO), 5 June 1995.

[18] K. Cheong and M. Mullins, 'International Telephone Service Imbalances: Accounting Rates and Regulatory Policy' *Telecommunications Policy* 15(3) (1991): 12.

[19] Also published in ITU and TeleGeography, *Direction of Traffic: Trading Telecom Minutes* (Geneva: ITU, 1999), p. 189, World Table 2, 'International Traffic Trends'.

[20] For example, Afghanistan 0.5 million minutes, Georgia 0.2 million minutes.

[21] Data available in ITU, *World Telecommunications Development Report and Basic Telecommunications Indicators: Mobile Cellular* (Geneva: ITU), pp. A-49, A-50 and A-51.

elastic with respect to prices.[22] The introduction of competition has had a tremendous impact on collection charges for international telecommunications services. According to a study conducted by the FCC in 1992, calls to the US can exceed by as much as 80 per cent the outbound rate of calls.[23] There exists a close nexus between collection charges and the balance in traffic flows. According to the FCC, evidence suggests that telecommunications traffic is 'reasonably well balanced' with regard to countries with collections rates that are comparable to the US collection rate.[24] Countries, which have not introduced competition, do have higher collection rates and generate less outgoing traffic. Traffic between the US and Africa highlights this point. The African market is the least open to competition.[25] One result is that call prices in African countries are way above cost and their outgoing traffic is very limited compared to their incoming traffic. The study of telephone traffic between African countries and the US shows that in African countries incoming traffic from the US was almost eight times the outgoing traffic in 1999.[26]

The second phenomenon, which put further strain on the accounting rate regime, is the appearance and evolution of alternative calling procedures. Alternative calling procedures have different forms. They include: calling cards, country direct services, refile, international simple resale, international virtual private network services, voice-over-networks, and callback.[27]

According to the ITU, the portion of international traffic settled outside accounting rates is as high as 30 per cent.[28] This proportion will grow

[22] See Kenneth Stanley, 'Balance of Payments, Deficits, and Subsidies in International Communications Services: A New Challenge for Regulation', *Administrative Law Review* 3 (1991), n. 11.

[23] FCC, Common Carrier Bureau, 'Calling Prices for International Message Telephone Service Between the US and Other Countries', Washington DC: FCC, October 1992.

[24] FCC, 'International Accounting Rates and the Balance of Payments Deficit in Telecommunications Services', FCC, Common Carrier Bureau, December 1988, p. 45, cited by K. Cheong and M. Mullins, 'International Telephone Service Imbalances: Accounting Rates and Regulatory Policy', *Telecommunications Policy* 15(3) (1991): 117.

[25] The African countries have only a very limited participation in the basic telecommunications agreement, with very weak commitments to market opening and liberalisation. See Summary of Country Commitments under WTO Agreement on Basic Telecommunications, in ITU, *World Telecommunications Development Report 1996/1997* (Geneva: ITU, 1997), p. 103, Table 6.3.

[26] See the Common Carrier Bureau statistics at www.fcc.gov/Bureaus/common-carrier/reports/fcc-stste-link/Intl/4361-f99/pdf.

[27] For a brief description of each of these forms, see ITU, *World Telecommunications Development Report 1996/1997* (Geneva: ITU, 1997), pp. 92–3.

[28] ITU, *Direction of Traffic: Trading Telecoms Minutes* (Geneva: ITU, 1999), pp. 4–7.

even faster with the exponential growth of voice travelling over Internet-based protocols in lieu of the traditional PSTN. In 2000, 4 billion minutes travelled over IP networks. As mentioned in the ITU's Internet Reports, with the economies of scale enjoyed by IP networks and the possibility to conduct international calls at a fraction of the price, it is very likely that IP networks will grow to provide an attractive alternative to the traditional PSTN for international traffic.[29]

In the US, for example, the FCC has reported a total traffic of 28.4 billion minutes in 1999. The traditional accounting rates system handled 19.3 billion minutes, while the remaining 9 billion minutes were settled by international simple resale and hubbing arrangements.[30]

The common denominator between the different alternative calling procedures is that they depart from the concept of telecommunications services as a jointly provided service and provoke service competition in countries that do not permit infrastructure competition. Of these different procedures, callback[31] is the most relevant to the purpose of our investigation. Callback simply converts incoming traffic into outgoing traffic and exacerbates the problem of settlement payment.[32] The rationale behind this practice is the ability of callback operators to offer customers in monopolistic markets the possibility to conduct international calls at collection rates offered by the competitive market where the callback provider is located rather than at collection rates charged by the national carriers. The large discrepancy between collection charges at

[29] It is reported that voice-over-Internet doubles every 100 days. ITU, *Internet Reports: IP Telephony* (Geneva: ITU, 2000).

[30] See the latest Industry Analysis Report, 'International Traffic Data Pursuant to Section 43.6', FCC Common Carrier Bureau statistics, available at www.fcc.gov/Bureaus/common-carrier/reports/fcc-stste-link/Intl/4361-f99/pdf.

[31] Callback has developed as a result of two phenomena. First, the development of technology, and, secondly, the asymmetry in market structures. As to the first point, technology has developed to permit evolution in switching devices. The caller sends uncompleted call signals by dialing a number in the country of destination. The callback operator identifies the caller through computerised switching and places a call back to him with a foreign dial tone.

[32] It should be emphasised here that the alternative calling procedures have differing impacts on accounting rates. For example, virtual private networks and simple resale ignore the accounting rates system. In these procedures, private operators do not pay accounting rates to the terminating carrier. They pay annual fees for the leased circuit in question irrespective of the actual flow of traffic over the circuit. Of these procedures, the calling-card-based service is the one with the closest effect on accounting rates to callback. It increases the trade imbalance by allowing subscribers abroad to bypass the local network and have the call conducted by their own carriers and have the calls billed to their home account. Country direct services and refile are a form of call reorigination services.

both ends explains to a large extent how callback grew to be an attractive option for consumers in high collection rate markets. The result is that, in many instances, the callback provider can offer its customer rates of up to 50 per cent lower than the rate that the customer would have paid under the conventional method.[33]

The attractive price cut leads to further intensifying the phenomenon of traffic imbalance. In the case of India, for instance, callback was responsible for 63 per cent of India's outgoing traffic being rerouted to the US by callback providers.[34]

These various factors culminated to create a situation in which developing countries stood to be net importers of international traffic and beneficiaries of substantial sums of settlement payments. Developed countries, led by the US, become net exporters of international traffic suffering from deficits in settlement payments. This situation created a conflict in the position of each group towards the accounting rate regime and a difference in approaching a satisfactory solution.

Opposing concerns and reactions of the different parties involved

The differing concerns about the current international accounting rates have been nicely summarised by the ITU: 'Those that propose reform face one stark problem: those that do well out of the existing system greatly outnumber those that fare badly.'[35]

The developed countries' positions

Developed countries, led by the US, have fiercely criticised the accounting rate regime. According to US officials, the regime is a complete anachronism in need of urgent reform. The main concern outlined by developed countries is the discrepancy between the cost of delivering international services and the charges under the accounting rate regime. High charges and traffic imbalances culminated to create trade deficits in many developed countries, most notably the US.

The US is a major exporter of telephone traffic, with outgoing traffic exceeding incoming traffic for all region of the world. In 1999, the US

[33] Estimate by Kenneth Propp, 'The Eroding Structure of International Telecommunication Regulation: The Challenge of Call Back Services', *Harvard International law Journal* 37 (1996): 499.

[34] ITU, *World Telecommunications Development Report 1996/1997* (Geneva: ITU, 1997), p. 115.

[35] *Ibid.*, p. 93.

sent 28 billion minutes, up from 22.6 billion minutes in 1997. Incoming traffic to the US amounted to only 10.6 billion minutes, which translates into a deficit of 18 billion minutes.[36] Between the early 1970s and the late 1990s, the US net deficit for settlement payments jumped from 40 million minutes to 5 billion minutes.[37]

The reaction of the US is central to our analysis. The focus of the US was to address the problem within the accounting rate regime by advocating cost-based, non-discriminatory and transparent accounting rates. To this extent, the US approach to the problem is different from the approach of the European Union or the OECD, both of which advocated solutions that call for the departure from accounting rates altogether in favour of new ways of revenue-sharing.

In 1997, the FCC adopted a new Order, which established benchmarks for settlement rates that US carriers are allowed to pay to foreign carriers for terminating calls originating in the US.[38] The Order is by far the most far-reaching step towards putting an end to the above cost accounting regime.[39] The benchmarks proposed by the US have three different rates: 15.4 cents per minute for upper-income countries; 19.1 cents per minute for middle-income countries; and 23.4 cents per minute for lower-income countries. The regime took effect in January 1998, and is scheduled to be in operation in 1999 for upper-income countries, 2000 for upper middle-income countries, 2001 for lower middle-income countries, 2002 for lower-income countries and 2003 for countries with a teledensity less than 1.

[36] FCC, Common Carrier Bureau statistics, 2000, www.fcc.gov/wcb/.

[37] ITU, *World Telecommunications Development Report 1996/1997* (Geneva: ITU, 1997), p. 91. It should be mentioned here that, unlike the US, few other countries publish accounting rates data. Most examples in the literature focus on the US. The US is of course of particular importance given that the problem of accounting rates is most heavily felt in the US. In addition, the US situation is central to the discussion of accounting rates reform, given the large share of international traffic generated by the US. According to an INTELSAT estimate, the US terminates or originates over half of the traffic carried by INTELSAT.

[38] FCC, In the Matter of International Settlement Rates, IB Docket No. 96-261, Report and Order Adopted 7/August 1997, released 18 August 1997, available on the FCC website, www.fcc.gov/bureaus/international/orders/1997/fcc97280.html, accessed February 2002.

[39] The US battle against above cost accounting rates started in 1984. The FCC adopted its 'International Settlement Policy' (ISP) in 1986. See 'Implementation and Scope of International Settlement Policy for Parallel International Communications Routes', Docket no 85-204, 50 Federal Register 28418 (1985), Report and Order 51, Federal Register 4736 7 February 1986. Under the ISP, US carriers are prevented from agreeing on a division for accounting rates other than 50/50. They are also obliged to follow uniform settlement rate agreements on parallel international routes.

The US position has triggered immense controversy and mounting dissatisfaction from foreign carriers,[40] many of which have joined forces to challenge the order in the US Court of Appeals. Critics agree that the benchmark approach has many flaws and is an inadequate solution to the problem of international accounting rates.[41] The first flaw relates to the danger of unilateralism in dealing with the issue of international accounting rates. The US is unilaterally dictating the price of terminating a telephone call in a foreign country, an issue that has always been a matter of bilateral negotiations. This policy is an undue interference with the national sovereignty of other countries, as it directs the other countries to reconsider their national policies.[42]

The second flaw in the Benchmark Order relates to the method used to calculate the benchmarks. The Benchmark Order is based on the tariffed prices for the three components of international services: the international transmission facilities, the international switching facilities and the national extension component.[43] For the international transmission facilities, the FCC used a tariffed component price based on the price of private leased high-speed digital circuits. For international switching, the FCC used data published by the ITU on the existing settlement charges among forty-two countries of TEUREM (the Tariff Group for Europe and the Mediterranean Basin). The switching component of these settlements was used by the FCC as a proxy for international switching services in all countries. Finally, the national extension prices are based on the average of different domestic prices as published by national operators. The approach is based on tariffs charged for domestic calls travelling equivalent routes over the national network. According to commentators from the ITU, the method used for the calculation of benchmarks is not accurate because it is based on tariffed prices and not on real costs and because it

[40] For an the overview of the different reactions to the Order, see David Melony, 'FCC Wins Accounting Rate War', *Communications Week International*, 23 November 1998; Larry Luxner, 'Back and Forth on Foreign Billing: FCC Embroiled in International Accounting Rate', *Telephony*, 5 October 1998; and Jeremy Scott Joynt, 'First Law Suits Fly as KDD Challenges FCC's Unilateral Accounting Rates', *Total Telecom*, 3 September 1997. See also Jeremy Scott Joynt, 'C&W Set to Challenge FCC in Court Over Accounting Rates', *Total Telecom*, 11 August 1997.

[41] United States Court of Appeals for the District of Columbia Circuit, *Cable and Wireless plc* v. *FCC*, 12 January 1999. The court's opinion is available at www.fcc.gov/ogc/documents/opinion/1999/cable.html.

[42] The Court of Appeals, studying the issue of jurisdiction, held that the FCC Order was a valid exercise of the FCC's regulatory authority under the Communications Act.

[43] For a more detailed description of US methodology, see Annex E to the benchmark Order, 'Tariffed Components Price Methodology'.

ignores fixed charges as a tariff element. In addition, the FCC approach neglected the fact that in most developing countries socio-political considerations keep local call prices low to encourage affordability of the service. As to the switching cost, the FCC did not take into consideration that switching costs are lower in European countries (subject to TEUREM) and in developing countries.

The final flaw in the benchmark Order is that it contains enforcement measures that are in violation of WTO principles and US commitments on the Agreement on Basic Telecommunications. Under the Order, the FCC can prohibit US carriers with foreign affiliates and foreign carriers with a US presence from operating in the US market unless the carriers' foreign affiliates settle at the benchmark or below. Furthermore, for foreign carriers not willing to agree to the new benchmarks with in the specified time, the FCC could order US carriers not to pay settlement rates in excess of the benchmark rate. Both of these enforcement measures constitute barriers to entry to the US market in contradiction to GATS principles. In 1999, the FCC denied a petition for the reconsideration of the Benchmark Order. In its report on reconsideration, the FCC reaffirmed that the Benchmark Order is consistent with both domestic and international law.[44]

The level of implementation of the Benchmark Order can be deduced from data gathered by the FCC International Bureau on accounting rates between the US and over 250 international points.[45] Data show that for many destinations accounting rates have dropped closer to the benchmarks. The immediate impact of the entry into force of the Order for the overall US settlement deficit is already apparent. In 1999, the US net settlement payment has declined by US$1 billion as compared to 1997, despite the growing imbalance of traffic in 1999 (18 billion minutes in 1999, up from 13.4 billion minutes in 1997).

In addition to the US initiative to resolve the problem of international accounting rates, other efforts were deployed in other fora, although these other initiatives do not solve the problem of accounting rates but rather find new ways to replace the current regime. The example of the European Union is worth noting here. In 1998, as part of the liberalisation of basic telecommunications services, the European Union opted for replacing

[44] FCC, Report and Order on Reconsideration and Order Lifting Stay, IB Docket No. 96-261, released 11 June 1999.

[45] Current US accounting rates as well as historical data from 1985 to 2002 are published by the FCC's International Bureau. See www.fcc.gov/ib/td/account.htnnl, accessed February 2002.

international accounting rates between member countries with cost-based interconnection systems.[46] In other words, carriers conducting calls from France to the UK will not have to pay the UK carriers a settlement rate per minute of international traffic but an interconnection charge to the UK network. So far, implementation of the new arrangement has not resulted in the disappearance of accounting rates in European traffic. The old regime is still covering a major part of intra-European traffic.

The developing countries' position

Developing countries receive large amounts of settlement payments each year. According to ITU calculations, developing countries receive an average of US$10 billion of settlement payments per year. The sums at stake are very high if one considers for instance that the cash flow from

[46] See Commission of the European Communities, Commission Recommendation on Interconnection in a Liberalised Telecom Market, Part I, Interconnection Pricing, Brussels, 15 October 1997, available at http://europa.eu.nt/ISPO/infosoc/telecompolicy/en/r3148-en.htm. The liberalisation of trade in telecommunications services in the European Union was a gradual process. Trade in telecommunications services emerged as an issue of paramount interest for European policy in 1980 after the success of the liberalisation of the UK market. EC policy on the telecommunications sector is outlined in the famous Green Paper on the development of the common market for telecommunications services and equipment of 30 June 1987. The aim of the liberalisation is to strengthen the EU position in the world market for telecommunications and computer services. The aim set out in the Green Paper is to 'establish competitive market structures which will allow the community to match the dynamism developed by the US and Japan'. See Communication by the Commission, 'Towards a Dynamic European Community, Green Paper on the Development of the Common Market on Telecommunications Services and Equipment', COM(87)290 final. For a discussion of the Green Paper, see J. Scherer, 'European Community Opens its Telecommunications Networks: Legal Aspects of the Green Paper', *International Computer Law Adviser* (1987): 4–8. Many Council directives followed the policy proposals set out in the Green Paper. Phase one of the liberalisation extended to liberalisation of telecommunications equipment: Commission Terminal Equipment Directive 88/301 and Mutual Recognition of Terminal Equipment Directives 91/263 and 93/93. In addition to terminal equipment, the liberalisation extended to value-added services in Directives 90/388, 94/96 and 96/2. All these documents can be found in Nexis-Lexis library: Europe, File LEGIS. In addition to these general directives, the Commission adopted numerous other documents pertaining to specific areas of telecommunications: the Satellite Communications Directive 94/46, OJ 1994 L268/15; the Mobile Communications Directive 96/2, OJ 1996 L20/59; and the Cable Infrastructure Directive 95/51, OJ 1995 L256/49. For a discussion of the EU telecommunications legislations, see J. Scherer, 'Telecommunications Law and Policy of the European Union', in J. Scherer, ed., *Telecommunications Laws in Europe* (3rd edn, The Hague, London and Boston: Kluwer Law International, 1995), p. 1. The final step was the liberalisation of basic telecommunications services on 1 January 1998 and the replacement of accounting rates by interconnection charges in the intra-European market.

settlement payments for one year is more than twice the annual amount of telecom investment in all of Africa (as noted in a recent ITU publication). It is also estimated that net settlement payments to developing countries from 1992 to 1998 were sufficient to fund 45 million new lines.[47]

Developing countries derive at least three benefits from the current accounting rate system. First, for many countries international settlement constitutes a huge portion of their telecommunications revenues. In Latin America, settlement from the US alone can contribute more than half of total revenue, as demonstrated for example in the case of Haiti.[48] It should be mentioned, however, that the impact of the reduction of accounting rates on developing countries depends on the extent operators rely on accounting rates.

A study conducted by the ITU on the impact of accounting rates on developing countries shows that each country fares differently under a reformed accounting rates system.[49] For countries with high dependency on accounting rates, such as Samoa (40.8 per cent of telecommunications revenue) or Senegal (29.3 per cent), the impact of a reduction on accounting rates will prove to have dramatic results on national operators and on national foreign currency reserves. The study also argues that, even for countries which do not depend heavily on revenues from accounting rates, such as India (12.6 per cent) or Colombia, the effect of a reduction of accounting rates will also have dramatic results given the huge amounts involved.

Secondly, settlement payments constitute an important source of hard currency for developing countries, which enable them to purchase new telecommunications equipment and to improve their networks generally. The higher the level of hard currency income in developing countries, the better protection these countries will have against currency fluctuations. In India, net settlement payments are an important source of income to subsidise investment in domestic infrastructure. Settlement payments accounted for 17 per cent of telecommunications expenditure

[47] ITU, *Direction of Traffic: Trading Telecom Minutes* (Geneva: ITU, 1999), p. 73.

[48] See FCC Common Carrier Bureau statistics at www.fcc.gov/Bureaus/common-carrier/reports/fcc-stste-link/Intl/4361-f99/pdf, accessed February 2002.

[49] In his consultation paper on accounting rates reform, the Secretary General of the ITU emphasised the necessity of conducting case studies on the impact of accounting rates reform on developing countries. Eight studies were conducted by independent consultants. The studies followed an outline provided by the ITU. For an overview of the studies and the report of the consultants, see the ITU website on accounting rates reform.

in 1997.[50] In the case of Mexico, which is one of the top ten recipients of settlement payments, especially from the US, more than half (in 1996 as much as 90 per cent) of settlement payments from the US are passed on to US manufacturers in payment for telecom equipment imports.[51]

The truth is that, even in cases in which only small amounts of settlement payments flow to developing countries, the amount can still have a significant impact on small economies. This is because foreign exchange is a precondition to network growth. The case of Mauritania is worth noting here. For Mauritania, settlement payments constitute only 3.2 per cent of total telecommunications revenues. Despite the small amount involved, the case study on Mauritania concluded that the amount paid in hard currency remains important for a country whose currency is not convertible.[52]

Finally, developing countries have for a long time opted for keeping international telecommunications services way above cost in order to cross-subsidise local telecommunications services as well as network access cost. The reform of international accounting rates inevitably raises concerns about the affordability of universal telecommunications services in developing countries. It puts enormous strain on developing countries to restructure their cost strategies. In the case of Senegal, for instance, analysis of the income provided by local services and by international services proved that international services yield a surplus of US$0.93 per minute, which is used to subsidise local telephone services.[53]

The antagonistic positions of developed and developing countries *vis-à-vis* international accounting rate reform has led to institutional contradiction within the regime of telecommunications services.

[50] 'The Changing International Telecommunications Environment: India', Case Study prepared by Phillips Tarifica Ltd for the ITU, February 1998, p. 32. The study includes a detailed analysis of the revenue-sharing arrangement between VSNL, which has a monopoly of international telecommunications services in India, and the Department of Telecommunications. The arrangement testifies to the importance of the settlement revenues in subsidising the domestic market.

[51] ITU, *Direction of Traffic: Trading Telecom Minutes* (Geneva, ITU, 1999), p. 73, Figure 7.3.

[52] The study on the impact of accounting rates on Mauritania is published at www.itu.int/wtdf/cases/Mauritania/index.htm.

[53] The study of the impact of accounting rates on Senegal is published at http://www.itu.int/wtdf/Senegal/index.htm.

International accounting rates and the regime under GATS: a peculiar coexistence

Of all the aspects of international telecommunications services, international accounting is the trade question *par excellence*.[54] The traditional form of international telecommunications is a service that crosses national borders. The country that makes the call exports a service, and the country which receives the call imports the service. However, as mentioned by the ITU, unlike the traditional pattern of trade, the country which exports the call must pay the country that imports the call for its part in terminating the service.[55] Being an international trade issue, international accounting rates should have been the first element to be modified to match the multilateral trade liberalisation framework under the GATS. However, the issue of accounting rates proved to be one of the most stubborn questions in the negotiations. Failure to address the issue of accounting rates resulted in the survival of a mechanism that is in contradiction to the letter and spirit of the GATS and the liberalisation philosophy that is guiding sector reform at the international level.

The old inheritance is in conflict with the letter of GATS

The architectural design of the GATS is based on a distinction between general obligations, which apply to all members, and specific obligations, which are triggered only if a country made specific commitments in its schedule.[56] The current regime of accounting rates is in contradiction to the basic general principles of liberalisation under the GATS. A case for

[54] We recall here how the idea of trade in telecommunications services was difficult to grasp in the beginning, and how trade is considered as related mainly to goods not services. It took numerous research and studies to ascertain that trade principles do apply to services in general and that telecommunications services are indeed one of the most important sectors to which trade principles should be extended. For the tradability of services, see G. Fetekuty, *International Trade in Services: A Blue Print for Negotiations* (Cambridge: Balling, 1988); see also P. Sauvant, P. Robinson and V. P. Govitrikar, *Electronic Highways for World Trade* (Boulder, CO. Westview, 1989).

[55] ITU, *World Telecommunications Development Report 1996/1997* (Geneva: ITU, 1997), p. 91.

[56] For an overview of the GATS, see H. G. Broadman, 'GATS: The Uruguay Round Accord on International Trade and Investment in Services', *World Economy* 17(3) (1994): 181; Tuch H. E. Stahl, 'Liberalizing Trade in Services: The Case for Sidestepping the GATT', *Yale Journal of International Law* 19(2) (1994): 402; and P. Sauve, 'Assessing the General Agreement on Trade in Services: Half-Full or Half-Empty', *Journal of World Trade Law* 29(4) (1995): 125.

saying that it contradicts specific commitments can also be made, albeit on a more cautious basis.

The international accounting rate regime as it operates today is discriminatory. It is in contradiction to the most-favoured nation (MFN) principle under GATS and to the principle of transparency. The MFN principle is the core principle of trade liberalisation. Under this principle, parties to the GATS are under an obligation to treat services and service providers from one party in the same way as services and service providers from any other party. In the current accounting rates regime, however, prices charged for the same service, namely, termination of international calls, are different for different users. For example, in 1999, the settlement rate to terminate calls in Bosnia is 2.09 Bosnian dinars for calls originating from the US and 3.08 Bosnian dinars for calls originating from Canada.[57] This example shows a discriminatory approach to treatment of the same service accordance to its national origin. The case shows an artificial variance not justified by the difference in the cost of terminating a call whether originating from Canada or from the United States. The problems of discriminatory accounting rates may have deep adverse effects on the flow of traffic and the price to the consumers. Indeed, this discrimination creates incentives for refile, transit and other routing practices to profit from the least expensive routing.

The accounting rate regime is also in conflict with the transparency requirement under the GATS. The bilateral secret mechanism of negotiating accounting rates lacks transparency and does not provide carriers with a scale of reference to compare accounting rates with a particular country. The latter issue gave rise to intense debate led by the United States during the drafting of the Reference Paper. The United States stressed the case that accounting rates should be published for transparency reasons, but the other countries heavily rejected the proposition. Many countries argued that accounting rates should be negotiated on a commercially confidential basis.

Assessing the compatibility of the accounting rates regime with the second pillar of non-discrimination (namely, the principle of national treatment) is a more delicate task. Data gathered by the FCC in its benchmark order revealed that in many cases foreign carriers are overcharged for the national component element of the network in comparison with domestic calls travelling equivalent routes over the national network. Overcharging this part in the case of international services is a case of discriminatory

[57] ITU, TeleGeography, *Direction of Traffic*, p. 216.

treatment of foreign carriers in violation of the national treatment principle. It should be noted, however, that assessing the compatibility between international accounting rates and the national treatment principle under the GATS is not as easy as it looks. The difficulty stems from the fact the principle of national treatment under the GATS is fundamentally different from the principle of national treatment under the GATT.[58] Whereas under the latter national treatment is applied generally to different trade relations, national treatment under GATS is not a general principle. It is rather a specific commitment undertaken by countries in their schedule of specific commitment. A study of specific commitments undertaken by developing countries in basic telecommunications liberalisation shows that these countries undertook fewer commitments in the area of market access and national treatment than developed countries.[59]

The same can be said about accounting rates as a barrier to entry. New entrants might be discouraged because of the necessity to negotiate bilateral correspondent agreements with every individual country.[60] It is true, however, that the regime of bilateral negotiations as it operates today creates a burden on the carrier's ability to align accounting rates with the evolution of the market. The bilateral negotiating regime is a rigid mechanism in a liberalised environment. Here again we should be cautious in this judgment, as market access commitments like national treatment demonstrate specific commitments under GATS and not general applications. In other words, judging the compatibility of the accounting rates regime with these two principles cannot be made in the abstract but rather on a case-by-case basis.

Whether blatant (in the case of general obligations) or more dubious (in the case of specific obligations), the conflict between the current international accounting rates and the GATS principles is a proven fact

[58] A. Mattoo, 'National Treatment in the GATS: Cornerstone or Pandora's Box?', *Journal of World Trade Law* 31(1) (1997): 107.

[59] For an overview of developing countries' commitments, see Council for Trade in Services, 'Telecommunications Services: Background Note by the Secretariat', S/C/W/74, 8 December 1998; M. Mary, 'An Evaluation of the basic Telecom Services Agreement', Center for International Economic Studies, Policy Discussion Paper No. 98/109 (1999), available at www.adelaide.edu.au/CIES/98109, accessed February 2002; and B. Petrazzinni, *Global Telecom Talks: A Trillion Dollar Deal* (Washington, DC: Institute for International Economics, 1997).

[60] P. Tarjanne, 'How Will the Accounting Rate System Need To Be Modified in a Liberalized Market: Liberalization and Privatization of the European Telecommunications Sector Preparing for 1998 and Beyond', speech, Rome, 25 March 1996.

which constitutes one of the most important shortcomings of the new Agreement on Basic Telecommunications.

The regime is at odds with the spirit of GATS and the liberalisation efforts under the WTO

The problems associated with the current regime of accounting rate go beyond a mere conflict with the multilateral trade principles upon which the GATS is based. The regime is at odds with the spirit of the GATS. It should be emphasised here that the goal of trade liberalisation revolves around diminishing barriers to entry to achieve freer trade and more competition. The ultimate goal is that the new liberalised environment will have beneficial effects worldwide leading to the growth in new international markets of opportunities that will benefit all countries and translate into lower prices for telecommunications users and consumers. A closer analysis of the accounting rates system as it operates today shows that the system acts as a brake to the above goals.

The most apparent anomaly with accounting rates is market distortion. Petrazinni nicely summarises the accounting rate problem when he argued that 'high accounting rates create an odd mix of rewards and punishments. It rewards the inefficient carrier, which originates less traffic and bills high collection rates to its customer, while it punishes active carriers, which originate outbound traffic and charge their customers low rates.'[61]

In addition, the way international accounting rates are concluded slows the gradual move witnessed in the telecommunication sector from a bilateral regime to a multilateral regime. The problem with accounting rates is that the levels of rates for international services is determined by arbitrary methods and is not dictated by effective competition. In addition, the second element in the accounting rate – the principle of equal revenue division – may prevent the occurrence of full competition since carriers are prevented from offering lower rates in exchange for higher traffic flow. The 50/50 rule limits the scope of competitive negotiation and encourages a 'cartelised behaviour' which distorts market prices.[62]

Finally, high international accounting rates constitute an impediment to international trade in telecommunications services and a distortion of

[61] Petrazzini, *Global Telecom Talks*, p. 65.

[62] P. Tarjanne, 'The 1998 Telecommunications Revolution', Study Group 3, Meeting of 27 May 1997, p. 5.

trade in general. Indeed, excessive accounting rates inflate the prices of international services; and they curtail the growth of international services by raising rates to consumers. To the extent that accounting rates exceed the cost of terminating an international call, high accounting rates are today an obstacle which prevents consumers from enjoying the cheaper telecommunications services made possible by technological developments in transmission and switching facilities and by the unleashing of market forces. Deeper repercussions would be felt on the economy as a whole. As the global economy moves forward to be an information-based economy, high accounting rates curtail trade in services and slow the progress toward global markets.

After revealing the conflicts and contradictions underlying the issue of accounting rates reform, the intellectual challenge of this paper is to propose a compromise to the problem.

A possible consolation: applying the preferential treatment theory to accounting rates with developing countries

The move towards cost-based accounting rates seems to be an inevitable development due to the mounting pressure on the current level of accounting rates. Developing countries, although they benefit from the current system, are faced with a big dilemma. First, once the FCC successfully implements its benchmarks in different US–developing country routes, the rates would necessarily drop for bilateral relations with other countries. In addition and perhaps most importantly, developing countries eager to preserve the *status quo* would find themselves in a larger deficit with traffic diverting away from their PSTN to other competing networks. As mentioned earlier, the rise of IP telephony is indeed a serious concern for operators in developing countries. In 1999, the Republic of Korea had 9 per cent of its traffic with the US handled by IP network. The same is true for other large developing countries like India and China, which lost US$37 million and US$43 million respectively in settlement payments from the US for traffic handled by the Internet.[63]

If the reform of the international accounting rate regime is inevitable, developing countries should work in concert to ensure a multilateral approach to the reform. In this regard, the ITU's efforts to bring the regime closer to cost should be endorsed by developing countries as a better solution to the problem of accounting rates than the unilateral approach of

[63] ITU, *Internet Reports: IP Telephony* (Geneva: ITU, 2000).

the US or the collapse of the accounting regime altogether. As from 1992, ITU-T Recommendation D.140 stipulated that accounting rates should be cost-oriented, transparent and applied in a non-discriminatory fashion. The move towards cost has been slow and the ITU has been criticised for failing to find a satisfactory solution to the accounting rate problem.[64] The adoption of the fourth protocol as well as the FCC Benchmark Order, have further highlighted the need for the ITU to work with its members on a multilateral framework for bringing accounting rates closer to cost. The second World Telecommunications Policy Forum has focused on the issue of accounting rates and a group of experts have been appointed to deal with the issue. The group has successfully conducted its mission and the report of the focus group was adopted by Study Group 3 of the ITU Standardisation Sector. The proposal of the focus group is appended as Annex E to Recommendation ITU-T D.140. Annex E set a schedule for indicative target rates for direct and transit relations to be achieved by each group of countries over a three year period with the possibility of further extension in special circumstances.

Our proposal is to endorse the ITU's approach to accounting rate reform but to go a little bit further in responding to developing countries' concerns through the adaptation of the preferential treatment institution to accounting rates reform. In dealing with the reform of international accounting rates special attention should be devoted to the needs of developing countries. Soft landing measures can be made available through a development-oriented interpretation of preferential treatment under the trade principles. In order to justify the call for a preferential approach to the accounting rate problem, this section starts by highlighting the importance of accounting rates as a method of financing network growth in developing countries. The institution of preferential treatment is then defined, and proposals for adapting the institution to the accounting rate regime are attempted.

Why are accounting rates still needed?

There are many aspects for the development challenge in the telecommunications sector. The thrust of the challenge, however, is to fill the

[64] The FCC considers its unilateral action a necessary reaction to the failure of the ITU to come up with an acceptable multilateral solution to reform of accounting rates. See, for example, Vineeta Shetty, 'ITU in Knots Over Accounting Rates', *Communications International*, 2 November 1998; and Sheridan Nye, 'FCC Launches Unilateral Attack on International Settlement Rates', *Total Telecom*, 7 August 1997.

enormous gap between the telecommunications needs of developing countries on the one hand and the scarcity of resources on the other hand. The role of international settlement revenues as a means to subsidise network development in developing countries should be preserved, especially in light of the shortcomings of alternative funding mechanisms.

Foreign direct investment is increasingly recognised as a primary source for funding telecommunications infrastructure in developing countries. By incorporating mode 3 as a method of delivery of services to foreign countries, the GATS and the Agreement on Basic Telecommunications promise an increase in foreign direct investment inflows to developing countries. However, the prospect that increased foreign direct investment could bridge the telecommunications gap soon fade away if one considers the markedly uneven distribution of private capital among developing countries. A recent study by the South Center documented that only twelve developing countries account for 80 per cent of private flows to developing countries, with China alone accounting for over 25 per cent of all foreign direct investment flows to developing countries.[65] This leaves the majority of developing countries with little access to private capital. The lack of access is particularly acute for poorer countries. As reported by the UNCTAD in the 2001 World Investment Report, developing countries' share of global foreign direct investment flows declined in 2001 to 19 per cent compared with the much higher level of 41 per cent in 1999.[66] The share of the least developed countries has further deteriorated to 0.3 per cent of world inflows compared to 1 per cent in 1996.[67]

This pattern of unequal distribution is particularly apparent in the telecom sector where foreign operators compete fiercely for investment opportunities in large and lucrative markets in general and in the most lucrative sectors of these markets in particular. The case of the Latin American market is worth noting here, where a high level of foreign presence can be recorded.[68] Brazil, for instance, because of its large population and low teledensity, is viewed by foreign investors as 'the world's larger

[65] South Institute, *Financing Development: Issues for a South Agenda* (Geneva: South Institute, April 1999) available at www.southcenter.org/publications/financing/.

[66] UNCTAD, *World Investment Report: Promoting Linkages* (Geneva: UNCTAD, 2001).

[67] UNCTAD, *The Least Developed Countries: 200 Report: Aid, Private Capital Flows and External Debt: The Challenge of Financing Development in the LDC* (Geneva: UNCTAD, 2000).

[68] See Larry Luxner, 'The Dream of Mobility: Cellular Meets Pent-Up Demand and Sparks Explosive Growth in Latin America', *Global Telephony*, 1 December 1997.

potential phone market'.[69] Similar interest of foreign investors has been expressed in the Chinese telecom market, also considered as a lucrative market mainly because of its size and the huge demand for connection, despite the numerous regulatory hurdles encountered by foreign investors investing in China.[70] With concentration on these large markets, only 2 per cent of total telecom foreign direct investment reached Africa. Even then, most investment was concentrated in South Africa.[71] For other African countries, foreign investment is mostly restricted to the lucrative mobile sector.[72]

Other traditional sources of financing telecommunications infrastructure have also come under tremendous pressure lately. For instance, the latest available data from the Development Assistance Committee (DAC) of the OECD revealed a further decline in the level of foreign aid in 2000. Estimated to be around US$53.1 billion, the level of official aid from DAC countries underwent a 6 per cent decrease over the 1999 level.[73]

Sectoral breakdown of official aid to developing countries does not treat telecommunications as a distinct sector.[74] Instead, flows to the telecom sector are reported with transport and communications sectors under an 'economic infrastructure' category. A study of the 1999 data published by the DAC shows that less than 10 per cent of total aid flows to developing countries goes to transport and communications.[75] Except for Japan, which allocates 21 per cent of its aid to these sectors, most other countries give higher priorities to other sectors. It is interesting to note that Canada's aid to communications and transport is around 0.6 per cent,

[69] This explains to a large extent the fierce competition between numerous bidders to operate two cellular networks in the two largest cities of Brazil. See Larry Luxner, 'US Carriers Head South: Latin America Proves a Sunny Climate for Formerly Provincial Telecos', *Telephony*, 2 June 1997.

[70] See Vincent Ryan, 'Golden Opportunities, Hidden Difficulties', *Telephony*, 3 December 2001.

[71] E. M. Noam, ed., *Telecommunications in Africa* (New York: Oxford University Press, 1999), p. 6.

[72] See Ada Karina Izaguirre, 'Private Participation in Telecommunications: Recent Trends', Public Policy for the Private Sector Series, World Bank, Note No. 204, p. 3.

[73] See 'Development Assistance Committee Announces ODA Figures for 2000: Special Factors Explain Lower ODA Outcome', available on the OECD website at www.oecd.org/oda, accessed February 2002.

[74] Information on the sectoral and geographical distribution of international development assistance is recorded in the Creditor Reporting System created jointly by the OECD and the World Bank.

[75] See Table 19, 'Aid by Major Purposes 1999', available at www.oecd.org/xls/M000020000/M00002855.xls, accessed 24 January 2002.

while the US is reported to give a low priority to economic infrastructure development in its aid program, only 0.2 per cent.[76] A closer look at selected developed countries' official development assistance programmes in the area of communications and information technology reveals, however, that most activities fall within the technical cooperation category of development assistance. Examples include assistance in establishing regulatory policy and institutions, providing training, and promoting the use of information technology for development assistance.[77] It is important to stress here that the problem with official development assistance is not only a matter of decline in value. Perhaps the most troublesome aspect for telecommunications development is the practice of aid tying. Tying aid consists in conditioning aid to the obligation to purchase goods and services from donor countries. Aid tying is an anti-competitive process, which results in overpricing of goods and services. According to a recent study on the reality of aid, it is reported that in 1994, for example, aid tying resulted in 15 per cent overpricing which translates into US$1,900 million of the global aid budget.[78] According to a recent study on telecommunications in sub-Saharan countries, because the aid is tied to the obligation to purchase the equipment from a particular country, beneficiary countries are obliged to procure equipment at high costs in spite of the competitive tendering process. This results in an increase in the cost per line and higher rates for consumers.[79]

[76] For an overview of US official aid programmes, see USAID, 'Performance Report of Fiscal Year 2000', available at www.usaid.gov/pubs/apr00, accessed January 2002.

[77] For example, Japan's new commitment to help in bridging the digital divide in the information and communications sector is available from Japan's Ministry of Foreign Affairs' website at www.mofa.go.jp/policy/economy/it/index.html, accessed January 2002. The US international development agency (USAID) reported that foreign aid to the communications and information sector is focused mainly on providing technical assistance for regulatory reform and establishing regulatory institutions. In addition, USAID is involved in numerous initiatives to help developing countries become part of the global information revolution through improved access to the Internet and the use of the Internet for economic development. Examples include the Leland Initiative and the AfricaLink project. See USAID's information technology website at www.usaid.gov/info_technology for a list and a description of USAID's activities in bridging the digital divide. In Canada, the situation is not much different, with most official assistance being geared towards strengthening the policy and regulatory framework of the telecom sector of many countries, including Vietnam, India and Colombia.

[78] Tony German and Judith Randel, 'Trends in Aid and Development Cooperation', in *Reality of Aid: An Independent Review of Development Cooperation 1997–1998* (London: Earthscan, 1998), pp. 247–57.

[79] *Telecommunications in Sub-Sahara Africa.*

Finally, multilateral debt financing mechanisms are also available either on a regional or a global level. Although the development of telecommunications infrastructure is increasingly considered as a major element for economic growth, and despite the huge need for telecommunications investment in many regions, the percentage of total funding available to telecommunications projects is minimal. The European Bank for Reconstruction and Development is the only regional bank to allocate 10 per cent of its lending activities to telecommunications projects.[80] All the other development banks allocate a much smaller percentage (between 2 and 4 per cent) to telecommunications.[81]

On the global level, the World Bank, through its various agencies, has been involved in telecommunications projects. It provides long-term loans at market interest rates to governments and private parties. Since 1992, the World Bank group has been involved in forty telecommunications projects, involving a total of US$2.4 billion, covering wireline, wireless networks and earth stations.[82]

Despite the growing evidence of the crucial role that telecommunications play in economic development, the World Bank allocates only a minimal percentage of its funds to telecommunications development. In 1990, the Bank embraced a new policy towards telecommunications development. Instead of providing direct financing, the Bank's emphasis shifted towards enhancing private participation and creating competitive market structures. This shift was criticised by commentators as a shift that 'links developing country telecommunications development explicitly to the needs of private interest telecommunications companies and financial institution on industrialized countries'.[83]

In addition, the Bank's role in telecommunications development was criticised as being of uneven regional distribution Almost 50 per cent of

[80] The European Bank for Reconstruction and Development (EBRD) established in 1991 provides financing for telecommunications projects in countries of Central and Eastern Europe and the Commonwealth of Independent States. As of 31 December 2000, the Bank provided financing for fifty-six telecommunications projects totalling $1.5 billion with a total cost of $8.1 billion. See EBRD, Approved, Signed and Disbursed Telecommunications Projects as of 31 December 2000, available at www.ebrd.com/english/opera/sector/.

[81] OECD, *Communications Outlook 1999* (Paris: OECD, 1999), p. 239.

[82] For an overview of all the telecommunications projects, see www4.worldbank.org/sprojects/., accessed February 2002.

[83] G. Urey, 'Infrastructure for Global Financial Integration: The Role of the World Bank', in B. Mody, J. M. Bauer and J. D. Straubhaar, eds., *Telecommunications Politics, Ownership and Control of the Information Highway in Developing Countries* (Mahwah, NJ: Lawrence Erlbaun Associates Publishers, 1995).

the Bank's involvement was centred on the Latin American region, with US$1.1 billion invested in eleven projects. In Asia and Europe, the Bank provided more than US$600 million for each region, while, in the case of Africa and the Middle East, the Bank has contributed only US$150 million since 1992.[84]

This brief overview of the shortcomings of alternative financing mechanisms highlights the principal thesis of this paper, namely, that settlement payments constitute an important source of telecommunications financing. They are indeed the most stable source of revenue, and their importance today is more apparent than ever. In the words of the ITU, '[b]y shifting resources from developed economies to developing ones, the accounting rate process serves to promote organic or self-sustaining network growth'.[85]

Applying preferential treatment to accounting rates with developing countries could translate into agreed upon exceptions allowing a departure from uniform, cost-oriented accounting rates for calls terminating in developing countries. To be effective, however, the preferential regime needs strong institutional safeguards.

Preferential treatment

The institution of preferential treatment can be perfectly adapted to resolve the issue of accounting rates reform. To do so we need first to ascertain that the institution has a legal presence in the new regime for trade in telecommunications services and that beyond the legal consecration of the principle, collateral economic and telecommunications policy arguments uphold the necessity of preferential treatment.

Legal basis for preferential treatment

The preferential approach to trade relations grew after the decolonisation movement as a reaction from the developing countries to the inequities of the trading regime. The institution is today a cornerstone in developed/developing country relations and constitutes a well-established

[84] For an overview of the World Bank's projects, see www4.worldbank.org/sprojects, accessed February 2002.

[85] ITU, *World Telecommunications Development Report: Trade in Telecommunications services 1996/1997* (Geneva: ITU, 1997), p. 94.

principle of international trade and development laws.[86] The thrust of the institution is to provide exceptions to the most-favoured nation principle by allowing developing countries a more favourable treatment in trade relations.[87] The same philosophy could be extended to trade in telecommunications services and support a development-oriented approach to international accounting rate reform.

It should be noted from the start that the GATS, contrary to the GATT, does not contain a special section to address the concerns of developing countries. However despite the absence of a crystal-clear sanctification of the principle of special and differential treatment in a separate and distinct section in the GATS,[88] the institution of preferential treatment is indirectly embodied in GATS and in the telecommunications annex.

Taking into account the situation of developing countries, the GATS preamble stipulates that the fundamental objective of the new regime for free trade in services is the economic growth of all trading partners and the development of developing countries. The preamble puts emphasis on the need to increase the participation of developing countries in trade in services and the expansion of their trade exports including the strengthening of their domestic market and efficiency and competitiveness. Although the regime of international trade in telecommunications services as embodied in the basic telecommunications agreement falls short of concretising the principles in the preamble to the GATS, applying preferential treatment to international accounting rates will prove a good tool to improve the domestic market and the efficiency of the telecommunications market of developing countries.

The text of the GATS and the telecommunications annex contain differing provisions on the situation of developing countries. For example, Article 19 of the GATS provides that there should be appropriate flexibility for developing countries in opening fewer sectors, liberalising fewer

[86] For an overview of the concept and philosophy of preferential treatment in trade relations, see Robert E. Hudec, *Developing Countries in the GATT Legal System* (Sydney: Gower, 1988).

[87] During the Tokyo Round, the idea of non-reciprocity found a new illustration in the enabling clause. Under this clause, developing countries are not expected either to provide reciprocity for concessions made in trade negotiations or to make contributions that are inconsistent with their development. Finally, the theory of non-reciprocity was behind the generalised system preferences (GSP) adopted by UNCTAD on the basis of Part IV and the enabling clause.

[88] Murray Gibbs, 'Special and Differential Treatment in the Context of Globalization', Note presented to the G-15 Symposium on Special and Differential Treatment in the WTO Agreements, New Delhi, 10 December 1998.

types of transactions, and progressively extending market access in line with their development situation. Article 4 deals with the increased participation of developing countries. The Article conceives their increased participation through specific negotiated commitments relating to the strengthening of their domestic services capacity; its efficiency and competitiveness through access to technology on a commercial basis; the improvement of their access to the distribution channels and information networks; and liberalisation of market access in sectors and modes of delivery of export interest to developing countries. The language of this Article draws directly on the preamble to the GATS. It embodies important guidelines on matters of specific interest to developing countries.

In addition, the telecommunications annex allows developing countries to impose reasonable conditions on the access to and use of telecommunications networks that they consider necessary to strengthen domestic telecommunications infrastructure and to increase their participation in international trade in telecommunications services. The reasonable conditions can be extended to embrace conditions related to preferential pricing for the access and use of developing countries' networks.

In addition to the provisions of the GATS, special attention was devoted to the least developed countries in the WTO and in the ministerial declaration launching the Uruguay Round. Those elements can also provide a good foundation for providing least developed countries with extra attention in the problem of accounting rates. The Decision on 'Measures in Favor of Least Developed Countries' annexed to the Final Act of the Uruguay Round, stipulated that least developed countries will only be required to undertake commitments and concessions to an extent consistent with their individual development, financial and trade needs. In addition, the Final Act of the Uruguay Round incorporated measures for technical and financial assistance for least developed countries. Giving less developed countries extra flexibility in issues related to accounting rates reform will prove to be one important form and modality of international support measures for these countries.[89]

It follows from this overview of legal provisions that the various elements outlined above offer a good basis to treat developing countries on a different scale in issues related to the reform of international accounting rates.

[89] Decision available at www.wto.org/wto/legal/31-dlldc.wp5.

Paragraph 2: supporting arguments in favour of a preferential approach to accounting rates reform

Improvement to the network of developing countries through the maintenance of a certain level of hard currency income is in both the short- and long-term interest of developed countries. The problem with deficits encountered by developed countries in settlement payment is not due exclusively to the accounting rates being set above cost. It is also due to the existence of calling imbalance. Preserving a certain amount of settlement outpayment would prove to be an important element in diminishing the imbalance and reducing the deficit of developed countries interconnecting with developing countries.[90] It is well established today that improvements in the telecommunications sector lead to economic development and wealth.[91] This leads to improved use of telecommunications services for both personal and business reasons and to better connection to the world. Developed countries will undoubtedly witness an increase in the number of calls originating in developing countries and a decrease in deficit. In addition, securing a continuance in the flow of foreign currency in the form of settlement payments for developing countries does have more immediate benefits to developed countries. As long as developing countries are willing and able to finance telecommunications network development, this would translate into larger bills to developed countries in the form of equipment purchases, requests for technical assistance, and consultancy. The market in developing countries is mostly characterised by low penetration rates. High demand and outdated networks

[90] The idea was highlighted by Dawson Walker, who argued that cost-based accounting rates might not improve the situation of the United States towards developing countries. It is important, according to the author, to dig deeper to gain a truer perspective of the causal factors of deficit levels. The traffic imbalances are indeed a major cause of the problem. Dawson emphasises the case that the continuous flow of hard currency under accounting rates to developing countries is the 'best remedy for narrowing the calling imbalance and . . . the quickest way to diminish call and cost imbalances between developed and developing countries'. Dawson Walker, 'International Accounting Rates: A Perspective', *Telecommunications Policy* 20(4) (1996): 240.

[91] The relationship between telecommunications and economic development is well established today. The interaction was neglected in the beginning, but studies carried out by the ITU and the World Bank as well as by other institutions demonstrate the direct relationship between economic advance and the availability of telephone penetration. The first and most comprehensive study is by Robert J. Saunders, Jeremy J. Warford and B. Wellenius, *Telecommunications and Economic Development* (2nd edn, Baltimore: Johns Hopkins University Press, 1994).

constitute huge opportunities for developed countries.[92] In 1992, for example, developing countries spent more than US$4.6 billion on digital switching. According to Robin Bromby's study of digital switching markets in developing countries, this market will exceed US$7 billion by the year 2000.[93] What is more significant is that in many cases the flourishing or even the survival of certain telecommunications industries depends on developing countries. The cases of the wireless local loop (WLL) and the satellite industries are worth noting here.

The last few years witnessed an increase in the use of WLL technology in both developed and developing countries.[94] In developed countries, WLL is increasingly being used by new operators to unlock competition in the local loop, allowing new operators to bypass existing wireline networks and to deliver services to their customers without having to lay costly cables.[95] The economics of wireless are becoming irresistible even for well-established incumbents in developed countries who in many cases prefer to use WLL technologies to add advanced broadband features to their services.[96]

Despite its growing use around the world, much of the growth is taking place in developing countries. The WLL industry is focused principally on developing countries. An increasing number of tenders for WLL infrastructure originate in developing countries. WLL infrastructure manufacturers are targeting big developing countries like India, Brazil, China and Mexico for their products.[97] According to market projections, WLL technology could grow to satisfy as much as 70 per cent of excess demand

[92] Few developing countries have developed domestic telecommunications equipment sectors. The most important examples are the newly industrialised Asian countries such as South Korea and Taiwan, which supported local equipment industries. Because of market size considerations and the lack of economies of scale, most developing countries remain dependent on developed countries in this area.

[93] Robin Bromby, 'Digital Switching Markets in Developing Countries Report', *Telecommunications* 27 (1993): 16.

[94] In a WLL system, the connection between the customer and the public switched telephone network (PSTN) is not provided by the traditional copper or coax wire but rather by radio signals. Radio signals may include cordless access systems, proprietary fixed radio access and fixed cellular systems. For a technical description, see William E. Webb, *Introduction to Wireless Local Loop* (Boston and London: Artech House, 1998). See also the wireless local loop tutorial by the Institute of Engineering Consortium, available at www.iec.org/tutorials/wll/index.html.

[95] E. Thoreson, 'Farewell to Bell Monopoly? The Wireless Alternative to Local Competition', *Oregon Law Review* 77 (1998): 309.

[96] David Melony, 'Wireless Steps Out of the Local Loop Shadow', *Total Telecom* 19 January 1998.

[97] Web tutorial available at www.iec.org/tutorials/wll/index.html.

in developing countries by 2002. It is estimated that, by 2002, the total number of WLL lines would reach 339 million, 88 per cent of which would be deployed in developing countries.[98]

The satellite industry is also increasingly targeting the developing world market. In developed countries, satellite technology is widely challenged by technological development in fibre optic transcontinental fibre. Voice and data services are increasingly migrating to terrestrial networks to benefit from higher capacity. According to TeleGeography, the capacities of a single undersea cable system at 640 gigabits per second (TAT-14) now exceed the combined throughput of all the world's commercial communications satellites.[99] The latest industry forecast expects that the satellite industry is shifting back to broadcast and media applications in developed countries while, in developing countries, satellite technology is increasingly called upon to fill the missing link.[100]

In addition to these benefits, one can even argue that international efforts to boost telecommunications development and improve developing countries' access to telecommunications and information resources is a global public good with benefits transcending national borders to reach global dimensions.[101] This logic takes the form of a network externalities argument. Applied to a national setting, the network externality argument means that each additional subscriber increases the value of the entire network because millions of other subscribers have access to the new subscriber.[102] The same rational is perfectly applicable in an international setting. Indeed, given the information-based nature of the modern economy, the development of the telecommunications industry as more

[98] The reason why developed countries have a much smaller share of WLL lines is that in these countries there is no major problem of excess demand. Operators are in most cases able to serve demand with existing wireline structures. That is why WLL technology has developed mostly as a bypass technology.

[99] TeleGeography, *International Bandwidth, 2001* (Overview)

[100] For an overview and analysis of the latest developments in the satellite industry landscape, including technological developments, applications, satellite companies and market forecasts, see Theresea Foley, 'Features: Satellite Surge', *Communications Week International*, 24 September 2001.

[101] The global public goods doctrine has developed in recent years as a global policy response to today's global challenges. The doctrine applies to public goods whose benefits spill over national borders. Examples of global public goods include financial stability, international peace and environmental sustainability. See Inge Kaul, Isabelle Grunberg and Marc Stern, *Global Public Goods: International Cooperation in the 21st Century* (New York: Oxford University Press, 1999).

[102] For a description of the theory of economic infrastructure, see Cristino Antonelli, ed., *The Economics of Information Networks* (Amsterdam and London: North-Holland 1992).

global in nature, and the independent global environment, the value of the global network grows as more national networks and users are linked together.

Viewed in an economic light, preferential treatment in accounting rates reform (if the outcome is to ensure network development in developing countries) is bestowed not just for the sake of the recipient countries but also (and most importantly) for the sake of the information society as a whole. Given the importance of the telecommunications sector as a key component of the emerging information economy, the importance of creating a worldwide network should not be underestimated.

From the above-mentioned considerations, it follows that general trade principles can give rise to a preferential interpretation of accounting rates and that additional arguments support such a vision. It remains to be seen how preferential treatment can be applied to accounting rates reform.

Application of preferential treatment to accounting rates reform

Applying preferential treatment to accounting rates with developing countries could translate into agreed upon exceptions allowing a departure from uniform, cost-oriented accounting rates for calls terminating in developing countries. To be effective, however, the preferential regime needs strong institutional safeguards.

Exegesis of the preferential treatment regime

Defining a preferential regime requires, first, the definition of the beneficiaries; secondly, the determination of the constituents of the regime; and, finally, devising implementation measures.

Beneficiaries of preferential treatment

Defining the beneficiaries of preferential treatment is an essential preliminary step to define tailored transition paths for developing countries. The best method to define the beneficiaries of preferential treatment is to use a variety of criteria, which mix both socio-economic criteria and telecommunications variables including teledensity and the level of dependence on settlement payments. Indeed, the level of economic development of a country is a good indicator of the level of its telecommunications development and provides a reasonable indication of a country's ability to cope with a cost-based system of settlement rates.[103] However, such a classification does not suffice to determine adequate and differentiated treatment to developing countries for the transition to cost-based accounting rates. In its Benchmark Order, the FCC rightly decided to further divide the category of developing countries and create a new category, the 'least telecommunications developed', countries, defined as countries with a teledensity of less than 1. In 1992, the ITU defined the least telecommunications developed countries as economies with a teledensity of less than 1. The rationale behind this new category is outlined in the report and order adopted on 7 August 1997. The GNP per capita may not adequately reflect the level of telecommunication network development for the least developed countries. According to the FCC, the strong link between the level of economic development and telecommunications development is, substantially weaker in poorest countries.[104] Focusing on teledensity, in addition to socio-economic classification to divide developing countries for the purpose of applying preferential treatment to developing countries is a more accurate indicator to determine the need for and the duration of preferential treatment. Indeed, the group of developing countries is formed by different categories, which comprise both countries with a developed telecommunications infrastructure and very poor countries. A comparison of network development in South Asia and Latin America with the situation in sub-Saharan Africa justifies to a large extent the need to further distinguish the heterogeneous group of developing countries for the purpose of the application of preferential treatment. Teledensity in sub-Saharan Africa amounts to less than half the density in low income Asia.[105] While sub-Saharan Africa has 1 per cent of the world's telephone lines to serve 12 per cent of the world's population, many countries in the Asia Pacific region have graduated from the low to the high teledensity category.[106]

Even within the category of low-income countries, the use of telecommunications indicators suggests a large difference between least developed

[103] The approach is plausible, given the well-established and well-documented relationship between economic development and telecommunications.

[104] FCC, In the Matter of International Settlement rates Report and Order, IB Docket No. 96-261, adopted 7 August 1997; para. 189.

[105] W. L. Guttman, 'Telecommunications and Sub-Saharan Africa: The Continuing Crisis', *Telecommunications Policy* 10(1) (1986): 325.

[106] For an overview of the achievement in Asia, see Peter L. Smith and Gregory Staple, 'Telecommunications Sector Reform in Asia: Towards a New Pragmatism', World Bank Discussion Paper No. 232.

countries and other low-income countries. While the former are expanding their networks at a rate of less than 7 per cent per year, the latter have a network growth at a rate of 30 per cent per year.[107]

Working on its mandate to develop 'proposals for solutions for transitional arrangements towards cost-orientation beyond 1998', the focus group from the ITU Secretariat focused mainly on teledensity as a means to classify for the purpose of transitional paths. Using this variable, the report distinguished six groups of countries.[108] The category of least developed country is also retained as a distinct category, by the ITU focus group. The group has also elucidated an eighth category, small island countries, defined as countries with inhabitants of 300,000 or less and which rely exclusively on satellites for their international telecommunications.

Teledensity and the level of economic development are insufficient criteria by themselves to determine a list of eligibility for preferential treatment. The level of dependence on settlement payment is a third and necessary criterion which needs to be taken into account. This is because, as outlined above, the impact of accounting rate reform depends on the level of dependence on settlement payments. Developing countries with a high dependence on settlement payments are the ones that will suffer the most from a decrease in accounting rates. If we take the FCC benchmark scenario and apply it to three different developing countries, India, Senegal and Mauritania, we find that the greatest impact will be felt by Senegal, followed by India and Mauritania. Senegal, which derives over 30 per cent of its revenues from settlement payments, is likely to lose up to 70 per cent of its international revenues when the Benchmark Order is implemented. India, on the other hand, with 12 per cent dependence on settlement payments, is likely to lose less than 30 per cent of its revenue. The impact of the benchmark on Mauritania, with only 3 per cent dependence, will be secondly noticeable.[109]

[107] 'Methodological Note Concerning Classification of Economies by Socio-Economic Group', contribution to the SG3 Focus Group from the ITU Secretariat, 1 July 1998.

[108] Those with a teledensity of less than 1 (forty-two countries), those with a teledensity between 1 and 5 (thirty-six countries), those with a teledensity between 5 and 10 (twenty-eight countries), those with a teledensity between 10 and 30 (forty-seven countries), those with a teledensity between 30 and 40 (seventeen countries), and finally those with a teledensity exceeding 40. Focus Group Chairman's working document (rev. 2, 25 August 1998).

[109] For an overview of the different scenarios on case studies by the ITU, see ITU and TeleGeography, *Direction of Traffic: Trading Telecom Minutes* (Geneva: ITU, 1999). The scenario was calculated using different assumptions. It is assumed that the level of traffic

Constituents of preferential treatment

Preferential treatment should have two different components. The first element consists in keeping accounting rates for relationships involving beneficiary developing countries above cost for a certain period of time. The second element involves opting for a more favourable division of accounting rates. The series of studies conducted by the ITU on the issue of international accounting rates and developing countries[110] shows that either option may be more appropriate depending on the level of dependency on settlement payments and the pattern of international traffic.

Keeping accounting rates above cost for traffic involving developing countries This paper calls for the resurrection of a 1984 idea voiced by the Maitland Commission.[111] In its report, the Commission proposed that a proportion of revenue from calls between developed and developing countries could be used to boost telecommunications infrastructure development. The proportion in this context is the amount that exceeds the cost of providing the service. Developed countries would be encouraged to adhere to this programme because restructuring the accounting rates system to reflect cost will create a greater balance between developed countries, and will legitimise the concept of the transfer of resources to developing countries.

The idea that we are advocating here mirrors a very well established practice in national jurisdictions. A survey of the universal service policies of many developed countries reveals that in many jurisdictions interconnection charges include a sum that should be deployed for universal

will be growing at the same level as in the last six years with the same outgoing/incoming split formula. The percentage of the decline in international revenues is calculated in comparison with a baseline scenario, which assumes that the accounting rates are kept at their current level.

110 The case studies on the new environment of telecommunications and developing countries were requested by the Secretary General when he first considered the issue of accounting rates reform and created a study group on the issue of accounting rates. According to the Secretary General, conducting case studies on the impact of a reform of accounting rates on developing countries should be treated as a necessary step to guide the standardisation sector in its efforts to reform the accounting rates regime. ITU, Secretary General's Paper on Accounting Rates Reform (November 1996), available on the ITU website, www.itu.int.

111 ITU, *The Missing Link: Report of the Independent Commission for Worldwide Telecommunications Development* (Geneva: ITU, 1984). The Commission was created by the 1982 plenipotentiary conference to study network disparity and to propose ways to improve telecommunications access in developing countries.

service.[112] There is a wide body of economic literature that treats international accounting rates as a specific form of interconnection.[113]

According to the FCC chairman, international settlement rates are simply a specialised form of interconnection involving services that cross national borders.[114] The chairman suggested that the same rules of cost-based non-discriminatory interconnection applicable in a national setting should be transferred to the international arena. If we follow that reasoning to the end, we will find in the suggested analogy the very foundation of preferential treatment. Applying the same rationale, foreign carriers interconnecting to the national network might be required to pay a subsidy for network growth in developing countries in addition to the interconnection charge.

This first exception seems clear and easy to define at first glance. Yet it is tricky, as the whole idea is dependent upon setting acceptable rules and methods for determining appropriate cost to use as a basis for revised accounting rates.[115] Different approaches are under investigation at the international level to determine target rates. Such proposals include determination of price caps,[116] designated target ranges,[117] estimated cost elements[118] and best practice rates. Although each methodology has its inherent defects, we think that the last method is best suited to accounting

[112] For an overview of the international experience with universal service instruments measures and requirements, see S. O. Siochru, 'Telecommunications and Universal Service: International Experience in the Context of South African Policy Reform' (Working Paper, International Development Research Centre, 1995). The use of interconnection charges to finance universal service obligations is a well-established practice in liberalised markets (especially in the US and the UK). Incumbent carriers adjust the interconnection fee to raise funds from the interconnecting carriers. The funds are then allocated in order to meet the incumbent's universal service obligations.

[113] For a review of the literature and a list of articles, see James Alleman and Barbara Sorce, 'International Settlement: A Time for Change', Proceedings of the Global Networking '97 Conference, 15–18 June 1997, www.colorado.edu/engineering/alleman/print_files/inter-acct.pdf.

[114] Separate Statement by Chairman Hundt on International Settlement Rates Report and Order, 7 August 1997.

[115] The need to find acceptable methods to determine cost-based accounting rates is particularly important taking into account that the transition of the international telecommunications market to a purely market-based global industry where cost and prices are determined by market forces is not likely to be in the immediate future.

[116] 'Methodological Note Concerning the Use of cost Proxies', contribution to the SG3 Focus Group by the ITU Secretariat, 7 August 1998, available at www.itu.intset.focus/.

[117] The method is used in the work of the African Regional Tariff Group.

[118] 'Methodological Note on Developing 'Ranges of Indicative Target Rates', contribution to the Focus Group on Accounting Rates Reform, from the ITU Secretariat, available at www.itu.intset.focus/.

rates reform. The focus group defined target rates as the rate corresponding to the lowest 20 per cent of published rates for each group. Using this approach, the group has emphasised the idea that the move to cost-based accounting rates should be narrowly tailored for each group of countries. In addition, the group recognises that exceptional factors should be taken into account for least developed countries and whenever the gap between the best practice and current settlement rate is wide. Using this rationale, the amount of subsidy would equal the amount that exceeds the level of best practice rates for a given group.

The second practical question is how to determine the amount of the subsidy. One approach would be to keep accounting rates for beneficiary countries at their current level. In a paper on the telecommunications revolution, the Secretary General of the ITU argued that one possible way to provide a soft landing for developing countries is that major international carriers from developed countries might undertake to guarantee a certain settlement payment at a set level for a certain period of time.[119] This approach is unlikely to be welcomed at the international level, as it shows no intent to move towards cost-oriented accounting rates.

The studies conducted for the ITU in the case of eight developing countries is a good precedent for determining the level of accounting rate necessary to keep up with telecommunications development in developing countries. In the case of Senegal, for example, the study asserted that the use of a price cap under the US benchmark would have an adverse effect on Senegal which would translate into a net cumulative loss of US$42 million.[120] Keeping international accounting rates at a high level and the gradual reduction by 6–10 per cent per year will create favourable results with a cumulative net gain of US$17 million. This estimate takes into account the impact of new policies and the reduction in accounting rates on outgoing and incoming traffic and price elasticity.[121]

The ITU focus group on accounting rates has concluded that the reduction in accounting rates should be at an average of 12 per cent per year until best practice rate is achieved. However, exceptions to the 12 per cent reduction are warranted in specific cases. In any case, the reduction should not be less than 5 per cent per year. If this approach were endorsed

[119] It should be mentioned here that the proposal of the Secretary General relates mainly to the situation of the least developed countries and other low-income economies with small populations. P. Tarjanne, 'The 1998 Telecommunications Revolution', Study Group 3 Meeting, 27 May 1997, p. 12.

[120] See www.itu.int/wtdf/senegal/index.htm, p. 36.

[121] *Ibid.*, p. 38.

by members of ITU, the subsidy for each country would be the difference between the actual rate after a reduction of 12 or 5 per cent and the best practice rate for the country concerned.

Opting for asymmetric division of accounting rates Splitting the accounting rate on an equal basis is unfavourable to developing countries, which incur a higher cost in providing international services than developed countries. A preferential approach to accounting rates reform should include a more appropriate division of accounting rates. In this case, the idea of preferential treatment is very clear. Indeed, carriers in liberalised developed markets would agree to offer to terminate incoming calls from certain countries at a cost-based rate and to waive their right to have reciprocal access to the same market at the same rate.

A recent study conducted by the ITU ascertained that developing countries incur higher costs for international services by a factor of 2.08.[122] Although the reasons for such a discrepancy are not well documented, it has been argued that the reason has to do with the cost of building the infrastructure in developing countries. Indeed, as mentioned by Tim Kelly,[123] the average cost of installing a new line ranges from a few hundred dollars in economies such as China to several thousands dollars in some parts of Africa. Figures presented by the World Bank are astonishing; the cost per line in sub-Saharan Africa is estimated at US$5,600 compared to an average of US$1,500 for other developing countries. The study considers that the difference in cost is mainly due to the methods of financing.[124]

Another element worth mentioning here is the cost incurred by the lack of direct links between least developed countries and other parts of the world. Transit traffic represents a high proportion of the total traffic of many countries in Africa. According to the ITU, transit traffic originating in Africa and passing through the United States represents 36 per cent of total telephone traffic to the United States. African operators pay up to US$1 million per year for transiting the international calls through

[122] The cost study was commissioned by the ITU in response to the request by the Maitland Commission in 1984. ITU, *The Missing Link: Report of the Independent Commission for Worldwide Telecommunications Development* (Geneva: ITU, 1984).

[123] Tim Kelly, 'Ten Propositions for Accounting Rate Reform', paper prepared for ITU Asia Telecom 1997, Tariff Workshop, 22 April 1997.

[124] *Telecommunications in Sub-Sahara Africa* (World Bank 1995), p. 3.

a hub.[125] This practice inevitably has the effect of increasing the cost of terminating a service by a least developed country.

As early as 1985, the International Telegraph and Telephone Consultative Committee recognised that proportions other than 50/50 might be used when the facilities made available by each of the administrations of the terminal countries are not approximately equivalent, or if administrations reach agreement on a different proportion as in the case where the costs differ greatly.[126] At the 1994 plenipotentiary conference held in Kyoto, governments adopted Resolution 22, entitled 'Apportionment of Revenues in Providing International Telecommunications Services'. Under the resolution, governments can diverge from the 50/50 split of accounting rates in favour of a different formula. According to the ITU, a fairer splitting formula would be 66/33 rather than 50/50.

This second pillar of preferential treatment is best applied in countries like Mauritania with a low dependence on international settlement (international settlement represent 3.2 per cent of turnover in Mauritania) and high routing costs. Preferential treatment for Mauritania needs to be based on a different apportionment of the accounting rates rather than focusing on the level of accounting rates. The study conducted for the ITU ascertained that the cost of international services in Mauritania is very expensive due mainly to the high cost in the national extension component. The small number of subscribers, coupled with the extensive areas to be covered and the high network connection charge culminated to make the cost of routing international calls particularly high.[127] In the case of Mauritania and countries with similar conditions, a sound preferential approach would translate into a regime that takes into account the asymmetry in cost and network density.

Implementation of preferential treatment It is a delicate task to determine a schedule for the transition period for developing countries. Indeed, as noted by the ITU, '[a] soft landing at the end of a transition period may not be very soft and the transition period may not be very long'. This paper calls for using an innovative approach that measures the transition period with the achievement yardstick rather than the usual

[125] It was only recently that the ITU started to throw some light on the issue of transit rates. See 'Methodological Note on Transit Rates', contribution to the SG3 Focus Group by the ITU Secretariat, 12 August 1998.

[126] ITU, General Tariff Principles Charging and Accounting in International Telecommunications Services, Recommendations of the D series 1985, p. 107.

[127] The cost is estimated at 45–60 cents per minute.

proposed timescale. Instead of choosing three, five or seven years, a better approach is for the transition period to be measured against implementation of structural change in the telecommunications sector of developing countries. Developing countries benefiting from preferential treatment in accounting rates should undertake a commitment to overcome the deficiencies of their system.[128] For the purpose of setting acceptable transition periods, a set of indicators could be used to determine whether a particular developing country is ready to graduate from the exception to the rule:

Those signs include:

1. Improvement of telecommunications penetration through a commitment to allocate gains from settlement payments to network growth and expansion. Developed countries have argued that maintaining above cost accounting rates does not by itself promise an improvement in the telecommunications sector in developing countries. In many developing countries, income from settlement payments is diverted to other sectors of the economy. Most people agree that each country has the sovereign right to determine its public spending according to national priorities. However, if above cost accounting rates should continue to flow to developing countries in the form of a transparent subsidy, developing countries have to undertake to allocate this income to improving their telecommunications sector.
2. Adoption of new pricing policies to gradually reduce dependence on international accounting rates. This issue is politically sensitive, as such an undertaking might oblige developing countries to rebalance local and international tariff rates. Indeed, as outlined above, revenues from international telecommunications services have served for a long time in developing countries to cross-subsidise local services and make the services available to consumers. A decrease in revenues from international services will translate into a price jump in local services and

[128] This idea had found strong support in the seventh regulatory colloquium under the ITU. The colloquium dealt with the transformation of economic relationships in international telecommunications. The colloquium's conclusion was that the level of international accounting rates and the length of the transition period are not the fundamental problems to be addressed. The real problem is the lack of network development in developing countries. The solutions should be found by linking the restructuring of the international payments system with the restructuring of other international economic relations and the broader telecommunications policy of developing countries. ITU, 'The Changing Role of Government in an Era of Telecom Deregulation: Transforming Economic Relationships in International Telecommunications', Report of the Seventh Regulatory Colloquium held at ITU headquarters, 5–7 December 1997. A summary is available at www.itu.int/wtpf/trade/reg-coll/7th/chair-report.htm.

will widen the already apparent tendency in developing countries for telecommunications to be a luxurious commodity for the richer class of society. The necessary relation between moving to cost-based accounting rates and rate rebalancing has also been outlined by many critics of the FCC Benchmark Order. For example, CANTO argued that a country's transition period should not end until a rate rebalancing plan has been enacted and completed.[129] Telecommunications pricing is a complicated matter. It lies at the heart of policy issues and complex matters related to economics and regulatory structures, which will face developing countries when considering innovative and modern pricing approaches. However, regulators in developing countries, when they set prices, should deploy efforts based on cost and demand.

3. The necessary modernisation of traditional forms of ownership and market structure of the telecommunications industry of developing countries. This includes rethinking the public ownership and monopolistic structure of the telecommunications sector. Experience in developed countries over the last decade has demonstrated that both privatisation and the introduction of competition have positive effects on network growth and the expansion of services. For developed countries there is ample and undisputed evidence on the benefits of liberalisation on teledensity and network quality. An historical overview of the US experience demonstrates to a large extent this observation, and the same can be said of Japan, New Zealand and the United Kingdom. A study conducted by the ITU in 1994, which compared lines added in OECD countries, competitive markets versus non competitive markets, found that, from 1990 to 1994, provision of new lines grew by 21 per cent in competitive markets and decreased 28 per cent in closed markets.[130] The same result can be tested in the case of developing countries that have undertaken sector reform in the last few years. Figures collected by the ITU, the World Bank and the FCC show similar benefits of liberalisation in developing countries. The most widely cited example is that of the Philippines. Since 1990, the Philippines has undertaken liberalisation strategies. The result is a growth in main line installation from 19,625 main lines for the seven years preceding

[129] The same position has been defended by GTE and Telefonica of Spain, which argued that the transition period should be tied to rate rebalancing. See FCC, In the Matter of International Settlement Rates, IB Docket No. 96-261, Report and Order, 7 August 1997.

[130] See Figure 4.3, in B. Petrazzini, *The Telecom Talks: A Trillion Dollar Deal* (Washington, DC: Institute of International Economics, 1996), p. 39.

liberalisation to 224,500 lines per year in 1993 and 1994. The new policies also led to network modernisation of the Philippines where 64 per cent of the network has been digitised.[131] The ITU also cites the example of liberalisation in Peru, which created a network growth of 336,000 lines, more than the previous eight years combined.[132] In the Benchmark Order, the FCC stresses the importance of competition in increasing service and network availability. The FCC cites the example of China, where network growth reached 58.9 per cent in one year after the introduction of competition. Indeed, the experiences of developing countries show that teledensity in developing countries has grown twice as fast in countries with privatised telecommunications as in countries that have retained a public monopoly.[133]

The proposal of measuring the transition period using the achievement yardstick might prove to be difficult to manage without institutional safeguards.

Institutional safeguards for a successful implementation of preferential treatment

Two safeguards are necessary for a successful implementation of preferential treatment: transparency, and a multilateral supervision of the regime.

The requirement of transparency

To be acceptable, the system should identify the proportion of accounting rates that represents a subsidy in a transparent fashion. The subsidy portion should be exclusively allocated to telecommunications development and ensure investment in new infrastructure during the full transition period to cost-based accounting rates. An explicit, transparent subsidy mechanism targeted at network infrastructure to promote universal service is a more acceptable arrangement than the current system based on the non-transparent and poorly targeted transfer of resources. The system of explicit subsidy (in addition to being in conformity with preferential

131 ITU, *World Telecommunications Development Report 1996/1997* (Geneva: ITU, 1997).

132 *Ibid.*

133 For an overview of developing countries' experience with privatisation, see B. Mody, J. M. Bauer and J. D. Straubhaar, *Telecommunications Politics, Ownership and Control of the Information Highway in Developing Countries* (Mahwah, NJ: Lawrence Erlbaun Associates Publishers, 1995).

treatment under the WTO) also conforms to the principles of universal service embodied in the Reference Paper.[134] Under the Reference Paper, countries are allowed to impose universal service obligations on foreign carriers operating in their market. This possibility is restricted only by the conditions under which the obligation is imposed. A universal service obligation in a competitive environment should be administered in a transparent, non-discriminatory and competitively neutral manner.

For transparency reasons, the annual amount should be identified, and used only for the purpose of telecommunications development rather than diverted to other uses.

The requirement of institutional supervision

The successful implementation of preferential treatment in accounting rates reform requires that the whole mechanism be supervised by an international institution. The reason for insisting on this point is that very little has been achieved by developing countries to upgrade their infrastructure even though accounting rates have always been set above cost. An institutional mechanism to supervise the allocation of the surplus in the telecommunications sector will prove to be a worthwhile endeavour. The second reason for insisting on institutional intervention is inspired by the problems faced by developing countries in the issue of graduation in the GATT context.[135] The GATT's preferential treatment arrangements proved to be of very limited importance. The regime was inherently defective as it was based on unilateral concessions. Developed countries were free to set their own rules for preferential treatment in determining the beneficiaries and the quantities of imports subject to preferential treatment. In addition, because of a lack of multilateral discipline, the criteria for revoking the privileges are set by individual donor countries for reasons related to other priorities such as human rights violations in the recipient countries.[136]

[134] The Reference Paper contains a set of pro-competitive safeguards for the Agreement on Basic Telecommunications. It is appended to the Agreement on Basic Telecommunications for adoption by countries as additional commitments to their obligations in the basic telecom sector. Fifty five countries adopted the Reference Paper. See Reference Paper to the Fourth Protocol to the General Agreement on Trade in Services, ILM 36 (1997): 367.

[135] Lunt, 'Graduation and the GATT: The Problems of NIC', *Columbia Journal of Transnational Law* 31(3) (1994): 611–43. See also Robert Hudec, *Developing Countries in the GATT Legal System* (Sydney: Gower, 1986). Valerie J. Dellegrini, 'GSP: A System of Preference Not a Bargaining Lever', *Law and Policy in International Business* 17(4) (1985): 879–906.

[136] The US GSP scheme is a good example of the wide discretion that an individual country can have in determining GSP recipients, product coverage and criteria for unilaterally

The ITU is the institution best suited to supervise the transition period and the preferential treatment. Indeed, the ITU has long focused on issues of telecommunications and development. Since 1959, the need for cooperation and coordination related to development assistance has occupied an important place in the ITU agenda.[137] The 1959 International Telecommunications Convention required the CCIR (International Radio Consultative Committee) and CCITT (Consultative Committee on the International Telephone and Telegraph) to pay due attention to the formulation of recommendations directly connected with the establishment, development and improvement of telecommunications in developing countries in both regional and international fields. The idea of telecommunications cooperation for development has arisen in most of the plenipotentiary conferences, and ideas for cooperation were put forward by developing countries at the negotiating table.[138] The 1989 plenipotentiary conference went a step further in telecommunications development by the creation of a special sector in the ITU: the development sector, in addition to the radiocommunication and standardisation sectors. The roles of the sector are oriented towards encouraging technical cooperation. The ITU constitution stipulates that the Telecommunications Development Bureau is '[t]o facilitate and enhance telecommunications development by offering, organizing and coordinating technical cooperation and assistance activities'.[139] The institutional structure of the ITU, and its long

excluding or accepting countries. In the last few years, the regime of GSP was extensively used by the US as a tool to promote US foreign policy goals in the areas of workers, rights, intellectual property and other practices. The cases reported in the literature of the US revocation of GSP for the above reasons are numerous. We recall the revocation of the system from Sudan, Syria, Liberia and Mauritania for inadequate protection of workers, rights, and the revocation of the system from India and Thailand for lack of intellectual property protection. The US law of GSP is embodied in Title V of the Trade Act of 1974, codified at 19 USCA §§ 2461–6.

137 F. Lyall, 'The International Telecommunications Union and Development', *Journal of Space Law* 22 (1994): 22.

138 The suggestion that reappeared every time is the need to finance telecommunications development from the ITU budget and the creation of a special ITU development fund. See the negotiations at the plenipotentiary conference of 1965 and 1973. In 1982, the idea was reshaped by developed countries towards the creation of a special voluntary programme for cooperation instead of financing telecommunications development from the ITU budget.

139 B. Harris, 'The New Telecommunications Development Bureau of the International Telecommunications Union', *American University Journal of International Law* 7 (1991): 88. It should also be mentioned that ITU voting rules are friendly to developing countries. The ITU functions on the 'one-nation, one-vote' system, which enhances the power of the developing countries, numerically a majority. The voting power proved very helpful

tradition in telecommunications development, makes it a good institution to supervise the preferential arrangement.[140]

Different mechanisms can be discerned to supervise the implementation of the preferential treatment. One possible approach was inspired by the Trade Policy Review Mechanism TPRM under the WTO.[141] Under the TPRM, a special body, the Trade Policy Review Body, carries out trade policy reviews. The objective of the procedure is to review the overall trade policies of each Member on a regular basis. Applying a similar mechanism in the context of accounting rates would enable the ITU to undertake the regular collective appreciation and evaluation of the achievements of the beneficiaries of preferential treatment and their readiness to graduate to cost-based accounting rates.

Despite the attractiveness of this idea, we must be aware that establishing such a mechanism will not prove to be an easy task. Different contentions might be presented. Chief among them is that a telecommunication policy review mechanism might be a breach of the principle of state sovereignty to choose and implement telecommunications policy at the national level without international scrutiny. The issue is indeed very sensitive. Even though the object of the review mechanism is not to impose new policy commitments on Members, the impact would certainly amount to an indirect oversight of national policies in pricing, industrial structure, allocation of telecommunications revenues, etc. However, countries should be aware of the fact that a multilateral framework based on agreed upon procedures and criteria is more transparent and predictable than a system of bilateral negotiations in which weaker parties are not protected from a unilateral revocation of privileges from donor countries. Furthermore, the mechanism that we are advocating here would only apply to the subsidy part of the above cost accounting rates. Countries which refuse the mechanism can still opt for cost-oriented accounting rates and face different challenges.

to developing countries through the years as they succeeded in drawing the attention of the ITU to their specific demands.

140 Trade Review Policy Mechanism, Annex 3 to the WTO Agreement; see www.org/legal/29-tprm.wp5.

141 'The Right to Communicate: A New Declaration is Born', ITU News No. 6/97. The right to communicate, understood as defined by the ITU Secretary General in the above quoted statement, was endorsed by the United Nations General Assembly in December, 1997.

Conclusion

The international accounting rates regime is today a heavily debated theme in international telecommunications policy at national, regional and international fora. This paper tried to propose ways to accommodate developing countries' concerns in the new liberalised environment for telecommunications services. It defended the idea to fund telecommunications development from the current regime of accounting rates. Our proposal is motivated mainly by the importance of accounting rates for network development of developing countries and the importance of ensuring global universal access to telecommunications services. The issue of universal access is a very important element, which should be considered when addressing international telecommunications issues. Access to universal service is considered a fundamental principle given the importance of communications for economic growth in the new information-driven society. Indeed, as powerfully stated by the ITU Secretary General, '[t]he right to communicate understood as the access to universal service has to be viewed as a basic human right failing which the information age would have bypassed the majority of humankind'.[142]

However, despite the importance of preferential treatment in the area of accounting rates and its contribution to telecommunications development, one should not lose sight of the fact that many developing countries will remain untouched by the reform. According to the ITU, many developing countries, in Africa make settlement payments to developed countries. This is to say the goal of universal access to basic telecommunications services cannot be reached without additional international commitments alongside the preferential approach to accounting rates.

142 For an overview of universal access at a global level, see ITU, *World Telecommunications Development Report: Universal Access* (Geneva: ITU, 1998).

6

Levelling the playing field: is the WTO adequately equipped to prevent anti-competitive practices in telecommunications?

DAMIEN GERADIN AND MICHEL KERF

Introduction

On 15 February 1997, sixty-nine WTO Members reached an agreement, taking the form of a protocol to be attached to the General Agreement on Trade in Services (GATS), whereby they would open to foreign competition some or all of their basic telecommunications services markets.[1] This agreement, the 'Agreement on Basic Telecommunications', came as a result of several years of negotiation, and was welcomed as a major breakthrough in the liberalisation of basic telecommunications services.[2] The Agreement is of considerable importance, as its sixty-nine contracting parties represent over 90 per cent of the world's basic telecommunications revenues.[3]

While the removal of barriers to entry into the telecommunications markets is a major step forward, it might not be sufficient in itself to create thriving competition in such markets. As will be seen below, this is because the telecommunications sector has a certain number of features that allow the incumbents to retain a substantial degree of market power.[4] Controlling market power in telecommunications is usually achieved through a combination of competition rules and sector-specific legislation. In the European Union, for instance, the telecommunications

1 Fourth Protocol to the General Agreement on Trade in Services, ILM 36 (1997): 366.

2 For a discussion of the negotiating history of this agreement, see Laura B. Sherman, 'Wildly Enthusiastic About the First Multilateral Agreement on Trade in Telecommunications Services', *Federal Communications Law Journal* 51 (1999): 61.

3 *Ibid.*, p. 62.

4 See Damien Geradin and Michel Kerf, *Controlling Market Power in Telecommunications: Antitrust vs. Sector-Specific Regulation* (Oxford: Oxford University Press, 2003), pp. 8–10.

sector is extensively regulated by a set of detailed directives.[5] In addition, the EC competition authorities have often intervened to prevent abuses of market power on the part of the incumbents. Not all contracting parties to the Agreement on Basic Telecommunications, however, possess adequate tools to control market power in their telecommunications market. This raises the question of whether the WTO is able to provide remedies to foreign telecommunications operators suffering from abuses of market power on the part of the local incumbent. This issue is the theme of this paper.

This paper is divided into eight parts. After the present introduction, the second part reviews the benefits which have been derived from the introduction of competition in telecommunications markets. The third part analyses the reasons why public intervention remains necessary in the telecommunications sector even after barriers to entry have been lifted. The fourth part analyses the respective advantages of general competition rules and sector-specific rules to control market power in telecommunications. The fifth part then presents an overview of the rules that can be found in the WTO framework. As will be seen, WTO Members have so far failed to agree on general competition rules. By contrast, the vast majority of the Members that are party to the Agreement on Basic Telecommunications have also agreed to a set of sector-specific rules designed to provide safeguards against anti-competitive practices in the telecommunications sector that are contained in the so-called Reference Paper. The sixth part analyses whether the Reference Paper is an adequate document and the extent to which it could be strengthened. The seventh part addresses the question of whether, assuming that the Reference Paper could be strengthened, there would remain a need for general competition rules at the WTO level. Finally, The eighth part contains a brief conclusion in which we make some suggestions. First, we argue that, while the Reference Paper is a step in the right direction, it could, however, be strengthened to reach a better balance between the three following objectives: precision, simplicity and flexibility. In most cases, this would mean increasing the degree of precision of the provisions of the Reference Paper, as the current document tends to be very general. However, in order not to lose too much flexibility, increased precision may at times be obtained, not by specifying substantive provisions in great detail, but by offering Members a choice between different, well-defined solutions, or by strengthening

[5] See Pierre Larouche, *Competition Law and Regulation in European Telecommunications* (Oxford: Hart Publishing, 2000).

procedural rather than substantive rules. Secondly, we argue that, even if the Reference Paper could be strengthened along the aforementioned lines, a case could still be made for adopting a WTO Agreement on Trade and Competition Policy. Such an agreement could be helpful to prohibit some anti-competitive behaviour that would still remain unaddressed in the Reference Paper and to protect operators against anti-competitive behaviour beyond the narrow scope of telecommunications activities. We believe, however, that, if such additional competition provisions were to be adopted, they should focus on improving market access.

The benefits of liberalisation

Emphasising the importance of the changes, which have affected the telecommunications industry over the past decade, has become somewhat trite. Yet, such changes have been so profound indeed, that it is easy to forget that less than fifteen years ago most telecommunications services were provided, in almost all countries, by single state-owned operators and that most commentators considered that the characteristics of the sector justified such monopolistic arrangements. Today, experts almost unanimously argue in favour of opening telecommunications markets to competition and the extent to which competition-enhancing reforms have actually taken place is truly remarkable. About 40 per cent of all countries (including all countries with real GDP per capita of US$20,000 or more) have opened all or part of the fixed telephony market to competition,[6] about 50 per cent have opened the market for leased lines to competition, and 80 per cent or more have opened the cellular, cable TV, VSAT and ISP markets to competition.[7] By the beginning of 2001 for example, all OECD countries except for Hungary and Turkey had opened all their telecommunications markets to competition.[8]

Three main types of reason explain this shift from monopolistic to competitive market structures. First, technological changes are fast reducing the scope of the activities that do retain natural monopoly characteristics, and progress in information technology has made it easier and less costly to interconnect different networks and to let users change

[6] *Ibid.*

[7] See ITU, *Trends in Telecommunication Reform 2002: Effective Regulation* (Geneva: ITU, 2002), p. 6.

[8] See OECD, *Telecommunications Outlook 2001* (Paris: OECD, 2001), p. 25.

service providers.[9] Secondly, the performance of state-owned monopolistic operators proved disappointing: various studies demonstrated that monopolistic companies, in general, tended to be less efficient than those subjected to competitive pressures, and these results certainly held in the telecommunications sector.[10] Thirdly, policy makers increasingly came to realise that social objectives could be achieved in telecommunications without having to rely on a monopolistic incumbent to cross-subsidise the provision of services between different categories of users.[11]

On the whole, the elimination of barriers to entry has had the expected effects, starting with the capture, by new entrants, of substantial market shares, sometimes over relatively short periods of time. France and Germany, for example, opened their fixed telephony market to competition in 1998, and two years later, new entrants had captured 20 per cent of the national long-distance market and 27 per cent of the international market in France, and 40 per cent of both segments in Germany. New entrants' gains in mobile markets have been even more remarkable. As of 2000, the incumbent's share of that market had fallen below 60 per cent in two-thirds of the OECD countries. Competition is also fast developing in the market for the provision of Internet services with the number of ISPs skyrocketing in recent years.[12]

On the other hand, the fixed local market tends to remain heavily dominated by the incumbent. Given the large economies of scale, which exist in the fixed local loop, there is little facilities-based competition for the provision of fixed residential local voice telephony services. For instance, at the end of 2000, competitive local exchange providers (CLECs) provided only 16.4 (or 8.5) per cent of the approximately 194 million nationwide local telephone service lines to end-user customers. In addition,

[9] See James Bond *et al.*, *The Information Revolution and the Future of Telecommunications* (Washington, DC: World Bank Group, Finance, Private Sector, and Infrastructure Network, June 1997), pp. 4 and 12.

[10] See, for example, Ahmed Galal *et al.*, *Welfare Consequences of Selling Public Enterprises – An Empirical Analysis* (Oxford: Oxford University Press, 1994), which examines in detail twelve specific cases of liberalisation and privatisation (including three cases in the telecommunications sector) in Chile, Malaysia, Mexico and the UK. See also Bjorn Wellenius and Peter A. Stern, *Implementing Reforms in the Telecommunications Sector – Lessons from Experience* (Washington, DC: World Bank, 1994), which discusses the international experience of telecommunications sector reform, covering a wide range of issues and countries.

[11] See, for example, Werner Neu and Ulrich Stumpf, 'Evaluating Compensation Requirements by Telecommunications Universal Service Providers: A New Challenge to Regulators', *Communications and Strategies* 26 (1997): 165.

[12] See OECD, *Telecommunications Outlook 2001* (Paris: OECD, 2001), pp. 30–3 and 111.

about 60 per cent of the CLEC local telephone lines served medium and large businesses and institutional and government customers; which suggests that, while competition for business customers is growing, individual users largely continue to be served by the local incumbent.[13] In addition, local loop unbundling has proven very difficult to implement and therefore competition remains very limited in markets such as that for ADSL services where new entrants need to get access to some elements of the incumbent's fixed local infrastructure. For instance, according to figures from OFTEL (the UK regulator), at the beginning of 2001, only a fraction of British Telecom's telephone lines (approximately 50,000 lines out of 35 million) had been upgraded to provide ADSL services.[14]

More intense competition has, in many cases, had a visible impact on prices. One clear trend is the closer alignment of prices with underlying costs. For example, as new technologies have rendered distance increasingly irrelevant from a cost point of view, a growing number of operators facing competitive pressures have eliminated the difference between local and long-distance tariffs. The incumbents in Iceland, Norway, Sweden, Denmark and Belgium, for instance, now apply a tariff to all domestic calls that is independent of distance, and new operators in Ireland, the United Kingdom and Italy have introduced the same policy. Another trend is a reduction of prices in competitive markets. The OECD published, in 1999, some comparisons between the prices of business and residential baskets of telecommunications services in competitive and non-competitive markets. The data show that, by 1998, in both cases, prices were about 50 per cent higher in non-competitive than in competitive markets.[15]

The opening of telecommunications markets to competition has also been associated with increased teledensity. A recent report by Kirkman *et al.* compares the number of fixed and mobile lines as well as the rate of Internet penetration in 1996 and 2000 between those countries that opened their telecommunications markets to competition, those that only privatised the incumbent, and those that did not implement any reforms. It shows that, at various income levels, teledensity increased most in countries which had opened their markets to competition, and least in countries which carried out no reforms at all, with countries which only

[13] See FCC, 'Trends in Telephone Service', Industry Analysis Division, Common Carrier Bureau, August 2001, section 9.1.

[14] See OFTEL, 'Local Loop Unbundling Fact Sheet – April 2001', available at www.oftel.gov.uk/publications/local_loop/llufacts0401.htm.

[15] OECD, *Telecommunications Outlook 2001* (Paris: OECD, 2001), pp. 171–2.

privatised the incumbent somewhere in the middle.[16] The positive impact of liberalisation upon teledensity has also been confirmed by a number of recent econometric studies.[17]

Finally, there is substantial evidence that opening telecommunications markets to competition leads to the offering of a wider range of services and to higher service quality. A positive correlation has been established, for example, between liberalisation and certain quality indicators such as the waiting time for the installation of a fixed telephone line,[18] as well as the share of digital mainlines among total mainlines.[19]

The adoption of the Agreement on Basic Telecommunications on 15 February 1997 reflected to a large extent the fact that, by the second half of the 1990s, the benefits of telecommunications mentioned above had become increasingly clear. The negotiation and adoption of the Agreement, in turn, prompted parties to accelerate the pace of their telecommunications liberalisation reforms.

Continuing need for intervention by public authorities

While the liberalisation of telecommunications markets has, in many cases, yielded substantial benefits, the removal of barriers to entry, in itself, will rarely be sufficient to ensure that such benefits can be reaped. To a large extent, this is because telecommunications markets exhibit a number of specific features that enable incumbents to maintain some degree of market power over competitors and users, even when formal barriers to entry have been removed.[20]

[16] See 'The Networked Readiness Index: Measuring the Preparedness of Nations for the Networked World', in Geoffrey Kirkman *et al.*, *The Global Information Technology Report 2001–2002: Readiness for the Networked World* (Oxford: Oxford University Press, 2002), Chapter 2, pp. 124 and 129.

[17] See, for example, Carsten Fink *et al.*, '*Liberalizing Basic Telecommunications: Evidence from Developing Countries*', Preliminary Draft of 21 February 2002, World Bank mimeo; Charles Kenny, 'Prioritising Countries for Assistance to Overcome the Digital Divide', *Communications and Strategies* 41 (2001), www.idate.fr/an/publi/revu/num/n41/kenny_a.html; Augustin J. Ros, 'Does Ownership or Competition Matter? The Effects of Telecommunications Reform on Network Expansion and Efficiency', *Journal of Regulatory Economics* 15 (1999): 65; Scott Wallsten, 'An Econometric Analysis of Telecom Competition, Privatisation, and Regulation in Africa and Latin America', *Journal of Industrial Economics* 49 (2001): 1.

[18] See Kenny, 'Prioritising Countries'.

[19] See Fink, et al., 'Liberalizing Basic Telecommunications', p. 13.

[20] See Geradin and Kerf, *Controlling Market Power*, pp. 8–10.

First, in spite of the technological changes mentioned above, various segments of the telecommunications market might still retain, at the present time, some natural monopoly characteristics and may also be non-contestable (the fixed local loop is often mentioned as an example).[21] In such conditions, direct controls over the price and quality of services provided by monopolistic operators might still be required to protect users. In addition, measures might be needed to prevent such operators from using the market power they enjoy in monopolistic segments to distort competition in the potentially competitive segments of the industry.

Secondly, even in the absence of non-contestable natural monopolies, incumbents may be able to stifle competition by preventing new entrants from gaining access to their subscribers. Incumbents could, for example, impose anti-competitive interconnection conditions on their competitors, force their subscribers to dial longer numbers to access competing long-distance carriers, or prevent their subscribers from keeping the same telephone number when they choose another service provider. In order to maintain a level playing field between the incumbent and its competitors, steps may therefore need to be taken to ensure that interconnection agreements can be concluded under equitable conditions and to impose number portability and dialing parity.[22]

Thirdly, there are a number of scarce resources in telecommunications. The radio spectrum comes immediately to mind, and easily 'recognisable'

[21] A market is perfectly contestable when entry into the market, and exit from it, involves no cost (for example, because the facilities which need to be deployed to operate in the market can be sold easily or transferred to other markets). In such a case, the incumbent – even if it is in a monopolistic situation – is unable to exercise market power because of the threat of entry by potential competitors. When entry and exit are costly, however, competitors might then refrain from attempting to challenge an incumbent, thus leaving the latter with substantial market power. This is arguably still the case in the fixed local segment of the telecommunications market as long as alternative modes of communications remain more expensive. Many of the costs of developing a fixed local network would not be recovered by an enterprise forced to exit the market, and an incumbent for which the costs of building such a network are sunk could be expected to remain in the market as long as it could cover its marginal cost (likely to be much lower than the average costs because of the existence of the fixed costs). In such conditions, other operators might understandably be reluctant to challenge the monopolistic position of the incumbent. For an exposition of the 'contestability theory', see William Baumol *et al.*, *Contestable Markets and the Theory of Infrastructure* (New York and London: Harcourt Brace Jovanovich, 1982).

[22] Ensuring number portability means ensuring that users are able to keep the same telephone number when switching telecommunications operators. Ensuring dial parity means ensuring that users do not have to dial additional numbers when they choose certain telecommunications operators rather than others.

telephone numbers, for example, may also constitute a scarce resource. Specific measures might be needed to ensure non-discriminatory access by all competitors to such scarce resources. In fact, the allocation of subsidies to achieve social objectives in a liberalised telecommunications market raises similar issues.[23] Cross-subsidies built into the rate structure of incumbent operators are incompatible with competition as new operators can enter the profitable segments of the market and eat away the profits on which the incumbent relies to subsidise the unprofitable services. When authorities decide that some services should remain subsidised, new mechanisms need to be designed to fund such subsidies and specific steps need to be taken, once again, to ensure that the allocation of such subsidies does not distort competition between operators.[24]

Fourthly, state-owned incumbent telecommunications operators frequently maintain very close links to political and regulatory authorities. In order to ensure a level playing field between the incumbent and new competitors, such links may have to be severed. This might, for example, entail eliminating any direct or indirect anti-competitive subsidies which the incumbent might be receiving, taking steps to require the incumbent to operate as any other commercial entity, or even privatising the incumbent.

Finally, as in any other sector, once competition has been introduced in the telecommunications sector, it may be desirable to take specific steps to maintain it, in particular by preventing agreements or mergers that would stifle competition. In most regimes, such anti-competitive behaviours will be addressed by the application of antitrust laws.

Controlling market power in telecommunications: antitrust v. sector-specific rules

The rules which can be used to facilitate or maintain competition in the telecommunications sector or to prevent telecommunications operators from abusing their market power when that power cannot be taken away from them fall broadly into two categories: antitrust rules and telecommunications-specific rules. Both types of rules are summarily presented below together with a brief discussion of their respective advantages and disadvantages.[25]

[23] See Geradin and Kerf, *Controlling Market Power*, pp. 56–7.
[24] *Ibid.*
[25] This part of the chapter draws on Geradin and Kerf, *Controlling Market Power*.

While the exact characteristics of each type of rule will of course differ to a certain extent from country to country, the description presented here focuses only on the main features of these rules and would hold true in most contexts. Competition rules are applicable to most economic activities (including telecommunications and other network industries), unless specific exemptions are granted.[26] They fall broadly into three categories.

The first type of rule prevents the conclusion of anti-competitive agreements between operators. Prohibited behaviours will usually include agreements aimed at fixing purchase or selling prices, limiting or controlling production or investments, sharing markets or sources of supply or bid rigging. Such rules usually recognise, however, that some agreements between operators might be competitively beneficial: they may foster efficiencies, help create new products or services or methods of distribution, or improve information flow and, thus, facilitate the functioning of the market.[27]

The second type of rule deals with firms that enjoy substantial market power.[28] The rule's objective is to prevent those firms from abusing their dominant or monopoly position *vis-à-vis* end-users or other operators. Examples of prohibited behaviours might include, for instance, limiting production, refusing to deal with particular buyers or sellers, imposing excessive or predatory prices, raising rivals' costs, imposing discriminatory prices on different buyers for the provision of similar services under similar conditions, or conditioning the sale of a product to the purchase of another unrelated one (i.e. tying).

[26] For a good discussion of the application of such rules in the telecommunications sector, see Roger G. Noll, 'The Role of Antitrust in Telecommunications', *Antitrust Bulletin* (1995): 501.

[27] This might be the case, for example, when competitors together conduct research and development that none could have carried out independently, jointly purchase supplies or distribute products and thereby reduce their costs, or form a trade association that gathers statistics and other data that each can use to make their operations more efficient. In some legal systems, a notification mechanism has been set up to enable operators to obtain authorisation from the competition authorities prior to concluding or implementing an agreement. In others, controls are exercised *ex post* only. See, for example, World Bank and OECD, *A Framework for the Design and Implementation of Competition Law and Policy* (Washington and Paris: World Bank and OECD, 1998), p. 19.

[28] Several factors will generally be used to determine whether a firm holds 'market power' in a given market: a high market share, the presence of barriers to entry, the holding of an essential facility, a strong vertical integration, etc. For a good discussion of the concept of market power, see Simon Bishop and Mike Walker, *The Economics of EC Competition Law* (London: Sweet and Maxwell, 1997), paras. 2.25 *et seq.*

The third type of rule prohibits mergers that would 'substantially lessen competition'.[29] Given the difficulty of unscrambling merged companies once they have operated together, most legal systems which contain rules in this regard provide for *ex ante* control of proposed agreements. At the end of their inquiry, competition authorities will have to take one of the following decisions: clearing the merger in its entirety; prohibiting the merger in its entirety; requiring a partial divestiture of assets or operations sufficient to eliminate the anti-competitive effects while allowing the underlying transaction to proceed; or imposing a range of conditions designed to regulate the conduct of the merged firm so as to prevent anti-competitive effects.[30]

Given their wide scope of application, competition rules tend to be relatively general: they tend to prohibit or impose broad categories of behaviours defined in relatively general terms. This may be an advantage in a sector such as telecommunications that is characterised by rapid technological evolution and in which very specific and detailed rules may quickly become obsolete. At the same time, and precisely because they are expressed in relatively general terms, competition rules leave a wide degree of discretion to enforcing authorities. This in turn can be a problem when there are reasons to believe that the regulator may use this discretionary power unwisely. Finally, while competition rules are often expressed in rather simple terms, their application in practice may, in some cases at least, be far less than straightforward.[31]

Telecommunications-specific rules, on the other hand, may be adopted to deal with market power specifically in the telecommunications sector.[32] Like competition rules, telecommunications-specific rules may be classified into three broad types.

The first type of rule is primarily designed to promote or preserve competition. It might, for example: (i) identify the segments of the telecommunications sector in which the entry of new operators is permitted;

[29] This is the criterion imposed by US law. The precise criterion under which mergers are examined may vary from one jurisdiction to another, but a strong negative impact on competition is generally required to prevent a merger from taking place.

[30] See World Bank and OECD, *Framework*, p. 53.

[31] To take but one example, determining whether a firm occupies a dominant position presupposes a clear understanding of the size of the relevant market, and that, in turn, may require sophisticated economic analysis to evaluate the extent to which various goods or services may be substitutes for one another.

[32] For an excellent overview of such laws and regulations, see Colin D. Long, *Telecommunications Law and Practice* (2nd edn, London: Sweet & Maxwell, 1995).

(ii) define the entry process to be followed by those new operators; (iii) set technical, procedural and pricing conditions pertaining to interconnection agreements in order to ensure that all competing operators seeking access to an essential facility are granted access to that essential facility under the same conditions; (iv) impose some type of separation between the entities controlling access to an essential facility and the entities which operate in competitive markets and seek access to that facility, in order to eliminate the incentives which those who control the essential facility might have to discriminate among those seeking access to it; (v) determine conditions for number allocation, number portability and dialing parity; (vi) determine how frequencies are to be allocated; and (vii) prohibit the transfer of public resources or the granting of other advantages to certain publicly owned companies in order to maintain a level playing field between those companies and their private counterparts.

Other telecommunications-specific rules are aimed primarily at preventing abuses of market power by firms that possess a dominant position in some segments of the market. Some of those rules are designed to prevent abuses *vis-à-vis* other operators. For example, interconnection rules designed to prevent those who control an essential facility from overcharging the operators seeking access to that facility. Other rules are designed to prevent abuses *vis-à-vis* end-users. For example, price and quality requirements for various types of telecommunications services provided to end-users in markets that are not competitive.

Finally, an additional category of sector-specific rules comprises rules designed to ensure that various public service obligations are being met. Such obligations may comprise, for example, minimum geographical coverage requirements for certain types of services at pre-specified prices, special tariffs for low-income households, as well as free access to certain emergency numbers and directory services.

Typically, telecommunications-specific rules are relatively precise. They tend to leave less discretion to enforcing authorities than do competition rules. In that regard, the relative advantages and disadvantages of telecommunications-specific rules tend therefore to be the converse of those displayed by competition rules. On the other hand, the complexity of the wording of telecommunications-specific rules and the extent to which such rules are difficult to implement in practice can vary enormously from rule to rule and so therefore does the degree of technical sophistication required of the regulators.

Overview of regulatory tools provided by the WTO to control market power

While all the countries seeking to liberalise their telecommunications markets and to promote competition in those markets do face some similar challenges, the extent to which they have chosen to rely on the types of regulatory tools described above varies greatly from country to country. The richest countries, for example, all of which have opened their telecommunications markets to competition as pointed out above, almost always rely on both competition rules and telecommunications-specific rules. However, the emphasis put on each type of rule can be vastly different in different countries. For instance, while the US relies to a large extent on a set of very detailed sector-specific rules embodied in the Telecommunications Act of 1996, New Zealand had, until recently, chosen to adopt very few telecommunications-specific rules and to rely instead almost exclusively on general antitrust rules.[33] In poorer countries, the options that have been chosen can vary even more markedly.

In the face of such heterogeneity, efforts have been made to introduce some common instruments at the international level through the WTO. This section of the paper will examine, in turn: (i) the unsuccessful attempts to negotiate competition rules; and (ii) the telecommunications-specific rules which can be found in the so-called Reference Paper.

Failed attempts to negotiate competition rules

One of the most contentious issues of international trade law relates to whether or not the WTO should draw up a set of competition rules.[34] While some observers argue that international competition rules are needed and that the WTO is the appropriate forum to negotiate and enforce them,[35] others consider that such rules are not desirable.[36]

[33] See Geradin and Kerf, *Controlling Market Power*, Chapters 4 and 5.

[34] There is an abundant literature on the subject. See, for instance, Daniel K. Tarullo, 'Norms and Institutions in Global Competition Policy', *American Journal of International Law* 478; 94 (2000): Eleanor M. Fox, 'Competition Law and the New Millennium Round', *Journal of International Economic Law* 2 (1999): 665; Andrew Guzman, 'Is International Antitrust Possible?', *New York University Law Review* 73 (1998): 1501; and Eleanor M. Fox, 'Toward World Antitrust and Market Access', *American Journal of International Law* 91 (1997): 1.

[35] See, for instance, Guzman, 'Is International Antitrust Possible?'; and Fox, 'Toward World Antitrust and Market Access'.

[36] See Diane P. Wood, 'The Impossible Dream: Real International Antitrust', *University of Chicago Legal Forum* (1992): 277.

The two main trading blocks, the European Union and the United States, have traditionally held opposing views on this issue, with the former supporting the adoption of a global competition framework and the latter opposing it.[37]

Whether or not the multilateral trading system should draw up competition rules is hardly a new issue in international trade law. By 1947, the Havana Charter and the International Trade Organization (ITO) contemplated it, envisaging a chapter of the Charter containing provisions for the regulation of restrictive business practices.[38] The ITO failed, however, in part because of objections by the US Government to its antitrust policy provisions. No competition-related rules were eventually included in the original GATT. Discussions over multilateral competition rules continued in a variety of international fora. For instance, in the early 1950s, the Economic and Social Council (ECOSOC) of the United Nations attempted to formulate an international agreement on restrictive business practices, which was also rejected by the United States.[39] In the 1970s, developing countries decided to pursue the negotiation of a multilateral code on restrictive business practices. These efforts led to the adoption in 1980 of a 'Set of Multilaterally Agreed Equitable Principles and Rules for the Control of Restrictive Business Practices'.[40] The practical importance of this code was, however, limited by its purely voluntary nature. While efforts to develop binding international competition rules remain fruitless, many states engaged in bilateral cooperation agreements.[41] Pursuant to these agreements, the parties agree to cooperate in the context of international antitrust investigations (e.g. by providing that each party notify the other of a pending enforcement action that could impact upon important interests of the other party). Some of these agreements also identify a set of negative and positive comity principles that can guide both parties as they decide whether or not to exercise or forego jurisdiction over a case. These agreements do not lead, however, to any coordination of substantive competition laws. In the absence of multilateral competition

37 See Eleanor M. Fox, 'Antitrust Law on a Global Scale: Races Up, Down, and Sideways', in Daniel C. Esty and Damien Geradin, eds., *Regulatory Competition and Economic Integration – Economic Perspectives* (Oxford: Oxford University Press, 2001), p. 348 at p. 361.

38 See Wood, 'The Impossible Dream', p. 281.

39 *Ibid.*, pp. 284–5.

40 *Ibid.*, pp. 285–7.

41 See, for instance, the Agreement Between the Government of the United States of America and the European Communities Regarding the Application of Their Competition Laws, OJ 1995 L132.

rules, some nations also started to coordinate their competition policy on a regional basis.[42] Examples include the EC, NAFTA and Mercosur.[43]

In the 1990s, the internationalisation of competition rules remained at the forefront of international trade discussions. The European Union in particular pressed its trading partners for the adoption of a competition law framework in the context of the WTO.[44] This approach was supported by some major trading nations. It was, however, opposed by the United States.[45] As a result, while the Uruguay Round negotiations led to the adoption of specific agreements over issues, such as intellectual property rights (TRIPs) and international investments (TRIMs), these negotiations did not lead to the adoption of global competition rules. Several agreements that are part of the WTO framework, however, contain competition-related provisions. For instance, the TRIPs authorises Members to specify, in their legislation, licensing practices or conditions that may, in particular cases, constitute an abuse of intellectual property rights having an adverse effect on competition in the relevant market.[46] The TRIMs requires, within five years of the date on which it becomes enforceable, consideration of whether the agreement should be complemented with provisions on investment and competition policy.[47]

In 1996, the WTO Ministerial Meeting held in Singapore created a Working Group on the Interaction between Trade and Competition Policy.[48] The mission of this Working Group was to 'study issues raised by Members relating to the interaction between trade and competition policy, including anti-competitive practices, in order to identify any areas that may merit further consideration in the WTO framework'.[49] This Working Group has produced several reports, which will provide support to further WTO initiatives in the competition field. In this regard, the recent Doha Ministerial Declaration represented another major step forward, as it provided that negotiations over competition will take place after the next WTO Ministerial Meeting, probably in 2003, based

[42] See OECD, 'The Relationship Between Regional Trade Agreements and the Multilateral Trading System: Competition', TD/TC/WP(2002)19/FINAL, 7 May 2002.
[43] *Ibid.*
[44] See Fox, 'Toward World Antitrust and Market Access', pp. 8–9.
[45] *Ibid.*
[46] Article 8.2 of the TRIPs Agreement.
[47] Article 9 of the TRIMs Agreement.
[48] Singapore Ministerial Declaration, 13 December 1996, para. 20.
[49] *Ibid.*

on modalities to be decided at the time.[50] It is, of course, too early at this stage to predict whether these negotiations will lead to the adoption of a WTO competition law framework.

The Reference Paper

While WTO Members have so far failed to agree on competition rules, the Members that are party to the Agreement on Basic Telecommunications Services managed to agree on a set of specific regulatory principles designed to ensure that the commitments made by the participating countries would not be compromised by anti-competitive practices. These principles, which are comprised in the so-called Reference Paper,[51] complement the general principles that are included in the General Agreement on Trade in Services (GATS) and which also apply to the telecommunications sector.[52] The Reference Paper is a truly remarkable document as it is the first time in the history of WTO negotiations that market access commitments are complemented with regulatory principles.[53] Adoption of such principles was seen by many delegations as necessary given the specific features of the telecommunications sector and, in particular, the risks that competition in the market may be restricted by the incumbent's abuses of market power.

The Reference Paper comprises many of the commitments that are typically found in a domestic telecommunications regulatory framework, such as the right of telecommunications operators to interconnect with the network of the incumbent. The principles found in the Reference Paper are, however, drafted in a less specific manner than comparable principles in domestic legislation. The reason is that the negotiators of the Reference Paper considered that these principles needed to be sufficiently flexible to accommodate the different regulatory philosophies of the countries involved.[54] As a result, it was decided that the Reference Paper would

[50] Doha Ministerial Declaration, 14 November 2001, paras. 23–5.

[51] See Reference Paper, Fourth Protocol to the General Agreement on Trade in Services, ILM 36 (1997): 354 at 367. For a discussion, see Chapter 3 above.

[52] For a discussion of these principles, see Marco Bronckers and Pierre Larouche, 'Telecommunications Services and the World Trade Organization', *Journal of World Trade* 31 (1997): 5 at 14–16.

[53] See Petros C. Mavroidis and Damien J. Neven, 'The WTO Agreement on Telecommunications: It's Never Too Late', in Damien Geradin, ed., *The Liberalization of State Monopolies in the European Union and Beyond* (Boston, MA: Kluwer Law International, 2000), p. 307.

[54] See Sherman, 'Wildly Enthusiastic', p. 73.

focus on effective outcomes, rather than on the means or processes by which such outcomes could be achieved.

The Reference Paper applies to basic telecommunications services, although it can be assumed that it also covers value-added services.[55] By contrast, the Reference Paper does not cover audio-visual services. This is due to the fact that the WTO framework follows a pre-convergence approach, whereby telecommunications services and audio-visual services are treated separately. In a context of growing convergence between telecommunications and audio-visual services, this limitation could affect the effectiveness of the Reference Paper, unless the scope of the Reference Paper was extended to audio-visual services as well.

The Reference paper is divided into six paragraphs. The first two paragraphs (competitive safeguards, interconnection) contain requirements that exclusively apply to 'major suppliers'.[56] The Reference Paper thus provides for asymmetric regulation. The four remaining paragraphs (universal service, licensing, independence of the regulator, allocation of resources) deal with general regulatory issues. They essentially seek to protect service providers from discriminatory or arbitrary regulatory actions. A more thorough discussion of the paragraphs is provided below.

One strength of the Reference Paper is that the principles it contains are not mere guidelines, but represent binding commitments, which means that their inadequate implementation is challengeable through the WTO dispute settlement system.[57] So far, there have not been any WTO panel or Appellate Body decisions interpreting Reference Paper provisions. This is about to change. In February 2002, the US Government requested the establishment of a panel to examine the compatibility with WTO law of certain Mexican measures affecting trade in basic and value-added

[55] The WTO Framework introduces a distinction between basic and value-added services. During the Uruguay Round negotiations some countries made commitments in the telecommunications fields, but these were limited to value-added services. Basic telecommunications services were liberalised subsequently through the Agreement on Basic Telecommunications. As the Reference Paper was negotiated at the same time as the Agreement on Basic Telecommunications, this explains why it applies only to basic telecommunications services. Some authors have, however, argued that it must be assumed that it also applies to value-added services. See Bronckers and Larouche, 'Telecommunications Services', p. 23.

[56] The Reference Paper defines a 'major supplier' as 'a supplier which has the ability to materially affect the terms of participation (having regard to price and supply) in the relevant market for basic telecommunications services as a result of: (a) control over essential facilities; or (b) use of its position in the market'.

[57] Bronckers and Larouche, 'Telecommunications Services', p. 23.

telecommunications services.[58] Among the issues addressed in the request was Mexico's failure to ensure that Telmex (the Mexican incumbent) provide interconnection to US cross-border basic suppliers on reasonable rates, terms and conditions, as required by Mexico's commitments under Section 2 of the Reference Paper.

Critical analysis of the Reference Paper

In the absence of general competition rules, the Reference Paper is a key instrument as it provides the main basis on which anti-competitive practices in the provision of telecommunications services can be challenged through the WTO dispute settlement process. Yet, the Reference Paper has been criticised by several observers as being a weak instrument.[59] One critique formulated against the Reference Paper is that many of its provisions are vague and that key concepts are not defined. Another critique is that the Reference Paper fails to include some important regulatory principles, such as number portability or carrier selection. To remedy these problems, some suggest that the Reference Paper should be strengthened by making existing commitments more specific and by including new commitments on a range of additional issues.[60]

While this assessment might have some merits, we believe that, in order to determine whether and how the Reference Paper should be strengthened, careful attention should be paid to the context in which this agreement operates. A first point to be taken into account is that the Reference Paper has a large number of contracting parties.[61] Such parties include

[58] The United States had sent an initial request for a panel in February 2000. 'Mexico – Measures Affecting Telecommunications Services, Request for the Establishment of a Panel by the United States', WT/DS204/2, 16 November 2000. Following this request, the United States and Mexico held consultations and managed to resolve some of the issues. However, the United States alleged that Mexico continued to maintain several measures that violated its obligations under the GATS. In February 2002, it therefore sent a new request for a panel. 'Mexico – Measures Affecting Telecommunications Services, Request for the Establishment of a Panel by the United States', WT/DS204/3, 18 February 2002.

[59] See, for instance, Markus Fredebeul-Krein and Andreas Freytag, 'The Case for a More Binding WTO Agreement on Regulatory Principles in Telecommunications Markets', *Telecommunications Policy* 23 (1995): 625.

[60] *Ibid.*

[61] All sixty-nine countries that are party to the Agreement on Basic Telecommunications (except for Ecuador and Tunisia) also agreed to be party to the Reference Paper. Some countries (Bolivia, India, Malaysia, Morocco, Pakistan, the Philippines, Turkey and Venezuela) did not adopt the whole of the Reference Paper, while others (Bangladesh, Brazil, Mauritius and Thailand) indicated they will follow the Reference Paper at a later point in time. See Bronckers and Larouche, 'Telecommunications Services', p. 22.

nations at different stages of economic development, as well as at different stages of telecommunications sector reform. A second point is that the institutional endowments of the contracting parties also differ greatly. While developed countries generally possess well-organised and competent regulatory authorities, the regulatory authorities of transition economies, when they exist, are generally poorly equipped to handle the complex issues of telecommunications regulation.

In light of the above context, we believe that the principles contained in the Reference Paper should meet three criteria. First, they should be flexible enough to allow Members to cater for differences in local circumstances. For instance, a principle that would require Members to systematically impose vertical separation between the local and long-distance markets in order to remove incentives on the part of the local service provider to discriminate between long-distance operators would probably be excessively rigid. While structural remedies are often effective to prevent discriminatory practices and may facilitate the task of the regulator, there may be circumstances in which behavioural remedies might be preferable.[62] Secondly, the principles of the Reference Paper should be simple enough to maximise the likelihood that they can be effectively implemented by the regulatory authorities of all Members. For instance, as we will discuss below, it is not clear that a principle requiring all Members to unbundle their local network would be desirable. Unbundling of the local loop is an extremely complex matter that places heavy demands on the regulator.[63] Rules imposing unbundling may thus not be desirable in countries which lack a sufficiently competent regulator. Finally, the principles contained in the Reference Paper should be sufficiently precise. Vague principles leave a large degree of discretion to the regulator and are therefore ill-suited when the risks of regulatory capture or of regulatory mistakes are high. In addition, vague principles are generally poorly enforced, as it is difficult to prove that they have been violated.

There is clearly a certain degree of tension between some of these criteria. For instance, it is not always easy to develop rules that will, at the same time, be flexible and precise. However, the tension between these criteria should not be exaggerated. First, the same degree of flexibility is not necessarily required with respect to all provisions contained in the Reference

[62] See Geradin and Kerf, *Controlling Market Power*, pp. 59–60.
[63] *Ibid.*, p. 313.

Paper. Flexibility will be particularly important when local variations determine to a large extent the types of rule that need to be implemented. On the other hand, some principles should arguably be applied in the same way independently of variations in local conditions (e.g. rules requiring transparency in licensing requirements). Moreover, various techniques can be used to ensure a balance between flexibility and precision. One technique is to offer Members a choice between several options and possibly to provide guidance as to when one option might be preferable to others. Another technique is to insist perhaps not so much on rules of substance than on the adoption of precise rules of procedure.

We proceed hereinafter with an analysis of the principles included in the Reference Paper with a view to assessing whether the way in which they are formulated fits with the criteria described above.

Paragraph 1.1 requires that 'appropriate measures shall be maintained for the purpose of preventing suppliers who, alone or together, are a major supplier from engaging in or continuing anti-competitive practices'. In Paragraph 1.2, the Reference Paper lists three examples of such anti-competitive practices, including: (i) cross-subsidisation; (ii) use of information obtained from competitors to restrict competition; and (iii) failure to provide other suppliers with the technical or commercial information they need to provide their services.

Paragraph 1 of the Reference Paper is thus extremely flexible as it only requires Members to adopt measures to prevent 'anti-competitive practices' and gives some examples of such practices. It is also formulated in fairly simple terms, although, as will be seen below, its application in practice may involve complex assessments. The main weakness of this provision is that it lacks precision in several respects.

First, it is not entirely clear what the Reference Paper understands by 'anti-competitive practices'. The three examples cited are examples of behaviours that are generally considered to be abuses of dominant position. This seems to support the view that such abuses are the only type of anti-competitive practices prohibited by Paragraph 1. Since the list of practices mentioned in Paragraph 1.2 is not exhaustive, other forms of anti-competitive practices, such as collusive behaviour (e.g. price-fixing, market-sharing, etc.), may fall under the prohibition of Paragraph 1.1. There is little doubt that, when it suits them, the parties will seek to interpret this provision extensively.

Secondly, even some of the practices referred to in Paragraph 1.2 remain undefined. For instance, Paragraph 1.2 provides no definition of the concept of 'cross-subsidisation'.[64] It is generally admitted that cross-subsidisation arises when a single company uses revenues derived from one activity to subsidise the performance of another activity. However, there is no unanimity as to when exactly the performance of a given activity is indeed being 'subsidised'. Is it when provision of goods or services takes place below marginal costs or below marginal costs plus a 'fair' allocation of common costs? In addition, it is not clear whether cross-subsidisation should always be prohibited or whether it should be prohibited only when the subsidies are derived from activities for which the company has exclusive rights (as opposed, say, to activities open to competition for which the company happens to hold some *de facto* market power because of a superior technology for instance).[65]

Thirdly, Paragraph 1 does little to specify the measures that Members should take in order to prevent the prohibited practices from occurring. The successful implementation of some of the requirements contained in the Reference Paper requires that some additional measures be taken. For instance, experience teaches that it is extremely difficult to challenge anti-competitive cross-subsidisation in the absence of separate subsidiaries for monopolistic and competitive services or rules mandating accounting separation between such services.[66] While a number of Members have adopted legislation imposing such remedies, others have not. We believe, along with other observers, that more specific requirements should be inserted into Paragraph 1 of the Reference Paper.[67] We also believe, however, that it is important to maintain a degree of flexibility in the requirements imposed on the Members. For instance, Members should probably be free to choose between structural (e.g. the creation of separate entities) and behavioural (e.g. accounting separation) solutions to prevent anti-competitive cross-subsidisation. Instead of imposing a specific method to address this problem, the Reference Paper could contain a provision

[64] For a discussion of that concept, see Leigh Hancher and José Luis Bundia Sierra, 'Cross Subsidization and EC Law', *Common Market Law Review* (1998): 901.

[65] Note that cross-subsidies derived from activities for which the company hold special or exclusive rights could fall under Article VIII:8 of the GATS that requires Members to ensure that monopoly suppliers do not abuse their dominant position in the reserved markets in relation to those activities in which they operate in competition and which are outside the scope of their monopoly rights. See David Luff, 'International Trade and Broadband Regulation: Towards Convergence?', *Journal of Network Industries* 3 (2002): 239 at 247.

[66] See Larouche and Bronckers, 'Telecommunications Services', p. 27.

[67] See, for instance, Fredebeul-Krein and Freytag, 'The Case for a More Binding WTO Agreement', pp. 628–9.

requiring Members to enforce behavioural or structural measures to prevent anti-competitive cross-subsidisation. It could also mention the key factors – such as the degree of market power which incumbents maintain, the track record of the regulatory authorities, etc. – which should be taken into account when choosing between structural and behavioural remedies.

Paragraph 2 contains a set of requirements regarding interconnection.[68] As in Paragraph 1, the objective of this provision is to prevent major suppliers from engaging in anti-competitive practices, in this case by denying interconnection rights or providing interconnection under unduly harsh or discriminatory conditions to other suppliers. The Reference Paper states that:

- interconnection must be provided at any technically feasible point in the network;
- it must be provided under non-discriminatory terms (relating to conditions and rates) and it must be of a quality no less favourable than that provided for its own like services or for like services of non-affiliated service suppliers or for its subsidiaries or other affiliates;
- it must be provided in a timely fashion;
- it must be provided at cost-oriented rates;
- the terms, conditions and rates must be transparent and reasonable, having regard to economic feasibility;
- there must be sufficient 'unbundling' so that the 'supplier need not pay for network components or facilities that it does not require to be provided'; and
- interconnection must be provided at points other than the network termination points used by the majority of users, subject to charges covering the costs for additional facilities.

Paragraph 2 also contains transparency requirements whereby '[t]he procedures for interconnection to a major supplier will be made available' and 'it is ensured that a major supplier will make publicly available either its interconnection agreements or a reference interconnection offer'. Finally, Paragraph 2 requires the availability of a dispute settlement

[68] Interconnection is defined as the 'linking with suppliers providing public telecommunications transport networks or services in order to allow the users of one supplier to communicate with users of another supplier and to access services provided by another supplier'.

mechanism in case of a disagreement with a major supplier over the terms, conditions and rates of interconnection.

Paragraph 2 is drafted in fairly general terms. It is thus sufficiently flexible to allow Members to take local circumstances into account when implementing that provision. As is the case with Paragraph 1, it could, however, be argued that Paragraph 2 is not sufficiently precise in a number of respects. In this regard, two requirements included in Paragraph 2 have attracted the attention of observers. First, Paragraph 2 provides that interconnection rates must be 'cost-oriented'. Cost-orientation is a very broad concept and it will generally be possible for a major supplier to claim that its interconnection rates meet this requirement even if such rates are unfavourable to new entrants. What matters in practice is the specific methodology used to determine the interconnection price. Secondly, Paragraph 2 requires that there be a 'sufficient' degree of unbundling so that suppliers do not have to pay for network elements or facilities that are not required. This provision is particularly vague and it seems that major suppliers will always be able to claim that their interconnection rates are sufficiently unbundled as the Reference Paper does not specify the degree of unbundling that has to be achieved.

The vagueness of these provisions has led several observers to suggest that they should be complemented by much more specific regulatory requirements. Specifically, they argue that Paragraph 2 should provide for a specific methodology to calculate interconnection rates.[69] Given the pro-competitive features of the long-run incremental costs (LRIC) methodology, these observers consider that this method should be imposed by the Reference Paper. These authors also claim that Paragraph 2 should comprise a list of network elements that need to be unbundled.[70] While there is some logic to this position, we believe that expressly providing in the Reference Paper for a specific pricing methodology or a list of network elements to be unbundled would be both extremely difficult and probably undesirable. Pricing and unbundling issues are extremely controversial, and it is highly unlikely that Members could agree on a specific methodology.[71] But even if a single methodology were to be adopted, it is

[69] *Ibid.*, p. 629.

[70] *Ibid.*, pp. 629–30

[71] In the United States, for instance, the methodologies chosen by the FCC for the calculation of interconnection charges and the prices of unbundled network elements led to a legal battle that delayed the implementation of the 1996 Telecommunications Act. See Timothy J. Tardiff, 'New Technologies and Convergence of Markets: Implications for Telecommunications Regulation', *Journal of Network Industries* 1 (2000): 447.

not clear that it would necessarily be desirable.[72] First, some methodologies are too complex from an implementation perspective to be imposed upon all the signatories to the Reference Paper. LRIC is in fact quite complex as it requires, *inter alia*, the regulator to determine what equipment a benchmark efficient firm would need in order to provide interconnection as well as to correctly forecast the rate of technological evolution in order to calculate appropriate depreciation rates. By focusing on incremental costs, LRIC also leaves open the question of how to recover the fixed costs that are not exclusively related to the provision of interconnection.[73] In addition, the choice of a pricing methodology should take into account a series of factors that may vary across countries. For example, application of the LRIC methodology – precisely because it tends to keep interconnection rates down and therefore promotes entry by new entrants – also provides strong incentives to the incumbent to erect non-price barriers to entry.[74] Where regulatory capacity is weak, it may therefore ultimately be advisable to opt for a pricing methodology that limits to some extent the incentives of the incumbent to resist entry. Similarly, the degree of unbundling imposed on interconnection rates may depend on local circumstances. Once again, the technical capacity of the regulator may need to be taken into account as the pricing of unbundled elements is particularly challenging.[75]

A related issue is whether Paragraph 2 should be extended to require that major suppliers unbundle their local loop. This goes beyond the interconnection requirements indicated above as unbundling of the local loop requires physical access to elements of the local infrastructure.[76] We believe the answer should be negative. First, the desirability of local loop unbundling depends upon the specific characteristics of the market under consideration. Unbundling may be a particularly advisable strategy when there is little or no competition in the local loop and a growing demand for high-bandwidth services. While many Members will be in that situation, some Members may have sufficient competition in the local segment to render local loop unbundling unnecessary. Moreover,

[72] See Jeffrey H. Rohlfs and J. Gregory Sidak, 'Exporting Telecommunications Regulation: The US–Japan Negotiations on Interconnection Pricing', AEI-Brookings Joint Center for Regulatory Studies, Working Paper 02-3, March 2002.

[73] See Jean-Jacques Laffont and Jean Tirole, *Competition in Telecommunications* (Cambridge, MA, and London: MIT Press, 2000), p. 159.

[74] *Ibid.*, p. 161–2.

[75] *Ibid.*, p. 313.

[76] *Ibid.*, p. 312.

the successful implementation of local loop unbundling requires complex regulatory assessments on the part of the regulator. A first difficult task is to define the individual network components to which access must be granted by the local loop owner. In addition, an appropriate price needs to be established for each of these individual components. Finally, implementing unbundling may require additional intervention by the regulator to ensure, for instance, that space within the (hundreds of existing) local exchanges is adequately shared between the incumbent and the access seekers. As many of the world's most competent regulators find it very difficult to successfully implement an unbundling strategy, there is no doubt that this objective is very unlikely to be successfully met in at least some developing economies.

Thus, unlike many observers, we therefore believe that Paragraph 2 should not necessarily contain more specific substantive requirements. One should avoid imposing very specific rules that would turn out to be too difficult to implement for some regulators. In addition, given the variations that exist between the conditions prevalent in the telecommunications market of different countries, the setting of substantive access requirements is an area in which flexibility is important. By contrast, we believe that the procedural requirements that are contained in Paragraph 2 could be usefully strengthened. For example, one could specify that incumbents be obliged to prepare and publish standard terms and conditions under which they are prepared to offer interconnection. The powers of the authority in charge of settling interconnection disputes could also be more clearly established. This authority could, for instance, be given the power to approve or reject the incumbent's standard interconnection offer and to impose specific terms of interconnection when the parties fail to reach an agreement.

While imposing interconnection requirements is critical in order to prevent abuses of market power on the part of major suppliers, other regulatory requirements such as number portability[77] or carrier selection are important as well.[78] Experience teaches that such requirements are necessary to create a true level playing field between incumbents and new entrants. Moreover, such requirements have been successfully implemented in a large number of states, including transition economies. For instance,

[77] Number portability means ensuring that users are able to keep the same telephone number when switching telecommunications operators.

[78] Carrier selection means users can choose between the services of competing carriers on a call-by-call basis or to pre-select the carrier of their choice on a permanent or default basis.

it has been reported that carrier selection has largely contributed to the competitiveness of the Chilean long-distance market.[79] There is therefore no reason why such requirements should not be included in the Reference Paper.

As pointed out above, the remaining paragraphs of the Reference Paper do not specifically apply to major suppliers, but instead comprise general obligations that must be adhered to by the Members.

Paragraph 3 guarantees that Members have the right to define the kind of universal service obligations they wish to maintain. The Reference Paper requires, however, that such obligations be 'administered in a transparent, non-discriminatory and competitively neutral manner and not more burdensome than necessary for the kind of universal service defined by the Member'. The authors of the Reference Paper were right to leave Members free to define the scope of universal service obligations that will apply on their territory, as there are major disparities in, for example, wealth and geographic circumstances among participating nations.

It seems, however, that the Reference Paper would gain by providing for more concrete requirements to ensure that universal service obligations are administered in a transparent, non-discriminatory and competitively neutral manner. As in the first two paragraphs, one main challenge is to strike the right balance between flexibility and precision. It would not be, for instance, appropriate to impose a single method on the basis of which universal service providers should be chosen, or a specific mechanism on the basis of which universal service obligations should be funded, as in both cases several methods can be relied upon and the choice of a specific method should be guided by the policy objectives being pursued as well as by local circumstances.[80]

[79] See Michel Kerf and Damien Geradin, 'Post-Liberalization Challenges in Telecommunications: Balancing Antitrust and Sector-Specific Regulation – Tentative Lessons from the Experiences of the United States, New Zealand, Chile and Australia', *World Competition* 23 (2000): 27 at 51.

[80] For example, countries whose first priority is to minimise the costs of universal service provision may wish to select the universal service provider on the basis of the lowest required subsidy (a system put in place with much success in Chile, for instance). On the other hand, if the main priority is to encourage innovation and quality on the part of universal service providers, it may be advisable to rely on a system of portable subsidies whereby multiple providers compete to provide services to users and receive the subsidy upon delivery of the services from the individual users whom they serve (a system which is being put in place in Australia, for example). As far as the source of the subsidies is concerned, the effectiveness of the general tax system, for example, may determine whether funds should be raised through general taxation or through other ways, such as levies imposed upon the telecommunications operators for instance.

Procedural guarantees could, however, help. For instance, the Reference Paper should require that Members publish the method they will use to select their universal service provider(s), as well as to calculate, fund and allocate universal service subsidies (in the event such subsidies are granted).[81] This would increase the level of transparency and, thus, discourage Members from opting for mechanisms that may lead to discriminatory or anti-competitive results.

Paragraph 4 provides that, when Members require that telecommunications operators obtain a licence, they have to make public 'all the licensing criteria and the period of time normally required to reach a decision concerning an application for a licence' and 'the terms and conditions of individual licences'. In addition, Paragraph 4 states that the 'reasons for the denial of a licence will be made known to the applicant upon request'. While this provision encourages transparency in the licensing process, it lacks precision and fails to provide sufficient guarantees that the licensing process will not be used for protectionist ends. Licensing requirements can represent a substantial barrier to entry for telecommunications suppliers and there is thus a need to impose additional requirements. These requirements could be of both a substantive and a procedural nature.

First, the Reference paper should define the circumstances in which a licence can be required. In theory, licences should only be required in two circumstances: when the provision of a given type of service requires access to scarce resources (e.g. spectrum); or when there is a need to prevent market failures by subordinating market entry to certain conditions (e.g. safety standards that may be needed in the face of an information deficit on the part of the users and in order to prevent the imposition of large negative externalities on society as a whole by negligent or unscrupulous service providers).[82] Secondly, the Reference Paper should specify the type of conditions that can be imposed on the licensees. Members often impose conditions on operators that are not needed to control market failures.[83]

[81] Such guarantees are arguably already imposed under Article III of the GATS, which contains an obligation of transparency that requires that all WTO Members promptly publish all laws, regulations and administrative guidelines that significantly affect trade in services. See Luff, 'International Trade and Broadband Regulation', p. 241.

[82] See Damien Geradin and Christophe Humpe, 'Regulatory Issues in Establishment and Management of Communications Infrastructure: The Impact of Network Convergence', *Journal of Network Industries* 3 (2002): 99 at 103.

[83] For instance, it is reported that the French Government included a provision in an operator's licence that at least 5 per cent of the company's investment had to be spent on research and development. See Thomas Kiessling and Yves Blondeel, 'The EU Regulatory Framework in Telecommunications', *Telecommunications Policy* 22 (1998): 571 at 585.

Thirdly, the Reference Paper should specify the cases in which limitations on the number of licences, and therefore of operators, is authorised. There is ample evidence today that limiting the number of licences for reasons other than scarcity of resources is often a bad policy and delays the arrival of competition in the market.[84]

Some procedural requirements could also be helpful. First, Members should be required to publish the details of the licensing process. In addition, the Reference Paper should specify that all decisions to refuse a licence should be justified and made public.

Paragraph 5 requires that Members guarantee the separation of the regulatory authority from any supplier of basic telecommunications services. Regulatory authorities must also act impartially.[85] This requirement that regulatory bodies be independent from telecommunications suppliers is of great importance. The Reference Paper is right in leaving Members free to decide how their regulatory authority should be organised (e.g. whether there should be a specific telecommunications authority or whether regulatory duties in telecommunications could be accomplished by a competition authority). On the other hand, several widely accepted principles of good governance could be added to the Reference Paper. First, there should be a requirement that, when one or several telecommunications suppliers remain owned by the state, the regulatory authority should be structurally separated from the ministries or departments in charge of exercising control on these suppliers. In practice, structural separation means that, at a minimum, the regulatory authority should not be under the authority of the minister in charge of managing the state's interests in these suppliers (ideally, measures should be taken to try to minimise the risks that the regulators be subjected to undue political pressures by any

[84] Note that the three requirements we are proposing here could also be adopted under Article VI:4 of the GATS, which authorises the Council for Trade in Services to adopt disciplines to ensure that qualification requirements, technical standards and licensing are 'inter alia: (a) based on objective and transparent criteria, such as competence and the ability to supply the service; (b) not more burdensome than necessary to ensure the quality of the service; (c) in the case of licensing procedures, not in themselves a restriction on the supply of the service'. In the absence of such disciplines, Article VI:5 of the GATS provides that Members shall not apply licensing and qualification requirements and technical standards that 'nullify or impair specific commitments in a manner which: (i) does not comply with the criteria outline in subparagraphs 4(a), (b) or (c); and (ii) could not reasonably have been expected of that Member at the time the specific commitments in those sectors were made'.

[85] See Geradin, 'Institutional Aspects of Telecommunications Regulatory Reforms in the European Union: An Analysis of the Role of National Regulatory Authorities', Journal of Network Industries 1 (2000): 5–32 at 19–20.

part of the executive).[86] Such a structural separation appears necessary to avoid conflicts of interest. Secondly, provisions could also be added in order to ensure the accountability of the regulator. For instance, the Reference Paper should require that all decisions adopted by the regulator be made for the benefit of and disclosed to the public.

Finally, Paragraph 6 requires that the procedures for the allocation and use of scarce resources, including frequencies, numbers and rights of way, be carried out in an 'objective, timely, transparent, and non-discriminatory manner'. Once again, this paragraph is extremely flexible as it leaves Members free to decide how to allocate scarce resources. But, as in the case of the paragraphs dealing with universal service obligations and licensing, we believe that additional procedural guarantees could be helpful. For example, the Reference Paper should require Members to publish the methods on the basis of which scarce resources should be allocated.

In sum, the Reference Paper is a valuable document that provides a set of safeguards against anti-competitive practices that could limit market access. The fact that the Reference Paper requires Members to impose obligations on certain private entities (e.g. the interconnection requirements applicable to major suppliers) is remarkable and clearly a breakthrough in trade negotiations. The Reference Paper has, however, a number of weaknesses. As pointed out above, some of its provisions lack precision and are therefore likely to create enforcement difficulties. Adoption of more specific rules will therefore often be desirable. In addition, important regulatory requirements to create a level playing field between incumbents and new entrants – such as number portability and carrier selection – are missing, thereby weakening the effectiveness of the Reference Paper as a tool to control market power. At the same time, in order to maintain a sufficient degree of flexibility, it may be advisable in certain cases to keep substantive rules somewhat general and to focus on devising more specific procedural rules.

Do general competition rules remain necessary?

Assuming that the effectiveness of the Reference Paper could be strengthened along the lines described above, a question arises as to whether there would still be a need for general competition rules. Two factors suggest that the answer to this may be positive.

[86] *Ibid.*

First, competition rules are needed to deal with a range of anti-competitive practices that are not necessarily addressed by sector-specific rules such as those contained in the Reference Paper. It could, of course, be argued that the Reference Paper does contain some competition rules. It is true that Paragraph 1 clearly echoes the type of provisions that can be found in competition legislation. Unless it is interpreted extensively, this provision seems, however, to focus on one specific type of anti-competitive practice, which is the abuse of a dominant position. Controlling market power in telecommunications involves preventing other types of anti-competitive practices, such as collusive behaviour between competitors.

One approach to remedy this problem would be to expand Paragraph 1 to address all types of anti-competitive practices, including collusion or even mergers leading to excessive market consolidation. But, even in this case, there would be a second factor justifying the adoption of horizontal competition provisions. One considerable limitation of the Reference Paper is that it only applies to basic telecommunications services and the anti-competitive practices that one might want to prohibit are likely to be just as harmful across a broad range of economic activities as they are with respect to telecommunications. This argues in favour of the adoption of horizontal competition rules applicable across sectors.

A case may therefore be made for seeking to negotiate a WTO Agreement on Trade and Competition Policy (here in after, the 'Competition Agreement'). Whether such an agreement would prove to be useful in practice would depend, to a large extent, upon whether it meets the same requirements of flexibility, simplicity and precision discussed above with respect to the principles of the Reference Paper. To meet these criteria, a Competition Agreement should not contain rules that are excessively vague or, at the extreme opposite, unnecessarily complex. In addition, such an agreement should not provide for a set of rules that would be too rigid and thus leave no scope to the Members to develop their own approaches to competition law. In the paragraphs that follow, we propose an approach which would allow Members to adopt a Competition Agreement meeting our requirements.[87] This approach can be summarised in six main points.

First, we believe that a Competition Agreement should focus exclusively on rules that address cross-border issues of market access such as

[87] This proposed approach shares many similarities with the proposal made by Eleanor Fox in 'Competition Law and the Millennium Round', *Journal of International Economic Law* 4 (1999): 665.

horizontal and vertical restraints designed to foreclose market access on the part of foreign competitors or abuses of dominant position seeking to exclude such competitors. Ensuring such market access is arguably one of the most powerful tools that can be used to promote competition in the telecommunications sector, as well as in the other sectors where Members have made commitments, and even an imperfect application of such rules would likely bring some benefits (the same would not necessarily be true of rules designed to prevent, for example, mergers that would lead to an excessive consolidation of the market, as an imperfect application of those rules might well prevent certain types of merger that would be competitively beneficial). Focusing on cross-border issues of market access would have the additional advantage that the objectives of such rules would be very closely aligned with the overall objectives of the WTO.

Secondly, in order to provide for a maximum degree of flexibility, a list of prohibited practices could be inserted in the Competition Agreement but the precise content of the rules would, however, be left to the discretion of the Members, which would only be bound by an obligation of 'result'.

Thirdly, while a Competition Agreement should leave Members free to develop their own approaches to meet the requirement of protecting market access, it should, however, contain a number of core principles on which there is a large international consensus and which can already be found in several WTO instruments, including transparency, non-discrimination and procedural fairness in the application of competition law.[88] This would ensure that the effectiveness of the national rules developed to protect market access would not be impeded by opaque or discriminatory procedures putting foreign operators at a disadvantage.

Fourthly, in order to address the concern expressed by some Members, in particular the United States, that the WTO panels and the Appellate Body might be tempted to second-guess the decisions adopted by national competition authorities, we propose that WTO dispute settlement bodies should only be authorised to verify whether a Member has complied with its obligation to adopt domestic rules necessary to ensure that market access is not impeded by public or private anti-competitive practices, as well as to uphold the core principles we described in the preceding paragraph.

[88] See Robert D. Anderson and Peter Holmes, 'Competition Policy and the Future of the Multilateral Trading System', (2002) *Journal of International Economic Law* 5 (2002): 531 at 550.

Fifthly, any agreement on competition rules should also include an obligation that Members set up an enforcement body. Once again, Members should be free to decide on the specific features of this body, but they should be bound to create formal institutional mechanisms to ensure that competition rules are properly enforced. In addition, the Competition Agreement should include modalities for cooperation between Members on competition policy issues, as well as a series of measures designed to provide technical assistance to the competition authorities of developing countries. Technical assistance is already provided in many countries by the EC and the United States, but some degree of coordination at WTO level might be helpful.

Sixthly, we suggest that, if a Competition Agreement were to be adopted, some amendments to existing agreements would be necessary. Paragraph 1 should be taken out of the Reference Paper and all competition-related provisions found in other WTO agreements should probably be eliminated as well. In order to ensure that a coherent approach is adopted across sectors, it would indeed be preferable that competition issues be addressed by a single set of rules. Note, however, that the other paragraphs of the Reference Paper would remain entirely relevant as they go beyond what is generally found in competition law provisions.

It is difficult to know at this stage whether the results negotiations taking place in the framework of the Doha Round will be compatible with our proposed approach.[89] The proposals submitted by the delegations appear to share some of the elements of our proposed approach.[90]

First, current proposals do not aim at a comprehensive 'harmonisation' of competition rules, but instead suggest that, if some competition rules and principles were adopted at the WTO level, Members should be left with broad scope to develop their own national approaches. This is consistent with our view that Members should only be bound by an obligation of 'result' (i.e. to adopt rules necessary to prevent anti-competitive measures impeding market access), while they should to a large extent be free to choose the means of achieving that result.

Secondly, like our proposed approach, current proposals foresee a limited role for the WTO dispute settlement system. Delegations in favour of a Competition Agreement suggests that the WTO enforcement bodies should only be allowed to check whether Members have complied with the

[89] For a good discussion of these proposals, see *ibid.*, p. 557.

[90] See the 2002 Report of the Working Group on the Interaction Between Trade and Competition Policy to the General Council, WT/WGTCP/6, 9 December 2002.

basic commitment to adopt a national competition legislation complying with the rules and principles contained in the Competition Agreement, and to set up an enforcement body. By contrast, the content of the decisions adopted by the national enforcement bodies should not be reviewed by the WTO dispute settlement system.

Thirdly, like us, the authors of these proposals insist on the importance of establishing modalities for cooperation between Members over competition issues, as well as providing technical assistance programmes to developing countries. Most delegations appear to be in favour of an approach whereby cooperation between Members should be on a purely voluntary basis.

A point of disagreement, however, between these current proposals and our proposed approach is that these proposals do not seem to place much emphasis on cross-border market access.[91] Rather, they suggest that a Competition Agreement should contain a commitment by Members to a set of core principles, including transparency, non-discrimination and procedural fairness in the application of competition law and policy, as well as a commitment to adopt measures against hardcore cartels. We agree that these core principles should be found in any Competition Agreement, but we do not see any reason why Members should only commit themselves to take measures against hardcore cartels. This approach is under-inclusive because hardcore cartels are only one kind of anti-competitive practice that may impede cross-border market access. To the extent that other practices, such as abuses of a dominant position or vertical restrictions, can have a negative impact on market access, we see no valid reason not to commit Members to adopt measures to prevent such practices. It is also probably over-inclusive because the anti-competitive effects of hardcore cartels may, in some cases, be entirely contained within a single domestic market and it can be argued that the WTO is not the right forum to tackle purely domestic issues.

Conclusions

Controlling market power and preventing anti-competitive practices is of central importance to ensure that liberalisation of telecommunications markets yields its full potential benefits. National legislations are very unequal in that respect. Some countries are better equipped than others and the variance between different national approaches is very large. Attempts

[91] See Anderson and Holmes, 'Competition Policy', p. 559.

to provide a more uniform framework at the international level should therefore be encouraged.

The Reference Paper is a step in the right direction. It could, however, be strengthened to reach a better balance between three main objectives: precision, simplicity and flexibility. In most cases, this would mean increasing the degree of precision of the provisions of the Reference Paper, as the current document tends to be very general. This can be achieved by tightening existing substantive rules or by adding new ones. However, in order not to lose too much flexibility, increased precision may at times be obtained, not by specifying substantive provisions in great detail, but by offering Members some choices between different, well-defined solutions, or by strengthening procedural rather than substantive rules.

Assuming that this could be done, a case could still be made for adopting a Competition Agreement. Such an agreement could be helpful to prohibit some anti-competitive behaviour that would still remain unaddressed in the Reference Paper and to protect operators against anti-competitive behaviours beyond the narrow scope of telecommunications activities. We believe, however, that, if such additional competition provisions were to be adopted, they should probably focus only on improving cross-border market entry. Indeed, improving cross-border market access is arguably one of the most powerful tools for promoting competition in liberalised markets; it is also an objective that is very closely aligned with those of the WTO; and, last but not least, the risk that regulatory capture or incompetence might spawn decisions that would actually have a harmful impact on competition is arguably more limited when regulators are asked to implement market-opening rules than when they have to apply other types of competition rules.

PART III

International regulation of audio-visual services

7

Audio-visual policy: the stumbling block of trade liberalisation?

CHRISTOPH BEAT GRABER

A historical perspective

Observers of recent developments in international trade law may remember that audio-visual media was a hot issue at the end of the Uruguay Round in 1993. There was a dispute dividing two groups of countries. The first group was made up of governments conceiving audio-visual media as entertainment products, which do not differ from any other products. They wanted audio-visual media to be subject to the rules of trade liberalisation in the services sector. The second group consisted of countries conceiving audio-visual media as cultural products, i.e. as vectors of the fundamental values and ideas of a society. The slogan of this second group was the notorious 'cultural exception'.[1] The whole debate had the structure of an all-or-nothing issue and provoked highly emotional reactions in the media. The general impression was that of a wide gap dividing two completely different ways of conceiving audio-visual media without much hope for bridging it. In the very last moment of the negotiations, however, it was possible to find a compromise: while it was decided that audio-visual services are covered by the GATS, Members agreed on a flexible method of liberalisation[2] allowing each country to refrain from making any specific commitments on market access and national treatment in relation to audio-visual services and to put measures related to film and television programmes on a list of exceptions to the general obligation of most-favoured nation treatment.[3] But this time off

[1] See C. B. Graber, 'Exception culturelle. Une revendication dépassée', *Courrier de la Planète* 55 (2000): 46.

[2] This flexibility of the GATS is not limited to audio-visual services but applies to all sectors.

[3] See C. B. Graber, 'WTO: A Threat to European Films?', in Enrique Banus, ed., *Proceedings of the V Conference 'European Culture', 28–31 October 1998* (Elcano: University of Navarra at Pamplona, Aranzadi Editorial, 2000), pp. 865–78 at p. 865.

for culture would only last for a certain period of time because Members have furthermore agreed that audio-visual media are subject to the principle of progressive liberalisation (Article XIX of the GATS) obligating them to reconsider the respective lists in future rounds of negotiation.

This paper aims at providing an analysis of the tension between trade liberalisation and audio-visual policy with a view to the services negotiations within the Doha Round. It starts with an assessment of the proposals related to audio-visual services which were submitted by Members. After a short overview of the structure of the relevant WTO law, the paper proceeds to undertake a typology of measures of national audio-visual policy in order to get a better view on actual and potential conflicts with principles of trade liberalisation. The paper then explores the range of flexibility the law of the WTO is able to offer to countries which – because of cultural policy reasons – may not be able or may not wish to accept a higher level of liberalisation in the area of audio-visual media. It concludes by addressing some open questions which most probably will be of importance in the realm of audio-visual services negotiations of the Doha Round.

Audio-visual services in the Doha negotiations

General remark

Following the built-in agenda of Article XIX of the GATS, Members started negotiations in January 2000 in order to achieve a higher standard of liberalisation of services, including audio-visual services. These negotiations remained dormant until they were fuelled by the positive results of the Doha Ministerial Conference in November 2001 to follow a request-offer approach based on the existing lists of commitments.[4] While initial requests were due for 30 June 2002, initial offers had to be presented before 31 March 2003.

In the context of these negotiations, at the time of writing five countries made submissions relevant to audio-visual media. Of these, three countries presented specific communications and two dedicated a section of their horizontal GATS communications to audio-visual services. Before a detailed analysis of the specific communications from the United States,

[4] According to Paragraph 15 of the Doha Declaration (World Trade Organization, Doha Ministerial Declaration, adopted on 14 November 2001, WT/MIN(01)/DEC/1), these negotiations are to be integrated into the larger framework of the new comprehensive trade round.

Brazil and Switzerland is provided, a brief look at the two horizontal communications submitted by Japan[5] and Canada,[6] might be helpful in order to provide a full view of the situation. Japan[7] states that the liberalisation of audio-visual services 'is important for respecting the right of the citizens of each Member to free access to a variety of cultures and information'. Japan expects from the negotiations in this sector that progress in liberalisation will be achieved with regard to the following issues: exemptions of MFN treatment in providing services; quantitative limitations; and deviations from the obligation of national treatment. Canada's communication in pertinent part is radically different, declaring that it 'will . . . not make any commitment that restricts our ability to achieve our cultural policy objective until a new international instrument, designed specifically to safeguard the right of countries to promote and preserve their cultural diversity, can be established'.[8]

Communication from the United States

The Communication from the United States[9] is the most important and influential of the three specific submissions. It is based on three interrelated elements. First, the United States wants to trigger a discussion on whether the classification of the different activities within the Members' lists of commitments should be reviewed. One option – with regard to audio-visual services – would be to replace the old 'services sectoral classification list' with a new structure consisting of 'theatrical motion pictures' (production, distribution and exhibition of movies); 'television' (production and sale of programmes including advertising); 'home video entertainment' (production, duplication and distribution of home video entertainment); 'transmission services' (terrestrial, cable- and satellite-based transmission of broadcasts); and 'recorded music' (production,

[5] Communication from Japan, 'The Negotiations on Trade in Services', S/CSS/W/42, 22 December 2000, paras. 36–7.

[6] Communication from Canada, 'Initial Canadian Negotiating Proposals', S/CSS/W/46, 14 March 2001, and S/CSS/W/46/Corr.1, 23 March 2001.

[7] According to Paragraph 15 of the Doha Declaration, these negotiations are to be integrated into the larger framework of the new comprehensive trade round.

[8] On the French-Canadian project for a new international instrument protecting cultural diversity, see I. Bernier and H. Ruiz Fabri, 'Evaluation de la faisabilité juridique d'un instrument international sur la diversité culturelle', available at www.mcc.gouv.ca/international/diversite-culturelle/publications.htm (5 May 2002).

[9] Communication from the United States, 'Audiovisual and Related Services', S/CSS/W/21, 18 December 2000.

duplication and distribution of sound recordings). Secondly, Members are requested to increase their commitments in the audio-visual sector. Thirdly, the US proposes to develop an agreement concerning disciplines for subsidies in the area of audio-visual services. Such an agreement 'will respect each nation's need to foster its cultural identity by creating an environment to nurture local culture'. The proposed disciplines might follow the example of the existing Agreement on Subsidies and Countervailing Measures (SCM).

All of the above three proposals may have far-reaching consequences, as will be argued below. Furthermore, some interesting insight may be drawn from the analysis of Annex B of the US proposal. In an apparently neutral manner, the United States lists a number of companies engaged in global activities in the audio-visual sector and therefore supposed to have a natural interest in trade liberalisation. However, the list cannot truly qualify as being exhaustive. The companies listed are mainly based in developing countries. Brazil, for instance, is mentioned several times, and some smaller European and Canadian companies also appear, while the big US multinational media companies are missing. This very list turned out to be a subtle wake-up call for those developing countries possessing expanding export industries in the area of audio-visual services, which is particularly the case for Brazil, India and Mexico.

Communication from Brazil

It appears that Brazil was woken up by the US proposal. As a consequence, in its submission Brazil requests Members to generally increase their level of commitments in the audio-visual services sector.[10] Brazil stresses that special attention should be given to the interests of developing countries; television services are mentioned in particular. On the other hand, Brazil is willing to assure the margin of flexibility which governments need for achieving their cultural policy objectives. Therefore Brazil explicitly respects the Member's rights 'to preserve and promote cultural identity and cultural diversity'. Furthermore, Brazil proposes to create an agreement concerning subsidies for the production and distribution of motion pictures. Brazil wants to assure that such subsidies have the least trade-distorting effect, given the very different capacities of Members to subsidise domestic industries. Finally, Brazil proposes to develop rules against dumping and unfair trade. Such rules should serve to fight

[10] Communication from Brazil, 'Audiovisual Services', S/CSS/W/99, 9 July 2001.

unfair advantages and behaviour resulting from an oligopolistic structure of global media markets, particularly the dominance of the global media enterprises.

Communication from Switzerland

The Swiss submission is phrased more as a discussion paper than as a formal proposal.[11] Members are invited to overcome the all-or-nothing type of discussion of the Uruguay Round in the area of audio-visual media. The aim is to find ways for a sustainable protection of cultural diversity in the area of audio-visual media. According to Switzerland, a safeguard for cultural diversity is necessary, because cultural diversity has emerged as a broadly accepted short-cut formula for a public policy objective to counterbalance cultural dysfunctions of the global media markets. The Swiss submission, however, does not specify what exactly the notions of cultural diversity and cultural identity mean.

Switzerland furthermore suggests thinking about disciplines for subsidies in the area of audio-visual services. Finally, it proposes to consider the introduction of some kind of competition rules. According to Switzerland, such rules would be desirable because 'a growing vertical integration across the industry reinforces the fears of anti-competitive behaviours such as abuse of dominant positions'.

Preliminary conclusion

The discussion concerning the liberalisation of audio-visual media in the Doha Round once again risks becoming the stumbling block for the whole services sector. As shown by the above-outlined submissions, there is still a very wide gap separating the countries with strong export interests from those wanting to protect their domestic industries for cultural and/or economic reasons. The proposed reclassification of the lists of commitments appears at first glance as only a mere technical endeavour. A closer look reveals that it might have quite far-reaching consequences leading to a situation in which issues that previously were ruled under the title of broadcasting now become subject to regulation as telecommunications.[12] This change could be difficult to accept for those countries which agree on liberalisation in telecommunications but exclude it in the sector of

[11] Communication from Switzerland, 'GATS 2000: Audiovisual Services', S/CSS/W/74, 4 May 2001.

[12] For a detailed discussion of this issue, see pp. 208–10 below.

audio-visual services for media policy reasons. As will further be shown below, developing disciplines for subsidies in the audio-visual sector may challenge the system of public service broadcasting operated in Europe and Canada.

It is clear that the United States – as the strongest proponent of further liberalisation in this sector – will again face radical opposition mainly from the European Communities[13] and Canada. Developing countries like Brazil, Egypt and Mexico are likely to play a more active role in defending the specific interests of their emerging media industries. In this situation, the Swiss proposal advocating a cultural diversity safeguard as a counterbalance to a further liberalisation could be helpful. As a precondition, however, it would be necessary to find a definition of cultural diversity which does not further economic protectionism. This latter issue will be elaborated on below.

Agreements currently relevant to audio-visual media: a rough overview

General remark

Trade in audio-visual media is a crosscutting issue which in principle can be relevant under the GATT, the GATS and the TRIPs Agreement. The TRIPs Agreement cannot be analysed in this study due to space limitations, but it should be mentioned that it is of crucial importance for audio-visual media because the TRIPs Agreement incorporates the Berne Copyright Convention into WTO law.[14] This leads to two important consequences: first, the national treatment obligation of the Berne Convention applies to all WTO Members including those states which are not parties to this Convention. And, secondly, conflicts concerning the international protection of copyrights are subject to the compulsory dispute

[13] In the ongoing negotiations, the EC remained silent on audio-visual media. But in a meeting which took place immediately before the Doha Ministerial Conference, the Council of the EC agreed on a resolution recalling a decision made preparatory to the Seattle Ministerial Conference in 1999 that '[d]uring the forthcoming WTO negotiations the Union will ensure, as in the Uruguay Round, that the Community and its Member States maintain the possibility to preserve and develop their capacity to define and implement their cultural and audio-visual policies for the purpose of preserving their cultural diversity'. See 2381st Council Meeting, Cultural Audiovisual Meeting at Brussels, Press Release, Brussels, 5 November 2001, Press: 377 No. 13126/01.

[14] Berne Convention for the Protection of Literary and Artistic Works, revised at Paris on 24 July 1971. This Convention, *inter alia*, obliges contracting states to treat foreign holders of copyrights no less favourably than their own nationals.

settlement procedures of the WTO. This is a fact which constitutes an important change in the enforcement of existing international copyright conventions.[15]

GATT or GATS?

According to the 'services sectoral classification list',[16] which is used by the WTO as a structural framework for the audiovisual sector,[17] all types of production, distribution and exhibition of audio-visual media are subject to the GATS. Nevertheless, some issues remain not entirely clear, for example whether a tax on the ticket sale of movie theatres or trade in television programmes should be considered as covering trade in services exclusively. In its 'Canada – Periodicals' and 'Banana' judgments, the Appellate Body held that GATT and GATS do not exclude each other.[18] On the contrary, it may be possible that certain aspects of the same governmental measure are subject to the GATT and others are subject to the GATS. Since the effects of the non-discrimination principles in the GATT are stronger than in the GATS,[19] the preferred strategy of a plaintiff naturally is to allege a violation of the GATT in order to challenge another Member's trade-restrictive measures of cultural policy. One example may confirm this thesis: in June 1996, the US requested consultations with Turkey regarding the taxation of foreign film revenues.[20] The object of the dispute was a tax which Turkey levied on box office receipts from the exhibition of *foreign* films exclusively. The US took the view that this cinema tax infringed upon the national treatment commitment of Article III of the GATT. The dispute was settled by mutual agreement on 24 July

15 B. de Witte, 'Trade in Culture: International Legal Regimes and EU Constitutional Values', in G. de Burca and J. Scott, eds., *The EU and the WTO: Legal and Constitutional Issues* (Oxford and Portland, OR: Hart, 2001), pp. 237 ff. at p. 247.

16 Multilateral Trade Negotiations, the Uruguay Round Group of Negotiations on Services, Services Sectoral Classification List, Note by the Secretariat, MTN.GNS/W/120, 10 July 1991.

17 World Trade Organization, Council for Trade in Services, Audiovisual Services, Background Note by the Secretariat, S/C/W/40, 15 June 1998, p. 1.

18 WTO Appellate Body Report, 'Canada – Certain Measures Concerning Periodicals', WT/DS31/AB/R, 30 June 1997, para. IV; WTO Appellate Body Report, 'European Communities – Regime for the Importation, Sale and Distribution of Bananas', WT/DS27/AB/R, 9 September 1997, para. IV.C.1.

19 For an explanation, see p. 172 below.

20 'Turkey – Taxation of Foreign Film Revenues', WT/DS43/1, Request for Consultations by the United States of 17 June 1996.

1997 after Turkey accepted to equalise the tax in such a way that domestic films would be covered by it as well.[21]

Coverage of the GATS and summary of specific commitments of WTO Members

GATS coverage

According to Article I of the GATS, all internationally traded services are covered by the GATS. One exception applies: Article I: 3(b) states that 'services supplied in the exercise of governmental authority' are excluded. Article I: 3(c) gives some further indication, stating that such governmental services include any service which is supplied neither on a commercial basis nor in competition with other service suppliers. But would this mean that public service broadcasting meeting the conditions of Article I: 3(c) is excluded from the GATS? Article VIII indirectly gives a negative answer setting specific rules for monopolies and exclusive service suppliers. Since public service broadcasters generally benefit from exclusive or monopolistic rights granted by national law, they are covered by this Article and thus are subject to the GATS.

The principles of national treatment and most-favoured nation treatment were originally developed for trade in goods. In order to apply these principles to the particularities of trade in services some adaptations were necessary. Market access to trade in goods can be limited through customs tariffs. Thus the elimination of quantitative import restrictions does not prevent governments from imposing import regulations, which can be politically essential in areas of sensitive goods like agriculture. As services are naturally without frontiers, there is no possibility of regulating the imports of services by means of customs tariffs. Hence, it was necessary – in the Uruguay Round – to find another solution to give governments an appropriate instrument for dealing with the market access of foreign services and service suppliers. The solution found consists of lists of specific commitments for market access and national treatment. According to Article XVII of the GATS, a Member is obliged to apply the principle of national treatment only to those sub-sectors and divisions of sub-sectors which are listed in its individual list.

[21] 'Turkey – Taxation of Foreign Film Revenues', WT/DS43/3, Notification of Mutually Agreed Solution, 24 July 1997.

Summary of specific commitments

Table 7.1 shows that until November 2001 only twenty-four countries accepted commitments in the sector of audio-visual services.

Most of these commitments are listed in the category 'Motion picture and videotape production and distribution services' (02.D.a). Full commitments in all six categories were accepted only by Albania, the Central African Republic and the US. New Zealand and Kyrgyzstan committed to five, Panama, Lesotho, Georgia and Gambia to four and Hong Kong, Japan and Jordan to three categories. Neither the EC, its Member States nor Canada made any commitments.

Typology of specific measures of national cultural policy in the area of audio-visual media

The aim of this part of the paper is to offer a *typology* of measures of governmental audio-visual policy. Hence, it is not about establishing an exhaustive inventory, but rather about identifying typical measures as well as some of their actual or potential points of conflict with the law of the WTO. The compatibility with the law of the WTO will be examined in some detail only in those cases which, in the past, led to formal or informal disputes. The focus is on measures of *audio-visual and cultural policy* which excludes all those national regulations serving the cause of public morals, the rights of privacy, the protection of minors, and so on.

Subsidies

Level of the individual states

Subsidies are the financially most important governmental measures in the audio-visual area. In Europe particularly, but also in Canada, the domestic audio-visual industry is, to a great extent, supported by public funds. In Europe, France offers the largest amounts for the promotion of the national film industry,[22] followed by Germany[23] and the United

[22] Every year, the French audio-visual industry is subsidised by €33.5 million from the budget of the Ministry for the Arts. In addition, there are payments of about €200 million generated by contributions from cinema admissions and turnovers from television companies and video dealers (see also pp. 185–6 below). Although these funds come from the audio-visual industry itself, it can be assumed that they will be viewed as subsidies under the law of the WTO. For a definition of 'subsidy' within the law of the WTO, see pp. 207–8 below.

[23] According to Paragraph 1 of the *Gesetz über Massnahmen zur Förderung des deutschen Films* (FFG) of 6 August 1998, BGB1. I 2046, the *Filmförderungsanstalt* (FFA) is responsible

Table 7.1

Country	Motion picture and videotape production and distribution services (02.D.a)	Motion picture projection services (02.D.b)	Radio and television services (02.D.c)	Radio and television transmission services (02.D.d)	Sound recording (02.D.e)	Other (02.D.f)	Total
Albania	•	•	•	•	•	•	6
Central African Republic	•	•	•	•	•	•	6
Dominican Republic						•	2
El Salvador				•		•	2
Gambia	•	•	•	•			4
Georgia	•	•	•		•		4
Hong Kong	•				•	•	3
India	•						1
Israel	•						1
Japan	•	•			•		3
Jordan	•	•			•		3
Kenya	•	•					2
Korea (South)	•				•		2
Kyrgyzstan	•	•	•	•	•		5
Lesotho	•	•	•	•			4
Malaysia	•			•			2

Mexico	•	•					2
New Zealand	•	•	•	•		•	5
Nicaragua	•	•					2
Oman	•	•					2
Panama	•	•	•		•		4
Singapore	•				•		2
Thailand	•		•				2
United States	•	•	•	•	•	•	6
Total	22	15	11	10	10	7	75

Source : WTO Secretariat, November 2001.

Kingdom.[24] The main focus of these state aids is on supporting the *production* of films with national origin. While traditional schemes of film promotion funded projects on a selective basis, the instrument of *automatic* support has become more and more significant in the last few years. This scheme aims at automatically rewarding the success of a film at the box office thus supplementing existing selective film promotion with a measure responding to market performance.[25] Furthermore, most European countries have a system of *public service* television, thus rewarding certain broadcasting operators with subsidies or revenues from licence fees for supplying a valuable service with regard to cultural policy.

To give an example of a country with a small audio-visual industry, Switzerland has a total annual budget for the promotion of cinema which amounts to about half of what is being spent on advertising for an average Hollywood movie.[26] More notable, though, are the annual funds from licence fees which go to the *Schweizerische Radio- und*

for the support of films on the national level. Section 2 of the FFG entrusts the FFA with supplementing the activities of the federal states in the promotion of films, and provides for financing from public funds. In 2000, the FFA invested a total of about DM120 million in support of films (see FFA intern, No. 1/2001 of 5 February 2001, p. 16). The FFA must use 40 per cent of its funds for promoting the production of full-length films (reference films, see section 22 of the FFG), 30 per cent for marketing, and the remainder for the support of screenplays and projects and further education (Section 67a of the FFG). In addition to the FFA, in 2000 the federal government official responsible for cultural affairs and media invested DM26.6 million on the national level. The majority of film subsidies, though, came from the governments of the German *Länder*, which contributed a total of about DM220 million. See FFA intern, No. 1/2001 of 5 February 2001, p. 16.

[24] The Films Act 1985 ended the tax on cinema admissions, which had been the main source of income for film support in the UK since 1951, and replaced it by a system of loans by the National Lottery and tax incentives. See British Film Institute, *BFI Film and Television Handbook* (London: British Film Institute, 2000), p. 250. Using National Lottery funds, the Films Council grants loans to film projects which would not otherwise be financially viable. In 1999, a total of €27.8 million flowed from this source into the production of cinematographic works. Although in principle these loans are repayable, in reality less than 10 per cent are paid back (*ibid.*, p. 31).

[25] In France, today's share of the automatic film support is 60 per cent. See M. Zitzmann, 'Asterix contra Sauron: Die französische Filmwirtschaft und ihre Erfolgsrezepte', *Neue Zürcher Zeitung*, 7 January 2002.

[26] In 1998, the Swiss Confederation had CHF 21 million at its disposal for all activities in the audio-visual sector, of which about 45 per cent flowed into the production of films. See Botschaft des Bundesrates zum Bundesgesetz über Filmproduktion und Filmkultur, 18 September 2000, BB1. 2000, 5436. In comparison with this, in the same year the average marketing budget for an Hollywood movie amounted to US$25.3 million. See Motion Picture Association of America (MPAA), 'Worldwide Market Research 1998', www.mpaa.org/useconomicreview/1998/sld018.htm (19 December 2001).

Fernsehgesellschaft (SRG), the Swiss public service broadcasting company, amounting to more than CHFn 1.1 billion 2000.

Outside Europe, Canada is the biggest subsidiser of the audio-visual industry. The Canadian state supports public broadcasting with more than C$1 billion per year.[27] From 1996 to 1997, more than C$30 million flowed from the Feature Film Fund to the production of cinematographic works, and the Canadian Television Fund fosters domestic television film production by granting an annual sum of approximately C$200 million. Furthermore, Canada subsidises the music industry, the publishing industry and the press with non-repayable state subsidies, interest-free loans or reduced transport charges.[28]

In the US, governmental support of film production is non-existent.[29] The National Endowment for the Arts (NEA) supported movie projects on a modest scale until the 1990s, but then withdrew from the audio-visual sector.[30] Nonetheless, state subsidies have been flowing indirectly into the broadcasting sector since 1998 as part of the US anti-drug policy. The US government places anti-drug commercials with TV companies whose programmes are in accordance with the official anti-drug policy. Thus, the US government indirectly helps these companies to bear their costs.[31]

European level

The European Community The EC's Media Programme supports the audio-visual industry. As a result of the EC's limited remit on cultural affairs,[32] the funds available are far lower than those of some of the

[27] See Canadian Industries Cultural Advisory Group on International Trade, 'Canadian Culture in a Global World', February 1999, www.infoexport.gc.ca/trade-culture, p. 8 (26 October 2001).

[28] *Ibid.*, pp. 11–12. For more information on Canada's support of the domestic periodicals industry, see WTO Appellate Body Report, 'Canada – Certain Measures Concerning Periodicals', WT/DS31/AB/R, 30 June 1997.

[29] See D. E. Biederman *et al.*, *Law and Business of the Entertainment Industries* (4th edn, Westport, CT: Praeger, 2001), p. 639.

[30] See C. Vachon, *Shooting to Kill: How an Independent Producer Blasts Through the Barriers to Make Movies that Matter* (New York: Avon, 1998), pp. 297ff. In the GATS commitment list of the US, there still exists an entry enabling the National Endowment for the Arts to restrict its aid exclusively to US citizens or foreigners with an establishment permit.

[31] Until autumn 2000, public funds of US$21.8 million flowed to television companies. See the report of M. von Arx, *Neue Zürcher Zeitung*, 3 November 2000.

[32] Because the EC's cultural mandate is not an exclusive responsibility of the Community, the subsidiarity principle applies (Article 5 of the EC Treaty). See G. Ress and J. Ukrow, 'Article 151 EGV', in E. Grabitz and M. Hilf, eds., *Das Recht der Europäischen Union: Kommentar*, 16th Supplement, Munich: C. H. Beck, 2000), para. 16. Accordingly, Article 151(2) of the EC Treaty limits the cultural competence of the Community to promoting

individual Member States. In contrast to the support given by the Member States or by the Council of Europe, the EC's Media Programme refrains from production funding. Instead, it centres on three activities of support: development of audio-visual projects; promotion of audio-visual programmes;[33] and the training of professionals.[34] 'Media Plus', which has been in force since 1 January 2001, has taken over the reins of the Media II programme. All three pillars exclusively foster projects which (within the Community) cross the borders of Member States. In the distribution sector, even more markedly than in the past, Media Plus puts particular emphasis on *automatic* support.[35] Whereas Media II was endowed with €310 million, Media Plus now has €400 million at its disposal.[36] The programme is now also open to the associated countries of Central and Eastern Europe, as well as to the parties to the Council of Europe's Convention on Transfrontier Television.[37]

The Council of Europe 'Eurimages' is a fund established by the Council of Europe which primarily promotes co-production in Europe.[38] In addition to production, Eurimages also supports on a modest scale film distributors as well as cinemas, restricting this aid to those states which do not already take part in the EC's Media Programme.[39] Eurimages may

the co-operation of the Member States and supporting and complementing the activities of the Member States.

[33] Council Decision 2000/821/EC of 20 December 2000 on the implementation of a programme to encourage the development, distribution and promotion of European audiovisual works (MEDIA PLUS – Development, Distribution and Promotion) (2001–2005), OJ L13/34, 17 January 2001.

[34] Decision No. 163/2001/EC of the European Parliament and of the Council, of 19 January 2001, on the implementation of a training programme for professionals in the European audio-visual programme industry (MEDIA training) (2001–2005), OJ L26/1, 27 January 2001.

[35] See European Commission, Principles and guidelines for the audio-visual policy of the Community in the digital age. Announcement of the Commission to the Council, to the European Parliament, to the Economic and Social Committee and to the Committee of the Regions, in COM(1999)657 final, 14 December 1999, pp. 22ff.

[36] In May 2001, the establishment of an investment fund aimed at the promotion of risk capital for film production was agreed upon. See Commission Press Release IP/01/717 of 18 May 2001. The European Investment Bank allocates €500 million in long-term loans to specialised banks intended for the production of major pan-European film projects.

[37] See Ress and Ukrow, 'Article 151 EGV', para. 127.

[38] Council of Europe, Resolution (88)15 of 26 October 1988.

[39] Thus the scope of this support is restricted to Bulgaria, the Czech Republic, Hungary, Poland, Romania, Slovakia, Slovenia, Turkey and Switzerland. See Article 1.2.1 of the Regulations (of the Board of Management) concerning distribution support for full length feature films, animation and documentaries, www.culture.coe.fr/

support the financing of a film with a repayable loan on condition that the film in question is a co-production in which at least two parties from two different contracting states participate.[40] Furthermore, the project is required to be European. In the appendix to the European Convention on Cinematographic Co-production, there is a schedule of European elements defining which cinematographic works qualify as European.[41] Economically promising and culturally interesting projects have to be pre-financed to different extents: while the financing of the former has to be secured by 75 per cent, Eurimages requests a coverage of only 50 per cent for the latter. There is a general upper limit for promotion funds which does not apply to culturally interesting projects; in return, proof of the participation of a public institution for support must be produced.

Restrictions on market access and national treatment

Import quotas

The general prohibition of quantitative import restrictions in Article XI of the GATT[42] also applies to the imposition of quotas in the film industry. Before the WTO Agreement came into effect, a 'grandfather-exception' applied for Switzerland. If, at the moment of Switzerland's accession to the GATT of 1947, its national law already intended the imposition of import quotas, then the requirements of Part II of the GATT acknowledged this legal situation.[43] The WTO law put an end to the grandfather-rights of the GATT of 1947, so that they now can no longer be appealed to.[44]

Duties

Duties coming into effect when goods are crossing national borders are of secondary importance for the audio-visual sector. However, making use of customs duties in order to achieve cultural policy objectives is not excluded

Eurimages/eng/eeurprof.dis.html, 29 November 2001, and Article 1 of the Regulations (of the Board of Management) concerning assistance to cinemas, www.culture.coe.fr/Eurimages/eng/eeurprof.sal.html, 29 November 2001.

[40] Council of Europe, Resolution (88)15 of 26 October 1988.

[41] Council of Europe, European Convention on Cinematographic Co-production, of 2 October 1992, ETS No. 147. On this schedule, see in more detail p. 206 below.

[42] See pp. 197–200 below.

[43] See T. Cottier, 'Die völkerrechtlichen Rahmenbedingungen der Filmförderung in der neuen Welthandelsorganisation WTO-GATT', *Zeitschrift für Urheber- und Medienrecht* (1994): 749 at 751.

[44] See Articles XVI: 4 and XVI:5 of the Marrakech Agreement Establishing the World Trade Organization.

by the GATT. Recent decisions of the WTO Dispute Settlement Body show that national governments are given a certain leeway in specifying customs tariffs, provided that they comply with commitments in tariff schedules and are imposed in a non-discriminatory manner.[45]

Exhibition quotas

Cinema screen quotas Regulations which reserve a certain share of the total screen time in cinemas to domestic works fall into the category of measures restricting access to the domestic film market. Such *screen quotas* for cinemas are allowed by Article IV of the GATT and exist in France, Mexico, South Korea and Spain, to mention a few. The South Korean quotas and their compatibility with the GATT will be examined in detail below.

Television quotas Measures aiming at the promotion of programmes of a certain national origin exist, for instance, in the EC,[46] in the Council of Europe,[47] and in Australia,[48] Canada[49] and France.[50] Their effect is to

[45] See WTO Appellate Body Report, 'European Communities – Customs Classification of Certain Computer Equipment', WT/DS62/AB/R, WT/DS67/AB/R, WT/DS68/AB/R, 5 June 1998, paras. 74–99.

[46] See Articles 4 and 5 of Directive 97/36/EC of the European Parliament and the Council, amending Council Directive (89/552/EEC) of 3 October 1989 on the co-ordination of certain provisions laid down by law, regulation or administrative action in Member States concerning the pursuit of television broadcasting activities, OJ L202/60, 30 July 1997.

[47] Council of Europe, European Convention on Transfrontier Television (ECTT) of 5 May 1989, ETS No. 132, text amended according to the provisions of the Protocol (ETS No. 171) which entered into force on 1 March 2002. The relevant requirements of the ECTT concerning the cultural quotas (Article 10 in conjunction with Article 2(e)) have a weaker effect, though, due to the Council of Europe not disposing of a monitoring procedure comparable to the one the Commission of the EC successfully uses to implement its Directive.

[48] The Australian Content Standard was defined by the Australian Broadcasting Authority on 15 December 1995. Regulation 9 in Part 5 stipulates that 55 per cent of all programmes being broadcast between 6 a.m. and midnight must be of Australian origin. A second quota obliges pay-TV operators oriented towards fictional programmes to devote 10 per cent of their programme budget for new, domestically produced contents. The industry criticises these directives for being too narrow, particularly since they cover only fictional programmes and not pure entertainment shows. See also *Variety*, 1 May 2000.

[49] For further information on the fostering of Canadian content, see Canadian Industries Cultural Advisory Group on International Trade, note 27 above, pp. 10–13.

[50] France requires that a minimum of 60 per cent of all programmes broadcast between 6 p.m. and 9 p.m. (prime time) are of European origin. See J. D. Donaldson, '"Television Without Frontiers": The Continuing Tension Between Liberal Free Trade and European Cultural Integrity', *Fordham International Law Journal* 20 (1996): 90 at 103, n. 66.

restrict market access for other foreign TV programmes which are not subject to the privilege.

Taking a closer look at the cultural quotas set forth in the EC Directive 'Television Without Frontiers',[51] one has to distinguish two provisions: Article 4 of the Directive requires broadcasters to reserve for European works a majority of their transmission time in 'fiction' programmes.[52] According to Article 5 of the Directive, broadcasters must reserve at least 10 per cent of their transmission time in 'fiction' programmes or, alternately, at the discretion of the Member State, at least 10 per cent of their programming budget for European works created by producers independent of broadcasters. The difference between these two quotas lies in the fact that the former aims at increasing the diffusion of European works, whereas the latter aims at furthering the production of European works on the condition that producers are independent of broadcasters.[53] Article 6 of the Directive defines European works mainly as programming produced in the EU or in European third states which are parties to the European Convention on Transfrontier Television (ECTT) of the Council of Europe. According to Article 6(2), these works are mainly made with the participation of authors and workers residing in one or more European states, provided that they comply with one of the following three requirements:

1. they are made by one or more producers established in one or more of those states;
2. production of the works is supervised and controlled by one or more producers established in one or more of those states; or
3. the contribution of co-producers of those states to the total co-production costs is predominant and the co-production is not controlled by one or more producers established outside those states.

[51] Council Directive 89/552/EEC of 3 October 1989 on the coordination of certain provisions laid by law, regulation or administrative action in Member States concerning the pursuit of television broadcasting activities, OJ L298/23, as amended by Directive 97/36/EC of the European Parliament and of the Council, OJ L202/60.

[52] More precisely, Articles 4 and 5 of the TV Directive require EU Member States to observe the quotas in all programmes, excluding 'news, sports events, games, advertising, teletext services and teleshopping'.

[53] The term 'production', used in conjunction with cinematographic works, has a specific meaning, including both raising the funds necessary for the financing of the project and the creative function of initiating, controlling and supervising the whole process of the film production.

Furthermore, Article 6(5) provides that works which are not European works (in the sense explained above), but made mainly by authors and workers residing in one or more Member States, shall be considered to be European works to the extent corresponding to the proportion of the contribution of Community co-producers to the total production costs.

Both quotas shall be respected 'where practicable'. Although they are not formulated in a legally binding way, they are in fact binding due to an obligation on Member States to report on a biennial basis to the Commission on their observation of Articles 4 and 5 and to give reasons for any deviations therefrom. In particular, this report must contain a statistical overview from which it can be determined to what extent these quotas were respected. The Commission then informs the rest of the Member States as well as the European Parliament of these reports. If necessary, the Commission is obliged to enforce Articles 4 and 5 by means of a complaint to the European Court of Justice.

The Motion Picture Association (MPA), representing the export interests of the US entertainment industry, considers these quotas as a tool of protectionism. According to the MPA, these cultural objectives are merely a pretext and, in reality, the quotas mainly serve the purpose of protecting the economic interests of domestic producers. This criticism, voiced not only by US authors,[54] but also by European authors,[55] is not completely unjustified. With regard to the principle of non-discrimination in the GATS, Article 6(5) of the Directive in particular appears to be problematic. Assume a film with a total duration of 100 minutes is made by an author residing in Italy and mainly with workers residing in Italy, France, Spain and the United Kingdom. If this film is financed 20 per cent by a producer established or residing in Italy and 80 per cent by US capital, it is considered, according to Article 6(5), to be a 'European work' to the extent of 20 minutes. If, however, 60 per cent of the total co-production costs are financed by a producer established or residing in Italy, the entire work counts as a European work, provided that in the sense of Article 6(2)(c) the co-production is not controlled by one or more producers established or residing outside Europe. This example shows how these rules discriminate against service suppliers who are not established or residing in Europe. Because it is easier for European producers than

[54] See Donaldson, "'Television Without Frontiers'", p. 154.

[55] For a criticism of the quotas from a European point of view, see B. J. Drijber, 'The Revised Television Without Frontiers Directive: Is It Fit for the Next Century?', *Common Market Law Review* 36(1999): 87 at 117ff.

for foreign producers to have their films recognised as 'European works', foreign service suppliers are treated less favourably within the meaning of Article XVII of the GATS.[56] Moreover, the criteria operating in Articles 4 to 6 of the Directive do not focus on subjects, themes or other elements which might serve as a specific means for the protection of European cultural values, but merely on the national origin of the producers, authors and workers. The Directive's quotas appear not to support cultural policy objectives but economic goals or, at least, there is no clear criterion according to which such a distinction could be made. In this line of reasoning, the twentieth recital to the Directive states clearly that the first priority of the quotas is to generate economies of scale:

> It is, therefore, necessary to promote markets of sufficient size for television productions in the Member States to recover necessary investments not only by establishing common rules opening up national markets but also by envisaging for European productions where practicable and by appropriate means a majority proportion in television programmes of all Member States.[57]

In this context, a comparison with the Australian practice concerning the cultural quotas of the Australian Content Standard may be of interest. In a judgment of 28 April 1998, the Australian High Court interpreted the term 'Australian content of programmes' in such a way as to relate it more closely to criteria specific to culture.[58] Australian content is assumed primarily in those cases where the topic of the transmitted programme reflects the Australian identity, character or culture. It is only of secondary importance whether the actors, authors or producers of the programme are Australian nationals.

Dubbing restrictions

Regulations restricting access to the domestic market include special limitations on the dubbing of foreign films which can be found in the laws of various countries.

[56] This applies, provided that the sector is scheduled in the list of commitments and no limitations are taken. For an explanation of the functioning of the GATS schedules, see pp. 200–1 below.
[57] 20th recital to the TV Directive 89/552/EEC.
[58] See judgment of the High Court of Australia, *Project Blue Sky* v. *Australian Broadcasting Authority* (1998) HCA 28, 28 April 1998, S41/1997, available at www.austlii.edu.au/au/cases (10 October 2001).

While Mexico prohibits the dubbing of all foreign films, a Spanish law provided for a dubbing licence until the 1990s. As Spanish public preference is, to a large extent, for US films when they were dubbed into one of the official languages of Spain, this instrument served to limit the market access of Hollywood movies. Furthermore, film distributors were entitled to a maximum of four licences for dubbing films originating in third countries for each Spanish film for which they had concluded a distribution contract. The *Federación de Distribuidores Cinematográficos* (Fedicine) filed a complaint at the European Court of Justice(ECJ) against these measures. The Spanish government stated in its defence that the regulation in question aimed at the cultural objective of protecting the domestic film production. The ECJ rejected this argument on the ground that distribution of domestic films was treated in a privileged manner taking into consideration neither content nor quality. The ECJ therefore concluded that the measure was not backed by legitimate cultural objectives.[59]

Licensing requirements

Measures restricting access to radio or television transmissions by means of licence requirements or similar regulatory barriers are also common. Several states make the granting of licences to foreign broadcasters conditional upon the domestic operators being granted a reciprocal right in the country in question. Switzerland, for example, made a reservation of that kind in its exemption list to Article II of the GATS.[60]

The Canadian Radiotelevision and Telecommunications Commission's (CRTC) practice of granting licences led to disputes between Canada and the US which were settled outside the WTO.[61] In 1994, the CRTC licensed a series of new Canadian pay and speciality services. While the operator New Country Network (NCN) received a transmission permit, the US speciality channel Country Music Television (CMT) was removed from the list of eligible services in spite of CMT's presence in the Canadian

[59] See ECJ Case C-17/92, *Federación de Distribuidores Cinematográficos* v. *Estado Español* [1993] ECR I-2239.

[60] See pp. 203–4 below.

[61] For detailed information on this case, see A. M. Carlson, 'The Country Music Television Dispute: An Illustration of the Tensions Between Canadian Cultural Protectionism and American Entertainment Exports', *Minnesota Journal of Global Trade* 6 (1997): 585 at 586ff.; and A. E. Lehmann, 'The Canadian Cultural Exemption Clause and the Fight to Maintain an Identity', 23 (1997): *Syracuse Journal of International Law and Commerce* 187 at 207ff.

market for more than ten years. At first, according to section 301 of the US Trade Act, the United States Trade Representative (USTR) opened a proceeding against the decision at the Federal Court of Canada, but then halted it when NCN and CMT merged.[62]

Taxes

There are numerous forms of taxation of audio-visual works which differ considerably. In France, for instance, the revenues from the sale of cinema tickets,[63] the incomes of broadcasting operators[64] as well as the revenues from the sale of videotapes[65] are subject to tax. Most of the French film promotion organised through the *Centre National de la Cinématographie* (CNC) is financed by these tax proceeds. The German *Filmförderungsanstalt des Bundes* (FFA), the federal agency responsible for film promotion, obtains its income in a similar way. In Brazil, a new audio-visual law was introduced which rewards investment in production by granting a 100 per cent tax-exemption. On the basis of this law, since 1995 more than US$180 million have flowed into seventy Brazilian production projects.[66] To conclude this list of examples, even Italy grants a rebate of cinema tax to those cinema operators who exhibit domestic films.

Taxes on revenues of cinemas, television operators and video dealers

The taxation of cinema revenues is a means for financing domestic film production which is practised in several European countries. Thus, Sweden takes a 10 per cent share of the gross box-office takings to pay

[62] The maximum amount of foreign investments permitted by the Investment Canada Act of 1985 is 20 per cent.

[63] For more information on the French tax on cinema tickets see p. 186 below.

[64] This tax was introduced in 1986; 5.5 percent of the total income (including licence fees and income from advertising) of those broadcasters having a French licence must be paid to the tax authorities. In 1996, a sum of €257 million was generated by this source. The *Centre national de la cinématographie* (CNC) spent 62 per cent thereof financing selected television programmes and 38 per cent on producing French cinema films. In a similar way, Switzerland levies a 2 per cent licence tax on the net incomes of private broadcasters and spends these funds on the promotion of the Swiss film industry.

[65] Since 1993 a 2 per cent tax has been charged on the sale and rental of recorded videotapes, which has contributed a total of €11.5 million to the CNC's budget. The CNC spends 15 per cent of this sum on financing movies and 85 per cent on the production of television programmes.

[66] See P. Straumann, 'Renaissance des brasilianischen Films? Positive Folgen des Audiovisions-Gesetzes', *Neue Zürcher Zeitung*, 20 April 2000.

for the Swedish Film Institute.[67] The Institute uses these funds to support the production of Swedish films.[68] France has imposed the *taxe spéciale additionnelle* on cinema tickets since 1948 which makes cinema admissions more expensive by 11 per cent. For 2001, the revenues generated by this tax were estimated to be €96.7 million.[69] This cinema tax was the main source for financing the activities of the CNC for a long time.[70] But nowadays much more significance is attached to the *compte de soutien de l'industrie cinématographique et de l'industrie des programmes audiovisuels* (COSIP) which has been in existence since 1984. In 2001, approximately €118 million flowed from this source to the CNC, equivalent to 36 per cent of the total revenues of the COSIP.[71] The COSIP is paid by television operators, which remit an average of 5.5 per cent of their annual incomes to this fund. Finally, there is also a 2 per cent tax imposed on the sale of videotapes for financing the CNC's activities. In Germany, too, a similar tax is levied. Section 66 of the *Gesetz über Massnahmen zur*

[67] According to the Swedish Film Institute, the proceeds from the levy on cinema tickets amounted to about €12 million in 2000. The legal basis for this financing may be found in Article 5 of the 2000 Film Agreement between the Swedish State, the film industry and the Swedish TV operators AB and TV 4 AB, which is valid from 1 January 2000 until 31 December 2004. Cinema operators are to remit contributions equivalent to 10 per cent of their gross box-office takings directly to the Swedish Film Institute (Article 7). Those operators refusing to agree to this commitment in writing are excluded from the distribution (Article 8). For further information on this topic, see www.sfi.se/eng/meng.htm (15 October 2001).

[68] According to Article 13 of the 2000 Film Agreement, the funds accruing to the Swedish Film Institute shall be used for subsidising the production of Swedish films (Articles 14ff) as well as for the distribution and exhibition mainly of Swedish films in Sweden (Articles 22ff) and film-related cultural activities in Sweden (Articles 29ff). According to Article 4, a film is deemed to be Swedish if its producer is Swedish and if a substantial proportion of the actors or other performers involved are Swedish. A 'Swedish producer' is defined as a natural person residing in Sweden or a legal person registered in Sweden. A film which does not have a Swedish producer in the above-mentioned sense may nevertheless be regarded as Swedish provided that at least 20 per cent of its production costs are financed by Swedish capital and a substantial proportion of the actors or other performers involved are Swedish.

[69] See Zitzmann, 'Asterix contra Sauron'.

[70] The CNC uses the funds at its disposal for financing the activities of the domestic film industry, mainly in the areas of production, distribution and exhibition. Although the CNC has the benefit of financial independence (being an institution incorporated under public law), it is under the control of the Ministry for the Arts. The ultimate responsibility for French film policy rests with the CNC, the legal basis of which is Decree 83-1084 of 8 December 1983. The Minister for the Arts acts as president of the CNC.

[71] See Zitzmann, 'Asterix contra Sauron'.

Förderung des deutschen Films (FFG)[72] provides that the FFA is financed by contributions imposed on the annual revenues of cinema operators (1.5–2 per cent) and of video dealers (1.8 per cent). According to Section 67 of the FFG, further proceeds flow to the FFA from contributions by private radio and television operators.

As a consequence of Hollywood's large share of the film market, the revenues used to foster domestic film production in the above countries are generated mainly by US works. Therefore, an interesting question is whether a contribution which is generated by products originating in one country only is in compliance with the obligation of national treatment. WTO law differentiates between receiving public funds and spending them. The exemption to the principle of national treatment, which is enshrined in Article III:8(b) of the GATT gives expression to this principle. This provision exclusively exempts *payments* of subsidies which flow directly to domestic producers.[73] Therefore, in 'Canada – Periodicals' the Appellate Body held that no exception applies in cases where a discriminatory *imposition of taxes* is practised:

> Indeed, an examination of the text, context and object and purpose of Article III:8(b) suggests that it was intended to exempt from the obligations of Article III only the *payment* of subsidies which involves the *expenditure of revenue* by a government.[74]

Conversely, it follows from this that Article III:8(b)of the GATT cannot be appealed to if the discriminatory imposition of a tax is challenged. This may be the reason why Turkey – in the dispute concerning the taxation of foreign film revenues as discussed above – was not able to neutralise the United States' contention of having violated Article III of the GATT. In contrast to the Turkish cinema tax, the taxes, as they apply in Sweden, France and Germany, are in accordance with Article III of the GATT from the outset due to their being imposed on all cinema admissions without differentiating between domestic and foreign films. From the perspective of the GATS, discriminatory cinema taxes, if any, are permissible, provided that the country in question has not accepted any specific commitment

[72] *Gesetz über Massnahmen zur Förderung des deutschen Films* (FFG) of 6 August 1998, BGBl. I 2046.

[73] See WTO Appellate Body Report, 'Canada – Certain Measures Concerning Periodicals', WT/DS31/AB/R, 30 June 1997, p. 23.

[74] *Ibid.*, p. 24 (emphasis added).

in its schedule.[75] With a view to ongoing negotiations, such measures are subject to potential requests for further liberalisation.

Tax cuts for domestic industries

Legislation in Canada[76] and in several European states provides for tax incentives for domestic film production. In the United Kingdom, for instance, UK film projects in the production phase are allowed to deduct a maximum amount of €15 million of the production costs from their taxable income. Completed films are subject to a 100 per cent tax-exemption.[77]

As explained above, discriminatory tax reductions cannot be justified under Article III:8(b) of the GATT, because they are related to the imposition of a tax. It is rather surprising that so far no proceedings have been initiated in connection with tax incentives for domestic film projects.

Copyright-based cultural funds[78]

Copyright laws in several European countries (and elsewhere, for example in Canada) guarantee secondary use rights such as a private copying right[79] or a retransmission right.[80] The revenues from these secondary use rights are often administered exclusively by a collecting society authorised by the government.[81] Such secondary rights schemes apply to national right holders as well as to foreign ones. Consequently, foreign

[75] Neither Turkey nor Sweden, France or Germany accepted any commitments in the audio-visual area. For an explanation of the functioning of the GATS schedules, see pp. 200–2 below.

[76] See I. Bernier, 'Cultural Goods and Services in International Trade Law', in Dennis Browne, ed., *The Culture/Trade Quandary: Canada's Policy Options* (Ottawa: Centre for Trade Policy and Law, 1998), p. 118.

[77] The legal basis of tax relief for UK film projects is the Finance (No. 2) Act 1997; see British Film Institute, *BFI Film and Television Handbook*, p. 252.

[78] Parts of this section are taken from M. Footer and C. B. Graber, 'Trade Liberalization and Cultural Policy', *Journal of International Economic Law* 3 (2000): 115 at 127f.

[79] As it is almost impossible to prevent private copying, many countries have introduced a private copying levy on blank audio and/or video recording media (audio and video cassettes and CD-ROMs), sometimes known as a 'blank levy'. For a presentation of the rules for compensation of private copying under Swiss copyright law, See Christoph Gasser, *Der Eigengebrauch im Urheberrecht* (Berne: Stämpfli, 1998), pp. 145–76.

[80] For an overview of the different schemes for collective administration of secondary use rights, see World Intellectual Property Organization, *Collective Administration of Copyright and Neighbouring Rights* (Geneva: WIPO, 1990).

[81] See Footer and Graber, 'Trade Liberalization', p. 128.

right holders, in order to be compensated for their works which subsist in these countries, are forced to have their secondary use rights administered by these collecting societies and to pay the relevant administration fee.[82] The collecting societies then reserve a proportion of the total revenues collected for their own cultural funds in order to subsidise projects involving local audio-visual production. Under French law, for instance, collecting societies use 25 per cent of their remuneration for private copies (including void videocassettes) for the promotion of local artists or artistic production.[83] Under Austrian law, less than 50 per cent of the proceeds go to the individual right holders.[84]

Since Hollywood movies generate the biggest share of the revenues flowing into the cultural funds, it comes as no surprise that the United States repeatedly alleged that these schemes of mandatory collective administration violate the national treatment obligation contained in Article 3 of TRIPs.[85] Although this was one of the contentious issues of the GATT Uruguay Round,[86] the US finally refrained from its claim for a just share in the benefits of such schemes in order not to endanger the conclusion of the negotiations. The US entertainment industry, however, was bitterly disappointed by this result of the Uruguay Round and appears unwilling to resign itself to this situation.[87]

Thus, it seems to be evident that in the Doha negotiations the United States will sooner or later request that the principle of national treatment

[82] Daniel Gervais, *The TRIPs Agreement: Drafting History and Analysis* (London: Sweet & Maxwell, 1998), pp. 74ff.

[83] See Article L 321-9 of the French *Code de la propriété intellectuelle* of 1 July 1992. See also Footer and Graber, 'Trade Liberalization', p. 128. The copying levy on blank audio-visual recording media was extended to digital data carriers such as blanks CDs or DVDs by means of a revision of the French copyright law which came into force on 22 January 2001. This tax increases the price for a recordable blank DVD by FFR24.75. For the situation in Canada, see Canadian Industries Cultural Advisory Group on International Trade, note 27 above, p. 16.

[84] See WIPO, note 80 above, p. 50.

[85] See Bernier, 'Cultural Goods and Services', pp. 142f.

[86] See T. P. Stewart, ed., *The GATT Uruguay Round: A Negotiating History (1986–1994)*, vol. IV, *The End Game* (Part I) (The Hague, London and Boston: Kluwer, 1999), p. 512; Gervais, *The TRIPs Agreement*, pp. 74ff.

[87] The International Intellectual Property Alliance, representing the interests of the US entertainment industry, commented on the conclusion of these negotiations as follows: 'The result is that, on the intellectual property issues, we are left with an inadequate national treatment provision which preserves in part the ability of the Europeans and others to discriminate against our works, and unless we are able to find a remedy in other forums, will cause continued losses to the United States.' Quoted in Stewart, *The GATT Uruguay Round*, p. 527, n. 476.

be applied to the spending of revenues from copying levies on blank audio-visual recording media.[88] The European and Canadian collecting societies, however, consider the retention of these revenues in favour of the national production as justified compensation for the inadequate protection of foreign right holders in the US.[89] In view of the substantial market share of US films, the provision of national treatment in the Berne Convention (which has been integrated by reference into Article 3 of TRIPs) leads to the consequence that European collecting societies have to pass on by far the biggest part of their proceeds to Hollywood studios. Since there are no collecting societies for films in the United States, remuneration flows in only one direction. European and Canadian collecting societies therefore take the view that they are justified by the principle of reciprocity in restricting the rights of US authors since the United States does not grant an equivalent right concerning the remuneration of private copying.[90] This argument rests on shaky ground, however, since the Berne Convention does not provide for exemptions to the principle of national treatment.[91]

Ownership rules

Measures restricting foreign investment or reserving the ownership of certain companies to its own nationals may be found in numerous legal systems. In the broadcasting area, this applies, for instance, to Australia,[92]

[88] Even the WIPO considers the non-observance of national treatment in the case of using the revenues from copying levies on blank video tapes a reason for conflict in future international negotiations on copyright. See WIPO, note 80 above, pp. 52f.

[89] See Canadian Industries Cultural Advisory Group on International Trade, note 27 above, p. 17.

[90] See *Ibid.*, p. 17.

[91] The reservation of the principle of reciprocity in the Berne Convention is restricted to works of applied art (Article 2(7) of the Berne Convention), the term of protection (Article 7(8)) and the *droit de suite* (Article 14*ter* (2)). See A. Staehelin, *Das TRIPs-Abkommen* (2nd edn, Berne: Stämpfli, 1999), pp. 45f.

[92] In 1997, the Australian Broadcasting Authority and Australia's treasurer ordered the Canadian broadcaster CanWest Global to partially divest its shares in Australia's Ten network in order to comply with ownership restrictions for broadcasting undertakings. Under Australian law, the maximum foreign investment allowed in Australian broadcasting companies is 15 per cent. See www.infoexport.gc.ca/trade-culture, p. 19 (20 November 2001).

Canada,[93] Austria[94] and the United Kingdom.[95] France restricts ownership in broadcasting companies to a maximum of 49 per cent of the share capital, though this requirement is not conditional upon the owner's nationality.[96] The Swiss Federal Council changed its licensing practice in February 1998 by granting equal treatment to foreign and Swiss applicants for transmission licences, provided that the country of establishment of the foreign broadcaster accords the same rights to Swiss nationals on a reciprocal basis.[97]

Under US law, there is a complex of regulations prescribing the upper limits of individual ownership in broadcasting corporations.[98] According to the regulations enacted by the Federal Communications Commission (FCC), based on sections 308–310 of the Communications Act of 1934,[99] the share of one individual television operator in for instance, the

[93] See the case of NCM and CMT noted at p. 184 above.

[94] In accordance with Article 5(1) of the Austrian Cable and Satellite Broadcasting Act of 1 July 1997, broadcasting operators transmitting their programmes via cable or satellite must be Austrian citizens (if natural persons) or have their registered office in Austria (if legal persons). Terrestrial broadcasting at the regional level is still monopolised by the ORF. The European Court of Human Rights, in its verdict of 21 September 2000 in the case of Tele 1, declared this contravention of Article 10 of the European Convention on Human Rights (ECHR) to be admissible provided that the transition to digital technologies had not yet taken place and therefore competition was not yet possible. See *Tele 1 Privatfernsehgesellschaft mbH* v. *Austria*, Application No. 00032240/96 (available at http://hudoc.echr.coe.int/hudoc/ViewRoot.asp?Item = 0&Action = Html&Notice = 1&NoticeMode = 2&RelatedMode = 0, 15 December 2001). In the meantime, the Austrian government submitted a draft law on the extensive liberalisation of the broadcasting sector. See W. Dillenz, 'Elektronische Medien: Entwicklungsschub in Österreich', *Medialex* 2/2001, pp. 64f.

[95] See T. Gibbons, 'Aspiring to Pluralism: The Constraints of Public Broadcasting Values on the De-Regulation of British Media Ownership', *Cardozo Arts and Entertainment Law Journal* 16 (1998): 475–500; and G. Doyle, 'Regulation of Media Ownership and Pluralism in Europe: Can the European Union Take Us Forward?', *Cardozo Arts and Entertainment Law Journal* 16 (1998): 451–73. The draft of the new UK Communications Bill with liberalised ownership rules is available at www.communicationsbill.gov.uk (15 May 2002). According to Chapter 9 of the Bill, remaining restrictions apply to owners of more than 20% of the national newspaper market, who will not be allowed to own ITV, though they can own Channel 5, a small commercial broadcaster. For a comment on the draft, see *The Economist*, 11 May 2002, pp. 37–8.

[96] See A. James and A. Dawtrey, 'Oui are the World', *Variety*, 19 June 2000, at 1, 85.

[97] For illustration, see 'Switzerland – List of Article II MFN Exemptions, Audiovisual Services' (GATS/EL/83), reprinted at pp. 203–4 below. In pertinent part, the entry states that 'concessions for the operation of radio or television broadcast stations may be granted, normally on the basis of bilateral agreements'.

[98] The FCC regulations are available at www.fcc.gov/resources.html (11 October 2001).

[99] 47 USCA.

nationwide broadcasting market, must not amount to more than 35 per cent.[100] Restrictions also apply to the ownership of local radio or television as well as to daily newspaper/broadcasting cross-ownership and cable operators/television cross-ownership respectively. The principal purpose of such laws is the safeguarding of diversity and competition in the broadcasting sector.[101] The share of foreign companies in US broadcasting operators is expressly regulated and limited in several ways by section 310 of the Communications Act of 1934: In principle, it is not possible for foreign natural or legal persons to be granted a licence.[102] Although foreign investors are allowed to possess a share in US companies holding such licences, no more than 20 per cent of the share capital may be owned or voted by aliens.[103] Furthermore, it is expressly provided that no more than 25 per cent of the share capital of a parent company of the US licence holder may be held by a foreign investor.[104] The Communications Act of 1934 leaves it to the discretion of the FCC, however, to decide whether the public interest will be served by a foreign investment or not. If the FCC decides to permit this, it is authorised to permit a vertical ownership which would be inadmissible *per se*.[105] This regulation was used in 1995 when the Australian based News Corporation controlled by Rupert Murdoch took over Fox Broadcasting Network. The FCC decided that the take-over, which did not comply with section 310(b)(4) of the Communications Act, was justified in the public interest.[106]

As regards the compliance of such ownership rules with WTO law, it can be stated generally that these rules are admissible, provided that the

[100] In 1996, the US Congress increased the admissible market share from 25 per cent to 35 per cent. In spite of several operators pressing for a further increase of this threshold, the FCC refrained from an amendment in the context of its ordinary review of ownership rules in June 2000. See Federal Communications Commission, Review of the Commission's Broadcast Ownership Rules and Other Rules Adopted Pursuant to Section 202 of the Telecommunications Act of 1996, MM Docket No. 98-35, 1998, Biennial Regulatory Review Report, FCC 00-191, 20 June 2000; C. Stern, 'Nets Push to Remove National Ownership Cap', *Variety*, 20 September 1999, p. 6.

[101] See Federal Communications Commission, Biennial Regulatory Review 2000, Staff Report of 18 September 2000, p. 144; Harvey L. Zuckman *et al.*, *Modern Communication Law* (St Paul, MN: West Publishing, 1999), pp. 1196f.

[102] See section 310(b)(1) and (2) of the Communications Act.

[103] See section 310(b)(3) of the Communications Act. The US has entered this 20 per cent restriction on foreign investment in broadcasting operators on its special commitment list.

[104] See section 310(b)(4) of the Communications Act.

[105] See Zuckman *et al.*, *Modern Communication Law*, p. 1209.

[106] *Ibid.*, p. 1209.

country in question did not accept any relevant obligations in its GATS schedules of commitments.[107] In any case, such measures are subject to potential requests in negotiations aiming at the progressive liberalisation of the services sector.

Agreements on cinematographic co-production

Numerous European states, and other countries such as Australia, Canada and Israel, concluded bilateral treaties on support for cinematographic co-production. In the context of the Council of Europe, the European Convention on Cinematographic Co-production (ECCC) is the relevant act in force serving as a multilateral instrument for financing larger cinematographic projects. As this type of instrument accords preferential treatment exclusively to partners of certain countries, the question arises as to whether this is a violation of the most-favoured nation obligation. Further observations on this question are set out below.

Competition rules protecting free access to information and media pluralism

The safeguarding of a diverse and high-quality supply of programmes is an objective of both film and television regulation, particularly in view of increasing market concentration. To this end, the legislation of several WTO Members provides for a series of measures which aim at safeguarding competition in the media sector in cases where competition law *per se* is insufficient. Competition law aims at preventing the emergence, and prohibits the abuse of, a dominant position and aims at preventing agreements between undertakings which may distort competition. General competition law rules cater for creating and sustaining markets with free access and multiple competitors. Nevertheless, since such disciplines can only exert an influence on economic competition, the experience of liberalised broadcasting markets shows that the existence of a multitude of legally independent broadcasting operators does not in itself guarantee a high quality supply of programmes expressing a variety of social, political, cultural and ideological views.

[107] This is the case for the United States; see 'Sector Specific Commitments United States' (GATS/SC/90). For an explanation of the functioning of the GATS schedules, see pp. 200–2 below.

Access to major events

On the European level, there are two basic types of rule which aim at ensuring access by the public to events of major importance. The first type of rule is represented by Article 9 of the European Convention on Transfrontier Television (ECTT) of the Council of Europe, which recommends to its contracting parties the introduction of a right to *short reporting*. This provision aims at ensuring that the right of the public to information is not undermined by the exercise by a broadcaster of exclusive rights to the transmission of a major public event. This right of access is regulated, for instance, in section 5 of the German *Rundfunkstaatsvertrag*[108] and in Article 7 of the Swiss *Radio- und Fernsehgesetz.*[109] The second type of rule is the lists embodied both in Article 3a of the EC Television Directive[110] and in Article 9*bis* of the ECCT. Both regulations aim at ensuring that important events are accessible to the wider public on free-to-air TV. To this end, Member States and contracting states respectively are authorised to take measures to prevent the less affluent audiences from being excluded from viewing because events of major importance are only available on pay-TV. The operators are obliged to respect the law of the receiving state which prescribes what qualifies as an event of major importance in the country in question.[111] To ensure transparency, both regimes oblige the individual state, where they make use of such access rights, to draw up a list of events which are considered to be of major importance and to determine the measures taken. Once a year, the authorised committees publish a consolidated list in order to avoid differences between the European Community provisions and those of the ECTT.[112]

Both the right to short reporting and the lists for major events may be combined with restrictions on exclusive rights of TV companies. As such restrictions apply in a non-discriminatory manner to both domestic and foreign operators, they give no cause for concern as regards WTO law. As far as copyrights are restricted, these limitations do not go further than is allowed by Article 13 of TRIPs.

[108] See H. Waldhauser, *Die Fernsehrechte des Sportveranstalters* (Berlin: Duncker & Humblot, 1999), pp. 297ff.

[109] See O. Sidler, *Exklusivberichterstattung über Sportveranstaltungen im Rundfunk* (Berne: Stämpfli, 1995).

[110] See Drijber, 'The Revised Television Without Frontiers Directive', pp. 117ff.

[111] *Ibid.*, p. 119.

[112] See the report of the EC Commission of 26 July 2001, with an overview of the lists of Denmark, Italy, the United Kingdom and Germany, OJ C208/25, 26 July 2001.

Competition measures against media concentration

Several states have instituted special measures both to combat the concentration of media and to protect media diversity. While the EC – in spite of ten years of effort – still has not succeeded in agreeing on a directive on media concentration,[113] various European countries have enacted their own measures. The German model, which takes account of a company's share in the viewing market,[114] or the complicated UK schedule of points, including rules concerning cross-media ownership, are among the better-known European examples.[115]

Such measures should not conflict with WTO law because WTO Members enjoy a very large leeway as regards the regulation of competition.[116]

Distribution privileges

Must-carry rules Cable operators in many countries are limited in their freedom of transmission by provisions of the broadcasting law which provide for obligations to transmit or retransmit certain programmes.[117] For example, under Article 47 of the Swiss Broadcasting Act (*Radio- und Fernsehgesetz*, or RTVG), cable operators may be obliged by the Federal Office of Communication (OFCOM) to transmit certain Swiss programmes. A licensed operator whose programmes are not being transmitted wirelessly and who wishes its programme to be distributed by means of the cable network must submit a request to OFCOM. The OFCOM may then oblige the cable operator to make transmission capacity available

[113] At the level of the EC, the most recent attempt was made in summer 2000. For an overview on regulatory instruments for combating media concentration existing in the EC Member States and corresponding unsuccessful initiatives of the EC Commission, see A. Harcourt, 'The European Commission and Regulation of the Media Industry', *Cardozo Arts and Entertainment Law Journal* 16 (1998): 425–49; and Doyle, 'Regulation of Media Ownership', pp. 468–72.

[114] See M. Stock, 'Konzentrationskontrolle in Deutschland nach der Neufassung des Rundfunkstaatsvertrags (1996)', in M. Stock, H. Röper and B. Holznagel, eds., *Medienmarkt und Meinungsmacht: Zur Neuregelung der Konzentrationskontrolle in Deutschland und Grossbritannien* (Berlin: Springer, 1997), pp. 1–70; F. Hoffet and T. Hoehn, 'Zusammenschlusskontrolle im Medienbereich, Anmerkungen zur bisherigen Praxis der Schweizerischen Wettbewerbskommission', (1999) *sic!* 232ff.

[115] Gibbons, 'Aspiring to Pluralism', pp. 489–500; B. Holznagel and A. Grünwald, 'Britisches Medienkonzentrationsrecht im Wandel', in Stock, Röper and Holznagel, 'Zusammerschlasskontrolle', pp. 109–59.

[116] See Cottier, 'Die völkerrechtliche Rahmenbedingungen', p. 752.

[117] For a detailed assessment of the duties to transmit and retransmit under US, UK and Canadian law, see W. Hoffmann-Riem, *Regulating Media: The Licensing and Supervision of Broadcasting in Six Countries* (New York and London: Guilford Press, 1996), pp. 49f, 76, 211ff and 295.

(Article 47(1)(b) of the RTVG) in case the cable network does not dispose of sufficient capacity for all applicants, on the condition that the programme contributes to the cultural policy mandate enshrined in Article 3 of the RTVG. In accordance with Article 47(2) of the RTVG, the OFCOM may, by way of exception, allow the cable operator to interrupt the retransmission of a foreign programme.

The rule established by Article 47(2) of the RTVG raises the question of a possible conflict with the WTO principle of non-discrimination. The OFCOM takes the view that Article 47(2) does not have a discriminatory effect in practice, since there are no economic incentives for a cable operator to replace an attractive foreign programme with a Swiss programme. However, Article 47(2), at least formally, is not free of discrimination and might be objected to in the ongoing negotiations for liberalisation of the GATS.

In addition to the above-mentioned transmission duties, Article 42(2) of the RTVG obliges cable operators to include certain programmes produced by licensed operators in their retransmission supply. This duty to retransmit is also called the 'must-carry rule'.[118] In accordance with Article 42(4) of the RTVG, cable operators are not permitted to collect a fee for the retransmission of non-encrypted programmes of Swiss operators. Foreign operators do not enjoy this privilege, unless the corresponding foreign state grants reciprocal rights (Article 42(5) of the RTVG).

The latter requirement for reciprocity contradicts the idea of national treatment. The OFCOM argues that the term 'Swiss' in this context means only that the operator must be licensed under Swiss law. Article 111(3) of the RTVG provides that the Swiss Federal Council, under certain conditions, may grant a licence to foreign natural persons or to legal persons controlled by foreigners. Again, the objection against this argument would be that conditions of reciprocity are attached to such licensing and thus the potential cause for conflict with the law of WTO remains.

Reservation of transmission capacity In the process of convergence of telecommunications and broadcasting, frequencies are used for both broadcasting and telecommunication services. Owing to the competition between broadcasting and telecommunications brought about by this convergence, and to the greater 'purchasing power' of the

[118] See M. Dumermuth, 'Rundfunkrecht', in H. Koller *et al.*, eds., *Schweizerisches Bundesverwaltungsrecht, Informations- und Kommunikationsrecht* (Basel and Frankfurt am Main: Helbing & Lichtenhahn, 1996), vol. 4, para. 395.

telecommunications industry, governments may decide for cultural policy reasons to reserve certain transmission capacities in the terrestrial frequency spectrum and in the cable network for broadcasting activities. The Swiss draft of a new Broadcasting Act provides for such compensating measures through its Article 38.[119] In order to avoid conflicts with WTO law, these measures must be implemented in a non-discriminatory manner.[120]

Provisions of WTO law providing for flexibility towards measures of national cultural policy

Screen quotas (Article IV of the GATT)

After World War I, many countries introduced import quotas and screen quotas as a reaction to the worldwide dominance of Hollywood films. This brought about an enduring conflict with the United States which would only be resolved in 1947 by establishing a compromise under the new GATT. While Article XI of the GATT prohibits quantitative restrictions on imports, including import quotas,[121] Article III:10 of the GATT provides for an exception from the obligation of national treatment for cinematographic films under conditions which are specified in Article IV of the GATT. The latter allows screen quotas as the only means for protecting domestic film industries. Article IV(a), first sentence, states that *internal* quantitative regulations shall take the form of screen quotas, making clear that import restrictions are not permitted. Further requirements are defined in Article IV(a) to (d). According to Article IV(a) screen quotas must be computed on the basis of screen time per theatre per year. If a theatre exhibits films totalling 1,500 hours per year, a screen quota of 50 per cent means that 750 hours are reserved for national films. Article IV(b) provides that screen quotas may only discriminate between foreign and national films, i.e. it is prohibited to accord preferential treatment to *certain* foreign films. Article IV(c) states an exception to Article IV(b) in the sense of a *grandfather clause.* Finally, Article IV(d) requests contracting parties to begin negotiations for the limitation, liberalisation or elimination of screen quotas. Negotiations to this effect had only just started at the time of writing.

[119] See the Federal Council's explanations attached to the draft of the new radio and television Act of December 2000, pp. 65ff, www.bakom.ch (15 October 2001).

[120] See pp. 208–10 below.

[121] See p. 179 above.

Screen quotas have been in operation in, for example, South Korea, where, since 1996, cinema operators have been obliged to exhibit Korean films for a certain number of days per year. These screen quotas are set out in Article 16 of the Korean Movie Act of 1995[122] and in a Presidential Decree of 1997.[123] Article 16 of the Movie Act provides that '[t]he person who operates a public performance place where the motion pictures are screened . . . shall screen the Korean motion pictures for more than such number of days as determined by the Presidential Decree'. Article 19 of the Presidential Decree provides as follows:

> (1) Any manager of a theatre who screens motion pictures as prescribed in Article 16 of the Act, shall exhibit Korean motion pictures for no less than two-fifths of the annual screening days.
> (2) If it is deemed particularly necessary to do so in consideration of the supply and demand situation of Korean motion pictures, the Minister of Culture and Tourism may, notwithstanding the provision of Paragraph (1) of this Article, reduce the number of the annual screening days of Korean motion pictures . . . .

Under the current system, Korean cinema operators are obliged to devote a minimum of 146 days per year to the exhibition of domestic films. The Korean Minister of Culture may, under certain conditions, reduce this number to 106 days[124] Cinemas infringing these regulations may face withdrawal of their business authorisation.

These Korean screen quotas are a thorn in the flesh of the US entertainment industry. Although the US government is trying hard to get rid of these quotas, it has so far refrained from instituting formal proceedings because the quotas are in accordance with Article IV of the GATT. The requirement for Korean films to be exhibited for a period of at least two fifths of the total annual screen time complies with the main condition set forth in Article IV(a) of the GATT requiring that screen quotas shall take the form of a quota computed on an annual basis. Since the Korean quotas

[122] Promotion of the Motion Picture Industry Act, 30 December 1995, Korea Legislation Research Institute, Statutes of the Republic of Korea 861, cited by C. Hyun-Kyung Kim, 'Building the Korean Film Industry's Competitiveness: Abolish The Screen Quota and Subsidise the Film Industry', *Pacific Rim Law and Policy Journal* 9 (2000): 353 at 356.

[123] Enforcement Decree of the Promotion of the Motion Pictures Industry Act, Presidential Decree No. 15085 of 29 June 1996, Korea Legislation Research Institute, Statutes of the Republic of Korea 861, according to: C. Hyun-Kyung Kim, 'Building the Korean Film Industry's Competitiveness', p. 356.

[124] *Ibid.*, p. 357.

accord preferential treatment to domestic films, but draw no distinction between foreign films, they are also compatible with Article IV (b) of the GATT, reserving the MFN principle. As Korea accepted national treatment commitments in its GATS list of specific commitments, including the distribution of audio-visual services,[125] alleging a violation of the GATS might be a strategy worth consideration by those opposed to the quotas. Korea may then object that Article IV of the GATT settles the matter of screen quotas explicitly and comprehensively with the consequence that a parallel application of the GATS should be excluded.

Since legal remedies seem to be burdened with uncertainty, the US government is putting political pressure on South Korea, and has recently made the abolition of the quotas a prerequisite for stronger trade relations. First, the US government postponed the conclusion of bilateral negotiations on a US–South Korean bilateral investment treaty until the screen quotas were eliminated. Secondly, in the run-up to the Seattle Ministerial Conference of the WTO, the US Trade Representative (USTR) put strong pressure on the South Korean government to repeal these quotas.[126] In response, South Korean film directors went on hunger-strike and organised mass demonstrations intended to force their own government to stand up to US pressure.[127] Simultaneously, the Motion Picture Association of America (MPAA) followed a different strategy: it made an offer to the Korean state to invest US$500 million in the Korean film industry, provided that Korea gives up its screen quotas. The MPAA's argument was that consumers must be the 'ultimate arbiters of the market place' and that after repealing the screen quotas the Korean film industry would become more significant.[128]

Apart from the Korean example, screen quotas have lost much of the importance they had until the 1950s. Nonetheless, Article IV of the GATT is of methodological interest because it can be interpreted as a proof of

[125] See the entries in the GATS commitment list of Korea concerning market access and national treatment, GATS/SC/48.

[126] C. Alford, 'Goliath Balks at David's Quotas', *Variety*, 9 August 1999, p. 34; C. Alford, 'S. Korea's Cultural Yen', *Variety*, 10 July 2000, p. 46; S. Rosenberg, 'Koreans Push Quota Issue', *Variety*, 31 July 2000, p. 49.

[127] See Hyun-Kyung Kim, 'Building the Korean Film Industry's Competitiveness', p. 362.

[128] *Ibid.*, p. 363. As to this, it is interesting to add that the South Korean film industry has been enjoying an increasingly high standing throughout the world, and that numerous prizes at important international cinematographic festivals were awarded to Korean directors. See P. Rist, 'An Introduction to Korean Cinema', at www.cinekorea.com/kc.html (26 March 2001) (translation of an article published in *Séquences*, September/October 1998).

an old tradition in world trade law of treating cultural issues in a specific way.

General exceptions

Article XX of the GATT and Article XIV of the GATS provide for an exception to the non-discrimination obligations of world trade law. The only provision specifically referring to cultural products is Article XX(f) exempting measures which are imposed for the protection of national treasures of artistic, historic or archaeological value.[129] Although this provision obviously cannot be alleged when trade in audio-visual media is concerned,[130] it shows that already the GATT of 1947 recognised the relationship between trade in cultural objects and national identity.[131] The question is whether the provisions of Article XX(a) of the GATT and Article XIV(a) of the GATS, providing for an exemption for public morals, could be more helpful. This seems unlikely because conflicts in the area of trade in audio-visual media are about the legitimacy of cultural policy measures, and there is no disagreement that national measures (e.g. of criminal law) protecting public morals are legitimate under WTO law.

GATS schedules

It may seem surprising that GATS schedules in this study are dealt with under the title of norms providing for flexibility for national policies, but, as already emphasised, GATS schedules of specific commitments and MFN exemptions are an expression of the flexible liberalisation method in the services sector, and thus their analysis is fitting.

Specific commitments

The meaning of Article XVII of the GATS is that a Member is obliged to apply the principle of national treatment only to those sub-sectors and divisions of sub-sectors which are included in its individual list. If a

[129] As a consequence of the *double test* which is generally required by both Article XX of the GATT and Article XV of the GATS, such measures must not be applied in a manner which would constitute a means of arbitrary or unjustifiable discrimination between countries or a disguised restriction on international trade. See WTO Appellate Body Reports, 'United States – Gasoline', WT/DS2/AB/R, 29 April 1996, p. 22, and 'United States – Import of Certain Shrimp and Shrimp Products', WT/DS58/AB/R, 12 October 1998, paras. 118ff.

[130] Cottier, 'Die völkerrechtliche Rahmenbedingungen', pp. 751f.

[131] See Bernier, 'Cultural Goods and Services', p. 114.

certain sub-sector or division is covered, the Member then has to specify any limitation of this commitment in its list. If the example of India's list of specific commitments (see Table 7.2) is examined, it is apparent that India included only one division of the audio-visual sector, that of distribution of motion pictures or videotapes.

Limitations on market access are specified in column 2. Paragraphs 1 to 4 correspond to the four possible modes of supply for services as defined in Article 1 of the GATS. 'Unbound' for the first two modes of supply means that India did not commit itself to any obligations with regard to these. Next to mode of supply 3 (commercial presence), India listed some limitations. Thus there is a commitment with regard to this mode of supply with the exception of the limitations specified in Paragraph 3. As an example, the listing in the 'Market access' column legitimates measures which restrict the import of foreign films to 100 per year. According to the listings in the 'National treatment' column, foreign films are treated like domestic films (e.g. with regard to distribution licences) only if the Indian film authority certifies that the film won an award, or participated in an international film festival, or received good reviews in prestigious film journals.

MFN exemptions

Article II of the GATS obliges Members of the WTO to giant most-favoured nation treatment. Paragraph 1 states that, with respect to any measure covered by the GATS, each Member shall accord immediately and unconditionally to services and service suppliers of any other Member treatment no less favourable than it accords to like services and service suppliers of any other country (not only WTO Members). However, Paragraph 2 opens the possibility to WTO Members to exempt certain measures from the MFN obligation, provided that at the moment of the entry into force of the WTO Agreement this measure was listed in the Member's list of exemptions.

Up to October 2001, forty-nine countries had listed MFN exemptions. Typically scheduled exceptions relate to co-production agreements, tax benefits, or simplified entry procedures for natural persons. To get a more concrete idea of the structure of such a list, it seems useful to take a closer look at Switzerland's list of MFN exemptions, which are set out in Table 7.3.

Column 2 describes the measures of audio-visual policy and their inconsistency with the MFN principle. While column 3 lists the countries to which preferential treatment is granted, column 5 explains the

Table 7.2 *Sector-specific commitments India (GATS/SC/42) (modes of supply: (1) cross-border supply; (2) consumption abroad; (3) commercial presence; and (4) presence of natural persons)*

Sector	Limitations on market access	Limitations on national treatment	Additional commitments	Notes
2. COMMUNICATION SERVICES D. Audio-visual Services a) Motion picture or videotape distribution services (CPC 96113)	1) Unbound	1) Unbound		
	2) Unbound	2) Unbound		
	3) i) Only through representative offices which will be allowed to function as branches of companies incorporated outside India ii) Import of titles restricted to 100 per year	3) Subject to the prescribed authority having certified that the motion picture has: a. won an award in any of the international film festivals notified by the Ministry of Information and Broadcasting, Government of India; or b. participated in any of the official sections of the notified international film festivals; or c. received good reviews in prestigious film journals notified by the Ministry of Information and Broadcasting, Government of India.		
	4) Unbound except as indicated in the horizontal section	4) Unbound except as indicated in the horizontal section		

Table 7.3 *List of Article II MFN exemptions for Switzerland (GATS/EL/83)*

Sector or sub-sector	Description of measure indicating its inconsistency with Article II	Countries to which the measure applies	Intended duration	Conditions creating the need for the exemption
Audio-visual services	To confer national treatment to audio-visual works covered by bilateral or plurilateral agreements on co-production in the field of audio-visual works, in particular in relation to access to funding and to distribution	All countries with whom cultural cooperation may be desirable (at present agreements exist with member countries of the Council of Europe and with Canada)	Indefinite	Promotion of common cultural objectives
	Measures granting the benefit of support programmes, such as MEDIA and EURIMAGES, and measures relating to the allocation of screentime which implement arrangements such as the Council of Europe Convention on Transfrontier Television and confer national treatment, to audio-visual works and/or to suppliers of audio-visual services meeting specific European origin criteria	European countries	Indefinite	Promotion of cultural objectives based on long-standing cultural links

Table 7.3 (*cont.*)

Sector or sub-sector	Description of measure indicating its inconsistency with Article II	Countries to which the measure applies	Intended duration	Conditions creating the need for the exemption
Audio-visual services	Concessions for the operation of radio or television broadcast stations may be granted, normally on the basis of bilateral agreements, to persons of countries other than Switzerland	All countries with whom cultural cooperation may be desirable	Indefinite	Promotion of common cultural objectives, and to regulate access to a market limited in scale (given the size of Switzerland) in order to preserve diversity of supply

conditions creating the need for the exemption. In column 4 carrying the title 'Intended duration', Switzerland listed 'Indefinite'. That raises the question of whether this entry conflicts with the GATS Annex to Article II exemptions providing that such exemptions are in principle limited until 2005.

Among other measures, column 2 exempts bilateral agreements on co-production of movies and the European Convention on Cinematographic Co-production (ECCC) from the MFN obligation. The aim of the ECCC is to promote the development of *European* cinematographic co-productions (Article 1). Following this purpose, Article 16 states that only European countries can be signatories to the Convention. It applies to co-productions involving at least three co-producers, established in three different parties to the Convention. Provided that this requirement is fulfilled, one or more non-European co-producers are admitted under the condition that their total contributions do not exceed 30 per cent of the total cost of the production (Article 2(2)(b)). In all cases, the convention only applies under the condition that the co-produced work meets the definition of a *European cinematographic work* as set in Appendix II to the convention. According to that Appendix, a cinematographic work qualifies as European if it achieves at least 15 points out of a possible total of 19, according to the schedule of European elements set out in Table 7.4.

The ECCC makes no statement concerning the question of whether, for instance, a director who was born in Europe but lives in the United States still qualifies as a European author, or whether an American actor living in Europe counts as European. These questions appear to be left to the discretion of the competent authorities of each party.[132] If the work reaches less than the required 15 points, the competent authorities may nonetheless grant co-production status to the work if they consider that, on the basis of the screenplay, the film reflects 'the European identity'. Since there is no definition of 'European identity', this provision is a rather elastic one.

Why is this co-production status so important? It is the raison d'être of this Convention that the parties involved in a co-production accord national treatment to films having received this co-production status by the competent national authorities. National treatment in the sense of the Convention means that such a film may benefit from the advantages granted to national films by the legislative and regulatory provisions in force in each of the parties to the Convention.

[132] Graber, 'WTO: A Threat to European Films', p. 870.

Table 7.4 *Schedule of European elements (Appendix II to the European Convention on Cinematographic co-production)*

European elements	Weighting points
Director	3
Script writer	3
Composer	1
First role	3
Second role	2
Third role	1
Cameraman	1
Sound recordist	1
Editor	1
Art director	1
Studio or shooting location	1
Post-production location	1

How does this conflict with the MFN principle? As already made clear, non-European films and producers are treated less favourably than equivalent services and service suppliers established in contracting parties to the Convention. In the ongoing services negotiations, the MFN exemptions are expected to be subject to requests and offers of progressive liberalisation. The parties to the Convention could thereby come under conflicting pressures.

Concluding observations concerning some open questions

The analysis undertaken above reveals the existence of a wide variety of governmental measures protecting cultural goals in the area of audio-visual media. As demonstrated, existing WTO law provides for some flexibility towards the various instruments of cultural policy. While at the end of the Uruguay Round a provisional compromise was accepted by net exporters and net importers of audio-visual media, it was not possible, however, to reconcile the conflict between liberal trade and cultural policy. With a view to the proposals submitted in the ongoing trade negotiations, a number of open questions appear on the horizon, which will be highlighted in this final section.

Disciplines concerning subsidies for audio-visual services

Several countries made proposals to developing disciplines concerning subsidies for audio-visual services.[133] As the United States suggests, these disciplines may follow the example of the Agreement on Subsidies and Countervailing Measures (SCM). The SCM Agreement applies exclusively to subsidies for goods. With regard to subsidies for services, the obligations up to now are limited to specific GATS commitments accepted by Members in their respective lists and general obligations such as MFN, although Article XV of the GATS requests Members to enter into negotiations with a view to developing additional disciplines. The SCM Agreement draws a distinction between prohibited and permissible subsidies. Prohibited subsidies are export subsidies.[134] The category of permissible subsidies is subdivided into non-actionable and actionable ones.[135] If this normative framework were transposed to the proposed new disciplines for audio-visual services, all measures of public funding discussed above would most probably fall into the category of actionable subsidies.[136] In view of the fact that funding for public service broadcasters in many countries derives from licence fees, a salient question is whether such funds have to be regarded as a subsidy. While EC institutions on several occasions decided that licence fees do not amount to state aid,[137] a broader definition of subsidies is operated in the context of the SCM Agreement, and therefore the question may be answered differently by the WTO institutions.

[133] According to the WTO Secretariat, the audio-visual sector is one of the most subsidised ones. See WTO Council for Trade in Services, 'Subsidies for Services Sector, Background Note by the Secretariat, Information Contained in WTO Trade Policy Reviews', S/WPGR/W/25 (26 January 1998), p. 4.

[134] See WTO Appellate Body Report, 'United States – Tax Treatment for "Foreign Sales Corporations"', WT/DS108/AB/R (adopted 4 February 2002).

[135] For detailed information concerning the functioning of the SCM Agreement, see T. Cottier and C. Germann, 'The WTO and EU Distributive Policy: The Case of Regional Promotion and Assistance', in G. de Burca and J. Scott, eds., *The EU and the WTO: Legal and Constitutional Issues* (Oxford and Portland, OR: Hart, 2001), p. 185 at pp. 198ff.

[136] A Member challenging actionable subsidies must demonstrate that these have adverse effects on its economy. In view of the United States' 80–90 per cent share of the world market in audio-visual services, it is unlikely that the US government could prove this. See Cottier, 'Die völkerrechtliche Rahmenbedingungen', p. 754.

[137] See Communication from the Commission on the application of state aid rules to public service broadcasting, OJ C320/04, 15 November 2001; Commission Decision of 22 May 2002 approving state funding to BBC digital television and radio channels, European Commission Press Releases IP/02/737; ECJ Case C-379/98, *PreussenElektra AG* v. *Schleswag AG*, [2001] ECR I-2099; ECJ Case C-53/00, *Ferring SA* v. *Agence centrale des organismes de sécurité sociale (ACOSS)*, [2001] ECR I-9067.

According to the SCM Agreement, a subsidy is defined by three elements: (1) a *cost* arising to the public body which does not necessarily consist in the payment of money but may, for example, be the consequence of tax credits, fiscal incentives or any other form of income or price support (Article 1(1)(a) of the SCM); (2) a *benefit* hereby conferred; which (3) is *specific* to certain enterprises or industries (Article 2(1) of the SCM). If this definition is to be integrated into the new regime discussed above, it seems likely that the funding of public service broadcasters from licence fees would meet all of the above-mentioned three conditions.

Classification issues

In their submissions made in the area of audio-visual services, several countries criticised the present classification system. Indeed, as a consequence of technological development, the GATS/UN Central Product Classification system no longer corresponds with reality. The digital revolution has changed the ways in which audio-visual programmes are created, produced and distributed. On the national level, there is a trend towards a technology-neutral regulation of audio-visual services.[138] This leads to the consequence that infrastructures necessary for the transmission of audio-visual content such as cable networks or radio frequencies which used to be regulated under broadcasting law will eventually be regulated exclusively within a framework of telecommunications law.[139] As

[138] Technological neutrality is now an underlying principle of the European Union's regulatory framework of electronic communications networks and services. The new package consists of one framework directive, Directive 2002/21/EC (OJ L108/33), and four specific directives, the Authorisation Directive 2002/20/EC (OJ L108/21), the Access Directive 2002/19/EC (OJ L108/7), the Universal Service Directive 2002/22/EC (OJ L108/51) and the Personal Data and Protection of Privacy Directive 97/66/EC (OJ L24/1). The framework directive explicitly puts a general requirement for the Member States to ensure that in carrying out their tasks national regulatory authorities take utmost account of the desirability of making regulations technologically neutral (Article 8). The principle of technological neutrality is further elaborated upon in the specific directives.

[139] The new regulatory framework of electronic communications networks and services builds upon the concepts developed in the 1999 Communications Review (The 1999 Communications Review, Towards a New Framework for Electronic Communications Infrastructure and Associated Services, Communication from the Commission to the European Parliament, the Council, the Economic and Social Committee and the Committee of the Regions, COM(1999)539, 10 November 1999), as well as on the basic suggestions made by the Green Paper on Convergence of the Telecommunications, Media and Information Technology Sectors, and the Implications for Regulation (COM(1997)623). It is based on a clear separation between networks and content, and regulates only the former. The separation is quite technical and is likely to cause problems in terms of the

already pointed out, the market sees the electronic delivery of telecommunications services as more profitable than the delivery of broadcasts. To counterbalance the advantages of telecommunications on the market and to ensure the achievement of cultural policy objectives, governments may wish to reserve capacity in terrestrial frequencies and cable networks for public service broadcasting (including radio).[140] Conflicts with the principles of WTO law may arise if governments do not implement such trade-restrictive measures in a transparent, non-discriminatory and proportionate manner. A different question arises with regard to the classification of video games. Since computer games can be played in groups linked to interactive digital TV services, it is not easy to draw the distinction between software and broadcasting.[141] Furthermore, the classification of 'knowledge and content management services' such as electronic programming guides (EPG) is disputed. While the information technology industry claims that such services be fully liberalised under the GATS, public service broadcasters reject this view, arguing that EPGs are important content-related services. Although they are built into a television set-top-box, they decide on the extent to which users have access to audio-visual content. As technology is developing so rapidly and without a predictable end, it is important to recall in this context the preamble to the GATS which recognises the right of Members to regulate and to introduce new regulations within their territories if this is necessary in order to meet national policy objectives.

A further point of conflict is the classification of a number of new services associated with electronic commerce.[142] With regard to the question of whether electronically delivered media are goods or services, two different views are taken.[143] Some governments argue that movies, television programmes or music delivered via the Internet are *virtual goods* because

accelerating process of convergence where content and infrastructure come together and cannot be treated as separate entities. For criticism on the latter issue, see 'European Communications at the Crossroads', Report of the CEPS Working Party on Electronic Communications, Executive Summary, available at www.ceps.be/pubs/2001/Eu-Com.pdf (12 May 2002).

140 See pp. 196–7 above. Governments want to assure to public service broadcasters terrestrial frequencies or cable capacities needed for the transmission of programmes.

141 See M. König, 'Was bringt eine neue GATS-Runde für die audiovisuellen Medien?', (2002) *Zeitschrift für Urheber- und Medienrecht*(2002): 271–83 at 274.

142 Paragraph 34 of the Doha Declaration instructs the General Council to continue the Work Programme on Electronic Commerce, and to report on further progress to the Fifth Session of the Ministerial Conference.

143 For a detailed discussion, see W. Drake and K. Nicolaïdis, 'Global Electronic Commerce and GATS: The Millennium Round and Beyond', in P. Sauvé and R. Stern, eds., *GATS 2000*:

they may have a tangible equivalent (e.g. a DVD, a videotape or a CD) and consequently should be subject to the GATT. Others object that this is also the case for many other categories, and that such a view would unduly restrict coverage of the GATS. A possible solution could consist in a distinction between goods and services based on the *economic purpose* of the transaction. Hence, the economic purpose of electronic on-demand delivery of, for example, a movie would be to provide a service regulated exclusively by the GATS. However, shipping a DVD of the same movie would be subject exclusively to the GATT.[144]

Structural discussion concerning 'domestic regulation' (Article VI of the GATS)

The aim of Article VI of the GATS is to introduce an obligation for Members to ensure a minimum standard of the rule of law while implementing national policy objectives. The provision aims to prevent national laws having the effect of technical barriers to trade.[145] Article VI, *inter alia*, sets rules for technical standards and licensing procedures. Until now, Article VI has not had much of an effect, but, in accordance with its Paragraph 4, a working group has been set up, mandated to develop 'any necessary disciplines', especially a necessity test for national provisions. Since licensing procedures are frequently used to regulate broadcasting and cinema, further discussions concerning Article VI are highly relevant for the audio-visual sector. The same is true for the development of technical standards, such as those for the transmission of digital television signals. Following an initiative of European market players co-operating in the

New Directions in Services Trade Liberalization (Washington, DC: Brookings Institution Press, 2000), pp. 399–437 at pp. 407ff.

144 For a similar solution, see ECJ Case C-275/92, *Schindler*, [1994] ECR I-1039, paras. 22–5. The case law of the ECJ generally favours a realistic approach and does not stick to the 'residual' nature of services, but rather to the economic reality. The rule whereby the accessory follows the principal is an important guide to the Court's action. In Case 155/73, *Sacchi* [1974] ECR 409, the ECJ held that the transmission of television signals is dealt with under the freedom to provide services although the circulation of more tangible items, such as films and recording equipment, falls within the free movement of goods. This reasoning of the Court was confirmed in Case 52/79, *Debauve*, [1980] ECR 833, with regard to cable signals. But, in the case of *Schindler*, the Court gave a judgment only on Article 49 of the EC Treaty and held that service activities having as an ancillary side-effect the circulation of goods should together be treated under the rules of services.

145 Since technical barriers to trade usually have the effect of indirect discrimination (prohibited under Article XVII of the GATS), it is not yet clear, in this regard, if Article VI of the GATS has an autonomous standing.

Digital Video Broadcasting Group, the European Telecommunications Standardisation Institute developed such a standard, which eventually became an International Telecommunications Union recommendation. The EC Framework Directive provides that Member States may decide to make the implementation of such standards mandatory.[146] Mandatory standards obviously may be perceived as technical barriers to trade in television services whenever they are used for restricting the market access of certain providers or services.

However, the question is not yet resolved as to whether disciplines to be developed under Article VI: 4 of the GATS apply independently of the inclusion of an entry by a Member in its list of specific commitments. While some countries respond positively, the majority of the Members reject this idea. In my view, it would contradict the structure of the GATS if new commitments for national treatment and market access were introduced by way of disciplines for domestic regulation. The structural choice of GATS was that such commitments are negotiable individually.

Competition policy and safeguards for cultural diversity

The audio-visual sector is characterised by a growing horizontal and vertical integration. A few multinational enterprises[147] increasingly dominate the production, distribution and exhibition of audio-visual content worldwide. This oligopolistic structure not only impacts on the functioning of the audio-visual media market *per se*, but also tends to induce a homogenisation of content.[148] Economies of scale and dysfunctions of the media market (externalities) work in favour of mainstream movies, but prove detrimental to arthouse films.[149] If the market has the decisive say, there is a real danger that, in the end, only mainstream products will survive. The same is true for high-quality television programmes in the sense of public service broadcasting. Although the so-called *digital revolution* reduced technical constraints and led to a rapid growth in the number of television stations worldwide, a closer look at the output of these stations

[146] Recital 30 of Directive 2002/21/EC of the European Parliament and of the Council of 7 March 2002 on a common regulatory framework for electronic communications networks and services (Framework Directive), OJ L108, 24 April 2002, p. 33 at p. 37.

[147] Consisting mainly of AOL/Time Warner, Vivendi/Universal, Walt Disney, Viacom, Bertelsmann and News Corporation.

[148] Communication from Switzerland, note 11 above, para. 15.

[149] See C. E. Baker, 'An Economic Critique of Free Trade in Media Products', *North Carolina Law Review* 78 (2000): 1357 at 1361.

reveals that consumers do not have wider choice, but – on the contrary – are confronted with a higher through put of the same mainstream food.

In the realm of the WTO, a first response to media concentration and homogenisation may be the development of a multilateral competition policy able to resist anti-competitive behaviour such as the abuse of dominant positions or export cartels. According to Paragraph 23 of the Doha Ministerial Declaration, Members agreed that negotiations on this issue should take place after the Ministerial Conference in Mexico in 2003, provided that an explicit consensus on the modalities of negotiation is achieved. Paragraph 25 stresses that the Working Group on the Interaction between Trade and Competition Policy will, in the meantime, focus on the clarification of the main principles of competition policy, including provisions on hardcore cartels. Recalling the strong opposition to any multilateral disciplines of competition policy demonstrated by the United States in the discussions of the Working Group since the Singapore Ministerial Conference,[150] a special effort by all Members will be necessary to avoid a deadlock in 2003.

A second response may be the development of a *cultural diversity safeguard* legitimising governmental measures such as subsidies for art-house films or for high-quality television programmes. Although both the Brazilian and the Swiss proposals submitted in the context of the ongoing services negotiations advocated such a safeguard, neither of the two offered a definition of *cultural diversity* or *cultural identity*. Without being able to discuss these complex issues in the required depth, I would nevertheless like to highlight some of their characteristics.

During the last two years, the concept of *cultural diversity* emerged as the supreme goal of cultural policy on the international level. This thesis is mainly backed by the Universal Declaration on Cultural Diversity adopted by UNESCO's General Conference on 2 November 2001.[151] Article 1 of the Declaration stresses that cultural diversity 'as a source of exchange, innovation and creativity', 'is as necessary for humankind as biodiversity is for nature'. The cultural diversity objective seeks a plurality of different media expressions without actually preferring domestic to foreign programmes. Hence, a country with no access to a foreign cultural content would be considered lacking in cultural diversity. Conversely, cultural

[150] See e.g. Report of the Working Group on the Interaction Between Trade and Competition Policy to the General Council, WT/WGTCP/4, 30 November 2000.

[151] UNESCO Press Release No. 2001-120 of 2 November 2001, www.unesco.org/opi/eng/unescopress/2001/01-120e. shtml (10 December 2001).

diversity in audio-visual media could be ensured by the existence of, and access to, a large variety of programmes differing in budget, style and national origin.

Cultural diversity produces a humus of creativity. It stimulates artists, authors, directors and other creative people to give expression to the identities of the societies in which they are living. The *cultural identity* of a pluralist state is the *unitas multiplex* of various self-descriptions of specific groups and societies belonging to its territory. Thus, the concept of cultural identity appears to be one methodologically dependent on the larger concept of cultural diversity. Why is it legitimate for a state to support its cultural identities? Under the conditions of globalised market, societies, individuals or groups face more complex conditions for creating their identities.[152] Ensuring, at the same time, the peaceful cohabitation of groups with different identities becomes more difficult.[153] As a consequence of the emergence of 'increasingly diverse societies, it is essential to ensure harmonious interaction among individuals and groups with plural, varied and dynamic cultural identities'.[154] In order to keep the peace and to guarantee social cohesion, governments therefore may decide to develop policies for the inclusion and participation of all citizens. Such a policy may consist in supporting the national audio-visual industry and for public service broadcasting. The creation of high-quality audio-visual media within a certain society may offer to individuals and groups a means of helping them to determine their cultural identities, and the dissemination and reception of those programmes across 'borders of identities' may further a better mutual understanding.

In the ongoing negotiations, the essential question will be whether net exporting countries accept that any discussion concerning a further liberalisation of audio-visual services needs to take account of problems of market failure, economies of scale and lack of cultural diversity. In order to achieve a fair trade-off between economic and cultural interests, it will be necessary for claims for market access, national treatment, disciplines for subsidies etc. to be linked with claims of competition policy. But rules against anti-competitive behaviours such as hardcore cartels and abuse of dominant positions are not sufficient. In addition, there needs to be an agreement on a cultural diversity safeguard, which recognises

[152] Jürgen Habermas, *Die postnationale Konstellation: Politische Essays* (Frankfurt am Main: Suhrkamp, 1998), pp. 91–167.

[153] Albert O. Hirschman, *Propensity to Subversion* (Cambridge, MA, and London: Harvard University Press, 1995), pp. 231–48.

[154] Article 2 of the UNESCO Declaration.

the legitimacy of domestic measures promoting high-quality television programmes and arthouse films produced and distributed with low budgets.[155]

[155] For an elaborate defence of this thesis, see C. B. Graber, *Handel und Kultur im Audiovisionsrecht der WTO: Völkerrechtliche, ökonomische und kulturpolitische Grundlagen einer globalen Medienordnung* (Berne: Stamptli Verlag: 2003).

8

Content regulation in the audio-visual sector and the WTO

IVAN BERNIER*

Introduction

Though the question of content regulation was not on the agenda of the GATS negotiations that led to the Annex on Telecommunications and the Fourth Protocol,[1] it is quite clear that the next steps in the gradual opening of national markets to foreign telecom service suppliers will touch directly or indirectly upon that question. The US–Mexico DBS Protocol of November 1996, annexed to the US–Mexico Satellite Agreement[2] signed earlier in April 1996, as well as the US–Argentina Framework Agreement and Protocol for Direct-to-Home Satellite Services and Fixed-Satellite Services[3] of 5 June 1998, can be seen as a prototype of things to come. Significantly, the two Protocols, according to the US Federal Communications Commission (FCC), limit domestic content restrictions either

* The discussion on pp. 222–33 below is based on Ivan Bernier, 'Trade and Culture', in Arthur Appleton, ed., *The Kluwer Companion to the WTO* (forthcoming).

1 Measures affecting the cable or broadcast distribution of radio or television programming were excluded under Paragraph 2(b) of the GATS Annex on Telecommunications. A number of states, in their commitments under the Fourth Protocol, have clearly indicated that commitments in their schedule did not cover the economic activity consisting of content provision which require telecommunications services for its transport: see European Union, GATS/SC/31/Suppl.3 (4 November 1997); see also Chile, GATS/SC/18Supp.12 (4 November 1997).

2 Agreement Between the Government of the United States of America and the Government of the United Mexican States Concerning the Transmission and Reception of Signals from Satellites for the Provision of Satellite Services to Service Users in the United States of America and the United Mexican States, signed 28 April 1996, and Protocol Concerning the Transmission and Reception from Satellites for the Provision of Direct-to-Home Satellites Services in the United States of America and the United Mexican States, signed 8 November 1996.

3 Federal Communications Commission (FCC), Report No. IN 98-27, 'International Bureau Announces Conclusion of US–Argentina Framework Agreement and Protocol for Direct-to-Home Satellite Services and Fixed-Satellite Services', 5 June 1998.

side can place on satellite programming to only a 'modicum' of total programming, 'thereby increasing opportunities for US programme content producers'.[4] Technological development, convergence and the globalisation of the economy, more than anything else, are at the root of this movement towards the opening of national telecommunication and communication markets and, as shown by the incredible development of the Internet, it will be difficult to stop that movement. But, at the same time, there are issues behind content regulation which are very real public concerns and often go beyond the parameters of trade. Content regulation, among other things, is an important part of cultural policy in many countries. To predict the disappearance of content regulation in the audio-visual sector from that point of view may be somewhat premature.

In order to get a better understanding of how content regulation in the audio-visual sector may be affected by the changes brought about by trade liberalisation in telecommunication and communication services and by convergence, it may be useful to begin by considering the type of use that is made of content regulation in that sector. Subsequently, we shall examine how content regulation is presently treated in the WTO context, distinguishing between what the texts themselves have to say and the actual practice of states. Finally, we shall consider the pressure that the new environment exerts on existing rules and suggest some plausible outcomes for the future.

Content regulation in the audio-visual sector

Content regulation is of interest to the WTO insofar as it entails some form of restriction on the international circulation of goods or services. From that point of view, the concept of content regulation is close to two other concepts frequently used in international trade practice to describe such situations which are those of 'content requirement' and 'content restriction'. Although often considered more or less as synonymous, these two concepts differ in the way in which they operate, the first one acting by way of affirmative obligations and the second one by way of prohibitions. Content requirement thus refers to regulations that usually prescribe a given percentage of local content in film and television programmes or a given percentage of television and radio programmes in the national language or languages; they are commonly referred to in such cases as local content requirements. The expression also covers obligations to provide a balance of viewpoints. The usual justification for regulations of that nature

[4] *Ibid.*

is that they are essential to preserve and promote cultural and linguistic diversity as well as freedom of expression and pluralism. The concept of content restriction for its part refers to regulations that exclude certain types of content (so-called illicit material) or allow them subject to certain conditions (unsuitable material); the regulations in question concern the protection of minors, the protection of human dignity and of public morals and the protection of consumers. But the concept of 'content regulation', being somewhat broader than those of 'content requirement' and 'content restriction', also encompasses a third type of intervention that intends to stimulate the development of local content, such as direct subsidies for the production of local programmes or an 'investment quota' obliging television operators to devote a percentage of their annual earnings on films deemed national or produced in the national language.[5] These three types of regulations, as we shall see now, raise different levels of concern in practice.

The type of content regulation that appears to raise most concern in trade practice so far is the one that imposes local content requirements. This does not come entirely as a surprise because local content requirements are assimilated to quotas which are generally viewed as more prejudicial than subsidies from an economic point of view.[6] In the 2002 National Trade Estimate Report on Foreign Trade Barriers, published by the United States Trade Representative, for instance, some 30 states, including the Member States of the European Union, are identified as trade partners of the United States which maintain local content restrictions in the audio-visual sector.[7] An earlier study in 1998 by Solon Consultants for the EU Commission, entitled 'Audio-visual Industry; Trade and Investment Barriers in Third Country Markets States', already pointed out that '[a]s a rule, audio-visual suppliers commonly encounter non-tariff measures in the form of law and practice barriers, such as quotas

[5] A discussion paper commissioned by the Asia-Pacific Broadcasting Union and entitled 'Trade Liberalisation in the Audio-visual Services Sector and Safeguarding Cultural Diversity' (1999) affirms in this regard: 'Content regulation can also foster the development of domestic production industries which create local programs' (*ibid.*, p. 7). See www.aba.gov.au/radio/research/projects/trade.htm.

[6] For a more elaborate and balanced view on the subject, see Martin Richardson, 'Cultural Quotas in Broadcasting: Local Content Requirements, Advertising Limits and Public Radio', University of Otago, Dunedin, New Zealand (2002), www.economics.utoronto.ca/roberts/quotas.pdf.

[7] See United States Trade Representative, '2002 National Trade Estimate Report on Foreign Trade Barriers'. Apart from the Member States of the European Union, those identified included Argentina, Australia, Brazil, Bulgaria, Canada, China, Egypt, Hungary, Malaysia, Mexico, Poland, Romania, South Korea, Ukraine and Venezuela.

that affect the theatrical distribution of films; [and] the broadcasting of foreign-made productions.'[8] Authors who have considered the question also come to similar conclusions. According to Gareth Grainger: 'Regulations for domestic content quotas for the television industries have been adopted by the majority of western countries. Noteworthy exceptions to this general pattern are the US and New Zealand. The mechanisms relied on are broadly similar in those nations with quota systems.'[9]

Concrete examples of local content requirements in national practice will help to explain how they operate. In most cases, the local content requirement is expressed in terms of national content. Thus, in Canada, the federal broadcasting regulator, the Canadian Radio, Television and Telecommunications Commission (CRTC), requires that for Canadian conventional, over-the-air broadcasters, Canadian programmes make up 60 per cent of television broadcast time overall and 50 per cent during evening hours (6 p.m. to midnight). It also requires that 35 per cent of popular musical selections broadcast on radio should qualify as 'Canadian' under a Canadian government-determined points system. For cable TV and direct-to-home (DTH) broadcast services, a preponderance (more than 50 per cent) of the channels received by subscribers must be Canadian programming services. For other services, such as specialty television and pay audio services, the required percentage of Canadian content varies according to the nature of the service.[10] A similar approach is used in the European Union where the Television Without Frontiers Directive requires that 'Member States shall ensure where practicable and by appropriate means that broadcasters reserve for European works . . . a majority proportion of their transmission time, excluding the time appointed to news, sports events, games, advertising, teletext services and teleshopping.'[11] The Directive also allows Member States to apply stricter

[8] Solon Consultants, 'Audio-visual Industry: Trade and Investment Barriers in Third Country Markets', Final Report prepared for the DG 1 Market Access Unit of the European Commission, November 1998, www.obs.coe.int/online_publication/reports/00002413.pdf.

[9] Gareth Grainger, 'Globalisation and Cultural Diversity: The Challenge to the Audio-visual Media', see also Franco Papandrea, 'Cultural Regulation of Australian Television Programs', Occasional Paper No. 114, Australia, Bureau of Transport and Communications Economics, 1997, Appendix II, p. 233.

[10] See the website of the Canadian Radio Television and Communications Commission, www.crtc.gc.ca/eng/INFO_SHT/G11.htm. For a condensed presentation of the subject, see Commonwealth of Australia, Productivity Commission, 'Broadcasting', Report No. 11, AusInfo, Canberra, Appendix F (2000).

[11] The Television Without Frontiers Directive 89/552/EEC was adopted on 3 October 1989 by the Council, and amended on 30 June 1997 by European Parliament and Council Directive 97/36/EC.

provisions where they are deemed necessary for national and cultural (notably linguistic) reasons, which a number of them have done. In France, for instance, terrestrial television must allocate 40 per cent of time to original French-language works. Similar requirements are also in use in a number of states for radio programming.[12]

Characteristic of this type of approach is the need to define what constitutes national content. Canadian content status is determined on the basis of a 10 point scale. Programmes are awarded points for each key creative person who is a Canadian citizen at the rate of two points each for the director and screenwriter and one point each for the highest and second highest paid actor, the head of the art department, the director of photography, the music composer and the picture editor. Programmes must be produced by a Canadian and have at least six points to be considered Canadian. To qualify for financial assistance, programmes must attain 10 points.[13] In Australia, the determination of what is an Australian programme follows a very similar procedure consisting of determining whether the programme in question is produced under the creative control of Australians.[14] Sometimes, the local content requirement is expressed in terms of a limit to foreign participation in the national audio-visual market. Thus, in Korea, local content in the free TV sector is favoured by limiting the percentage of monthly broadcasting time (not to exceed 20 per cent) that may be devoted to imported programmes. Annual quotas also limit, at a maximum of 75 per cent, 58 per cent and 40 per cent respectively, broadcast motion pictures, animation and popular music. Korea also restricts foreign participation in the cable TV sector by limiting per channel air time for most foreign programming to 50 per cent. Annual quotas are set at 70 per cent for broadcast motion pictures and at 60 per cent for animation.

State interventions to stimulate the production of local content in the audio-visual sector do not appear to generate the same level of concern, even if, as a 1998 WTO Secretariat study on audio-visual services noted,

[12] In France, a radio broadcast quota (40 per cent of songs on almost all French private and public radio stations must be Francophone) took effect on 1 January 1996: see Loi 9488 of 1 February 1994, Article 12. In Canada, all radio stations must ensure that 35% of their popular musical selections each week is Canadian, and French-language radio stations must ensure that at least 65 per cent of popular vocal music selections each week is in the French language: see note 10 above.

[13] See note 10 above.

[14] The detailed procedure is described on the website of the Australian Broadcasting Authority, www.aba.gov.au/tv/content/ozcont/std/index.htm#3.

'substantial subsidies are granted in a number of WTO members'.[15] More often than not, those subsidies are granted on condition that they contribute to the production of local programmes. In Germany, for instance, financial support for a full-length film requires that the film in question be identifiable to Germany, whether through the compulsory use of the German language, through requirements concerning the origin of the persons or enterprises involved in the production of the film or requirements concerning the location of the shooting itself.[16] As early as 1970, in the Tokyo Round catalogue of non-tariff barriers the United States had complained about the subsidies employed by twenty-one countries in order to support their cinema and television industries.[17] During the Uruguay Round, the uncertainty concerning the treatment of subsidies in the audio-visual sector was taken seriously enough to prompt the European Economic Community to include, in its last minute attempt to have a cultural clause included in the GATS, a provision guaranteeing the right of Member States to subsidise their audio-visual industry.[18] Since then, however, complaints regarding subsidies to producers of local programmes have been rare. It is interesting to note in that regard that in both the 2002 National Trade Estimate Report on Foreign Trade Barriers, and the Solon Communications study prepared for the European Commission, there is no reference to state interventions to stimulate the production of local programmes. But a particular case must be made in this respect of indirect subsidies which take the form of investment quotas obliging television operators to devote a percentage of their annual earnings on films deemed national or produced in the national language. Such interventions remain identified, both in US National Trade Estimate Report on Foreign Trade Barriers and the Solon study as trade barriers in the audio-visual sector. An example of such a type of intervention which operates as an

[15] See WTO Doc. S/C/W/40, 15 June 1998, p. 6, www.wto.org/english/tratop_e/serv_e/w40.doc.

[16] On this see Michel Gyory, 'Making and Distributing Films in Europe: The Problem of Nationality', www.obs.coe.int/online_publication/reports/natfilm.html, study carried out in cooperation with and commissioned by the European Audio-visual Observatory (January 2000).

[17] See GATT, Doc. MTN/3B1.

[18] See www.wto.org/english/tratop_e/serv_e/w40.doc. The attempt failed by only a small margin, because, according to Karl F. Falkenberg, the Community presented its position late in the negotiations: see 'The Audio-visual Sector', in Jacques H. J. Bourgeois, Frédérique Berrod and Eric Gippini Fournier, ed. The Uruguay Round Results: A European Lawyer's Perspective (Brussels: European Interuniversity Press/College of Europe, 1995), p. 432.

indirect subsidy is the legislation adopted in 1999 by the Spanish Parliament which obliges television operators to devote 5 per cent of their annual earnings to finance European feature-length films and films for European television. This investment quota was further defined in July 2001 in new legislation (60 per cent of the investment quota must be spent on audio-visual works in one of Spain's official languages).[19] Similarly, Australia's Broadcasting Services Amendment Act requires pay television channels which include more than 50 per cent drama programmes in their schedules, to spend 10 per cent of their programming budget on new Australian drama programmes.[20]

Rarely identified as a trade barrier until recently, content regulations regarding illicit and unsuitable material have become, in recent years, a subject of growing concern particularly in the context of the Internet. This type of regulation has been traditionally considered as falling within the category of measures that are necessary to protect public morals and the public order which is recognised as a general exception in Article XIV of the GATS.[21] The few references to such measures to be found in the US 2002 National Trade Estimate Report on Foreign Trade Barriers concern cases where the scope of the measures in question appears excessively broad or where they are applied in an inconsistent and subjective way.[22] Interestingly, the only case of cultural barriers in the form of censorship mentioned in the Solon report concern the United States where the interventions originate not from the government but from the industry[23]. More recently, however, the problem has taken a new dimension with the attempt of the French judiciary to affirm its jurisdiction to apply local regulations censoring certain types of information in a case involving foreign-based sites.[24] This case raises in broader terms the problem of the impact of new communication technology and the Internet on content regulation, which will be examined in more detail below.

[19] '2001 Country Reports on Economic Policy and Trade Practices', released by the Bureau of Economic and Business Affairs, US Department of State, February 2002 (under 'Spain'): see www.state.gov/documents/organization/8235.pdf.

[20] See Office of the United States Trade Representative, '2002 National Trade Estimate Report on Foreign Trade Barriers', under 'Australia'.

[21] See also, by analogy, Article XX(a) of the GATT 1994.

[22] The states concerned are China, the Gulf Cooperation Council, India and Singapore.

[23] See the discussion on this at pp. 229–30 below.

[24] *Tribunal de grande instance* of Paris, 20 November 2000, in *Association 'Union des Etudiants Juifs de France'*, la '*Ligue contre le Racisme et l'Antisémitisme*', le '*MRAP*' (*intervenant volontaire*) v. *Yahoo! Inc. et Yahoo France*. See also the decision handed down in the United States in *Yahoo! Inc.* v. *Ligue contre le Racisme et l'Antisémitisme*, US District Court for the Northern District of California, Case No. C-00-21275JF, 7 November 2001.

The present treatment of content regulation in the WTO

The three basic types of content regulation that we have identified in the audio-visual sector raise distinct legal problems in the context of the WTO and therefore must be examined separately. Although they are examined first and foremost under the GATS, since the audio-visual sector is generally considered as a service sector, the impact of other WTO agreements such as the GATT 1994 will be considered. This raises an issue that is not yet resolved and of which a word must be said at the outset.

To say that certain agreements are applicable to goods as opposed to services implies that there is a clear distinction between goods and services. Unfortunately, that is not always the case. Thus, although films are specifically mentioned in Articles III and IV of the GATT 1994 and duty concessions have been made in relation to films, cinema has been considered as a service in the GATS, in the OECD's Code on Invisible Current Transactions and in the United Nations Central Products Classification.[25] The same ambivalence is reflected in dispute settlement procedures. In 'Turkey – Taxation of Foreign Film Revenues',[26] the US complaint against Turkey was based on Article III of the GATT, but in 'Canada – Measures Affecting Film Distribution Services',[27] the EC complaint against Canada was based on Articles II and III of the GATS.

The possibility of conflict in the application of the GATT and the GATS raises a fundamental problem that was first examined in the WTO decision of June 1997 in 'Canada – Certain Measures Relating to Periodicals.' The finding of the Panel that '[t]he ordinary meaning of the texts of GATT 1994 and GATS as well as Article II:2 of the WTO Agreement, taken together, indicates that the obligations under GATT 1994 and GATS can co-exist and that one does not override the other' was supported by the Appellate Body.[28] Specifically with respect to periodicals, the Appellate Body went as far as to say that 'a periodical is a good comprised of two components: editorial content and advertising content. Both components can be viewed as having services attributes, but they combine to form a physical

[25] United Nations Central Products Classification, version 1.0, Code 96, Doc. ST/ESA/STAT/Ser.M/77/Ver. 1.0.

[26] Doc. WT/DS43 (1996).

[27] See 'Canada – Measures Affecting Film Distribution Services', WT/DS117/1 (1998).

[28] Doc. WT/DS31/AB/R, 30 June 1997, section 4. Canada was arguing in that case that the provision of the Excise Tax Act challenged by the United States was not a measure regulating trade in goods but rather a measure regulating trade in services (access to the advertising market).

product – the periodical itself'.[29] Needless to say, this last statement, interpreted literally, could have far-reaching consequences.

Barely two months later, in 'European Communities – Regime for the Importation, Sale and Distribution of Bananas,' the Appellate Body attempted to explain more fully its view on the subject of potential conflicts between trade agreements. It wrote:

> Given the respective scope of the two agreements, they may or may not overlap, depending on the measure at issue. Certain measures could be found to fall exclusively within the scope of GATT 1994, when they affect trade in goods as goods. Certain measures could be found to fall exclusively within the scope of GATS, when they affect the supply of services as services. There is yet a third category of measures that could be found to fall within the scope of both the GATT 1994 and the GATS. These are measures that involve a service relating to a particular good or service supplied in conjunction with a particular good. In all such cases in this third category, the measure in question could be scrutinized under both the GATT 1994 and the GATS. However, while the same measure could be scrutinized under both agreements, the specific aspects of that measure examined under each agreement could be different. Under the GATT 1994, the focus is on how the measure affects the goods involved. Under the GATS, the focus is on how the measure affects the supply of the service or of the service suppliers involved. Whether a certain measure affecting the supply of a service related to a particular good is scrutinized under the GATT 1994 or the GATS, or both, is a matter that can only be determined on a case-by-case basis.[30]

But this still leaves open the possibility that the exercise of a right under one agreement becomes the negation of a right under the other. This is what would have happened, for example, if India's limitations on film distribution in its specific commitments under the GATS, although in full conformity with the agreement and accepted by all the parties to it, had been successfully challenged under the GATT as a restriction on the import of a good.[31] Unless a line is traced somewhere between what

[29] *Ibid.*

[30] Report of the Appellate Body, 'European Communities – Regime for the Importation, Distribution and Sale of Bananas', AB-1997-3, WT/DS27/AB/R (1997), paras. 221–2. In 1998, in 'Indonesia – Certain Measures Affecting the Automobile Industry', the same reasoning was extended to a situation which involved an apparent conflict between the Agreement on Subsidies and Countervailing Measures and the Agreement on Trade-Related Investment Measures. WT/DS54/R, WT/DS55/R, WTDS59/R, WT/DS64/R, 2 July 1998, paras. 14.52–14.53.

[31] For the Indian exceptions in the film distribution sector, see GATS/SC/42, p. 8. Most of these limitations, however, have subsequently been dropped by India.

pertains to trade in services and what pertains to trade in goods, conflicts of this nature appear inevitable.

Content requirements

Interestingly, the best known and most explicit provision regarding content requirements is not to be found in the GATS but in the GATT 1994. It takes the form of an exception to the obligation of national treatment of Article III which is developed in Article IV. It provides that a Member may maintain or establish screen quotas requiring the exhibition of films of national origin during a specified minimum portion of the total screen time in the commercial exhibition of all films of whatever origin; such screen quotas, however, are subject to negotiations for their limitation, liberalisation or elimination. In its Communication on Audio-visual and Related Services of 18 December 2000, to the WTO Council for Trade in Services, the United States explains the *raison d'être* of that provision as follows:

> GATT Article IV provides a special, and unique, exception for cinematographic films to GATT national treatment rules. In 1947, in recognition of the difficulty that domestic film producers faced in finding adequate screen time to exhibit their films in the immediate post-World War II period, GATT founders authorised continuation of existing screen-time quotas.[32]

This explanation, however, appears quite recently and contradicts the one that was given by the main proponents of the exception during the negotiations of the GATT (the United Kingdom, Norway and Czechoslovakia) who advocated that in the case of films, important cultural considerations entered into consideration, which was not the case for other goods.[33] This last explanation is also taken up by John Jackson in his seminal work on the GATT[34] and is the one offered in the historical review of Article IV prepared by the GATT Secretariat in 1990 for the Uruguay Round Working Group on Audio-visual Services.[35] Interestingly, the United States, in its Communication on Audio-visual and Related Services of 18 December 2000, explicitly mentions Article IV of the GATT

[32] See WTO, Council for Trade in Services, Communication from the United States, Audio-visual and Related Services, 18 December 2000, Doc. S/CSS/W/21, para 8.

[33] Second Session of the Preparatory Committee of the United Nations Conference on Trade and Development (Geneva, 1947), Doc. EPCT/TAC/SR/10.

[34] John H. Jackson, World Trade and the Law of the GATT: *A Legal Analysis of the General Agreement on Tariffs and Trade* (Indianapolis: Bobbs-Merrill, 1969), p. 293.

[35] GATT Doc. MTN.GNS/AUD/W/1, 4 October 1990.

1994 as an example of the flexibility of the WTO system in answer to the argument that trade rules in the audio-visual sector are too rigid to take into consideration the special cultural qualities of the sector.[36]

In 1961, the question of the extension of the language of Article IV, which refers exclusively to cinematographic films, to cover television programmes recorded in video format was raised by the United States. It stated then that 'restrictions against the showing of television programs were technically a violation of the principles of Article III:4, but that some of the principles of Article IV might apply to them'.[37] Canada for its part took the position that Article IV covered the issue, even though the Article did not mention television programmes as such, because this was a development that could not have been foreseen in 1947. Unfortunately, the working group set up to examine the question was unable to reach a consensus on the subject.[38]

To the extent that films or video films are covered by the GATT 1994, the further question arises of whether other provisions could apply to content requirements. The immediate answer that comes to mind, in view of the fact that they are assimilated to quotas, is obviously Article XI. But it would appear (to say the least) awkward that measures that are protected by Article IV could be challenged under Article XI. The situation is different if the protection of Article IV does not apply. In 1991, a request for consultations with the European Community was addressed to the GATT by the United States concerning restrictions on the showing of non-European programmes in the Television Without Frontiers Directive; the United States, while recognising the existence of the Article IV exception, pointed out that it applied exclusively to cinematographic films and argued that such restrictions were incompatible with Article XI.[39] The matter was later dropped to become part of a wider debate in the context of the Uruguay Round negotiations on services. It was still unresolved

[36] This does not mean that film quotas are accepted in practice. In 1998–9, a vigorous debate emerged in South Korea following the decision of the government to gradually phase out the local screen quota which the US government, in the context of ongoing Seoul–Washington investment negotiations, had described as a protectionist policy and the elimination of which it had made a condition for the signature of a bilateral investment agreement. See 'Korean Film Industry's Plea for Screen Quota Turns Emotional', *Korea Herald*, 18 June 1999. The debate was still going on in early 2002 as evidenced by an article published in the *Korea Herald* entitled 'Film Industry Leaders Protest Gov't Bid to Ease Screen Quota Regulations', 29 January, 2002.

[37] See GATT Analytical Index 1994, p. 192.

[38] *Ibid.*

[39] *Ibid.*

at the end of these negotiations and, since then, neither the quotas of the Television Without Frontiers Directive nor other existing quotas, including the radio quotas maintained by France and Canada, have been challenged.

Another provision that could apply is Article I, which imposes the most-favoured nation (MFN) treatment. Thus, content requirements that would apply to certain Members of the WTO and not to others could be challenged. But Article IV does include an exception to the MFN treatment in the case of measures 'which reserve a minimum proportion of screen time for films of a specified origin other than that of the contracting party imposing such screen quotas',[40] the exception in question apparently concerning countries that shared the same language.

The situation of content requirements under the GATS is quite different. National treatment and market access obligations are determined by the specific commitments of the Members under Articles XVI and XVII of the GATS. Those Members that have not included the audio-visual sector in their specific commitments have no obligations in that respect and remain free to adopt or maintain content requirements. Those Members that have included the audio-visual sector in their commitments are bound by Articles XVI and XVII, subject to the terms, limitations and conditions agreed and specified in their schedule of commitments. In practice, few Members have made commitments in the audio-visual sector. A WTO document mentions in this respect that only nineteen Members (thirteen at the conclusion of the Uruguay Round negotiations, six more as a result of accession) have made market-opening commitments in the audio-visual sector, including four developed countries (the United States, Japan, New Zealand and Israel) and fifteen developing countries, and that many of these commitments include various types of limitations.[41] Clearly, there is some reluctance on the part of GATS Members to undertake obligations in this area.[42] The fact is that, once a Member

[40] Article IV(c) of the GATT 1994.

[41] WTO Council for Trade in Services,'Audio-visual Services', Background Note by the Secretariat, S/C/W/40, 15 June 1998, paras. 24–6 and Table 9.

[42] Christopher Arup, in *The New World Trade Organization Agreements: Globalizing Law Through Services and Intellectual Property* (Cambridge: Cambridge University Press), 2000. p. 301, writes in this regard: 'The GATS has added to the pressure on those national measures which were designed to ensure that less powerful and mainstream voices, particularly local ones, enjoyed access to distribution channels. Nevertheless, for the time being, many countries have availed themselves of the opportunities inherent in the GATS itself to maintain limitations on their exposure to the open-trade and free-market norms of the WTO.'

has made a commitment with regard to a particular category of services, it cannot easily withdraw the commitment.[43] New Zealand, which had committed in 1993 not to have recourse to quantitative restrictions in the audio-visual sector, was reminded of this fact in no uncertain terms following its government's pledge in 2001 to introduce format-specific quotas for local content for radio and broadcast television.[44] The United States Trade Representative, in its National Trade Estimate Report on Foreign Trade Barriers 2001, pointed out that such an action would violate New Zealand's commitments under the GATS.[45]

Content requirements in the audio-visual sector could also be challenged, whether specific commitments have been made or not, if they violate the MFN obligation of Article II of the GATS, which provides for the granting of most-favoured nation treatment to all services and service suppliers of all Members. However, under paragraph 2 of that same Article, a 'Member may maintain a measure inconsistent with paragraph 1 provided that such measure is listed in, and meets the conditions of, the Annex on Article II Exemptions'. The conditions in question provide that all exemptions granted for a period of more than five years should be reviewed and that in principle exemptions should not exceed a period of ten years. A large number of MFN exemptions have been taken in regard to audio-visual services. Counting the European Community as a single entity, a total of thirty-three MFN exemptions[46] specifically applying to the audio-visual sector are in place, most of which concern cinema and television co-production agreements inscribed in the Annex on Article II, for reasons having to do essentially with national and regional cultural

[43] Article XXI admittedly provides for modification or withdrawal of any commitment in a Member's schedule but subject to compensation.

[44] New Zealand, Ministry for Culture and Heritage, Department Forecast Report 2001, p. 9, www.mch.govt.nz/publications/dfr2001/.

[45] Office of the United States Trade Representative, 'National Trade Estimate Report on Foreign Trade Barriers 2001', under 'New Zealand'.

[46] The thirty-three exemptions covering audio-visual services are by Australia, Austria, Bolivia, Brazil, Brunei Darussalam, Bulgaria, Canada, Chile, Colombia, Cuba, Cyprus, the Czech Republic, Ecuador, Egypt, the European Community, Finland, Hungary, Iceland, India, Israel, Liechtenstein, New Zealand, Norway, Panama, Poland, Singapore, the Slovak Republic, Slovenia, Sweden, Switzerland, Tunisia, the United States and Venezuela. The eight general MFN exemptions potentially impacting audio-visual services are by El Salvador, Malaysia, Peru, the Philippines, Sierra Leone, Thailand, Turkey and the United Arab Emirates. WTO, Council on Trade in Services, Audio-visual Services, Background Note by the Secretariat, Doc. S/C/W/40, 15 June 1998, www.wto.org/english/tratop_e/serv_e/w40.doc, para. 29.

identity.[47] One such exemption that can be considered as covering a content requirement is that of the European Communities regarding measures which define works of European origin in such a way as to extend national treatment to audio-visual works which meet certain linguistic and origin criteria regarding access to broadcasting or similar forms of transmission.[48]

Content restrictions

Content restrictions that apply to illicit or questionable content, whether they take the form of a total prohibition or of conditional access, cannot easily be challenged as a violation of the GATS national treatment provision to the extent that they are normally applied without discrimination to national services and services providers and to foreign services and services providers. From that point of view they differ from content requirements which, by definition, discriminate between national and foreign services and services providers. To have a chance to succeed, a challenge under Article XVII of the GATS would require, first, a demonstration that a commitment regarding the audio-visual sector has been taken without reservations concerning national treatment, and, secondly, a demonstration that the complainant Member is not treated as favourably as the respondent Member. A more appropriate way of challenging content restrictions before the GATS would be to resort to Article XVI which deals with market access, provided once again that market access commitments regarding audio-visual services have been made without reservations. In both cases, however, the Member State author of the measure incriminated could always argue that the measure in question was authorised by Article XIV(a) of the GATS, which provides that:

> Subject to the requirement that such measures are not applied in a manner which would constitute a means of arbitrary or unjustifiable discrimination between countries where like conditions prevail, or a disguised restriction on trade in services, nothing in this Agreement shall be construed to prevent the adoption or enforcement by any Member of measures:
>
> (a) necessary to protect public morals or to maintain public order...

[47] For examples of specific exemptions, see GATS/EL/82 and GATS/EL/33 for Sweden and Finland, and GATS/EL/92 for Venezuela.

[48] GATS/EL/31, European Communities and their Member States, Final List of Article II (MFN) Exemptions, www.wto.org/english/tratop_e/serv_e/serv_commitments_e.htm.

A footnote annexed to sub-paragraph (a) specifies that 'the public order exception may be invoked only where a genuine and sufficiently serious threat is posed to one of the fundamental interests of society'.

In practice, although certain types of content restrictions in the audio-visual sector have been described as trade barriers,[49] and at least in one case have even given rise to an actual dispute,[50] no formal complaints have to this day been lodged before the WTO regarding the legality of such interventions.[51] But the possibility of having recourse to Article XIV(a) does exist and could find application in the audio-visual sector in the case of regulations intended to preserve public morality. The United States, in their Communication on Audio-visual and Related Services of 18 December 2000 to the WTO Council for Trade in Services, argued as further evidence of the flexibility of the WTO system in the audio-visual sector that 'in both the GATS (Article XIV(a)) and GATT (Article XX(a)), the general exception for measures necessary to protect public morals provides further reassurance for Members concerned that commitments relating to content mean that they will not be able to apply regulations intended to preserve public morality'.[52]

If a measure of that nature was to be effectively challenged before the WTO, the question would immediately arise of how to interpret the expression 'public morals', since standards of public morals may differ among participating states. It has been pointed out in that regard that only a case-by-case approach at the judicial level and strict compliance with the rules of the Vienna Convention on the Law of Treaties could provide predictability with respect to the 'public morals' exception.[53] Another question could also arise regarding the responsibility of the state due to the fact that content restrictions are not always implemented through government regulation but sometimes also through codes of ethics developed and applied by the private sector. In such a case, a distinction might have to be made between those interventions which are directly or indirectly mandated by the state and those where the private sector acts entirely on

[49] See notes 22 and 23 above.

[50] The dispute concerned import prohibitions on pornographic products. See Christoph T. Feddersen, 'Focusing on Substantive Law in International Economic Relations: The Public Morals of GATT's Article XX(a) and "Conventional" Rules of Interpretation', *Minnesota Journal of Global Law* 7 (1998): 75.

[51] A similar measure to be found in Article XX(a) of the GATT 1947 never came before a GATT panel.

[52] See note 32 above.

[53] See Feddersen, 'Focusing on Substantive Law'.

its own. In the first instance, GATT and WTO decisions regarding government involvement in general suggest that, where the implementation of a code of ethics is dependent on government action or intervention,[54] it would be open to Members to challenge the code in question if it restricts imports and the conditions of Article XIV(a) are not met. Thus, in Canada, where adherence to a code of ethics is a condition of the licence for conventional or specialty television programming as well as for pay television and pay-per-view programming, such a challenge would be possible.[55] In the second instance, where the private sector acts independently of the government, the state cannot be held responsible. Thus, the Motion Picture Association of America's classification code for films,[56] the application of which is totally independent of government, would not be open to a challenge before the WTO even if it was established that the classification of foreign films was discriminatory.

Content production

Content regulation, as explained above, is also used to foster the development of domestic production industries which create local programmes. This is done primarily through various types of subsidy programmes that act as an incentive to create local programmes. Such an approach, contrary to content requirements, is often described as a less intrusive way of ensuring local content. According to the European Commission, support mechanisms for audio-visual programmes are effectively needed due to market failure.[57] Article XV of the GATS, in that respect, simply recognises that, in certain circumstances, subsidies may have distortive effects on trade in services, and asks that Members enter into negotiations with a view to developing the necessary multilateral disciplines to avoid such distortive effects. According to Mario Kakabadse of the WTO Secretariat, '[t]here is no presupposition as to what the [disciplines] will contain or how different they will be from rules on subsidies in the goods area. Like all GATT/WTO negotiations, they will take place on the basis of consensus and it would seem unlikely that governments would abandon their

[54] See 'Japan – Trade in Semi-conductors', May 1988, BISD 35S/116, paras. 104–9.

[55] See Canadian Radio-Television and Telecommunication Commission, Public Notice CRTC 1996-135, 4 October 1996 and Public Notice CRTC 1994-155, 21 December 1994.

[56] See www.mpaa.org/movieratings/.

[57] See 'Regulating Audio-visual Content in the Digital Age', European Commission, Directorate-General for Education and Culture, Audio-visual Policy, http://europa.eu.int/comm/avpolicy/intro/show.pdf.

explicit right to support film production.'[58] In view of the substantial financial support given by many governments to their cultural industries, these negotiations should obviously be followed with care.[59] However, because of the inherent complexity of developing guidelines in this area, the negotiations in question have progressed very slowly since their beginning, in 1995, in the context of the Working Party on GATS Rules.[60] It remains unclear for the moment to what extent there is a real consensus on the need for such guidelines.

Even though there are currently no multilateral disciplines on subsidies as such in the GATS, subsidies are not totally beyond the reach of the GATS. The GATS does apply, for instance, in a situation where access to domestic subsidies is granted to certain states and not to others. A concrete example of this in the cultural sector is that of cinema and television co-production agreements which provide preferential access to funding: but for the exemption regime of Article II:2 of GATS, those agreements would clearly be in violation of the MFN obligation of Article II:1. Thus, in its list of Article II exemptions, the European Communities mention '[m]easures granting the benefit of any support programmes (such as Action Plan for Advanced Television Services, MEDIA or EURIMAGES) to audio-visual works, and suppliers of such works, meeting certain European origin criteria'.[61] The GATS also applies to subsidies when members list a

[58] Mario A. Kakabadse, 'The WTO and the Commodification of Cultural Products: Implications for Asia', Media Asia 22(2) (1995): 71–7. In its Communication on Audio-visual and Related Services of 18 December 2000 to the WTO Council for Trade in Services, the United States writes in this respect: '*Finally, in its current form, the GATS does not prevent governments from funding audio-visual services, a sensitive issue for many Members where local theatrical film production, for example, is dependent on government support. While the GATS provides for future negotiations to develop disciplines on subsidies that distort trade in services, there is no presupposition as to what those provisions will contain.*' See note 32 above.

[59] In a 1998 Background Note prepared by the Secretariat for the Working Party on GATS Rules which analyses, on the basis of information provided in the Trade Policy Reviews, subsidies for services sectors, aids to the audio-visual industries are the most frequently mentioned type of subsidy: see Doc. S/WPGR/W/25 (26 January 1998).

[60] See the note on conceptual issues relating to subsidies prepared by the Secretariat, Doc. S/WPGR/W9. For the most recent report of the Working Party on GATS Rules, dated 5 November 2002, see Doc. S/WPGR/8. See also Gilles Gauthier, with Erin O'Brien and Susan Spencer, 'Déjà Vu or New Beginning for Safeguards and Subsidies Rules in Services Trade', in Pierre Sauvé and Robert M. Stern, eds., *GATS 2000: New Directions in Services Trades Liberalization* (Cambridge, MA, and Washington, DC: Center for Business and Government, Harvard University, and Brookings Institution Press, 2000), p. 165 at pp. 176–81.

[61] WTO Doc. GATS/EL/31 (15 April 1994)

sector in their schedule of commitments without any limitation concerning national treatment. National treatment then requires governments providing subsidies to domestic services suppliers to make equivalent subsidies available to foreign services providers operating in the country. This explains why the United States, in one of its few limitations on specific commitments in audio-visual services, explicitly mentioned grants from the National Endowment for the Arts that are only available for individuals with US citizenship or permanent resident alien status, a clear indication that in its view such grants, in the absence of a limitation, would be incompatible with national treatment.[62] New Zealand has similarly indicated in its list that assistance to the film industry through the New Zealand Film Commission is limited to New Zealand films as defined in section 18 of the New Zealand Film Commission Act 1978.[63] In practice, the majority of members have included limitations to their national treatment commitments that apply to all subsidy practices.[64]

The treatment of content regulation fostering the development of local programmes through subsidies has been examined so far exclusively under the GATS. There remains to consider the possibility that a subsidy programme intended to stimulate the creation of local content might be investigated under one of the multilateral agreements on trade in goods of the WTO. Such a possibility is not to be excluded. It will be remembered in that respect that the United States complained in the 1970 GATT Catalogue of Non-Tariff Barriers about the subsidies granted by various states to their national film industries.[65]

The GATT provisions on subsidies having turned out to be largely ineffective, they have been completed by those of the Agreement on Subsidies and Countervailing Measures (SCM) which is much more constraining in that regard. Article 1:1 of the SCM Agreement contains a detailed definition of the term 'subsidy' that leaves very few financial contributions by a government or public body outside of the scope of the Agreement, provided that they are, in law or in fact, specific and a benefit is thereby conferred.[66] Subsidies subject to the Agreement fall into one of three

[62] GATS/SC/90, p. 46.

[63] GATS/SC/62, under audio-visual services.

[64] See Gauthier, O'Brien and Spencer, 'Déjà Vu', p. 177.

[65] GATT Doc. MTN/3B1. The countries in question were Argentina, Austria, Belgium, Brazil, Canada, Chile, Denmark, Egypt, France, Germany, Greece, Indonesia, Israel, Italy, Japan, the Netherlands, Norway, Pakistan, Portugal and the United Kingdom.

[66] The term 'specificity' is defined in Article 2 of the SCM Agreement, and essentially means that the subsidy is restricted, in law or in fact, to a limited number of enterprises or to a particular region of the country.

categories: prohibited subsidies (export subsidies and subsidies contingent upon the use of domestic over imported goods), non-actionable subsidies (subsidies that are not specific or which relate to research, regional development and environmental requirements and which meet certain criteria specified in the Agreement),[67] and actionable subsidies, which are not prohibited but can be challenged in the WTO dispute settlement system if they have an adverse effect on the interests of another Member (basically, all other subsidies).

Three types of adverse effect are envisaged in the category of actionable subsidies. First, injury to a domestic industry caused by subsidised imports in the territory of the complaining Member. Secondly, serious prejudice, which usually arises as a result of adverse effects (e.g. export displacement) in the market of the subsidising Member or in a third country market. Finally, nullification or impairment of benefits accruing under the GATT 1994, which arises most typically where the improved market access presumed to flow from a bound tariff reduction is undercut by subsidisation.

In practice, a challenge to a subsidy programme for the development of local content could be mounted in the WTO under Part III (actionable subsidies) of the SCM Agreement, or under a domestic countervailing law (which must comply with Part V (countervailing measures) of the SCM Agreement). In both instances, it would be necessary to demonstrate that the subsidised products and the affected products are 'like products', which is not particularly obvious in the case of cultural products.[68] According to Article 15:1, footnote 46, the expression 'like product' is to be interpreted throughout the SCM Agreement to mean a product that is identical, i.e. alike in all respects to the product under consideration, or in the absence of such a product, another product which, although not alike in all respects, has characteristics closely resembling those of the product under consideration'.

Content regulation in the new round of multilateral trade negotiations

There is manifestly a great deal of ambivalence in the way the present WTO legal regime deals with content regulations. However, as new

[67] The category of non-actionable subsidies no longer exists, since the relevant provision in the Agreement had a five-year term which was not renewed.

[68] See Articles 6:3 and 15:1 of the SCM Agreement.

communication technologies and convergence are forcing a re-evaluation of national approaches to content regulation at the national level, they are also challenging the present tolerance for content regulation in the context of the WTO. Two distinct arguments are made in that regard. The first argument is that, since the large number of available channels (due to the digitalisation and compression of the signal) and the tendency towards audience specialisation raise in more flexible terms the problem of compliance with positive (such as the programmes content and mix) and negative (such as the prohibition of specific materials) requirements, there is a growing and justifiable demand for less intrusive regulation, the technology and market characteristics of convergent services making such regulation less necessary.[69] The second argument is that traditional solutions regarding content regulation do not provide an adequate response to the legal problems raised by the trans-frontier nature of the new form of communication so well epitomised by the Internet.[70] Both arguments have significant implications for the present multilateral trade negotiations that must be considered.

The implications of the first argument are clearly articulated in the following presentation made by the Motion Picture Association of America (MPAA) before the US Congress in May 2001, a presentation which also reflects in essence the point of view of the US government. It starts with a recitation of the basic line of reasoning:

> Many countries around the world have a reasonable desire to ensure that their citizens can see films and TV programmes that reflect their history, their cultures, and their languages. In the past, when their towns might have had only one local cinema and received only one or two TV broadcast signals, the motivation for foreign governments to set aside some time for local entertainment products was understandable. In today's world, with multiplex cinemas and multi-channel television, the justification for local content quotas is much diminished. And, in the e-commerce world, the scarcity problem has completely disappeared. There is room on the Internet for films and video from every country on the globe in every genre imaginable. There is no 'shelf-space' problem on the net.[71]

[69] See François de Brabant, 'Some Comments on the Preparatory Document 'Working Group III' for the Birmingham Conference', http://europa.eu.int/eac/papers/debrabant3_en.html.

[70] As affirmed in the European Parliament's Resolution on the Commission Green Paper on the Protection of Minors and Human Dignity in Audio-visual and Information Services' (COM(96)483 – C4-0621/96), www.gilc.org/speech/eu/ep-minors-resolution-1097.html.

[71] 'Impediments to Digital Trade', Testimony of Bonnie J. K. Richardson, Vice President, Trade and Federal Affairs, Motion Picture Association of America, before the House Commerce

Then the MPAA goes on to explain to Congress the significance of this development for the ongoing trade negotiations:

> Fortunately, to date, we haven't seen any country adopt this form of market-closing measure for digitally delivered content. We hope this market will remain unfettered – and hope we can count on your support as we work with our international trade partners to keep digital networks free of cultural protectionism. Congressional authorization of Trade Promotion Authority will also be very helpful in empowering the Administration to negotiate these commitments in the WTO and other trade agreements.

The argument of the MPAA ends with a plea that the United States should ensure that digital goods retain the level of protection they currently enjoy under the GATT rules since it would be completely unacceptable if products that are currently classified as goods – motion pictures, magnetic tapes, DVDs, etc. – lost trade benefits through a reclassification process.

What attracts the attention at the outset in this argument is the demarcation that is made between the past and the future: if local content quotas were largely justified in the past and therefore tolerated, the situation has changed now with the development of new technologies, and they should either be negotiated away or, in the Internet and e-commerce world where the scarcity problem does not exist, purely and simply prohibited.

But before accepting this last conclusion, it may be useful to question the assumption that the justification for local content requirements is much diminished. This is all the more important since the pressure to have local content quotas gradually eliminated is already very much part of the present multilateral trade negotiations. The United States, in their specific requests to other countries to lower their trade barriers in audio-visual services, have asked that they schedule commitments that reflect current levels of market access in areas such as motion picture and home video entertainment production and distribution services, radio and television production services, and sound recording services.[72] Japan has also indicated in its general communication entitled 'The

Committee Subcommittee on Commerce, Trade and Consumer Protection, 22 May 2001, www.mpaa.org/legislation/. This viewpoint is also the one developed by the U.S. in their Communication to the WTO Council for Trade in Services, note **32** above.

[72] Office of the United States Trade Representative, Press Release 02-63, 1 July 2002, www.ustr.gov/releases/2002/07/02-63.htm.

Negotiations on Trade in Services' its desire to have issues such as quantitative limitations discussed in the audio-visual sector.[73]

But the claim that the justification for local content quotas for films and television programmes is much diminished in today's world appears at first sight at variance with statistics indicating that the degree of penetration of foreign audio-visual products in relation to local productions remains extremely high in many countries. Thus, regarding cinema, over one-third of all countries have practically no cinematographic image to reflect their own culture, and 'a characteristic feature of the situation in the 40 countries that do have a stable film production of between 10 and 200 films is dependence on direct government financing coupled with a high degree of legal protection which is even more important than public funding'.[74] In the case of television, the figures regarding local content are somewhat more favourable, but nevertheless remain problematic in many countries considering the importance of television as a means of social communication.[75]

Even among those countries that have a relatively acceptable level of production of films and television programmes of their own, there is no indication that the claim that content requirements are no longer justified in the new communications environment has led to a change of attitude concerning content requirements. A typical example of a country that has a relatively stable audio-visual production is Canada, with its well-developed subsidy programmes for films and television producers and its television and radio content requirements. Far from considering the new communication environment as a valid justification for doing away with content requirements, Canada has sought to respond in a timely and more open fashion to the development of new delivery technologies while still retaining a place for Canadian content across the

[73] Communications from Japan to the Council for Trade in Services, 'The Negotiations on Trade in Services', para. 37, 22 December 2000, www.wto.org/english/tratop_e/serv_e/s_propnewnegs_e.htm.

[74] See Luis Artigas de Quadras, 'Cultural Diversity in National Cinema', in UNESCO, *World Culture Report 2000* (Paris: UNESCO, 2000), p. 89. The affirmations are based on data taken from a survey of national cinema conducted by the Culture section of UNESCO which were published in May 2000; see www.unesco.org/culture/industries/cinema/html_eng/survey. shtml. See also Table 4 of the *World Culture Report* 2000.

[75] In many developing countries, consumption of locally produced television programmes is still marginal. As for developed countries, a certain number of them stand at the lower end of what would appear as a minimum requirement; see note 78 below.

broadcasting system.[76] Similarly, the European Commission, while recognising in its Communication of 1999 entitled 'Principles and Guidelines for the Community's Audio-visual Policy in the Digital Age' that the digital environment seemed to call for a wider approach at both national and Community level, has clearly reaffirmed that Europe's cultural and linguistic diversity had to be assured and, as such, had to be considered as a component of the development of the Information Society.[77] The only exception is New Zealand which, as indicated previously, committed in the Uruguay Round of negotiations not to have recourse to quantitative restrictions in the audio-visual sector, only to regret it later.[78] A recent study conducted in New Zealand has shown in that respect that the proportion of local content relative to total schedule time had diminished in recent years and that when compared with ten other countries New Zealand stood at the bottom end of the spectrum with a local content percentage of 24 per cent.[79]

All this seems to indicate that the problem of preserving, and *a fortiori* developing, a 'shelf-space' for national and regional cultures will remain a serious preoccupation for many countries in the foreseeable future. At the present time, it is difficult to predict how the divergence of view between those Members of the WTO who consider that local content requirements are no longer justified in the new communications environment and those Members who consider that they still remain justified will be resolved in the present negotiations. One scenario, suggested by the MPAA presentation to Congress, is that less pressure will be put in the present GATS negotiations on the elimination of existing content requirements in the traditional broadcasting framework and a great deal more on the pressure will be put prohibition of new content requirements in the digital networks.

Recent developments at the multilateral and bilateral level effectively tend to indicate that this is precisely the scenario adopted by the United States. Thus, in the GATS negotiations on services, the United States,

[76] As described by B. Goldsmith, J. Thomas, T. O'Regan and S. Cunningham 'Cultural and Social Policy Objectives for Broadcasting in Converging Media Systems', Australian Broadcasting Authority and Australian Key Centre for Cultural and Media Policy (KCCMP), May 2001, p. 73, www.aba.gov.au/tv/research/projects/pdfrtf/CMP_report.rtf.

[77] Commission of the European Communities, Brussels, 14 December 1999, Doc. COM(1999)657 final, p. 19.

[78] See notes 44 and 45 above.

[79] New Zealand On Air, 'Broadcasting and Cultural Issues at the Start of the New Millennium', www.nzonair.govt.nz/media/policyandresearch/otherpublications/issues.pdf.

while limiting themselves in their proposals for liberalising trade in audio-visual services to a request that countries schedule 'commitments that reflect current levels of market access in areas such as motion picture and home video entertainment production and distribution services, radio and television production services, and sound recording services',[80] strongly insist on the need to keep free of barriers trade in electronically delivered audio-visual products. This scenario finds further confirmation in the bilateral free trade agreements that they have signed[81] with Chile and Singapore in 2003 and more recently with Central American states and Australia. The agreements include a chapter on electronic commerce which has been described as 'a breakthrough in achieving certainty and predictability in ensuring access for products such as computer programs, video images, sound recordings and other products that are digitally encoded';[82] they establish a clear link between a pro-competitive and fully liberalised telecommunications sector and the development of electronic commerce, and assert, as one of their basic principles, that trade barriers to the free flow of content in digital products do not exist today and should not be created in the future. But, at the same time, they open the door in their service Chapter to cultural reservations with regard to conventional television, a possibility that has effectively been used. Thus, in the Chile–US Free Trade Agreement, Chile lists five cultural reservations in Annex I (existing measures that do not conform with obligations imposed) and Annex II (specific sectors for which a party may maintain existing, or adopt new or more restrictive, measures that do not conform with

[80] See United States Mission – Geneva, Press Release, 'US Proposals for Liberalizing Trade in Services', www.us-mission.ch/press2002/0702liberalizingtrade.html.

[81] For the text of the Chile–US Free Trade Agreement, see www.chileusafta.com or www.ustr.gov/new/fta/Chile/text/index.htm; and for the text of the US–Singapore Free Trade Agreement, see www.ustr.gov/new/fta/Singapore/final.htm or www.mti.gov.sg/public/PDF/CMT/FTA_USSFTA_Agreement_Final.pdf. For the Central American Free Trade Agreement, see www.ustr.gov/new/fta/Cafta/text/index.htm. In their chapters on electronic commerce, these agreements provide in essence: (1) that the supply of a service using electronic means (defined as means using computer processing) is covered by obligations set forth in the service chapter (MFN treatment, national treatment and market access) subject to reservations; (2) that the parties do not apply customs duties on digital products transmitted electronically (digital products being defined as 'computer programs, text, videos, sound recordings and other products that are digitally encoded and transmitted electronically, regardless of whether a party treats such products as a good or a service under its domestic law'); and (3) that trade in such digital products benefit from MFN treatment and national treatment.

[82] United States Trade Representative, Summary of US–Chile FTA Electronic Commerce Chapter, www.ustr.gov/new/fta/Chile/summaries/Chile%20Ecommerce%20Summary.PDF.

obligations imposed) to the Agreement; and, in the US–Singapore Free Trade Agreement, Singapore lists two cultural reservations in Annex II to the Agreement. Similar reservations are to be found in the Central American Free Trade Agreement and the US–Australia Free Trade Agreement.

This brings us to the second argument that has been put forward to justify the elimination of content regulation. The advent of direct-to-home satellite television had already given an indication of the difficulty of controlling content in a situation where the service provider is out of the country but has direct access to the consumer. With the Internet, as it quickly appeared, the difficulty was compounded. As explained by a representative of the Australian Broadcasting Authority at a conference held in Sydney in 1997:

> We recognized that the Internet cannot be regulated in the same manner as traditional media as there is no central control and content can be provided from anywhere in the world. And, unlike traditional mass media, such as broadcasting, the operators of the infrastructure, such as on-line service providers, are usually not aware of, and are not in a position to be aware of, much of the content which is being accessed or provided by users of their service, unless it is specifically brought to their attention.[83]

States quickly realised that this difficulty of regulating the content of the Internet would have a serious impact on their efforts to control illicit content or content unsuitable for children in the audio-visual sector: from a problem that up until then had been resolved essentially at the national level, it had become one that had an important international component and which seemed to require for its effective solution some degree of international cooperation. In 1998, Goldberg, Prosser and Verhulst could already predict that 'the international nature of the Internet and of other forms of new media will mean that future controls will have to be international in nature or involve self-regulation by parts of the industry itself. New attempts at content regulation are thus likely to look very different from techniques adopted in the past.'[84]

[83] Kaaren Koomen, 'Emerging Trends: Content Regulation in Australia and Some International Developments' www.aba.gov.au/abanews/speeches/online_serv/pdfrtf/kkaic_97.pdf, p. 4.

[84] D. Goldberg, T. Prosser and S. Verhulst, *Regulating the Changing Media* (London: Clarendon Press 1998), p. 16 (quoted in Tallach McGonagle, 'Does the Existing Regulatory Framework for Television Apply to New Media?', *Iris Plus, Legal Observations of the European Audio-visual Observatory*, Issue 2001-6).

This has not prevented some states from attempting to impose existing content restrictions on national service providers as well as on foreign service providers. A recent example of this is the attempt of the French judiciary in *Association 'Union des Etudiants Juifs de France,' la 'Ligue contre le Racisme et l'Antisémitisme', le 'MRAP' (intervenant volontaire)* v. *Yahoo! Inc. et Yahoo France*, to affirm its jurisdiction and apply local regulations censoring certain types of content in a case involving service providers based in the United States.[85] Following a preliminary decision rendered in May 2000 which ordered Yahoo Inc. to take all appropriate measures in order to deter and prevent any Internet visit from electronic visitors in France to the web pages and auction site of Nazi items on Yahoo.com, a final decision confirming that order was subsequently rendered in November 2000, after consideration of the written reports of experts establishing that the prescribed line of action was technically possible, at least sufficiently to establish an acceptable level of compliance. This last decision was immediately attacked by Yahoo.com in the United States on the ground that the First Amendment precluded enforcement within the United States of a French order intended to regulate the content of its speech over the Internet. On 7 November 2001, a motion for summary judgment was granted by the United States Court for the Northern District of California confirming in essence that the French decision was unenforceable in the United States.[86] The respondents in this last case, *La Ligue contre le racisme et l'antisémitisme*, lodged an appeal on December 2001 with the Ninth Circuit Court of Appeals in San Francisco, the decision of which is expected sometime in 2003.[87]

This trans-Atlantic legal struggle, which is far from over, seems to confirm the inappropriateness of the traditional broadcasting framework as a regulatory framework for the practices of the new media but also suggest at the same time that an international commitment to keep digital networks totally free of market-closing measures, as requested by the MPAA, is not something that will be readily acceptable in the near future. The fact is that states are truly concerned with the issue of illegal content on the Internet and have adopted or are in the process of adopting strategies to ensure that online content continues to be regulated whether formally or informally.[88] In most states, the general approach to online services

[85] Note 24 above.

[86] Case No. C-00-21275JF, 7 November 2001.

[87] Case No. 01-17424.

[88] A totally different situation of course is that of authoritarian governments who try to limit their citizens' access to the Internet through such censorship techniques as surveillance

regulation is based on existing legislative regimes for content that deals with subjects like obscene publications and the protection of children. Some states have gone further and adopted legislation dealing specifically with online content. The new Australian Broadcasting Services Amendment (Online Services) Act 1999, for instance, grants the government the power to force removal of sexually explicit or violent material from Australian web content hosts, the Australian Broadcasting Authority aiming to apply the same standards to Internet content as those applied to books and movies.[89] Quite a number of States have also chosen to complement their existing or newly introduced legislation with incentives for service providers to develop and comply with a self regulatory framework.

These developments, it must be pointed out, have taken place without any serious questions being raised concerning their compatibility with WTO obligations and without any serious attempts to resolve them at the international level. Whether it is because the states involved considered that they were covered by the public morals and public order exception of GATS Article XIV(a), or because they had made no commitments concerning audio-visual services and had no intention to take any in the present negotiations, the fact is that the immediate preoccupations with the problem of controlling illegal content have taken precedence over the search for an international solution.

Conclusion

The picture that emerges from our investigation of the treatment of content regulation in the WTO is one that is (to say the least) blurred. Content regulations in the audio-visual sector, although quite frequent in practice and often trade-distorting in their effect, seem to have been largely tolerated so far. A number of reasons can explain that situation. It could be because it is unclear to what extent they come under the GATT, the GATS or both, or because they are covered by an exception – the public morals exception – whose scope also remains to be determined, or because, in the case of GATS, there are no applicable obligations – as in the case of content production subsidies – or because the Members have

of e-mail and message boards, blocking content based on keywords, blocking individuals from visiting proscribed websites (often without those individuals even knowing the sites have been blocked), blacklisting users seeking to visit proscribed websites, and wholesale denial of Internet access.

89 For the text of the legislation, see: http://members.ozemail.com.au/~mbaker/amended.html.

taken no specific commitments regarding the audio-visual sector, or more simply because there is no will to challenge such content regulations, the justifications given for their existence being generally acceptable.

However, it is unclear to what extent this tolerance for content regulation will be allowed to continue in the future. New communication technologies and convergence are challenging in particular the 'scarcity' justification behind the use of local content requirements (the difficulty that domestic producers may have in finding adequate screen time to exhibit their films and television programmes); but at the same time, there is no evidence that these new technologies have significantly improved the situation of those states whose cinema and television are largely dominated by foreign products, with the result that such states have practically no image to reflect their own culture. More importantly, the transfrontier nature of the new forms of communication, so well epitomised by the Internet, have rendered the traditional solutions regarding content regulation inadequate. This has already forced a number of states to adjust their approach to content regulation with regard to the control of illegal content on the Internet. A similar process, characterised by an increasing recourse to subsidies, could take place with regard to local content requirements. Thus, for the moment, it seems that national attempts at content regulation are not about to disappear, but that they will nevertheless adjust with time to the particular conditions of the new telecommunication and communication environment.

9

International regulation of audio-visual services: networks, allocation of scarce resources and terminal equipment

DAVID LUFF

Introduction

The two previous chapters focused mainly on what is the essential policy objective surrounding many of the measures and discussions in the sector of audio-visual services: culture. This chapter will focus on the means used to convey and receive audio-visual products (whether content or services). It will examine whether WTO law provides an appropriate framework for the regulation of those means and to what extent culture is an issue in this area. After this introduction, the second part of the chapter will address the current application of WTO rules to the provision of and access to networks. The third part of this chapter will discuss the current principles and regulations concerning the allocation of scarce resources, such as frequencies and satellite orbits. The fourth part of this chapter will present the rules applicable to terminal equipment. The fifth and final part of this chapter will contain a small conclusion. Throughout this analysis, the consequences of convergence in the application of these rules will be addressed as well as the place that it left to cultural policies.

Networks (general rules)

Traditionally, audio-visual services have been conveyed either by air, through reserved frequency bands, or by cable. The latter generally provided a one-way communications path and could therefore be used only by broadcasting services. Presently, technological developments enable the fast conveyance of large quantities of sound, image and data in both one-way and two-way communication paths, through broadband infrastructure. Broadband networks thus support both telecommunications and audio-visual services. They enable their provision in an integrated manner. Broadband technology also facilitates the multiplication of such networks, generating new competitive relations in converged services.

It is therefore of some relevance to examine how current rules adapt to this new environment. Different facets of the general regulation of networks used to convey audio-visual services will be examined in this context: first, whether WTO rules mandate international competition in this sector; secondly, whether WTO law can be used by suppliers of audio-visual services to force access to existing networks; and, thirdly, what is the impact of convergence and broadband technology on these rules. Focus will be given to the trade in services aspect of networks, i.e. their function to transmit audio-visual signals through the radioelectric spectrum. Trade in goods aspects, such as those pertaining to the physical components of networks, do not present specific features here, which would distinguish them from trade in other relevant goods. We refer in this regard to the discussion below pertaining to terminal equipment.[1]

Liberalisation of networks?

Network services fall in principle within the scope of the GATS, to the extent they are not supplied in the exercise of governmental authority.[2] In other words, they are subject to GATS rules if they are supplied either on a commercial basis or in competition with other service suppliers,[3] which is now likely to be the case in most countries.

Under GATS, opening markets to international competition is obligatory for services for which commitments have been made. There is no such obligation for services for which no commitments have been made. It should be recalled that making a commitment for a service results from

[1] The issue of whether audio-visual content transmitted through telecommunications networks is a good or a service falls outside the scope of this paper. It should be noted, in this regard, that the WTO Secretariat considers that the electronic transmission of a message that can be downloaded and then printed or viewed is a service subject to the GATS. It may also constitute an input of a downloaded good (see WTO, Council for Trade in Services, 'The Work Programme on Electronic Commerce', Note of the Secretariat, S/C/W/68, 16 November 1988, paras. 36–8). Restricting this service may therefore have an impact on the trade in the good concerned. This, however, requires a determination of the origin of its good, i.e. whether or not it acquires the origin of the country where it is downloaded and sold. Probably the good would acquire the origin of the country where it underwent its last substantial transformation. This may be a complex determination, in particular concerning multinational productions.

[2] Article I:3(b) of the GATS.

[3] Article I:3(c) of the GATS.

its inclusion by WTO Members in their individual Schedules annexed to the GATS. Commitments may, however, be limited by specific indications in the Schedules.[4] Most commitments have been made according to a classification prepared by the WTO Secretariat during the Uruguay Round, on the basis of the United-Nations Central Product Classification List (CPC List).[5]

The difficulty arises here from the fact that there is no specific classification for networks used to provide audio-visual services. Furthermore, it is unclear whether commitments in audio-visual services themselves cover the networks necessary to supply them. In other words, does opening domestic markets to foreign audio-visual services also authorise their suppliers to operate their own networks? This very much depends on the interpretation given to current Schedules of commitments. As repeatedly indicated by the WTO's Appellate Body, such interpretations must abide by the rules of the Vienna Convention on the Law of Treaties.[6] The first rule in this regard is that of giving words their primary sense.[7] Thus, for instance, should a commitment be made on 'Radio and Television *Transmission* Services' (emphasis added), this arguably includes the networks necessary to *transmit* these services. The question remains open for 'Radio and Television Services' or for 'Motion Picture and Video Tape Production and Distribution'. It can be argued that networks are excluded for the first, considering the existing specific category of 'Transmission Services'. However, arguably, concerning 'Motion Picture Distribution Services', since they can now also be provided through broadband networks, commitments for them would include such networks.

In summary, liberalisation of networks used by audio-visual service providers depends on the types of commitment that are made for audio-visual services themselves. There is no separation in commitments between the networks and the content that can be supplied through them. Furthermore, current definitions are unclear as to the extent to which networks are included in commitments made for specific audio-visual services. As indicated below, such uncertainty and confusing commitments may be inappropriate in relation to broadband networks and for the definition of apposite domestic cultural policies.

[4] Article XX of the GATS.

[5] See Doc. MTN.GNS/W/120.

[6] See, by analogy with the GATT's tariff schedules, Appellate Body Report, 'European Communities – Customs Classification of Certain Computer Equipment', WT/DS62/AB/R, WT/DS67/AB/R, WT/DS68/AB/R, 5 June 1998, paras. 84ff.

[7] Article 31(1) of the Vienna Convention on the Law of Treaties, ILM 8 (1969): 679.

Should networks that are used for audio-visual services be covered by commitments, they would benefit from national treatment and market access obligations (respectively Articles XVI and XVII of the GATS), to the extent indicated in the Schedules. Should networks not be subject to commitments, which currently corresponds to the majority of the cases, then there is no obligation for WTO Members to open their markets to foreign network services. Only the general provisions of the GATS apply. These are, in particular, the MFN principle contained in Article II of the GATS and the rule of transparency contained in Article III of the GATS.

Access to public networks

Considering the uncertainty as to the right of providers of audio-visual services to operate their own networks, the question arises as to the extent to which they may force access to existing networks. The right of suppliers of audio-visual services to access existing networks clearly depends on commitments made for audio-visual services. When commitments are made, these services may in principle benefit from all provisions of the GATS, as well as from those of the Annex on Telecommunications, like any other scheduled service.

Right of access to public transport telecommunication networks and services: the Annex on Telecommunications

Scope of the Annex As previously indicated, the Annex on Telecommunications does not by itself command liberalisation of telecommunications services or of networks.[8] It only requires WTO Members to accord to suppliers of scheduled services access to 'public transport telecommunication networks and services'.[9]

'Telecommunications' is defined as 'the transmission and reception of signals by any electromagnetic means'.[10] Arguably, this also includes cable distribution of signals,[11] but it is not entirely certain. Furthermore, a 'public telecommunications transport *service*' is defined as:

[8] Article 2(c)(1) of the Annex on Telecommunications.

[9] Articles 1 and 5 of the Annex on Telecommunications.

[10] Article 3(a) of the Annex on Telecommunications.

[11] Cables transmit electromagnetic signals (whether digital or analogue) and themselves use the electromagnetic spectrum.

> any telecommunications transport service required, explicitly or in effect, by a Member to be offered to the public generally . . .[12]

while a 'public telecommunications transport *network*' is defined as:

> the public telecommunications infrastructure which permits telecommunications between and among defined termination points.[13]

Both notions cover network elements. Transport services indeed include specific means used to transport certain services, and networks refer to the general telecommunications infrastructure of a country. Access to the first depends on the degree of their public availability in the domestic market of the WTO Member taking the commitment. Access to the second is unquestionable. Consequently, should a country require specific network services to be offered to the public generally, such as satellite services, then arguably these services should be subject to the disciplines of the Annex, even if a message can be conveyed using other public infrastructure. However, as indicated above, the status of cable distribution could be made more explicit.

b) Cable or broadcast distribution of radio or television programming are excluded from the scope of the Annex on Telecommunications

Measures affecting cable or broadcast distribution of radio or television programming are explicitly excluded from the scope of the Annex.[14] Arguably, this is in line with the objective of the Annex, which is to promote the businesses of service providers by giving them access to essential telecommunications facilities. It is doubtful that radio or TV constitute such facilities.

It is less clear whether suppliers of radio or TV programmes can themselves benefit from the provisions of the Annex and thus have a right of access to the public telecommunications infrastructure necessary to supply these services. As indicated above, this infrastructure can be constituted of all public facilities making use of the electromagnetic spectrum. Arguably, however, considering the above exclusion, if such infrastructure is necessary to distribute radio or TV programmes, the right of access to

[12] Article 3(b) of the Annex on Telecommunications. It is specified that: 'Such services may include, "inter alia", telegraph, telephone, telex, and data transmission typically involving real-time transmission of customer-supplied information between two or more points without any end-to-end change in the form or content of the customer's information.'

[13] Article 3(c) of the Annex on Telecommunications.

[14] Article 2(b) of the Annex on Telecommunications.

it would not be guaranteed by the Annex. For example, should a country make a commitment on radio services, it may nevertheless not be obliged to grant access to its cable infrastructure, to its radio frequency spectrum or to its satellite services.

Such exclusion does not seem to be coherent with the objective of the Annex. Indeed, considering the remaining uncertainty as to whether or not network provision is included in the commitments made for certain audio-visual services (see above), the lack of access to existing networks may obviously undermine market access of the scheduled service. Despite the aforementioned points, the Annex may nevertheless benefit scheduled audio-visual services other than radio or TV broadcasting.

Exceptions to the right of access to networks Pursuant to the Annex on Telecommunications, access to and use of public transport telecommunication networks and services can be subject to certain restrictions, to the extent they are necessary:

- to ensure the security and confidentiality of messages;[15]
- to safeguard the public service responsibilities of suppliers of public telecommunications transport networks and services as public services;
- to protect the technical integrity of public telecommunications transport networks or services; or
- to ensure that services, not open to international competition, are nevertheless supplied.[16]

The second of these exceptions is interesting. Refusal to grant access to public networks may be justified if their lack of capacity jeopardises the supply of public services, such as a universal voice telephony service or educational audio-visual services. There is no definition of the expression 'public service', nor a limitation on the kind of public service responsibilities that can be imposed on suppliers of public telecommunications transport networks and services. This can be interpreted as meaning that WTO Members have a certain degree of discretion in this regard. Adopted measures, however, must be 'necessary', which means, if this term is applied like the one that is included in Article XX of the GATT, that they

[15] Article 5(d) of the Annex on Telecommunications.

[16] These last three exceptions are included in Article 5(e) of the Annex on Telecommunications.

must be the least restrictive measures that are reasonably available to reach the public service objective pursued.[17]

The Annex on Telecommunications furthermore explicitly limits the kind of restrictive measures that can be adopted:

- restrictions on resale or shared use of public telecommunications services;
- a requirement to use specified technical interfaces, including interface protocols, for interconnection with public transport telecommunications networks and services;
- requirements, where necessary, for the interoperability of such services and to encourage the achievement of the global compatibility and interoperability of telecommunication networks and services;
- type approval of terminal or other equipment which interfaces with the network and technical requirements relating to the attachment of such equipment to such networks;
- restrictions on the interconnection of private leased or owned circuits with such networks or services or with circuits leased or owned by another service supplier; or
- notification, registration and licensing'.[18]

All these measures and the necessity test that is attached to them are intended, as the WTO Secretariat appropriately indicates in its explanation of the Annex on Telecommunications, to 'strike a fragile balance between the needs of users for fair terms of access and the needs of the regulators and public telecommunications operators to maintain a system that works and that meets public service objectives'.[19]

Lack of adequate balance between the right of access and the protection of public objectives The Annex on Telecommunications is ambiguous. On the one hand, by according suppliers of scheduled services access to the public telecommunications networks and services, it is intended to improve the commitments that are made for them. On the other hand, it excludes outright from its scope cable and broadcast distribution of radio or television programming.

[17] See, for instance, Appellate Body Report, 'European Communities – Measures Affecting Asbestos and Asbestos-Containing Products', WT/DS135/AB/R, 12 March 2001, paras. 170ff.

[18] Article 5(f) of the Annex on Telecommunications.

[19] See the WTO Secretariat's explanation of the Annex on Telecommunications (www.wto.org/english/tratop_e/serv_e/telecom_e/telecom_annex_expl_e.htm.

Consequently, the only real balancing between the right of access to networks and the protection of a public service that is required from WTO Members is limited to audio-visual services that are not cable and broadcast distribution of radio or television programming. This can be regretted, not only for the uncertainty created in relation to these latter services, but also because it does not encourage the definition of explicit and transparent public policies with respect to them.

It should be noted that certain flexibility is also given by the Annex to developing countries. They maintain the possibility to place certain access restrictions 'on reasonable conditions' in order to 'strengthen [their] domestic telecommunications infrastructure and service capacity'. Such restrictions, however, must be 'necessary' and enable them 'to increase [their] participation in international trade in telecommunications services'.[20]

Market access for scheduled services

Article XVI of the GATS (market access) may remedy some of the above-mentioned problems of the Annex on Telecommunications. To the extent indicated in Schedules of commitments, it prohibits national measures limiting the number of service suppliers in a domestic market, or the value or the quantity of services supplied or the number of persons authorised to supply a service.[21] To the same extent, it also prohibits 'economic needs tests'. These are domestic regulations that give to public authorities discretionary powers to limit the supply of a service on the basis of criteria that are unrelated to its quality or to the qualifications of its suppliers.[22]

Consequently, if requirements for access to public networks are unrelated to the quality of the service or the qualifications of its providers and are so burdensome as to impede access to these networks, arguably, a violation of Article XVI of GATS can be found. However, as previously indicated, commitments under Article XVI of the GATS may be limited in the second column of the Schedules of commitments. In audio-visual

[20] Article 5(g) of the Annex on Telecommunications.

[21] Article XVI of the GATS applies to market access through the modes of supply identified in Article I. These are the supply of a service: (a) from the territory of one Member into the territory of any other Member (cross-border mode); (b) in the territory of one Member to the service consumer of any other Member (consumption abroad mode); (c) by a service supplier of one Member through a commercial presence in the territory of any other Member (commercial presence mode); and (d) by a service supplier of one Member through the presence of natural persons of a Member in the territory of any other Member (physical presence mode).

[22] See Article XVI:2 of the GATS.

services, for instance, countries may subordinate market access to conditions related to cultural content. Furthermore, should the restrictions on the access to public networks be objectively connected to the quality of the services or the qualifications of their suppliers, Article XVI of the GATS would no longer be relevant. The measure would then fall under the scope of Article VI:5 of the GATS (see below).[23]

National treatment for scheduled services

Domestic requirements for access to public transport networks and services may also be subject to Article XVII of the GATS containing the national treatment obligation. Should full commitments be taken for a specific audio-visual service, *de jure* and *de facto* discriminations between domestic and foreign service suppliers are prohibited.[24] An analysis under this provision requires one to examine to what extent the requirements and their application affect the competitive position of foreign service suppliers in relation to the domestic suppliers of like services. Similarly to the market access obligation, the national treatment obligation may be subject to limitations specified by WTO Members in the third column of their Schedules of commitments.

Reasonableness, objectivity and necessity of new domestic regulation

Provisions of the Annex on Telecommunications may also be complemented by the various paragraphs of Article VI of the GATS. Article VI:5 of the GATS, read in conjunction with Article VI:4 of the GATS, requires measures relating to qualification requirements and procedures, technical standards and licensing requirements that nullify or impair commitments of Members, to be based on objective and transparent criteria. They cannot be more burdensome than necessary to ensure the quality of the service and must reasonably have been expected at the time the commitments

[23] WTO Members generally agree that Articles XVI and VI:5 of the GATS are mutually exclusive. Therefore domestic regulations affecting the supply of a scheduled service, that are not listed in Article XVI:2 of the GATS, fall within the scope of Article VI:5 of the GATS (see WTO, Council for Trade in Services, 'Article VI:4 of GATS: Disciplines on Domestic Regulation Applicable to All Services – Note by the Secretariat', S/C/W/96, 1 March 1999, paras. 9, 13 and 14). This view is also reflected in common rules recently adopted in the accountancy sector (WTO, Council for Trade in Services, 'Disciplines on Domestic Regulation in the Accountancy Sector', adopted on 14 December 1998, S/L/64, 17 December 1998, para. 1).

[24] See Appellate Body Report, 'European Communities – Regime for the Importation, Sale and Distribution of Bananas', WT/DS27/AB/R, 9 September 1997, para. 234.

were made. Licensing procedures cannot themselves constitute a restriction on the supply of services. Articles VI:4 and VI:5 of the GATS do not further specify these rules, but negotiations are open on the subject.[25]

These provisions are relevant to the conditions that might be imposed on the access to networks and that are linked to the 'quality' of the service concerned or to the qualifications of its supplier. Such measures would indeed not fall under the scope of Article XVI of the GATS (see above). However, should they have a more restrictive effect than measures in place at the time commitments were made,[26] they must be based on objective and transparent criteria and they must be 'necessary' to ensure the quality of the service. This requires the notion of 'quality' of audiovisual services to be defined. Arguably, it could include objectives related to the supply of a universal service or to the need to protect cultural identities, cultural diversity and cultural 'quality'. Members seem to retain a certain discretion in this regard. Furthermore, the GATS intends to remain a flexible instrument and not to hamper Members' right to regulate the provision of scheduled services in their markets.[27] It only requires that any regulation adding new requirements constitute the least trade-restrictive regulation available to achieve the 'quality' objective pursued.

Article VI:3 of the GATS also imposes specific disciplines on the provision of authorisations and licences. Service suppliers applying for authorisations must be informed without delay of the status of their application and of the decisions taken.

Finally, Article VI:1 of the GATS imposes on governments a general obligation of reasonableness, objectivity and impartiality in the administration of domestic regulations affecting trade in services. This rule is similar to Article X:3 of the GATT concerning trade in goods. Accordingly, WTO Members must ensure that formalities imposed on foreign entrants are no more burdensome than necessary to achieve the objective sought, that those who are supposed to implement them are not

[25] Negotiations were first undertaken in a Working Party on Professional Services which were assigned the task to elaborate rules on these services (see WTO, Council for Trade in Services, 'Decision on Professional Services', adopted by the Council for Trade in Services on 1 March 1995, S/L/3, 4 April 1994). After this Working Party adopted common principles in the accountancy sector (see note 23 above), it was replaced by a working party with an enlarged mission, the 'Working Party on Domestic Regulation' (see WTO, Council for Trade in Services, 'Decision on Domestic Regulation', adopted by the Council for Trade in Services on 26 April 1999, S/L/70, 28 April 1999).

[26] This condition reflects the fact that only requirements and licensing procedures that nullify or impair commitments of Members are covered by Article VI:5 of the GATS.

[27] GATS, Preamble, fourth paragraph.

themselves competitors of foreign service suppliers, that they abide by minimum transparency requirements and a sense of equity and that they motivate all their decisions which affect trade in the services concerned.[28]

Exceptions

Exceptions to the above rules are possible pursuant to Article XIV of the GATS. According to this provision, WTO Members may impose measures inconsistent with the GATS and their commitments. to the extent they are necessary, including measures:

- to maintain public morals or public order; or
- to secure compliance with laws or regulations which are not inconsistent with the provisions of the GATS.

These measures must also be applied in a manner which would constitute a means of arbitrary or unjustifiable discrimination between countries where like conditions prevail, or a disguised restriction on trade in services. The analysis under this provision is therefore twofold. It is necessary to determine, first, whether the measure concerned pursues one of the objectives indicated in Article XIV, and, secondly, whether its application is made in good faith.[29]

The public morality and the public order exceptions were discussed in previous presentations. As to the need to secure compliance with laws or regulations which are not inconsistent with the provisions of the GATS, it may justify restrictive measures which are necessary to give effect to a particular cultural policy programme. Article XIV of the GATS thus complements the exception provisions of the Annex on Telecommunications

[28] Concerning Article X:3 of the GATT, see Appellate Body Report, 'United States – Import Prohibition of Certain Shrimp and Shrimp Products', WT/DS58/AB/R, 12 October 1998, paras. 182ff; WTO Panel Report, 'Argentina – Measures Affecting the Export of Bovine Hides and the Import of Finished Leather', WT/DS155/R, 19 December 2000, paras. 11.80ff; WTO Panel Report, 'United States – Antidumping Measures on Stainless Steel Plate in Coils and Stainless Steel Sheets and Strip from Korea', WT/DS179/R, 22 December 2000, para. 6.51.

[29] This sequence of analysis was set by the Appellate Body with regard to Article XX of the GATT, the corresponding provision to Article XIV of the GATS (see Appellate Body Report, 'United States – Standards for Reformulated and Conventional Gasoline', WT/DS2/AB/R, 29 April 1996, Section IV, first paragraph; Appellate Body Report, 'United States – Import Prohibition of Certain Shrimp and Shrimp Products', WT/DS58/AB/R, 12 October 1998, paras. 115 and 157; Appellate Body Report, 'Korea – Measures Affecting Imports of Fresh, Chilled and Frozen Beef', WT/DS161/AB/R, WT/DS169/AB/R, 11 December 2000, para. 156).

and contributes to striking a balance between market access of scheduled audio-visual services and non-trade objectives.

Summary

Access to public networks by suppliers of scheduled audio-visual services is guaranteed by the Annex on Telecommunications with respect to services that are not cable or broadcast distribution of radio and television programmes. This right may, however, be limited, when, *inter alia*, the supply of a public service is jeopardised due to scarce networks resources.

As far as cable or broadcast distribution of radio and television programmes is concerned, the market access and national treatment provisions of the GATS may help their providers to obtain access to relevant networks in accordance with scheduled commitments.

Access to networks may be generally restricted if this is necessary to protect one of the public policy objectives mentioned in the exception clause of Article XIV of the GATS. Furthermore, domestic regulation that is necessary to ensure the 'quality' of the services is generally admitted.

Unscheduled services

As already indicated, should audio-visual services not be scheduled, which occurs in most of the cases, the rules above do not apply. There is no right of access to an importing country's domestic telecommunications infrastructure. In this case, WTO Members must only apply the MFN and the transparency rules contained in Articles II and III of the GATS. In practice, this means that, if certain foreign suppliers of audio-visual services are accorded access to public transport telecommunications networks and services despite the lack of commitments, interconnection procedures must be published promptly. Furthermore, such access must be extended to other service providers, considering that preferential access to public networks for services originating in different countries is, in principle, prohibited.

Several WTO Members, however, exempted themselves from the MFN obligation, pursuant to Article II:2 of the GATS. For instance, the European Community reserved for itself the possibility to grant more favourable treatment to certain countries whose audio-visual works meet certain linguistic and origin criteria. The idea is, in this case, to 'preserve and promote the regional identity of countries within Europe which have long-standing cultural links'. Furthermore, the EC also reserved the possibility to impose corrective measures, similar to anti-dumping duties, when unfair prices for the distribution of audio-visual material cause injury to Community producers.[30] Theoretically, nothing in the GATS and in the Annex on Telecommunications would impede these corrective measures to be imposed at the level of access to the networks.

The impact of broadband technology

Increased relevance of the Annex on Telecommunications for audio-visual services

As indicated above, broadband networks enable the conveyance of both telecommunications and audio-visual services or of an integrated version of them. A typical broadband interface is provided by Internet. Pursuant to the Annex on Telecommunications, suppliers of scheduled services can choose how to supply their services, including by Internet. Indeed, they have the right to use their own operating protocols and to have access to international communications lines and to information contained in databases.[31] Furthermore, if broadband networks are available to the public generally in the country taking the commitments, access to such networks can be mandated.

Consequently, if commitments are made on telecommunications services, access to Internet protocols and broadband networks can be mandated for their suppliers. This may also be the case for Internet providers themselves, as arguably, Internet services qualify as 'packet-switched data transmission services' which is a category of telecommunications services. Such right of access may have favourable consequences for the above suppliers who are also providers of audio-visual content. They can indeed use the same broadband network and benefit *de facto* from an access to it for all their activities.

Incoherence would result from the possibility that broadband gateways are required to be made available for telecommunications services and can be used for the Internet transmission of TV and radio programmes, while limitations on traditional broadcast or cable distribution of such programmes would be maintained. Taking different commitments for directly competing, and, arguably, like services, may not make sense (see below). Obviously, it may be legally possible to prevent the transmission of TV and radio through broadband telecommunications networks. However, how in practice could one distinguish from the kind of use that is made of converged facilities?

[30] WTO Doc. GATS/SC/31/Suppl.3.

[31] Articles 5(b) and (c) of the Annex on Telecommunications.

Of course, this situation depends on the extent to which broadband technology is made available in WTO Member States. And the Annex on Telecommunications is only applicable upon the availability of such technology. The International Telecommunications Union (ITU) is committed to provide leadership for the general extension of broadband networks. Thus, awkward regulatory dichotomy may be expected in the next few years between services supplied through Internet and those supplied through traditional one-way networks.

Possible impact of the Reference Paper on audio-visual services

A similar reasoning applies to the provisions contained in the Reference Paper. As explained in previous chapters, the Reference Paper contains additional commitments by WTO Members which are party to the Agreement on Basic Telecommunications. It provides, among other things, that suppliers of essential facilities must not abuse their dominant position, by impeding, among other things, access to these facilities. Essential facilities are defined as:

> public telecommunications transport networks and services that:
> – are exclusively or predominantly provided by a single or limited number of suppliers; and
> – cannot feasibly be economically or technically substituted in order to provide a service.[32]

The Reference Paper enables providers of basic telecommunications services to interconnect to essential facilities supplied by local monopolistic suppliers.[33] To the extent such infrastructure is broadband, the Reference Paper may indirectly benefit those who are also suppliers of audio-visual content if they use the same broadband facilities. For broadband facilities to be qualified as essential facilities under the Reference Paper, one should examine actual conditions of competition in the relevant market and the number of suppliers of broadband networks. If there is only one or a limited number of such suppliers, then broadband networks can be considered as essential facilities. Broadband technology, however, enables higher substitutability of networks. Thus, arguably, in a converged environment, should there be full competition between networks, the provisions of the Reference Paper would not be applicable. This is, however, not yet the case in most countries.

[32] Article 1 of the Reference Paper.
[33] Article 2 of the Reference Paper.

In summary, the Annex on Telecommunications and the Reference Paper can be applicable to networks that can be used to provide both scheduled telecommunications services and audio-visual content. In this situation, restrictions on the supply of audio-visual content remain possible but in practice, when the same undertakings supply both kinds of service, it would be more difficult to implement them at the level of access by them to the network. There is indeed the risk that such restrictions would affect the supply of basic telecommunications services in a manner inconsistent with commitments made. Thus, limitations on the provision of audio-visual content, such as TV or radio programmes, if desired, must be implemented at the level of the control on the use that is made of the network. However, as indicated above, this might be difficult to achieve in practice.

Unexpected consequences of the application of the non-discrimination rules

The non-discrimination rules of the GATS might be violated if access to networks is restricted for providers of certain foreign audio-visual services, such as TV or radio broadcasting (see above), while being entirely open for providers of like Internet services of a different origin. The national treatment principle is relevant when the audio-visual services concerned are subject to commitments, while the MFN treatment applies to all services covered by the GATS.[34]

Clearly, the determination of the existence of discrimination entails a prior examination of the existence of like services. In the context of trade in services, a test based on the physical characteristics is by definition impossible. Similar functional characteristics may nevertheless be required. It may also be expected that, in light of the evolution of the jurisprudence related to the notion of like product, a test based on the existence of a competitive relationship between the services concerned will be authoritative.[35] This would be in line with the principle of technological neutrality recognised in the Agreement on Basic Telecommunications

[34] The fact that the measure appears on its face to be neutral from the point of view of the origin of the service concerned does not prevent a finding of a *de facto* discrimination, depending on the actual competitive conditions applicable to the affected services (see, by analogy, WTO Appellate Body Report, 'Canada – Measures Affecting the Automobile Industry', WT/DS139/AB/R, 31 May 2000, paras. 78 and 79 (among others).

[35] Appellate Body Report, 'European Communities – Measures Affecting Asbestos and Asbestos-Containing Products', WT/DS135/AB/R, 12 March 2001, paras. 98 and 99.

Services.[36] In other words, services providing the same functions and supplied in competition with each other in the same markets can be considered as like services even if the technology used to supply them is different.

On the basis of these principles, which are as yet speculative, TV or radio programmes transmitted through the Internet may be like services to TV or radio broadcasting, to the extent they are supplied in the same markets (which may not yet be the case). By analogy with trade in goods, the fact that they may be classified differently would not change this determination. Consequently, different treatment for providers of these services could constitute an illicit discrimination. This obviously leads to the question of whether restrictive regulations applied to providers of traditional audio-visual services only are WTO-compatible.

Necessary modifications of the regulatory focus concerning audio-visual services

As indicated above, under GATS rules, restrictions on access to and use of public transport telecommunications networks and services may be authorised if they are necessary to enable the supply of a public service or if they are necessary to ensure the quality of the service. Furthermore, certain market access restrictions are permitted if justified by a legitimate public policy objective pursuant to the exceptions clauses of Article XIV of the GATS.

In a converged environment, similar restrictions may not be workable. First, restrictions justified by the lack of capacity of the available public networks might become less relevant. Indeed, digital technology and broadband networks enable the conveyance of virtually an unlimited number of signals. Secondly, as indicated above, in order to avoid any undue discrimination, any restrictions should apply to both suppliers of traditional broadcasting services and to suppliers of like Internet services. The difficulty arises here from the fact that such restrictions might also affect the provision of telecommunications services by the same persons in a manner incompatible with commitments made. Restrictions on audio-visual services may be acceptable when they are linked to a legitimate cultural policy objective. The same restrictions, however, may not be justifiable if they affect services that do not carry audio-visual content.

[36] See WTO, Council for Trade in Services, Note by the Chairman for Scheduling Basic Telecom Services Commitments, S/GBT/W/2/Rev.1, 16 January 1997, para. 1(c).

Consequently, as indicated above, it would be difficult to implement restrictions on multimedia services, whatever technique is used for their supply, at the level of the access to networks by service suppliers. Control on content and on the use that is made of the network thus remains the only workable solution. As indicated above, this might be difficult to achieve in practice. It first requires policy-makers to define explicitly the kind of content that is acceptable or required, or objective 'quality' requirements, irrespective of the undertaking supplying it. Furthermore, considering the transboundary nature of services supplied, international cooperation to combat illegal content is indispensable, as argued earlier by Bernier in Chapter 8 above. In any event, purely restrictive audio-visual policies, based on the nationality of the service provider, may become less tenable in a converged environment, whatever commitments are taken on audio-visual services, as currently classified.

Assignment of scarce resources

This part of the chapter addresses the more specific issue of the assignment of scarce network resources. Networks may indeed be a limited resource. If the network is wireless, its operator must be assigned a frequency in the radioelectric spectrum. This usually requires prior authorisation, as well as rules to avoid congestion. If the network requires the use of a satellite, the satellite operator must be granted an orbital position, as well as an authorisation to install its terrestrial platform(s). Finally, if the network is cable, rights of ways must be granted to its owner. Assignment of these scarce resources responds to both international and domestic rules. It is thus interesting to examine to what extent WTO rules may have an impact on these rules and foster a fair assignment of scarce network resources for providers of audio-visual services. The impact of broadband technology will also be examined in this context.

Frequency assignment

Networks concerned by frequency assignment are wireless networks. Cable networks, although they also use the radioelectric spectrum, do not need to be assigned a specific frequency. They may indeed use any frequency which they need and can support. The only limit is that they must avoid causing undue electromagnetic interference.

The assignment of frequencies requires two sets of procedures. First, frequency bands must be allocated to different categories of radiocommunications applications, such as military/defence, emergency services, broadcast, telecommunications, etc. This allocation is coordinated internationally in order to avoid undue interferences between services and countries. It is done in the context of World Radio Communications Conferences, under the auspices of the ITU. The most recent took place in June and July 2003 in Geneva (the 'WRC-2003'). The previous conference took place in May and June 2000 in Istanbul (the 'WRC-2000').[37] The second type of procedure is the assignment of frequencies within the allocated frequency bands to the operators of the services concerned. This assignment is done domestically by the governments of the countries where the services must be supplied.

It should be noted that wireless networks, for which frequencies need to be assigned, can also be broadband. Typical examples include the so-called third-generation mobile communications networks (IMT-2000/UMTS), broadband satellite services (including third-generation Mobile Satellite Systems, such as 3G MSS, part of IMT-2000, and high-density fixed satellite services (HDFSS)), fixed wireless systems, and terrestrial microwave systems (such as High Altitude Platform Stations (HAPS)). They enable the provision of new types of multimedia and digital services (such as Digital Audio Broadcasting (DAB), Digital Video Broadcasting (DVB), video-on-demand, etc.) as well as enhanced Internet services.

Traditionally, competition between telecommunications services and audio-visual services occurs at the level of the international allocation of frequencies, while competition between operators of the same service takes place at the level of the domestic assignment of the frequency band. Increasingly, however, broadband networks are blurring this apparently clear distinction. First, eager to obtain space in the radioelectric spectrum, they compete with the more traditional applications for the allocation of frequency bands. Secondly, considering they enable the simultaneous provision of both telecommunications and audio-visual services, they also make competition possible between these two types of service at the domestic level.

International allocation of frequency bands

The process As previously indicated, the co-ordinated allocation of frequency bands to specific services operating with similar technical characteristics is indispensable to avoid undue interferences between countries. In Europe, such coordination takes place in two settings. A preliminary

[37] For further details, see www.itu.int/ITU-R/terrestrial/.

co-ordination is done in the context of the European Conference of Postal and Telecommunications Administrations (CEPT). CEPT has forty-four member countries and is responsible for the development of a co-ordinated spectrum-management policy on the European continent.[38] The European views are then promoted within the Radio Communications Conferences held under the auspices of the ITU. International co-ordination is less intense than that occurring at the level of the CEPT, despite the ITU's increasingly proactive role in this regard.[39]

Allocation of frequency bands is negotiated by governments, according to their public policy agenda. For instance, a policy fostering convergence and network competition, such as that of the EC, will promote the extension of frequency bands allocated to broadband networks.[40] The WRC-2000 and WRC-2003 were satisfactory in this regard for the EU.[41] This policy, however, may conflict with other public policy objectives such as those of national security (military applications), research and development (radio astronomy) or national culture for which public analogue broadcasting is still perceived by many as indispensable. Also, developing countries may not be entirely satisfied with the additional bands reserved to broadband applications, since they do not, as yet, necessarily possess such technology.

Thus, international harmonisation of frequency allocations reflects transnational rivalries between countries, in a manner relatively similar

[38] For the procedure to be followed for the next WRC-2003, see http://europa.eu.int/information_society/topics/telecoms/radiospec/radio/world_radiocomm_conf/wrc_03/index_en.htm.

[39] See T. Gavrilov, 'Regulatory Arrangements for Terrestrial Services', World Radiocommunications Seminar, Geneva, 11–15 November 2002, www.itu.int/ITU-R/conferences/seminars/geneva-2002/index.html.

[40] See European Commission, 'Green Paper on Radio Spectrum Policy in the Context of European Community Policies Such as Telecommunications, Broadcasting, Transport and R&D', Brussels, 9 December 1998, COM(1998)596 final; Communication from the Commission to the Council, the European Parliament, the Economic and Social Committee and the Committee of the Regions, 'The European Positions for the World Radiocommunications Conference 2000 (WCR-2000)', Brussels, 8 March 2000, COM(2000)8; Communication from the Commission to the Council, the European Parliament, the Economic and Social Committee and the Committee of the Regions, 'The World Radiocommunications Conference 2003 (WRC 2003)', Brussels, 14 April 2003, COM(2003)183.

[41] See Communication from the Commission to the Council, the European Parliament, the Economic and Social Committee and the Committee of the Regions, 'Results of the World Radiocommunications Conference 2000 (WCR-2000) in the Context of Radio Spectrum Policy in the European Community', Brussels, 6 December 2000, COM(2000)811 final. See also European Community, Brussels 'Commission Welcomes Outcome of the World Radiocommunication Conference 2003 (WRC-03)', IP/03/950, 4 July 2003.

to trade negotiations. The only difference probably lies in the fact that the frequency spectrum is a limited resource and that there may be optimal methods of exploiting it. The role of the ITU in providing guidance as to the most rational and efficient allocation methods is critical in this regard.

While international negotiation may involve conflicts between Members' public policies, it is clearly up to governments to define their own negotiating position and to take into account relevant national interests. This is when rivalry between telecommunications operators and audiovisual services providers is most obvious. Generally speaking, operators of telecommunications services promote broadband networks. In this respect, they are satisfied with current developments and the frequencies allocated during the WRC-2000. Traditional broadcasters, instead, complain that insufficient space is left to public broadcasting. They consider that analogue applications are still necessary, despite the gradual move to digital transmission of signals. They are of the view that a transition period during which frequencies are needed for both kinds of applications must be preserved. Other industries are also concerned. Transport companies, for instance, are dissatisfied with the WRC-2000, as they perceive it mainly promoted, to their detriment, the interests of the communications industry.

In conclusion, the allocation of frequency bands is as much a technical necessity as an arbitration process in which divergent economic interests are increasingly asserted.

Relevance of WTO law The issue of the allocation of frequency bands remains very much outside the scope of WTO law. There is not much the latter can do to protect the interests of dissatisfied countries and, through them, affected operators. While the implementation by a Member of an international agreement can be assessed in relation to WTO rules,[42] it appears difficult, in the case of the international allocation of frequencies, to establish a violation of the latter.

Indeed, international cooperation with respect to standards and interoperability of networks is not only tolerated, but encouraged by the Annex on Telecommunications.[43] The latter also provides that WTO Members 'recognise the role played by intergovernmental and non-governmental organisations and agreements in ensuring the efficient operation of

[42] See Appellate Body Report, 'Turkey – Restrictions on Imports of Textile and Clothing Products', WT/DS34/AB/R, 22 October 1999, para. 60.

[43] Article VI:5(b) of the Annex on Telecommunications.

domestic and global telecommunications services, in particular the International Telecommunications Union,'[44] This means that, most likely, ITU Radio Regulations, which set forth international frequency arrangements (the 'Regulations'),[45] are WTO-compatible.

A possible violation of WTO principles can nevertheless be found, not in relation to the Regulations themselves, but if a country is discriminated against in the context of the World Radio Communications Conference negotiations. There could be a violation of the most-favoured nation obligation contained in Article II of the GATS, if it was established that a differential treatment during those negotiations adversely affected the competitive position of services or service suppliers of a particular country. The differential treatment itself would result from the manner in which negotiations were held, such as insufficient opportunity to respond to negotiating positions, restricted meetings, etc.[46] The most-favoured nation principle contained in Article II of the GATS is a horizontal rule applying to all service sectors, whether or not commitments have been made for them. It may therefore be invoked for providers of audio-visual services, even in the absence of commitments.

Except for the above (theoretical?) violation of the MFN principle, the WTO is neutral with respect to the international allocation of frequency bands.

Domestic assignment of frequencies

Domestic assignment of frequencies also entails commercial rivalries. In this case, rivalries develop between providers of services for which a specific frequency band was allocated.

Domestic assignment procedures may vary from country to country. There is no international harmonisation for them, except concerning the international registration and protection of assigned frequencies.[47]

[44] Article 7(b) of the Annex on Telecommunications.

[45] See ITU, *Radio Regulations* (2001 edn, Geneva: ITU, 2001). These Regulations are a binding international treaty (see Article 31 of the ITU Constitution). For frequency allocations to defined services, see Article 5 of the Radio Regulations.

[46] Despite these, problems may also exist during international trade negotiations, violation claims arguably cannot be made there considering that the outcome of negotiations is incorporated in WTO law itself.

[47] See Article 11 of the Radio Regulations. It should be noted that frequency assignments might also have to comply with specific allotment plans which might be drawn for certain radiocommunications services, such as terrestrial broadcasting (see J. Fonteyne and J. M. Paquet, 'Terrestrial Broadcasting Plans in LF/MF/HF/VHF/UHF Bands, Including Procedures for Plans GE 75, GE 84 and GE 89', World Radiocommunications Seminar, Geneva, 11–15 November 2002).

Domestic procedures usually consist in licensing or authorisation procedures, or in more recent assignment methods such as auctioning.[48]

Barriers to trade may result from burdensome and discriminatory frequency assignment procedures. The relevance of WTO rules is obvious here. Their impact depends on whether or not a service is subject to specific commitments. The following analysis will therefore address the rules that are relevant to scheduled services and those that apply to unscheduled services.

Frequency assignment for scheduled audio-visual services Relevant WTO rules are similar to those that apply to the general right of access to public networks.

Arguably, the radioelectric spectrum is itself a public network falling within the scope of the Annex on Telecommunications. Indeed, as previously indicated, a 'public telecommunications transport network' is defined as 'the public telecommunications infrastructure which permits telecommunications between and among defined termination points'. Arguably, the radioelectric spectrum is such a public telecommunications infrastructure.

Thus, pursuant to this interpretation, a refusal, in law or in fact, by the domestic authority to assign an available frequency could constitute a violation of the obligations contained in the Annex, as far as services falling within its scope are concerned. As already indicated, radio or TV services are normally excluded, but other audio-visual services are not.

As also previously indicated, restrictions on the rights granted by the Annex on Telecommunications are possible if they are necessary to maintain the integrity of the network or the provision of a public service. For instance, a refusal to assign a frequency could be justified under the Annex if, due to the lack of available frequencies in the allocated band, the supply of a universal service or of educational audio-visual services would be jeopardised.[49] Flexibilities are also tolerated for developing countries willing to 'strengthen [their] domestic telecommunications infrastructure and service capacity'.[50]

As discussed above, the right of access to a public network, such as the radioelectric spectrum, is also complemented by other provisions of the

[48] See, for instance, as far as the US is concerned, National Telecommunications and Information Administration, Manual of Regulations and Procedures for Federal Radio Frequency Management (January 2000 edition with January/May/September 2001 revisions).

[49] Article 5(e) of the Annex on Telecommunications.

[50] Article 5(g) of the Annex on Telecommunications.

GATS applicable to scheduled services, such as the market access (Article XVI) and national treatment (Article XVII) provisions. Furthermore, pursuant to Article VI:5 of the GATS, new requirements imposed for the provision of a scheduled service must be necessary to achieve its 'quality'. As indicated above, there is no definition of the term 'quality', which could theoretically enable an interpretation compatible with a domestic cultural policy. Assignment procedures must also be administered in a transparent, reasonable, objective and impartial manner. Finally, restrictions on market access and national treatment of scheduled audio-visual services may be tolerated only if they are necessary to pursue one of the legitimate objectives indicated in the exceptions clauses of Article XIV of the GATS.

In summary, should audio-visual services be included in WTO Members' schedules of commitments, the rules of the GATS appear to provide several guarantees that foreign services and service providers could have access to the radioelectric spectrum and operate their own network in such a spectrum under fair, transparent, non-discriminatory and not unduly burdensome assignment procedures. This could solve, with respect to wireless networks, some of the above-mentioned uncertainties related to the question of whether or not networks are included in commitments on audio-visual services.

It should be noted that the rules of the GATS do not mandate that domestic assignment procedures be carried out in the most economically efficient manner.[51] Also, as indicated previously, the GATS theoretically enables national governments to implement cultural policies and to protect public services even if access to a frequency band is affected, provided that a balance is maintained, in accordance with relevant rules, between the public policy objectives pursued and the right of access to the radioelectric spectrum.

Frequency assignment for unscheduled audio-visual services As already indicated, should audio-visual services not be scheduled, which is usually the case, the rules described above do not apply. There is no specific

[51] See, in this regard, Article 44 of the ITU Constitution: 'In using frequency bands for radio services, Members shall bear in mind that radio frequencies and the geostationary-satellite orbit are limited natural resources and that they must be used rationally, efficiently and economically, in conformity with the provisions of the Radio Regulations, so that countries or groups of countries may have equitable access to both, taking into account the special needs of the developing countries and the geographical situation of particular countries.'

right for foreign services and their suppliers to be assigned a frequency in the relevant allocated band.

Assignment of satellite positions and authorisation of terrestrial platforms

Certain wireless networks may also require satellite transmissions of audio-visual signals. Thus, in addition to access to the radioelectric spectrum, network operators may need to be assigned an orbital slot for their satellites or to be authorised to use existing satellite capacity for the supply of their services.

The assignment process

For the radioelectric spectrum, allocation of orbital slots is handled internationally, at the level of the ITU. There are two kinds of slots: the geostationary orbit and the non-geostationary orbit. Both are scarce resources. The first is scarcer than the second. The existing rule is based on a 'first-come, first-served' principle, through a rather complex coordination procedure[52] or pursuant to a plan, even if no satellite is eventually launched.[53] This has often been criticised as an inefficient use of orbital capacities, but it is based on the objective of safeguarding the rights of countries which do not have, as yet, the capability to launch satellites.[54]

Once satellites are launched, the space segment between them and the earth is also a scarce resource which is administered by the government having jurisdiction over them.[55] This government therefore takes the responsibility of granting space segment licences to the network operators making use of the satellite facilities as well as authorisations to dispose terrestrial platforms. If satellite services must be provided in other countries as well, the satellite operators also need to obtain a space segment licence from the authorities of these other countries (the so-called landing rights). Obviously, important barriers to trade may exist both at the level of the initial space segment licences and at the level of landing rights.

[52] See Article 9 of and Appendices 4 and 5 to the Radio Regulations. See Danny TAM Weng Hoa, 'The Notification and Recording of Frequency Assignments in the Space Services', World Radiocommunications Seminar, Geneva, 11–15 November 2002.

[53] Appendices 30, 30A and 30B to the Radio Regulations.

[54] See Yvon Henri, 'Orbit/Spectrum Allocation Procedures Registration Mechanism', World Radiocommunications Seminar, Geneva, 11–15 November 2002.

[55] See NTIA Manual of Regulations and Procedures for Federal Radio Frequency Management, note 48 above, p. 49.

The role of WTO rules

As with the allocation of frequency bands, the international allocation of orbital slots appears unquestionably to be acceptable from the point of view of WTO law, unless discrimination can be established in the context of the radiocommunications conferences. WTO law, however, becomes more of an issue in relation to the granting of space segment licences and authorisations for the establishment of terrestrial platforms.

The analysis of the application of WTO rules to these issues is similar to that described above concerning frequency assignment. Reference is therefore made to the above discussion. It is worthwhile, nevertheless, to mention explicitly that, if satellite services are generally available in a specific country, they may be subject to the rules contained in the Annex on Telecommunications, as public transport telecommunications services. Therefore, access to such services may be mandated for suppliers of scheduled audio-visual services (that are not TV or radio broadcasting).

Furthermore, certain satellite operators may still benefit from special or exclusive rights. In this situation, they are themselves subject to the non-discrimination rules of the GATS pursuant to Article VIII:1 of the GATS. Furthermore, Article VIII:3 of the GATS requires WTO Members to ensure that privileged satellite operators do not abuse their dominant position to acquire undue advantage for activities in which they operate in competition and which are outside the scope of their monopoly rights. For example, if the satellite operator benefits from monopoly rights in relation to traditional broadcasting services, but not for telecommunications services, it cannot use its dominant position in the first market to unduly confer an advantage for its activities in the second market.

Impact of broadband technology

As already indicated, both wireless and satellite networks can be broadband. These networks have been allocated specific frequency bands during the WRC-2000.[56] Consequently, telecommunications and audio-visual services may compete with each other in the context of the domestic assignment of frequencies within the allocated bands and/or for space segment licences and landing rights. Although WTO rules do not specifically

[56] For instance, IMT-2000/UMTS networks were allocated to the frequency bands 806–960 MHz and 2500–2690 MHz (terrestrial networks), Ku (10–118 GHz) and Ka (18–30 KHz) (satellite applications), 1.9 and 2.2 GHz (HAPS), etc.

address this situation, the latter has in fact three major consequences on their application to audio-visual services.

The application of the non-discrimination principles

As previously indicated, non-discrimination principles prohibit less favourable treatment of like services of different origins. According to commitments taken, the national treatment and/or the MFN treatment rules might be relevant in this regard.

TV or radio programmes transmitted through the Internet may be like services to TV or radio broadcasting. Therefore, if the assignment of frequencies or the granting of space segment licences are more favourable for providers of one kind of service than for the other, then, arguably, it would be possible to make a complaint based on discrimination. However, different treatment may be due to different widths of allocated frequency bands for each kind of service. In this case, it could be argued that such discrimination is the necessary consequence of international allocation procedures which are not themselves contrary to the GATS. It would therefore be justified, pursuant to Article XIV(c) of the GATS, which authorises restrictive measures necessary to secure compliance with laws and regulations which are not inconsistent with the GATS.

Relevance of the Annex on Telecommunications and of the Reference Paper

As previously indicated, the rights of access to networks and essential facilities contained in the Annex on Telecommunications and in the Reference Paper, may also ultimately be of benefit to providers of audio-visual content through broadband networks, even if no commitments were made on audio-visual services. It should be noted in this context that Section 6 of the Reference Paper requires the assignment of scarce resources to be carried out in 'an objective, timely, transparent and non-discriminatory manner'. Consequently, even if restrictions are authorised for the supply of certain audio-visual services, it would be difficult in practice to implement them at the level of the assignment of a frequency and/or the granting of a space segment for a broadband network. This might indeed hamper the compliance with commitments on basic telecommunications services supplied through the same network.

Of course, divestiture policies prohibiting an undertaking to use a broadband network for the provision of both telecommunications services and audio-visual services are possible. However, these policies may not be in line with the promotion of convergence, impeding economies of scale in relation to the use of networks and thus hampering their development.

Difficult implementation of the exceptions related to public service

As indicated above, in a converged environment, it would be difficult to implement authorised restrictions at the level of the access to network infrastructures, such as the radioelectric spectrum or space segments, if the networks are broadband and can be used for the supply of both telecommunications and audio-visual services. Therefore these restrictions, when necessary, must be implemented at the level of the control on the use that is made of broadband networks. This, as discussed above, requires a change in the nature of the regulation adopted.

Terminal equipment

In addition to the use of networks, the provision of audio-visual services may require specific terminal equipment, such as computers, and access to several technical interface devices (decoders, navigation tools, etc.) Such items are goods[57] and, therefore, their trade falls within the scope of the GATT. Tariffs applicable to most of this equipment have been eliminated pursuant to the Information Technology Agreement. There is, however, no general right of access to terminal equipment should its suppliers be in a monopolistic position.

The Information Technology Agreement

The Information Technology Agreement (ITA) was concluded by WTO Members contributing more than 90% of the international trade in information technology products.[58] The Agreement provides for the gradual elimination of customs duties and other importation charges on these products from 1 July 1997 until 2000. The products concerned are classified into six categories: (1) computers; (2) telecommunications equipment; (3) semiconductors; (4) equipment required for manufacturing semiconductors; (5) computer programs; and (6) scientific instruments. Fifty-six countries or distinct customs territories are currently bound by

57 Decoders and navigation tools take the form of computer programs which are generally considered as goods.

58 See Ministerial Declaration of Singapore, 13 December 1996, WT/MIN(96)/DEC, 18 December 1996, para. 18 and the document annexed to this Declaration.

the ITA,[59] which covers most of the equipment relevant to the provision of telecommunications services and the deployment of broadband networks. As previously indicated, the latter may be used for the provision of audio-visual content. Pursuant to the GATT and the ITA, most of the relevant terminal equipment can be imported at a zero tariff.

Tariff classification

The difficulty with the ITA and tariff schedules is sometimes to determine the tariff classification of new types of goods, such as those designed for convergent applications. These goods include, among others, PC-TVs (the so-called multimedia computers) and network elements connecting computers with local area networks (LANs), the Internet and other telecommunications applications.

These products may be classified both as telecommunications or audio-visual apparatus (such as TVs) and as automatic data processing machines. Tariff reductions tend to be much higher for the second category than for the first, as a result both of commitments taken during the Uruguay Round and of the ITA.

The classification of LAN equipment and PC-TVs were the subject of the WTO dispute settlement case 'European Communities – Customs Classification of Certain Computer Equipment'. The WTO Panel considered that, in the EC, LAN equipment could not be classified as telecommunications equipment, but had to be classified as automatic data processing machines. Concerning PC-TVs, the Panel took the position that the EC was entitled to classify them as TV receivers. In both cases, however, the Panel admitted that schedules were not sufficiently clear.[60] The Appellate Body reversed the Panel's findings because, among other things, the Panel unduly relied on the legitimate expectations of WTO Members during the Uruguay Round in its determination of which classification had to prevail. The Appellate Body did not rule on the classification issue itself and thus left some uncertainty in this regard. However, it referred to the work

[59] For more current information regarding participation to the ITA, see WTO document series G/IT/1/Rev.

[60] See Panel Report, 'European Communities – Customs Classification of Certain Computer Equipment', WT/DS62/R, WT/DS67/R, WT/DS68/R, 5 February 1998, paras. 8.62 and 8.68.

carried out under the auspices of the World Customs Organization as the relevant and obligatory source concerning tariff classification.[61]

Currently, most of the terminal equipment used for converged telecommunications and audio-visual services is exempt from customs duties pursuant to the ITA. However, several classification issues are still pending before the WTO Committee of Participants on the Expansion of Trade in Information Technology Products.[62] In future, unless countries adapt their schedules, it may be expected that converged applications will entail several classification disputes.

It remains to be seen to what extent the product coverage of the ITA will follow the developments of convergence. Clearly, should the latter be promoted, differentiated tariffs for audio-visual, telecommunications or more general information technology applications should not cause undue discriminations with respect to the provision of like converged services.

Access to terminal equipment

Pursuant to the Annex on Telecommunications, suppliers of scheduled audio-visual services (except providers of radio or TV programmes) must be allowed to purchase or lease and attach the terminal equipment needed for their operations.[63] However, if terminal equipment and technical interface devices are traded by monopoly suppliers, access to them under competitive conditions does not seem to be guaranteed under current rules, despite the fact of their being an 'essential facility'.

Indeed, both the Reference Paper and the Annex on Telecommunications, which oblige governments to grant access to their public telecommunications infrastructure under reasonable and non-discriminatory conditions, refer to public telecommunications transport networks and services. Consequently, access to essential terminal equipment, decoders and navigation tools held by dominant suppliers would be mandated under such rules only if they were telecommunications services (which is not the case) or if they were considered to be network elements (which is unlikely). Therefore, the only way in which this deficiency could be remedied

[61] See Appellate Body Report, 'European Communities – Customs Classification of Certain Computer Equipment', WT/DS62/AB/R, WT/DS67/AB/R, WT/DS68/AB/R, 5 June 1998, paras. 74–98.

[62] See reports G/L/216 (1997), G/L/280 (1998), G/L/332 (1999), G/L/420 (2000), G/L/484 (2001) and G/L/577 (2002).

[63] Article 5(b) of the Annex on Telecommunications.

would be through the application of domestic competition laws. Clearly, a set of common international competition principles would be helpful in this regard.

Conclusion

This paper examined the impact of WTO rules on network liberalisation and on access to scarce network resources and to the relevant technical equipment to supply audio-visual services. It also examined whether WTO rules are sufficiently flexible and adapted to convergence in this context as well as in relation to the pursuit of cultural policies.

It was noted that, currently, WTO rules are uncertain in a number of respects regarding the liberalisation of networks. First, it is not obvious that, under current definitions, the scheduling of audio-visual services entails market access rights for providers of networks necessary to supply those services. Secondly, there is no certainty with respect to general access to cable networks under the Annex on Telecommunications. Arguably, however, to the extent cable networks are available to the public generally, they should be subject to the Annex. The latter, however, excludes from its provisions access to public networks, including cables, for broadcasters of radio and television programmes. We have noted that this exclusion, combined with the uncertainty surrounding the liberalisation of networks used for these services, could have the effect of preventing the adequate distribution of TV or radio programmes and thus hamper the liberalisation of scheduled TV or radio services in a manner incompatible with the objectives of the Annex.

It was argued that WTO rules concerning access to public networks are relevant to the assignment of frequency bands or satellite capacity within the jurisdiction of WTO Members. Under WTO rules, Members are in principle compelled to grant access to allocated frequency bands for scheduled audio-visual services to the extent they are available, on non-discriminatory conditions. Indeed refusal to assign a frequency band could amount to a violation of either the Annex on Telecommunications (except for TV or radio broadcasting) or, more generally, a violation of market access commitments if it is made on a discretionary basis. When it is connected to the quality of the service or the qualifications of service suppliers, it must be based on objective criteria, it must genuinely seek to increase the quality of the service, it must and be the least trade-restrictive measure available to achieve this objective.

The protection of culture is possible in several circumstances, due to the inherent flexibility of the GATS. First, in the absence of commitments, Members are free to implement a cultural policy, even in the form of restrictions to foreign audio-visual services. Secondly, if commitments are taken, access to the public networks can be restricted if necessary to enable the provision of a public service. This would be the case if enabling a foreign operator to access such network would jeopardise the provision of an educational audio-visual service, due to the lack of capacity of the available networks. Thirdly, Members may include limitations in their Schedules of commitments to protect national culture. These limitations can be inserted either in the second column of their Schedules, related to the market access obligation, or in the third column, related to the national treatment obligation. Fourthly, Members are free to enact domestic regulation, which is neither discriminatory nor more trade-restrictive than existing regulation, in order to guarantee the 'quality' of the service.

It should be noted that the notions of public service and quality of the service, providing grounds for restrictive regulations, are not defined in the GATS and in the Annex on Telecommunications. Consequently, it can be argued that, subject to a general obligation of good faith, WTO Members may define them by themselves in a manner compatible with their cultural policy.

The question then arises as to the extent to which convergence disturbs the above picture. We noted that convergence blurs the borders between telecommunication services and audio-visual services and enables them to use the same networks. Consequently, different regulations applicable to them at the level of networks may be more difficult to implement.

A first difficulty is related to the notion of like service. The non-discrimination rules in the GATS apply to like services. These are not defined, but, arguably, in the context of services, considering physical characteristics to be irrelevant, like services are services that are functionally equivalent and that are provided in the same market. This might be the case of multimedia services distributed by the Internet and those conveyed through more traditional broadcasting networks. These services are currently classified, respectively, as telecommunication services and as audio-visual services. Considering that the structure of the GATS is based on individual commitments per services sectors, different treatment, due to different commitments, on like telecommunications and audio-visual services may nevertheless constitute a prohibited discrimination. For instance, if access to a public network, including assignment of a frequency band, is granted to Internet services and not to similar broadcasting services, this could constitute either a violation of the MFN principle or the national treatment principle (assuming commitments have been made), depending on the origin of the service affected or the nationality of its supplier. This difficulty is also relevant at the level of frequency assignments for suppliers of Internet services or for broadcasters within the bandwidths allocated by the WRC-2000 to broadband networks.

Furthermore, technology itself may render restrictions on access to broadband networks difficult to realise in practice. Indeed, both telecommunications and audio-visual services can access these networks. In order to facilitate their expansion and the promotion of the Information Society, it would be inefficient to require that separate networks are used for each kind of service. Thus, restrictions on access to networks, including frequency bands, although they are authorised by the GATS for the pursuit of a public audio-visual service or quality, may be inappropriate in practice. Furthermore, subordinating the operation of broadband networks to conditions linked to audio-visual services may unduly affect the provision of scheduled telecommunications services in a manner incompatible with commitments taken and with the Reference Paper. Thus, it would be difficult to implement protective cultural policies at the level of access to the network. If needed, these should be implemented at the level of control of network use. This, however, may not be an easy task and might require cooperation among Members, considering the transboundary nature of the services affected.

One may conclude that, while current WTO rules are characterised by their flexibility, they are not, under current sectoral classifications, adapted to expected market developments. Perhaps, similarly to what was done during the World Radiocommunications Conferences, specific measures should be defined for broadband networks and for converged technology. In any event, culture would be separate from issues of access to networks, frequency assignments and terminal equipment. This would foster cultural policies that are more transparent and perhaps more proactive than based on prohibitions. Definitions and commitments should perhaps follow this trend.

10

Lack of clear regulatory framework on safeguards, government procurement and subsidies

JEAN-FRANÇOIS BELLIS*

Introduction

The Uruguay Round produced the first ever set of rules regulating the trade in services, the General Agreement on Trade in Services (GATS). For the first time since the GATT had came into effect in 1948, internationally agreed rules and commitments, broadly comparable with those of the GATT, became applicable to the trade in services.

That the GATS was created should not be interpreted as meaning that the many different views expressed during its negotiation were successfully resolved. An agreement on GATS rules could only be reached at the end of the Uruguay Round, and, in order to arrive at an agreement, Members decided to include only basic and commonly accepted rules. Contentious issues or rules, such as safeguards, government procurement and subsidies, which needed to be further defined, were not therefore included in the GATS.

Members generally agreed that the negotiations which were carried out during the Uruguay Round on an emergency safeguard mechanism, government procurement and subsidies and countervailing measures (hereinafter 'GATS rules') had to be continued. Members recognised that the relationship between these issues and the trade in services had to be addressed. The mandate to engage or conclude negotiations on emergency safeguard measures, government procurement and subsidies is, thus, provided for in the GATS.

In March 1995, the Council for Trade in Services established the Working Party on GATS Rules to carry out the negotiating mandates contained in the GATS on emergency safeguard measures, government procurement

* The author would like to thank Charles Julien and Tim Jordan for their assistance in the preparation of the present contribution.

and subsidies.[1] Since July 1995, negotiations on these three issues have been held within the Working Party.[2]

The negotiations held within the Working Party have not addressed issues directly related to telecommunications and audio-visual services. The broad set of rules which may result from these negotiations would, however, have a significant impact on these services. For this reason, it is particularly important not only for WTO Members but also for players in the telecommunication and audio-visual sectors to keep abreast of these negotiations.

Emergency safeguard measures in the GATS

The GATS framework: basic protection rules

The structures of the GATT and the GATS are inherently different. In the GATS, Members agreed on few broadly applicable rules but preferred to make commitments in the sectors in which they considered liberalisation was both possible and beneficial.

Despite the open nature of GATS rules, the right of Members to take emergency measures to safeguard their interests has not been taken away from them. Even in the absence of an emergency safeguard mechanism, which is currently the subject of negotiations, Members have always been granted the right to preserve the interests of their service suppliers in specific circumstances.

The structure of the GATS: an inherent protection of the interests of Members

Unlike the GATT, the GATS contains very few general obligations which are binding for all Members. One of the few general obligations provided for in the GATS, the most-favoured nation treatment clause of Article II, may even be bypassed by Members under certain conditions. Under Article II:2, Members can maintain measures inconsistent with their most-favoured nation treatment obligation provided that such measures are listed in their Schedule of commitments.

[1] Report of the meeting held on 30 March 1995, Note by the Secretariat, 28 April 1995, S/C/M/2.

[2] Report of the meeting held on 17 July 1995, Note by the Secretariat, S/WPGR/M/1. The reports of the Working Party meetings can be found on Documents online, http://docsonline.wto.org/, under the reference S/WPGR/M/.

The specific commitments each Member agreed to during the Uruguay Round are restricted to the sectors listed in its Schedule. Within a sector, scheduled commitments can be further limited to certain modes of supply and their precise terms can further be conditioned by market access or national treatment limitations.[3]

As a result of these inherent limitations, the desirability[4] of emergency safeguard measures is a central question in the negotiations conducted pursuant to Article X.

Article X:2: the guarantee of a minimum protection

Emergency actions available to Members during the negotiations on emergency safeguard measures are provided for in Article X:2[5] of the GATS.

Protection period The availability of these actions was initially limited to three years, i.e. the maximum duration of the emergency safeguard measures negotiations, by Article X:3. As a result of the inability of the Members of the Working Party on GATS Rules to conclude the negotiations, the Council for Trade in Services was forced on four occasions to extend the deadline within which the negotiations had to be completed.[6] On each of these occasions, the possibility for Members to invoke the provisions of Article X:2 was also extended for the entire estimated duration of the negotiations.[7] The latest deadline set for the completion of the negotiations on emergency safeguard measures is 15 March 2004. Consequently, Members which consider that some of their service suppliers

[3] Rules governing specific commitments are stipulated in Articles XVI and XVII of the GATS.

[4] The question of the desirability of an emergency safeguard mechanism is at the centre of the negotiations of the Working Party on GATS Rules. See below.

[5] Article X:2 of the GATS provides: 'In the period before the entry into effect of the results of the negotiations referred to in paragraph 1, any Member may, notwithstanding the provisions of paragraph 1 of Article XXI, notify the Council on Trade in Services of its intention to modify or withdraw a specific commitment after a period of one year from the date on which the commitment enters into force; provided that the Member shows cause to the Council that the modification or withdrawal cannot await the lapse of the three-year period provided for in paragraph 1 of Article XXI.'

[6] Decisions on negotiations on emergency safeguard measures, S/L/43, S/L/73 and S/L/90. Further to recommendations of the Working Party on GATS Rules, on 26 November 1997, 24 June 1999 and 1 December 2000, the Council for Trade in Services extended the deadline for completing the emergency safeguard measures negotiations to 30 June 1999, 15 December 2000 and 15 March 2002 respectively.

[7] See documents S/L/43, S/L/73, S/L/90 and S/L/102.

face unexpected adverse developments can resort to Article X:2 until 15 March 2004 in order to grant the necessary protection.

The duration of actions that may be adopted pursuant to Article X:2 is not defined. Unlike the Agreement on Safeguards,[8] Article X:2 does not limit the application of emergency actions to the period of time necessary to prevent or remedy serious injury and facilitate adjustment. The absence of such a provision is certainly due to the confidence of the drafters of the GATS that the emergency safeguards negotiations would be concluded before the deadline. Since the duration of provisional emergency actions was to be, *de facto*, limited to a period of three years, it was not considered necessary to legally determine their duration.

Scope of emergency actions The actions permitted under Article X:2 are the modification or withdrawal of the commitments listed by the Members in their Schedules. The possibility offered to Members to modify or withdraw some of their commitments relates only to those commitments which have been in force for more than one year. Recently negotiated commitments, i.e. commitments which entered into force within the last year, cannot be modified or withdrawn under Article X:2.

Article X:2 does not contain any other indications on the commitments which Members may modify or withdraw. Indeed, Article X:2 does not stipulate that the commitments to be modified or withdrawn must be closely linked to the activities of the service suppliers which are being injured or threatened by injury. It can, however, be assumed that the Council for Trade in Services, which is competent to examine whether commitment modifications or withdrawals can be made under Article X:2, would refuse to allow Members to modify or withdraw commitments which have no direct incidence on the activities of service suppliers suffering from injury.

Emergency action adoption procedure Members which decide to resort to Article X:2 will have to notify the Council for Trade in Services and show cause to the latter that the modification or withdrawal cannot await the lapse of the three-year period provided for in Article XXI:1.[9]

[8] See Articles 7:1 to 7:3 of the Agreement on Safeguards.

[9] Article XXI of the GATS concerns the modification of Schedules. Article XXI:1 (a) provides: 'A Member (referred to in this Article as the "modifying Member") may modify or withdraw any commitments in its Schedule, at any time after three years have elapsed from the date on which that commitment entered into force, in accordance with the provisions of this Article.'

Although not mentioned in Article X:2, it is generally agreed that the modification or withdrawal of commitments made under its provisions will have to follow the procedural requirements set forth in Article XXI.[10]

The modification or withdrawal of commitments under Article X:2 can give rise to compensatory adjustments. Indeed, under Article XXI:2, any Member which considers that its interests under the GATS may be affected by the proposed modification or withdrawal of a commitment may negotiate a compensatory adjustment with the Member modifying or withdrawing the commitment. In the event that the Members concerned cannot reach an agreement on the compensatory adjustment, it will be determined by an arbitration body. It is interesting to note that the Member intending to modify or withdraw a commitment will not be able to do so before a compensatory adjustment is granted. Under the Agreement on Safeguards, the Member applying a safeguard measure is not required, provided certain conditions are met, to compensate other Members for the adverse effects of the measure on their trade during the first three years the measure is in effect.[11]

Since the entry into force of the GATS, no Member has considered it necessary to resort to Article X:2.

Article XXI: a possible alternative protection mechanism

Article XXI sets forth the rules governing the modification of Schedules. Article XXI is not specifically intended to protect service suppliers faced with unanticipated adverse developments. However, since Article XXI does not limit the right of Members to modify their Schedules in response to certain specific circumstances, Members remain free to have recourse to Article XXI in circumstances in which they consider that their domestic service suppliers face unexpected difficulties.

Under Article XXI, a Member can modify or withdraw a commitment after three years have elapsed from the date on which the commitment entered into force. Modifications or withdrawals made pursuant to Article XXI are definitive, although Members, nevertheless, remain free to reinstitute any modified or withdrawn commitments.

[10] See below.

[11] Indeed, Article 8:3 of the Agreement on Safeguards provides: 'The right of suspension referred to in paragraph 2 shall not be exercised for the first three years that a safeguard measure is in effect, provided that the safeguard measure has been taken as a result of an absolute increase in imports and that such a measure conforms to the provisions of this Agreement.'

The steps which Members must observe to modify their Schedules are the following.

Notification During the first stage of the procedure, the Member intending to modify a scheduled commitment (hereinafter the 'modifying Member') shall transmit a notification to that effect to the Council for Trade in Services no later than three months before the intended date of implementation of such modification or withdrawal.

Information During the second stage, which lapses at the latest forty-five days after the date on which the intention to modify or withdraw a commitment has been notified, any Member which considers its interests under the GATS may be affected by the proposed modification or withdrawal (hereinafter the 'affected Member') will notify the modifying Member. If no such claim is raised, the modifying Member will be free to implement the proposed modification or withdrawal.

Negotiation If a claim is raised, during a third stage the modifying Member and any affected Member shall negotiate with a view to reaching an agreement within three months following the date on which the claim was raised. Members can agree on the nature of the modification or withdrawal and/or on any compensatory adjustments. In the event that the modifying and affected Members reach an agreement, they shall communicate their mutually satisfactory agreement to the WTO no later than fifteen days after the completion of their negotiations.

Arbitration If no agreement can be reached between the modifying and the affected Members within the three-month deadline, the affected Members can decide to proceed to the fourth stage. At this stage, the affected Members can request that the matter be referred to an arbitration body. Such a request must be made no later than forty-five days after the expiry of the three-month negotiation period. The arbitration shall be subject to the rules and procedures governing the settlement of disputes,[12] and must be completed within three months of the appointment of the arbitration body. Following the conclusion of the arbitration proceeding, the modifying Member is free to implement any modification or withdrawal that is in conformity with the findings of the arbitration

[12] These rules are to be found in the Understanding on Rules and Procedures Governing the Settlement of Disputes.

body. If the modifying Member does not comply with the findings of the arbitration body, any affected Member that participated in the arbitration may modify or withdraw substantially equivalent benefits in conformity with those findings.

Because Article XXI has never been enforced since its ratification, Members do not appear to have considered that they could no longer maintain the commitments made during the Uruguay Round, or that domestic service suppliers faced with unexpected adverse developments required the level of protection it allows.

Applicability of the concepts set out in the Agreement on Safeguards

At the request of the Members of the Working Party on GATS Rules, the WTO Secretariat prepared a note on the applicability of concepts used in the Agreement on Safeguards to trade in services.[13] The following section will examine the most important issues identified by the Secretariat in its Note and determine whether or not the concepts developed in the GATT context can be transposed to services.

Conditions for the application of a safeguard measure

Under Article 2:1 of the Agreement on Safeguards, a Member may apply a safeguard measure to a product only if it has determined that the product is being imported into its territory in such increased quantities, absolute or relative to domestic production, and under such conditions as to cause or threaten to cause serious injury to the domestic industry that produces like or directly competitive products.

Increase of imports The first condition is an increase of imports. The concept of importation with regard to the trade in goods is relatively simple. It implies the crossing of a border by the goods being imported. With regard to the trade in services, the concept of importation can have a wider meaning. Depending on the mode of supply, the concept of importation of services will be different. Under mode 1 (cross-border supply), the concept of importation is the same as for goods. Under mode 2 (consumption abroad), the consumption abroad falls within the concept of importation.

[13] Emergency Safeguard Measures in GATS, the Applicability of Concepts Applied in the WTO Agreement on Safeguards, Note by the Secretariat, 6 March 1996, S/WPGR/W/8 (see also Doc. S/WPGR/W/27/Rev.2, 16 September 1999; and Doc. S/WPGR/W/24, 3 September 1997).

Under modes 3 (commercial presence) and 4 (presence of natural persons), a distinction needs to be made between the establishment and the post-establishment phases. During the establishment phase, the establishment is considered as an importation, while in the post-establishment phase, the supply of services is considered as importation.

The determination of the volume of imports in absolute terms does not raise any particular difficulties. It only requires that statistics on the volume of services considered as imported be kept. The determination of the volume of imports in relation to domestic production is more problematic since it is linked to the concept of domestic production. In the Agreement on Safeguards, the domestic industry consists of the producers of the like or directly competitive products operating within the territory of a Member whose collective output of the like or directly competitive product constitutes a major total domestic production of those products. The definition of the Agreement on Safeguards can be applied without modification in GATS under modes 1 and 2. Under modes 3 and 4, the determination of the domestic industry is more complicated since a distinction needs to be established between the establishment and post-establishment phases. During the establishment phase, the domestic industry could include all the service suppliers, whether national or foreign, already established in a Member. In the post-establishment phase, a distinction would logically have to be made between domestic and foreign service suppliers. The domestic industry would, in this last case, be composed only of the domestic suppliers. As seen below, Members have different positions on the definition of the domestic industry.

Serious injury The second condition is the existence of serious injury or of a threat thereof.[14] A domestic industry is regarded as injured when it encounters a significant and imminent overall impairment of its position. The determination of injury is to be based upon relevant industry factors, the most important of which are listed in the Agreement on Safeguards. Notwithstanding the difficulties linked with the collection of relevant information, the factors listed in the Agreement on Safeguards could certainly be transposable in a GATS emergency safeguard measures agreement. The only difficulty would, again, be the determination of what constitutes the domestic industry.

[14] Agreement on Safeguards, Article 4.

Causal link The third condition is the existence of a causal link between the increased imports and the injury or threat thereof.[15] The causality requirement set out in the Agreement on Safeguards could in principle be developed in the context of services without any difficulty.

Application of a safeguard measure

The Agreement on Safeguards does not prescribe particular types of measure.[16] It only provides that safeguard measures are to be limited to the extent necessary to prevent or remedy serious injury and to facilitate adjustment. However, in practice, safeguard measures only take two forms: quantitative restrictions and tariff increases. Tariff increases are to be used at the provisional stage,[17] but definitive measures may normally take the form of quotas. If quantitative restrictions are used, they should not reduce the current average level of imports below the average level of imports of the product over the last three representative years for which statistics are available, unless it can be shown that a different level of imports is required to prevent or remedy serious injury. Where import quotas are allocated, a Member may seek agreement with respect to the allocation of the shares with all the Members having a substantial interest in supplying the product concerned. A discriminatory allocation of quantitative restrictions is only permitted in very limited circumstances.

The same choice between quantity-based or price-based emergency safeguard measures would also exist for services. Quantity-based measures would in addition, however, be enforceable by regulatory rules, which would limit the market access of imported services. A distinction would, again, have to be made between the different modes of supply. Under mode 1, the quantitative restrictions applicable under the Agreement on Safeguards would be transposable. Under mode 2, a different type of measure would have to be taken in order to limit the consumption of services abroad. Safeguard measures to limit consumption abroad could take the form of a tax, quantitative restrictions or measures restricting the physical movement of consumers. Under mode 3, during the establishment phase, the investment flow would have to be taxed or restricted. Under mode 4, the movement of natural persons would be restricted or taxed during the same phase. During the post-establishment phase, if an emergency safeguard measure was imposed under modes 3 and 4, the

15 *Ibid.*, Articles 2:1 and 4:2(b).

16 *Ibid.*, Article 5.

17 *Ibid.*, Article 6.

services provided by foreign, as opposed to national, service suppliers would have to be restricted or taxed.

The duration of safeguard measures and the period which must elapse before a new safeguard measure is introduced on a product that has previously been the subject of a safeguard action are provided in the Agreement on Safeguards.[18] These time limits vary depending on the nature of the action and the Members which apply them, and could also, as the case may be, be used for GATS safeguard measures.

Level of concessions and other obligations

A Member proposing to apply a safeguard measure or seeking an extension of a safeguard measure pursuant to the Agreement on Safeguards shall endeavour to maintain a substantially equivalent level of concessions and other obligations to those existing under the 1994 GATT, between it and the exporting Members that would be affected by such a measure.[19] In other words, a Member which intends to impose a safeguard measure must be prepared to compensate other Members for the adverse effects they would suffer as a consequence. The right to compensation is, generally, automatically available only to Members adversely affected by a safeguard measure three years after its ratification. During the first three years of application of a safeguard measure, the Member proposing to apply a safeguard measure only has to consult affected Members on the level of concessions and other obligations which are to be maintained. If, during that period of time, the consultations do not lead to a satisfactory outcome, a safeguard measure can be imposed.

The transposition of a compensation provision in a GATS emergency safeguard mechanism set of rules does not appear to raise any problems. As mentioned above, a compensation mechanism is already provided for in Article XXI. This mechanism could also be used in the context of emergency safeguard measures since it provides for a timely procedure pursuant to which arbitration on the level of the compensation to be granted can be requested by any affected Member. The procedures set out in Article XXI would only have to be adapted to satisfy the emergency requirement of a safeguard measure mechanism. In this regard, the provisions of Article XXI, which provide that modifications can only be brought to commitments of more than three years and that a three-month notification period must be observed, would certainly have to be

[18] *Ibid.*, Article 7.
[19] *Ibid.*, Article 8.

amended in order to permit Members to adopt safeguard measures more expeditiously.

The emergency safeguard measures negotiations: towards GATS rules?

Article X:1 of the GATS: an obligation to engage in negotiations

Article X:1 of the GATS invites WTO Members to conclude negotiations on the question of emergency safeguard measures within three years from the date of entry into force of the WTO Agreement, i.e. no later than 1 January 1998.[20]

Due to the inability of the Members of the Working Party on GATS Rules to reach an agreement before the initial deadline, the Council for Trade in Services was obliged to extend the negotiations deadline. The Council for Trade in Services extended the deadline first until 30 June 1999, then until 15 December 2000, then until 15 March 2002 and finally until 15 March 2004.

Since its first meeting in July 1995, the Working Party on GATS Rules has held thirty-nine formal meetings. The emergency safeguard measures negotiation has been addressed in all the meetings. In addition, the members of the Working Party have held numerous informal meetings with the sole aim of accelerating the emergency safeguard measures negotiation.

During the first two years, the discussions centred on the desirability of developing an emergency safeguard mechanism. The Working Party's members then agreed to set aside this fundamental question[21] and decided to examine four key substantive questions: (i) On whose behalf would emergency safeguard actions be taken? (ii) Under what circumstances would emergency safeguard actions be taken and what would be the purpose of such actions? (iii) What approach should be adopted with respect to injury/adverse effects, and what would be the relevant causal link between the injury/adverse effects and the commitments under the GATS? (iv) What measures would be available under the emergency

[20] Article X:1 of the GATS provides that: 'There shall be multilateral negotiations on the question of emergency safeguard measures based on the principle of non-discrimination. The results of such negotiations shall enter into effect on a date not later than three years from the date of entry into force of the *WTO* Agreement.'

[21] Report of the Meeting of 28 March 1996, Note by the Secretariat, 13 May 1996, S/WPGR/M/5.

safeguard mechanism, and, are some measures deemed more suitable than others?[22]

A questionnaire prepared by the WTO Secretariat was circulated to Members to collect the views of the Members on an emergency safeguard mechanism in the GATS.[23] Very few Members have, so far, replied to this questionnaire.[24]

Over the last two years, Working Party members examined the different themes which an agreement on emergency safeguard measures would have to address. These themes include the definition of the concepts of 'like services' and 'domestic industry'; the modal application of a safeguard mechanism; the identification of indicators and criteria for determining injury and causality; the possible forms of a safeguard measure; the questions of compensation and special and differential treatment; situations justifying safeguard actions; and relevant procedural matters. The themes on which diverging views were expressed are examined below.

Thailand, on behalf of the ASEAN members, circulated a concept paper in March 2000 that aimed to take into account the views expressed by all the members of the Working Party.[25] This concept paper was the first attempt to draft rules concerning a GATS emergency safeguard mechanism.

Contentious issues

First and foremost, the question of the desirability of an emergency safeguard mechanism in the GATS was addressed by the Working Party. Several Members, led by the United States, have questioned the desirability of an emergency safeguard mechanism in the GATS. The US position is that no Member has yet made a convincing case in favour of safeguards, and that the absence of recourse to Article X:2 actions during the first six years of existence of the GATS is a clear sign that the establishment of a

[22] Report of the Meeting of 22 May 1997, Note by the Secretariat, 30 June 1997, S/WPGR/M/11.

[23] Questions Relating to an Emergency Safeguard Mechanism in GATS, Note by the Secretariat, S/WPGR/W/15.

[24] Thailand (S/WPGR/W/15/Add.1), India (S/WPGR/W/15/Add.2), Poland (S/WPGR/W/15/Add.3), the European Communities (S/WPGR/W/15/Add.4), Egypt (S/WPGR/W/15/Add.5), Mexico (S/WPGR/W/15/Add.6) and Cuba (S/WPGR/W/15/Add.7) are the only Members which submitted responses to the questionnaire concerning the GATS emergency safeguard mechanism.

[25] Communication from ASEAN, Concept Paper: Elements of a Possible Agreed Draft of Rules on Emergency Safeguard Measures for Trade in Services (GATS Article X), 14 March 2000, S/WPGR/W/30.

safeguard mechanism in the GATS is not essential.[26] The US argues that a GATS safeguard mechanism only needs to be developed if it is linked with an obligation to make more extensive commitments to liberalisation. By contrast, a number of Members, led by Thailand, consider that the question of the desirability of a safeguard instrument should not even be addressed.[27] These Members consider that the mandate of the Working Party, which stems from Article X:1, only invites Members to negotiate the characteristics of safeguard mechanism.

The second question concerns the feasibility of a safeguard mechanism for services. The US, again, considers that such feasibility has not yet been demonstrated.[28] The US believes that the numerous approaches suggested by the different Members serve largely to raise the question of how safeguard measures could be applied in practice. Although most Members generally disagree with the US and consider that the establishment of a safeguard mechanism would be feasible,[29] these Members are also of the opinion that the instrument established would not necessarily cover all service supply modes.[30]

A third fundamental question concerns the scope of a GATS safeguard instrument, i.e. the Members' pre-existing commitments for which recourse to the safeguard instrument could be made. The first alternative would cover all existing commitments. This alternative is preferred by most of the Working Party's members. The second possibility would be to limit coverage to certain sectors or modes of supply. The US has suggested that sector-specific rules could include the requirement that a Member including a safeguard-type provision in its Schedule for a given sector would have to combine it with a commitment to liberalise that sector. A hybrid alternative combining both general and sector-specific rules would, of course, also be possible.

The other questions concern the underlying concepts of a GATS emergency safeguard measure.

[26] Communication from the United States, Desirability of a Safeguard Mechanism for Services: Promoting Liberalisation of Trade in Services, 2 October 2001, S/WPGR/W/37.

[27] Communication from Thailand, a Discussion Paper on GATS Emergency Safeguards, 18 December 1995, S/WPGR/W/6.

[28] Communication from the United States, Emergency Safeguards, 13 March 1997, S/WPGR/W/17.

[29] Report of the Meeting of 23 February 1996, Note by the Secretariat, 19 March 1996, S/WPGR/M/4.

[30] Contra: Communication from the European Communities and their Members, Modal Application of Emergency Safeguard Measure, 21 January 2002, S/WPGR/W/38.

The definition of the domestic industry is important in order to determine, in particular, both on whose behalf and against whom a safeguard action is being taken. This implies a choice between two alternatives. The first alternative would be to consider that all domestically established service suppliers, regardless of ownership, nationality and control, should be considered as the domestic industry.[31] The other alternative would be based upon the distinction established in Article XXVIII of the GATS,[32] which establishes a difference between domestic services and services of other Members or provided by natural persons of other Members on the basis of nationality. Under the second alternative, the domestic industry would, therefore, be limited to the national service suppliers. A number of Members argued that their domestic legislation does not authorise them to introduce such a distinction. Some Members in favour of the second alternative stated that in order to protect foreign investment they would have to guarantee the 'acquired rights' of domestically established foreign suppliers. This last approach would enable Members to take a safeguard measure only on behalf of the national industry, but exclude from its coverage domestically established foreign suppliers.

Most Working Party members agree that the determination of injury should be made according to the method set forth in the Agreement on Safeguards.[33] The reference to 'imports' would only have to be replaced by the notion of 'consumption of foreign services'. Other members argue that, given the problematic state of statistics concerning the trade in services, it may be difficult to use the methodology of the Agreement on Safeguards in order to determine whether a domestic industry is in fact suffering injury.[34] These members consider that, while the injury factors provided in the Agreement on Safeguards could be applied, it would be useful to consider also other factors. However, having an overly flexible definition of injury could open the door to abuse.

Finally, the question of compensation has been contentious. While some members consider that the provisions of the Agreement on Safeguards could be used as a model, other members believe that certain difficulties, notably the determination of the level of compensation itself,

[31] Communication from Cuba, Response to the Questions Relating to an Emergency Safeguard Mechanism in GATS, 25 August 1997, S/WPGR/W/15/Add.7.

[32] Communication from Poland, Response to the Questions Relating to an Emergency Safeguard Mechanism in GATS, 2 May 1997, S/WPGR/W/15/Add.3.

[33] Communication from ASEAN, Emergency Safeguards, 23 July 1997, S/WPGR/W/22.

[34] Communication from Switzerland, Safeguards and Trade in Services, 10 October 1996, S/WPGR/W/14.

would not be properly addressed if the rules of the Agreement on Safeguards were transposed. The role and importance of compensation has also been discussed. On the one hand, compensation can be seen to serve as a possible deterrent against protectionist use of the emergency safeguard mechanism.[35] On the other hand, a compensation requirement could render the invocation of a temporary measure overly burdensome and, therefore, create a bias in favour of using the permanent modifications or withdrawals provided for in Article XXI.

Possible outcome

In 2001, the Working Party on GATS Rules spent at least 80% of its time on GATS emergency safeguard measures in order to try to reach an agreement. Indeed, the negotiations on safeguard rules are the only ones which must be completed within a set deadline.

The members of the Working Party must now determine whether they will move on to the drafting phase of the negotiations. Unless this is done in the near future, it will be impossible for the Working Party to complete its work before the 15 March 2002 deadline. A number of members remain committed to concluding the negotiations within the set deadline, and will certainly make proposals in order to try to break the deadlock on certain issues.

Government procurement of services

Article XIII:1 of the GATS provides as a general rule that Articles II (most-favoured nation treatment), XVI (national treatment) and XVII (market access) shall not apply to laws, regulations or requirements governing the procurement by governmental agencies of services purchased for governmental purposes and not with a view to commercial resale or use in the supply of services for commercial sale.

A similar exemption from the national treatment obligation for the government procurement of goods is also provided for in Article III:8a of the GATT. Under both the GATS and the GATT, the right of Members to have the possibility to continue to favour local products and/or service suppliers when awarding contracts is guaranteed.

Despite an agreement on the exemption of government procurement from the fundamental GATS obligations, Members recognised that the

[35] Communication from Mexico, Response to the Questions Relating to an Emergency Safeguard Mechanism in GATS, 22 May 1997, S/WPGR/W/15/Add.6.

lack of rules covering government procurement was a significant gap which had to be remedied. Article XIII:2 of the GATS therefore stipulates that there shall be multilateral negotiations on government procurement in services under the GATS within two years of the date of entry into force of the GATS. In March 1995, the Working Party on GATS Rules received a mandate from the Council for Trade in Services to carry out negotiations on government procurement of services.[36] Having carefully examined the obligations already agreed upon by a limited number of Members in the Agreement on Government Procurement, the Working Party decided to use these obligations as a basis for negotiations.

The Agreement on Government Procurement and services: from Tokyo to Doha

Introduction

An Agreement on Government Procurement was first negotiated during the Tokyo Round and became enforceable on 1 January 1981. The initial parties considered that the purchases made by governments or their agencies, which typically represent 10–15 per cent of those Members' GNPs, could not be completely excluded from GATT rules. The purpose of the initial Agreement on Government Procurement was, therefore, to open to international competition government procurement to the greatest degree possible. This Agreement made law, procedures and practices regarding government procurement more transparent, and ensured that these measures did not protect domestic products or discriminate against foreign products. Twenty-five GATT Members signed the Tokyo Government Procurement Agreement.

During the Uruguay Round, most of the parties to the Tokyo Government Procurement Agreement negotiated to widen the scope of the Agreement and to reinforce the applicable provisions. The result of this ten-year negotiation process was the Agreement on Government Procurement, which entered into force on 1 January 1996. The Agreement was signed by twenty-two WTO Members.

The Agreement on Government Procurement, in comparison with the Tokyo Agreement, provides extended coverage of both the entities and the activities concerned: international competition has been extended to national and local government entities; and coverage has been extended

[36] Report of the meeting held on 30 March 1995, Note by the Secretariat, 28 April 1995, S/C/M/2.

to include certain service sectors. The rules guaranteeing fair and non-discriminatory conditions of international competition have also been reinforced.

Scope and coverage

The Agreement on Government Procurement applies to any law, regulation procedure or practice regarding any procurement made by the entities listed in the Annexes to Appendix I to the Agreement.[37] Annex 1 covers central government entities; Annex 2 covers sub-central government entities; and Annex 3 covers all other entities that procure in accordance with the provisions of the Agreement on Government Procurement. The definition of the entities listed in Annex 3 is broad because the parties could not agree during the negotiations on a common definition covering all other public entities and, in particular, public undertakings. The Agreement on Government Procurement only applies to procurement above a certain threshold value. Thresholds are determined, by each party, for each type of entity and transaction covered by the Annexes.

The types of transaction that may be covered by the Agreement on Government Procurement have been greatly extended as a result of the Uruguay Round negotiations, notably to include the procurement of services. However, the parties have adopted a position similar to that adopted during the GATS negotiations, by making only limited commitments by excluding numerous service sectors. The service sectors covered are listed by each party in Annex 4 to Appendix I. Each party's list can be positive, i.e. only listing the sectors covered, or negative, i.e. only listing the sectors excluded. The US is the only party to the Agreement on Government Procurement to have opted for a negative list. All parties have excluded basic telecom services from the coverage of the Agreement on Government Procurement. By contrast, all parties, with the exception of Israel, have indicated that value-added telecom services are covered. With regard to audio-visual services, the US is the only party to agree that these services fall within the scope of the Agreement on Government Procurement.

The scope of the Agreement on Government Procurement is also limited by the non-application and reciprocity provisions contained in the Annexes listing the services covered. Reciprocity provisions limit the benefit of a commitment to parties that have agreed to the same commitment. During the negotiations of the Agreement on Government Procurement,

[37] Agreement on Government Procurement, Article I:1.

parties were free to include in their Annexes non-application or reciprocity provisions pertaining to sectors, thresholds and the application of Article XX. Article XX sets out the rules concerning challenge procedures.

The scope of the Agreement on Government Procurement with regard to services is further limited by provisions of the GATS. The Agreement on Government Procurement only contains rules on the government purchase of services and does not concern market access and competitive conditions for services and service suppliers. The trade in services, regardless of whether it concerns government procurement, remains subject to GATS rules. As a result, a party to the Agreement on Government Procurement cannot fully benefit from its provisions for a particular sector that it covers unless another party has made GATS commitments in the same sector.

Basic provisions

Article III of the Agreement on Government Procurement establishes fundamental national treatment and non-discrimination principles. Pursuant to the national treatment provision of Article III:1, products, services and suppliers from other parties shall benefit from a treatment no less favourable than that granted to domestic products, services and suppliers. The most-favoured nation provision of Article III:2 establishes that discrimination between products, services and suppliers of other parties is prohibited.

The scope of the national treatment and most-favoured nation provisions of Articles III:1 and III:2 is limited by Article III:3. Article III:3 provides that the provisions of paragraphs 1 and 2 of Article III shall not apply to customs duties and charges of any kind imposed in connection with the importation, the method of levying such duties and charges, other import regulations and formalities, and measures affecting trade in services other than laws, regulations, procedures and practices regarding government procurement covered by the Agreement on Government Procurement.

The implementation of the national treatment and most-favoured nation rules are guaranteed by the detailed operational rules set forth in the Agreement on Government Procurement. The Agreement on Government Procurement ensures that the procurement process is fully transparent at each stage. During the first stage of an invitation to tender, the inviting party must make adequate efforts to inform potential bidders of relevant aspects of the procurement in question.[38] Following the award of a contract, the awarding party must provide adequate information regarding its decision. If requested, the entity concerned must also provide information justifying its decision and evidence that the procurement was made both fairly and impartially.[39]

An enforcement mechanism is also provided in the Agreement on Government Procurement.[40] The enforcement mechanism is based on the dispute settlement rules applicable to all WTO agreements. These rules were, however, adapted to provide appropriate remedies for disputes concerning government procurement. Indeed, government procurement is generally a single event, costly if not impossible to reverse, and is a sector in which modifications of national rules of non-application would not necessarily offer a guarantee of non-recurrence. The Agreement on Government Procurement therefore provides, for example, that, in situations where measures found to be inconsistent cannot be withdrawn, the parties collectively acting as the Dispute Settlement Body may authorise consultations regarding possible remedies. In addition to the dispute settlement instruments available pursuant to the Agreement on Government Procurement, each party shall provide non-discriminatory, timely, transparent and effective procedures enabling suppliers to challenge breaches of the Agreement arising in the context of procurements in which they have, or have had, an interest.[41] These challenge procedures must provide for rapid interim measures to correct breaches of the Agreement and to preserve commercial opportunities. Finally, these domestic procedures must provide for either a correction of the breach of the Agreement or compensation for the loss or damages suffered. This compensation may be limited to the costs for the tender preparation and the challenge of the public entity determination.

In order to encourage more Members to become party to the Agreement on Government Procurement, the latter contains provisions on special and differential treatment of developing countries.[42] Parties are obliged to take into account the development, financial and trade needs of developing Members, in particular less developed Members, in the implementation and administration of the Agreement on Government Procurement. Parties must also, in the application of laws, regulations

[38] *Ibid.*, Articles VII to XVII.

[39] *Ibid.*, Articles XVIII and XIX.

[40] *Ibid.*, Article XXII.

[41] *Ibid.*, Article XX.

[42] *Ibid.*, Article V.

and procedures affecting government procurement and in the preparation of their coverage lists, facilitate the increase of imports from developing countries. In addition, developing Members that become parties to the Agreement on Government Procurement are allowed, during their accession phase, to negotiate acceptable exclusions from the national treatment obligation for certain entities, products and services that are included in their lists. Even if they failed to negotiate such exclusions prior to their accession, developing parties can request the Committee on Government Procurement to grant to them similar exclusions. At the last WTO Ministerial Conference, which was held in Qatar on 9–14 November 2001, Members were not invited to join the Agreement on Government Procurement. Instead, Members preferred to agree to begin negotiations on transparency in government procurement after the next Ministerial Conference.

The existence of rules covering trade in services in the Agreement on Government Procurement should not hide the fact that these rules are only applicable to certain WTO Members, only cover limited service sectors – and to a great extent do not apply to the telecom and audio-visual sectors – and that exceptions or restricting provisions may limit their range. Consequently, it remains pertinent to negotiate a broad set of rules concerning government procurement of services.

The government procurement negotiations: a review of the fundamental principles

The negotiating mandate of Article XIII:2

Pursuant to the mandate it received from the Council for Trade in Services in March 1995, the Working Party on GATS Rules agreed to hold consultations on government procurement in services. Article XIII:2 provides that the negotiations shall be initiated within two years of the entry into force of the WTO Agreement, i.e. no later than 1 January 1997. The Working Party complied with the deadline set out in the GATS since it first examined the question of government procurement and services in December 1995.[43]

Article XIII:2 does not set a precise mandate for the Working Party. Members remain free to determine the scope of the negotiations and, in

[43] Report of the Meeting of 8 December 1995, Note by the Secretariat, 21 December 1995, S/WPGR/M/2.

particular, whether an agreement on GATS government procurement is even desirable.

Members agreed that accession to the Agreement on Government Procurement and the ongoing negotiations of government procurement in services constitute two different issues. However, Members also agreed that the experience acquired by parties to the Agreement on Government Procurement would have to be closely examined in the GATS government procurement negotiations.

During the initial negotiation phase, Working Party members considered it useful to improve the information base on government procurement by exchanging information on their relevant laws, regulations and procedures.[44] A questionnaire on government procurement of services was therefore circulated by the WTO Secretariat in April 1996.[45] Its questions were limited to existing procurement regimes in each Member or in multilateral, regional and/or bilateral agreements to which they were parties and to the economic importance of service procurement. The questionnaire did not request Members to present their views on either the desirability or the feasibility of implementing rules concerning government procurement of services, or on the more fundamental concepts which such rules would have to enforce. The Secretariat received a substantial number of responses to its questionnaire, and in July 1997 prepared a synthesis of all the responses received.[46]

During a second phase, although the information-gathering on national procurement regimes had not been completed, discussions focused on substantial issues such as the possible scope and coverage of government procurement disciplines. Discussions were also held on definitional issues. However, due to the importance of the emergency safeguard mechanism negotiations, no substantial progress was made during the last two years.

Possible alternatives

The first issue the Working Party members will have to address is whether the Article XIII:1 exemption should be maintained. A negative response

[44] Report of the Meeting of 23 February 1996, Note by the Secretariat, 19 March 1996, S/WPGR/M/4.

[45] Questionnaire on Government Procurement of Services, Note by the Secretariat, 2 April 1996, S/WPGR/W/11.

[46] Synthesis of the Responses to the Questionnaire on Government Procurement of Services, Note by the Secretariat, 7 July 1997, S/WPGR/W/20. Responses continued to be received after this synthesis was issued.

to this question would not necessarily imply that government procurement of services is fully covered by GATS rules, as an intermediary solution would be possible. This question also raises the further question of whether government procurement should be regulated by a separate and, possibly, multilateral agreement. These questions are open for discussion and have not yet properly been addressed by the Members.

If they were to agree to extend some of their GATS obligations to government procurement, Members could decide either to opt for any of the following approaches or to combine them.

Most-favoured nation and national treatment obligations Members could first take a very liberal approach and decide to apply most-favoured nation and national treatment principles to their procurement decisions. Considering that GATS Members only agreed to apply national treatment to scheduled sectors, it would appear unlikely that Members would decide to apply a national treatment clause to all sectors for government procurement. Members would also certainly limit the application of national treatment to procurement above certain thresholds.

An agreement on a set of rules incorporating most-favoured nation and national treatment obligations would not necessarily preclude developing Members from benefiting from special treatment. Similarly to the Agreement on Government Procurement, provisions regulating the procurement of services could contain dual-standard rules. Developing Members could be authorised, either during the negotiations or at a later stage, to exclude certain entities and/or sensitive sectors from the scope of the government procurement provisions. Developing Members could also continue to use offsets which would be forbidden to developed countries.

Regardless of their importance, government procurement rules should be ensured by procedural and enforcement mechanisms such as those provided for in the Agreement on Government Procurement. Parties to this Agreement have concluded that a simple national treatment requirement, as contained in Article III of the GATT, is insufficient to ensure equal treatment and non-discrimination in the area of government procurement, and that the enforcement of non-discriminatory provisions can only be guaranteed with procedural safeguards. These procedural safeguards would have to ensure that the rights of bidders are respected during the procurement process and that any supplier interested is guaranteed the right to challenge procurement decisions and obtain reparation if the rules were breached.

Transparency and procedural obligations The second alternative which could be followed by Working Party members would be less liberal and would continue to guarantee different treatment to government procurement. However, this alternative would be less restrictive than the current approach provided for in Article XIII:1 of the GATS. Under this alternative, Members would decide to increase transparency and strengthen enforcement procedures. This alternative would certainly be acceptable to those Members that are not yet ready to completely eliminate the discretion they enjoy over government procurement. This alternative would also encourage Members to gradually liberalise government procurement. Under this scenario, Members would first reach an agreement on generally acceptable principles pursuant to which procurement is to be made, and could then decide to slowly commit themselves to an opening of government procurement.

The Working Party's activities: towards an agreement on generally accepted principles?

The activities of the Working Party suggest that the majority of members is not yet ready to negotiate an agreement similar to the Agreement on Government Procurement that would cover services. Many Members, especially developing ones, are still deeply attached to the idea that government procurement should be excluded from the scope of trade liberalisation rules.

Since 1995, Working Party members have made substantial efforts both to exchange information on existing government procurement regimes and to develop common definitions. However, Working Party members have not yet been able to discuss substantially the basic concepts of government procurement because of the emphasis that has been placed upon the emergency safeguard mechanism negotiations.

Subsidies and countervailing measures in the GATS

Throughout history, subsidies have traditionally been provided to services or their suppliers. Subsidies may take very different forms despite not being covered by rules such as those provided for in the Agreement on Subsidies and Countervailing Measures or in other WTO agreements concerning the trade in goods.

Article XV:1 of the GATS nevertheless explicitly recognises that, in certain circumstances, subsidies may have distortive effects on trade in services. Article XV:2 therefore contains a procedure which enables any

Member which considers that it is being adversely affected by a subsidy of another Member to request consultations with that Member. Other provisions of the GATS also address, either directly or indirectly, the issue of the use of subsidies.

In order to avoid the trade-distortive effects of service subsidies over the long term, Members have been invited to enter into negotiations with a view to developing the multilateral disciplines necessary in this area. These negotiations are also aimed at addressing the appropriateness of countervailing procedures, and include the mandate to take into account the needs of developing Members. The role of subsidies in relation to the development of programmes of developing countries needs, in particular, to be approached with flexibility.

Service subsidies

Definition

The notion of 'subsidy' was first defined during the Uruguay Round in the Agreement on Subsidies and Countervailing Measures. Pursuant to this Agreement, a subsidy is deemed to exist if there is: (i) a financial contribution by a government or any public body within the territory of a Member or a form of income or price support; (ii) which confers a benefit.[47] Under the Agreement on Subsidies and Countervailing Measures, a subsidy can only be challenged if it is also specific, i.e. only available to a particular enterprise or industry or a group of enterprises or industries.[48]

The application of the definition provided for in the Agreement on Subsidies and Countervailing Measures to service sectors does not appear to pose serious problems in principle. In this regard, the only difficulty concerns the identification of the ultimate beneficiary of a subsidy which may be destined for downstream users rather than its immediate recipient. The use of different terminology in the goods and service sectors can also be misleading. However, in practice subsidies benefiting goods and services are generally similar.

Concepts developed in the WTO agreements on trade of goods

An examination of the existing subsidy rules and remedies available in the field of goods gives a valuable indication of both the rationale for adopting similar rules for services and the possible substance of such

[47] Agreement on Subsidies and Countervailing Measures, Article 1.
[48] *Ibid.*, Article 2.

rules. Rules concerning subsidies granted to goods are provided for in both the Agreement on Subsidies and Countervailing Measures and the Agreement on Agriculture.

A distinction between three types of subsidies, i.e. prohibited, actionable and non-actionable, is made in the Agreement on Subsidies and Countervailing Measures. Examples of prohibited subsidies include those that are contingent upon either export performance or the use of domestic over imported goods.[49] Non-actionable subsidies are those which do not satisfy the specificity requirement or which are aimed at developing research, regional development and environmental protection.[50] Actionable subsidies are defined by default as those that are neither prohibited nor non-actionable.

In the event that the Members decide to negotiate substantive rules concerning subsidies, they will also have to establish different categories. The distinction between different types of subsidies is even required by Article XV:1 of the GATS, which provides that negotiations should take into account both the role and the need for certain subsidies. Certain service subsidies which benefit developing countries, e.g. subsidies aimed at developing communication networks in less developed regions, could, consequently, be classified as non-actionable.

The remedies available to Members that are affected by a subsidy will therefore depend upon the measure's classification. As a general rule, non-actionable subsidies are neither subject to challenge in the WTO nor countervailable. The only exception to this general rule concerns cases where non-actionable specific subsidy programmes have a serious effect on the domestic industry of a Member, such as causing damage which would be difficult to repair, and the Committee on Subsidies and Countervailing Measures considers that a remedy is necessary. Prohibited and actionable subsidies can be either challenged in the WTO pursuant to the applicable dispute settlement rules or subjected to countervailing measures.[51] A Member which is adversely affected by a prohibited or actionable subsidy, therefore, has two options to remedy the consequences of the subsidy. It can challenge the subsidy before the Dispute Settlement Body with the aim of having it declared inconsistent with the provisions

[49] *Ibid.*, Article 3.

[50] *Ibid.*, Article 8. Subsidies aiming at developing research, regional development and environmental protection became countervailable on 1 January 2000 by effect of Article 31 of the Agreement on Subsidies and Countervailing Measures (see Doc. G/SCM/M/22 of 17 February 2000).

[51] Agreement on Subsidies and Countervailing Measures, Article 9.

of the Agreement on Subsidies and Countervailing Measures.[52] Alternatively, it can adopt countervailing measures against subsidised imports if, subject to a future investigation, it has concluded that its domestic industry is being injured or is threatened with injury by the subsidised imports.[53]

The transposition of the double-challenge option for service subsidies appears both reasonable and feasible. The incorporation of provisions concerning countervailing measures in a set of rules applicable to service subsidies would raise more questions. The definition of concepts such as the import of services, domestic industry or injury, among others, would raise difficulties similar to those the Working Party is currently experiencing in its attempt to negotiate an emergency safeguard mechanism.

In the area of agriculture, Members are authorised to maintain both domestic support and export subsidies provided that the levels of interventions are below established benchmarks.[54] With regard to remedies, the so-called 'peace clause' limits the circumstances in which agricultural subsidies may be challenged.[55] Domestic support measures with minimal impact on trade, e.g. research or disease control schemes, which are referred to as 'green box subsidies', are non-actionable for the purpose of countervailing actions, and are exempt both from challenge on the grounds of serious prejudice and from non-violation complaints. Domestic subsidies covered by reduction commitments and permissible export subsidies may be subject to countervailing measures, but Members are required to exercise 'due restraint' in exercising such actions. Also, domestic support subsidies cannot be challenged on serious prejudice or nullification grounds unless they exceed agreed thresholds. Finally, challenges to export subsidies on the basis of the provisions of the Agreement on Subsidies and Countervailing Measures are limited.

The approach adopted by the Agreement on Agriculture therefore appears very interesting as regards services. Indeed, unlike the Agreement on Subsidies and Countervailing Measures, the Agreement on Agriculture places an emphasis on the reduction of existing subsidies. The subsidy reduction commitments of each Member are subject to negotiation. A

[52] *Ibid.*, Articles 4 and 7.
[53] *Ibid.*, Articles 10–23.
[54] Agreement on Agriculture, Articles 6–11.
[55] *Ibid.*, Article 13.

Table 10.1 *WTO Members which maintain subsidies in the telecom and audio-visual sectors*

Telecom services	
India	preferential credit and guarantees and tax incentives
Peru	direct grants
Singapore	direct grants
Trinidad and Tobago	duty free inputs and free zones
Audio-visual services	
Argentina	direct grants
Canada	direct grants and tax incentives
Jamaica	tax incentives and duty-free inputs and free zones
Tanzania	tax incentives and duty-free inputs and free zones

progressive liberalisation of existing subsidies would be particularly appropriate for developing Members. Providing for a progressive availability of remedies would further ensure a smooth transition to a regulation of service subsidies.

Existing service subsidies

On the basis of the information contained in the trade policy reviews of each Member, the WTO Secretariat has prepared a background note on existing subsidy programmes.[56] Although the Secretariat's note is non-exhaustive – it only concerns thirty-seven trade policy reviews – it nonetheless serves to establish interesting patterns, suggesting that Members tend to concentrate their services-related subsidies in three sectors, i.e. maritime transport, tourism and financial services.

In the less-emphasised telecom and audio-visual sectors, the Members which maintain subsidies for the benefit of their domestic suppliers are set out in Table 10.1.

Subsidies in the service sectors, regardless of whether they are granted by developed or developing Members, may take numerous forms and pursue very different aims. In line with its mandate, which is to exchange information concerning all subsidies related to trade in services provided to service suppliers, the Working Party has requested the WTO

[56] Subsidies for Service Sectors – Information Contained in WTO Trade Policy Reviews, Background Note by the Secretariat, S/WPGR/W/25/Add.2. See also the last note, S/WPGR/W/25/Add.3, confirming trends noted so far.

Secretariat to prepare a questionnaire for Members on existing service subsidies.

GATS rules concerning the use of subsidies

Article XV:2: a basic protection mechanism

Under Article XV:2, any Member that considers itself to be adversely affected by a subsidy of another Member may request consultations with that Member. The consultation procedure available under Article XV:2 is aimed at ensuring that the distortive effects of service subsidies will not be left totally unaddressed before the negotiations on service subsidies are completed. Article XV:2 thus provides a minimal safeguard against the unreasonable and untimely use of service subsidies.

Article XV:2 only imposes three requirements for a Member to request such consultations: (i) the existence of a subsidy; (ii) an adverse effect; and (iii) a causal relationship between these two elements.

Since the entry into force of the GATS, no Member has had recourse to Article XV:2. This may be due to the nature of the remedy provided, i.e. consultations, which does not appear to be sufficient to guarantee that a subsidy which affects another Member will be amended or withdrawn or that compensation will be granted even if good cause is shown.

Article XXIII:3: non-violations complaints

Any measure, regardless of whether it is inconsistent with the GATS, which nullifies or impairs a benefit a Member could reasonably have expected to obtain under a specific commitment, may give rise to a so-called 'non-violation complaint'. If the Dispute Settlement Body concludes that the measure challenged nullifies or impairs a benefit, the Member affected shall be entitled to a mutually satisfactory adjustment on the basis of Article XXI:2. A mutually satisfactory adjustment can include a modification or withdrawal of the measure concerned, or in the event that no agreement can be reached between the Members concerned.

Non-violation complaints have been used in the GATT, and more recently in the WTO, to challenge subsidy schemes which were consistent with existing subsidy rules but which nullified or impaired a Member's reasonable expectations. Under the GATS, recourse to a non-violation complaint would be different since it contains no obligations concerning service subsidies. A non-violation complaint would, therefore, not be an alternative to a violation of the GATS. Nonetheless, in the GATS, a non-violation complaint can be an appropriate recourse against a service subsidy.

Since the entry into force of the GATS, no non-violation complaints have been lodged. This may be explained by the fact that the requirements for bringing a non-violation complaint is quite onerous. First, there must be a pre-existing scheduled commitment. Secondly, there must be either a nullification or an impairment of a reasonable expectation. As described above, Members have only made limited commitments under the GATS. The scope of potential non-violation complaints is therefore limited to certain service sectors. Furthermore, even if a sector is scheduled, it must be evidenced that, at the time of the commitment, the continuation of the subsidy alleged to be nullifying or impairing a benefit could not have been expected. In practice, the use of non-violation complaints therefore seems, *de facto*, to be exceptionally limited as regards recent service subsidies.

National treatment limitations: a tool for the protection of the interests of developing Members

Under Article XVII:1 of the GATS, scheduled sectors are subject to national treatment. In the sectors listed in its Schedule, each Member shall accord to service providers of any other Member, in respect of all measures affecting the supply of services, treatment no less favourable than that which it accords to its own like service providers. Under its national treatment obligation, a Member must, therefore, ensure that any subsidies granted do not discriminate between national service providers and those of other Members.

In order not to have to grant subsidies to both national and foreign services and service suppliers, Members have the possibility of inscribing sectors in their Schedules free of national treatment limitations under any or all modes of delivery. The exemption from the national treatment clause permits Members to continue to grant subsidies only to national services or service suppliers. This exemption would be very important, if disciplines on service subsidies were adopted, to enable developing Members, in particular, to continue to subsidise certain services. Indeed, developing Members do not generally have sufficient resources to grant subsidies to both national and foreign service providers. The national treatment exemption, which can also be seen as a discriminatory provision, could, therefore, be utilised in order to ensure greater liberalisation which would take into account the needs of certain Members. The benefit of the national treatment exemption provision for service subsidies would, however, have to be limited to certain Members.

For example, Bangladesh inserted a limitation on national treatment to restrict certain subsidies and tax benefits to telecommunication services in its Schedule. Korea, Slovenia, Bulgaria, Estonia, Qatar, the United Arab Emirates and Jordan also limit access to service subsidies. These Members have all restricted the eligibility or availability of subsidies in all of the sectors listed in their Schedules to national or domestically established entities.

Subsidies and countervailing duties negotiations

The Article XV:1 mandate

Article XV:1 stipulates that Members shall enter into negotiations with a view to developing the multilateral disciplines necessary in order to avoid the trade-distortive effect of subsidies. These negotiations are also aimed at addressing the appropriateness of countervailing procedures. The mandate of the negotiations also calls upon Members to recognise the role of subsidies in relation to the development programmes of developing countries and to take into account the needs of Members, particularly developing ones, for flexibility in this area. For the purpose of such negotiations, Members shall exchange information concerning all subsidies related to trade in services that they provide to their domestic service suppliers.

The service subsidies negotiations mandate differs from the emergency safeguard measures and government procurement negotiations' mandates because the former does not set a deadline within which negotiations have to be completed or even initiated. This is due to the fact that no systematic attempt was made to negotiate subsidy and countervailing disciplines in the GATS prior to the agreement on the Article XV negotiating mandate. Members also consider that the negotiations on service subsidies are less urgent than the negotiations held with regard to emergency safeguard measures and government procurement. At its inaugural meeting, the Working Party on GATS Rules decided to first take up the issue of emergency safeguard measures. Negotiations on service subsidies only began after six- and three-month periods of time following the initiation of the emergency safeguard measures and government procurement negotiations respectively.[57]

[57] Report of the meeting of 28 March 1996, Note by the Secretariat, 13 May 1996, S/WPGR/M/5.

The mandate provided for in Article XV:1 is very broad. Members are invited to negotiate disciplines on subsidies and countervailing measures while taking into account the role of subsidies in the service sectors and the needs of certain Members. Members are, at the same time, required to exchange information on the service subsidies. A footnote requires Members to determine a work programme and to decide in what timeframe negotiations should be held. At present, the Working Party members have not reached an agreement on a work programme. At the request of the chairperson, a checklist of issues for discussion was only circulated in 2000.

Status of ongoing negotiations

During the first two years, the Working Party members only considered the modalities of the information exchange called for in the negotiating mandate. At the beginning of 1997, the Working Party approved a questionnaire to facilitate the exchange of information.[58] However, too few responses were received from Members for the Working Party to request the WTO Secretariat to prepare a synthesis of the information provided by the Members.

In July 2000, the chairperson circulated a checklist of issues to be addressed. The issues listed by the chairperson include the following:

1. definition of a subsidy (including relevance of the definition in the Agreement on Subsidies and Countervailing Measures);
2. examination of any evidence of subsidies which may have distortive effects on trade in services (including production, distribution, consumption and export subsidies);
3. consideration of sources of information;
4. the extent to which WTO rules, in particular the GATS and its national treatment and most-favoured nation disciplines, already discipline service subsidies or provide the means to do so; this would include consideration of technical issues related to the GATS, including mode specificity and the concept of 'like service'.

These issues were each examined in turn by the Working Party at the meetings which were held in the second half of 2000 and in 2001. The discussions on these issues remained superficial, however, and did not permit any breakthrough to be made. In the absence of substantive con-

[58] Questions Relevant to the Information Exchange Required under the Subsidies Negotiating Mandate, Note by the Secretariat, 5 February 1997, S/WPGR/W/16.

tributions from Members, the Working Party decided in July 2001 that the chairperson's checklist would remain on the table and that the five topics it contains would remain open for discussion.[59] On 22 July 2001, the Working Party adopted a work programme on subsidies, without prejudice on the outcome of negotiations. Members are encouraged to 'continue discussions on the basis of submissions from Members and materials available' and to 'put forward submissions on subsidies as early as possible' before March 2003.[60]

A long road to a possible agreement

The primacy given to the emergency safeguard measures negotiations appears to have slowed the service subsidy negotiations. However, this cannot explain by itself the minimal progress achieved by the Working Party in more than six years. The limited number of responses to the questionnaire and of official communications from Members on this issue is evidence of the underwhelming inclination of the Members to engage in real negotiations.

An impetus for sector-specific negotiations could have come from the GATS negotiations. In a submission circulated in 2000 in the context of the GATS negotiations, Switzerland stated that subsidy rules under Article XV of the GATS have yet to be developed. Switzerland continued by stating that it is a matter of fact that most WTO Members do subsidise to different degrees the production and distribution of audio-visual products, at least in regard to motion pictures.[61] Therefore, in addition to the discussion on general subsidy rules, it would seem to be worth discussing subsidy practices and their foundational disciplines to be agreed as part of the solution to the audio-visual issue. A common understanding among Members about subsidies, the policy purposes justifying them, as well as their effect on trade, would represent a positive precondition both for the negotiation of specific commitments in the audio-visual sector as well as for the elaboration of general subsidy rules. The absence of support for the Swiss position, however, suggests that service subsidies negotiations will not be accelerated as a result of the GATS negotiations.

[59] Report of the Working Party on GATS Rules to the Council for Trade in Services, 4 October 2001, S/WPGR/6.

[60] Doc. S/WPGR/7, 25 July 2002.

[61] Communication from Switzerland, Guidelines for the Mandated Service Negotiations, 5 December 2000, S/CSS/W/16.

Conclusion

The negotiations engaged by the Working Party on GATS Rules are all at different stages, but none has yet to be concluded. Although the negotiations on emergency safeguard measures have addressed substantive issues, a draft is still to be negotiated and Members have still to determine whether a safeguard instrument is desirable and feasible in the GATS context. The negotiations on government procurement have enabled Members to exchange information and to begin clarifying certain concepts, but a choice remains to be made as to the type of rules that will be negotiated. The negotiations on subsidies and countervailing measures have suffered a slow start, as little information was exchanged and few positions were expressed.

Members have failed to attach great importance to the negotiations of GATS rules. This is partly due to their reluctance to make new commitments and to the conceptual questions these negotiations raise. Also, the core issues of the desirability and feasibility of GATS rules are still being questioned by a number of Members. For all of these reasons, it appears very uncertain that the negotiations, which began over six years ago, will soon be concluded. This should not, however, have any significant consequences on a further liberalisation of services in the telecommunication and audio-visual sectors.

PART IV

Towards convergence?

11

Convergence: a reality check

MILTON MUELLER

Introduction

The ability of technological change to subvert legal classifications is well known. But few technological changes are as radical and all-encompassing in this regard as digital convergence. Convergence is producing structural shifts in media industries that go well beyond simple notions of telecommunication and audio-visual services 'coming together'. This chapter describes the technological and economic forces that support digital convergence, and then considers some of the consequences for trade in communication industries.

My purpose is to emphasise the radicalism of the changes in store for us, but also to provide some perspective about the uneven pacing of the changes. Convergence is a solvent that dissolves broadcasting, postal and telephone networks, cinema, newspaper and book publishing, photography, musical recording, calendars, clocks, and money into One Big (distributed) Medium.[1] From this high-level perspective, the line between basic telecommunications and audio-visual services looks very thin and frail indeed. However, each of the traditional media will be affected by convergence at a different pace and in a different way. Whether and how classical trade barriers in audio-visual services can be reconciled with the WTO agreement in basic telecommunication services is a reasonably interesting question in the short term. In the long term it is a distraction. In a converged world the distribution of audio-visual services will take many new forms, producing new services and massive changes in market structures that will ultimately consume more regulatory attention than anything else. Most of these new forms of audio-visual distribution will not be subject to traditional trade protection or regulation. Attempts to

[1] See Ithiel de Sola Pool, *Technologies of Freedom* (Cambridge, MA: Harvard University Press, 1983).

impose trade protectionism on the older industries will simply diminish their strength and importance relative to the newer forms of distribution.

Defining convergence

Put simply, convergence means the digitisation of all media forms and the adoption of compatible digital formats by all networks and information appliances. Convergence makes information content, networks and terminals more interactive and interoperable. The technical substrate underlying convergence is Moore's law; i.e. the constant increase in the information processing power of integrated circuits.[2]

Convergence results in lower cost interoperability

Fundamentally, 'digital convergence' means an enormous reduction in the cost of interconnecting and interoperating various forms of communication and information technology. This cost reduction is driven by continuing increases in processing power and related technological advances that expand telecommunications bandwidth. The faster the processing speeds of computers and the more bandwidth available, the easier and more natural it becomes to utilise multimedia applications. Convergence is also advanced by the mathematical coding techniques of information theory, which makes it possible to represent more efficiently and to manipulate more easily large, complex information sources.

The link between the progress of media convergence and advances in integrated circuitry is well established in the literature.[3] Content and networks have gone digital in order to avail themselves of the power of integrated circuits. Most of the recent advances in digital video were not possible, for example, until a frame of digitised video could be stored on

[2] See David Farber and Paul Baran, 'The Convergence of Computing and Telecommunications Systems', *Science*, March 1977, p. 18; Gordon Moore, 'Moore's Law Revisited', keynote speech, IEEE International Electronic Devices Meeting, San Francisco, 10 December 1996, www.isdmag.com/Events/IEDM.html; Michael Slater, 'Living Without Moore's Law', *The Slater Perspective* (newsletter), 31 March 1997, www.chipanalyst.com/slater/perspective/1104sp.html; and G. Dan Hutcheson and Jerry D. Hutcheson, 'Technology and Economics in the Semiconductor Industry', *Scientific American*, January 1996, p. 54.

[3] See John Midwinter, in Institute for Information Studies, *Crossroads on the Information Highway: Convergence and Diversity in Communications Technologies* (1995 Annual Review of the Institute of Information Studies, Nashville, TN, and Queenstown, MD: Northern Telecom Inc. and the Aspen Institute, 1994), chapter 2, p. 29.

a single chip.[4] The Internet's ability to deliver voice and video signals to PC users required upgrades in the processing speed and memory of a typical PC and increases in the bandwidth and processing speed of the network and its routers. Likewise, the addition of data screens to mobile telephones and the adoption of CD-ROMs as a common storage medium for PC data, recorded music and movies all stem from a common root: lower priced and more powerful computer and laser components. The pace of convergence has thus been largely determined by the operation of Moore's law.

Converging content

Digitisation results in the technical homogenisation of all modes of information content. Indeed, the notions of 'content' and 'content industries' are very recent constructs. The use of those terms is probably related to the rise of digital technologies, because the term 'content' strips programming capabilities of any particular form or medium, collapsing literature and journalism, music, paintings, movies and interactive games into a single category. In digital media, sound (including the human voice), still and moving images, text and money can all be encoded as a stream of bits, and, as Nicholas Negroponte famously said, 'a bit is a bit'.[5] But that in itself is not the main point. Pre-digital analogue electronic networks could also encode most forms of content as varying waveforms. The revolutionary feature of digital media is that the various media forms can now be displayed, stored, transmitted and manipulated on a single end user platform. All forms of content are collapsed into a single format by developing information processing speeds that render irrelevant the difference between a page of text (which requires about 14,000 bits to represent digitally) and a video signal, (which in digitized NTSC format, without compression, requires continuously transmitting 90,000,000 bits per second).

[4] See George Gilder, *Life After Television: The Coming Transformation of Media and American Life* (2nd edn, New York: W. W. Norton, 1994); Midwinter, note 2 above; Milton Mueller, *Telecom Policy and Digital Convergence* (Hong Kong: Hong Kong Economic Policy Studies Series, City University of Hong Kong Press, 1997); and Milton Mueller, 'Digital Convergence and its Consequence', *Javnost/The Public* 6(3) (1999): 11–28.

[5] See Nicholas Negroponte, *Being Digital* (Cambridge, MA: MIT Press, 1990).

Convergence in terminals and networks

As the cost of computer processing power decreases, we have seen a dramatic movement of processing intelligence from the centre of network, where it was shared due to its high expense, to the edges, where it can be privately owned, controlled by and customised to the user. When this trend is combined with digital encoding of different types of content, the result is greater interoperability and versatility of different types of terminals and networks. In the past, different media forms such as film, television, print, radio, telegraph and telephone utilised separate distribution infrastructures and terminal devices with their own distinct and incompatible technical standards. The absence of integrated circuits made the input-output devices quite 'dumb' and dedicated to the display of the particular mode of communication for which it was engineered.

Once a network's encoding, signalling and storage functions are digital, however, a single network can offer voice, video and data services, and the devices for input, output and display of information become more easily interoperable. The different media forms suddenly become convertible into each other: printed documents can be translated into image files; a text message can be turned into a voice message, and so on. In the past, the owner of a phonograph or 'record player' could not do anything with the 'records' on a television set, and the owner of a telephone handset could not do anything with images. Each media form was technically isolated by the limited capabilities of the terminal equipment. Now, telephone handsets can display pictures and carry appointment books downloaded from a personal computer. Cameras can connect to networks, formats such as the Digital Versatile Disk (DVD) can carry sound, text or audio-visual information and be displayed on a variety of devices. A television set can display the information on a computer, and *vice versa.* Music can be downloaded from a network and stored and replayed on local playback devices. The old home movie camera and projector, which required its own klunky, dedicated display equipment, is being replaced by camcorders that can feed their output to a new world of digital devices.

False conceptions of digital convergence

Convergence as described above is a micro-level techno-economic phenomenon; in essence, it boils down to a huge reduction in the cost of encoding information, processing it, and establishing interoperability among different devices. What interests us most, of course, are the economic implications. It might be useful to begin discussion of that topic by dismissing some of the mythology that has grown up around it. Specifically, the notion of digital convergence is often confused with questionable economic predictions about market structure.

One appliance will do everything

One naïve conception of convergence is that one device, such as the PDA, the mobile phone, the home television set or the PC, will combine all functions into a single 'universal appliance'. In reality convergence is bringing about a proliferation of information appliances, leading to greater differentiation of markets and the specialisation of function. Thus, we see people owning PCs *and* digital organisers *and* MP3 players *and* mobile phones *and* televisions. What is new is the interoperability among these devices. The mobile phone can be plugged into the computer and used as a modem; the audio playback device can be connected to the computer and its network to download content. In that respect, one might say that all the diverse appliances are indeed integrated into a single 'appliance' with specialised components. But if any manufacturer bases their strategy on the marketing of one device or service that will integrate all our information needs, sell their stock. Human use of information technology is too diverse and multifaceted for that to ever happen.

One network will carry everything

With convergence, one network *can* carry every form of service and content, perhaps, but here, too, the reality is a proliferation of network infrastructures. The PSTN has gone from a single end-to-end network into multiple, competing but interconnected networks. Cable TV systems are supplemented by and compete with satellite distribution networks. Wireless networks are an increasingly viable alternative to the fixed network, and there are multiple, competing networks in that sphere as well. An inevitable consequence of multiple networks in a competitive environment is that the market will reward differentiation and specialisation of function. That is, competing network providers will play to their strengths and try to achieve dominance in particular segments of the market. So, paradoxically, in a converged environment, the likelihood of getting all services from a single network will diminish. The unique feature, once again, will be interoperability.

One industry will 'swallow' all the others

Sometimes convergence is misperceived as the incorporation of all the digitised products and services by a pre-existing industry. Some observers used to fear that telephone companies would take over mass media. Others predicted the reverse. A mindset that now seems quaint and archaic but was taken seriously only a few decades ago viewed postal systems as the most suitable institutional platform for convergence.[6] Today, we are more likely to fear that Microsoft will take over everything. But these scenarios underestimate the dramatic scope of digital convergence. It is not just television, computers and telephones. Convergence implicates a very broad range of industries, each with its own giants. Imaging companies like Kodak and Fuji bump up against consumer electronics and PC companies like Sony, Apple and Hewlett Packard. Web hosting companies and application service providers (ASPs) become potential entrants in the telephone industry. Software companies like Microsoft begin to impinge on broadband infrastructure service providers like AT&T and AOL-Time Warner while making incursions into the realm of content producers like Disney and Bertelsmann.

As convergence proceeds, there is increasing fungibility of communication products and services across the information industries. There is also massive growth in the scope of the market, leading to an increase in specialisation and division of labour. The simple fact is that no one company can do it all. The new market structure may well create new bottlenecks that can be exploited to achieve dominance of particular market segments. But the bottlenecks will indeed be *new* ones. It is fundamentally misleading to think of this process in terms of pre-existing industrial categories.

The limits of convergence

In the past decade, digital convergence has made huge strides forward. But it is also important to be aware of its limits and its uneven diffusion across media industries.

From the mid-1990s to the present, the Internet emerged as the global platform where digital convergence began to be realised. By 'the Internet' I mean the interconnection of private networks using the TCP/IP protocols, and the mass adoption of the World Wide Web protocols. The TCP/IP protocols were designed to facilitate the interconnection of separately

[6] See John Wicklein, *Electronic Nightmare: The New Communications and Freedom* (New York: Viking Press, 1980).

administered networks that used incompatible protocols.[7] The World Wide Web and the 'browser', on the other hand, provided an easy-to-use, graphical interface between the network and the user. That interface served as the catalyst for the transformation of internetworking into a mass medium. Because of the Internet's reliance on open standards and openly available, unedited content, it totally surpassed the (in retrospect) risible efforts of telephone and cable companies to construct their own proprietary and limited bundles of interactive media services. Today, Internet access coupled with broadband access and more powerful and intelligent web browsers or specialised multimedia players make it reasonably clear what a converged media world will be like.

Internet as convergence platform

On the Internet, one can engage in one-to-one 'postal' communications (e-mail), one-to-many text communications (e-mail lists and chat rooms), and the Internet equivalent of one-to-many publishing – only with much more extensive and powerful forms of interactivity. A new, popular form of communication that might be seen as a half-way house between older dreams of two-way audio-visual communication and e-mail is instant messaging. Instant messaging relies on a database that monitors the presence of various subscribers, allowing users who are on the Internet at the same time to engage in near-synchronous communication. Instant messaging that incorporates video is still experimental, but apparently not remote enough to prevent it from playing a significant role in the US Federal Communications Commission's decision to authorise the AOL – Time Warner merger.[8] With more sophisticated equipment, voice over IP (VoIP) is approaching commercial grade quality and reliability. Thus, in the realm of narrowband point-to-point communication, convergence is a reality.

The markets for still images and music also are already profoundly affected by the Internet and the digitisation of consumer equipment. With

[7] See Janet Abbate, *Inventing the Internet* (Cambridge, MA: MIT Press, 2000), p. 139.

[8] US Federal Communications Commission, Memorandum Opinion and Order, 'In the Matter of Applications for Consent to the Transfer of Control of Licenses and Section 214 Authorizations by Time Warner Inc. and America Online Inc., Transferors, to AOL Time Warner Inc., Transferee', CS Docket No. 00–30, adopted 11 January 2001, released 22 January 2001, www.fcc.gov/Bureaus/Cable/Orders/2001/fcc01012.txt. See also 'Statement of Commissioner Michael Powell, Concurring in Part and Dissenting in Part', Convergence A Reality Check, www. fcc.gov/Speches/Powell/Statements/2001/stmkp104.doc, p. 674.

the rapid diffusion of digital cameras, Internet-based albums and printing and storage services are starting to have a major impact on the photography market.[9] Because of its lower bandwidth relative to video, music has already crossed the threshold of the digital economy, with the Napster episode a milestone in its evolution. Ordinary end-users can download stored audio files, or listen to streaming audio files with reasonably good stereo speakers attached to a PC. They can burn their own CDs or DVDs, or store and play them back on specialised portable playback devices. In the wake of Napster and the continuing use of less visible forms of music file sharing, the recording industry is finally beginning to develop online business models.

With the Internet as the accepted convergence platform, most strategies for future development now involve Internet connectivity. 3G wireless handsets are incorporating Internet access and text- or image-based instant messaging capabilities. And because full exploitation of the capabilities of digital convergence over the Internet requires higher bandwidth than ever before, broadband development has become one of the key arenas for market and regulatory action.[10]

The 'special' case of audio-visual

In the audio-visual realm, progress is more limited. Less than broadcast-quality streaming video is routine. Educational institutions and corporations now routinely record and/or 'webcast' lectures or speakers, often supplemented by slides and images. Archives or libraries of public domain motion pictures or short films are beginning to appear.[11] Two-way

[9] See the website of the new International Imaging Industry Association (I3A), www.i3a.org, which in November 2001 proposed a 'Common Picture eXchange Environment', a network modelled after automatic teller machines, that will connect photo-finishers to digital camera users via the Internet.

[10] On recent efforts by European telephone companies to offer broadband capabilities in order to bundle voice, high-speed Internet access, and broadcast television services, see 'Telcos to Challenge Cable Multimedia', *Communications Week International*, 17 December 2001, p. 276. See Computer Science and Telecommunications Board, *Broadband: Bringing Home the Bits* (Washington, DC: National Academy of Sciences, 2001).

[11] See the Internet Archive's Movie Collection, www.archive.org/movies/index.html. The collection contains about 1,000 movies collected and digitised by the Prelinger Archives and donated to the Internet Archive. A related site, the Television Archive (www.televisionarchive.org), has posted a collection of television news coverage of the events of 11 September 2001 from around the world. Visitors can watch the broadcasts, read critical commentary, and see differing perspectives in the coverage from television stations worldwide.

videoconferencing using a PC is primitive but possible. But broadcast- and cinema-quality audio-visual content is not now delivered over the Internet except under experimental conditions.

The reason, of course, is that a high-quality video signal creates processing and bandwidth requirements that are thousands of times beyond what is required for music, and hundreds of thousands of times beyond what is required for text or still images. And video, like music, is isochronous; i.e. it requires delivery at a specific rate in a continuous stream. This is much more difficult for the Internet to accomplish than traditional transmission media, especially for large simultaneous audiences.

The Internet protocol (IP) breaks information down into pieces called 'packets'. TCP and various Internet routing protocols are just best-effort packet forwarding services. The routers read the packet header, figure out where to send the packet next, then send it one step closer to its destination. If any of the pipes or routers transmitting the packets are congested, the data simply waits, or its transmission rate is diminished.

As a mechanism for interactive, *asynchronous* point-to-point communications, the Internet is unparalleled; therefore it is already the undisputed platform for all types of information content and services that rely on two-way, asynchronous communication. Even some isochronous communication services that are point to point in nature and limited in bandwidth, such as voice telephony, are likely to be absorbed by the Internet fairly rapidly over the next decade.

On the other hand, for large-scale, broadband, simultaneous point-to-multipoint transmission, the Internet is currently much less efficient than broadcast media. Furthermore, non-TCP/IP broadcast transmission methods, such as cable television and over the air broadcasting, can take advantage of digital techniques that will make them faster and more efficient in the future. So the Internet may never be as efficient as the other methods.

The Internet has two methods of improving its performance to deal with isochronous, high-bandwidth media. One of them is a protocol called SIP (Session Initiation Protocol). The other is IP Multicast. Session Initiation Protocol, developed by the Internet Engineering Task Force, establishes, modifies and terminates 'sessions' over IP networks, thereby enabling IP to transcend simple packet forwarding to achieve the end-to-end quality of service required for isochronous communications. Moreover, once SIP has been implemented, a number of other multimedia services are enabled, such as instant messaging and unified messaging services.[12] IP multicast assigns a single address to a group of network participants and sends only one stream to that group address, which is then forwarded by routers to the individual receivers. Streaming video from a website is routed to local switching points first, and then distributed to individual customers' terminals. Multiple web viewers can watch the same stream, but multicasting reduces the traffic burden on the Internet backbone because of the splitting that occurs on a regional basis.[13] Multicast is currently exploited by content distribution networks (CDNs) and some broadband applications.

How far SIP, multicast, other quality-of-service-enhancing protocols and an improved broadband infrastructure can take the Internet remains to be seen. But one can get some sense of the distance we have to go from a press release from Apple Computer and Internet content distribution service Akamai. In the summer of 2000, the two companies worked together to broadcast Steven Jobs' keynote speech at the MacWorld exposition over the Internet. The broadcast, the companies announced proudly, set new records for the delivery of content at broadband rates over the Internet. The one-and-a-half-hour webcast attracted about 95,000 unique web visitors. During the peak of the webcast, more than 4.3 gigabits per second of video were streamed at broadband rates to more than 21,000 simultaneous viewers, including 5,000 visitors who watched 1 megabit-per-second (Mbps) streams.[14] For the Internet, this may be an impressive accomplishment, but for a broadcaster or nationwide cable system operator 21,000 simultaneous viewers is a puny audience.

Cinematic backwaters

If progress towards convergence is slow in the broadcast realm, the pace of change in cinematic production and distribution is even slower. One would think that duplicating and physically shipping gigantic rolls of 35mm film to places where they will be screened using mechanical projectors subject to manual loading, hairs, dust and the tears of sprockets would be an arena ripe for change.

[12] See www.sipworld.com for a contemporary commercial survey of developments and applications.

[13] Camden Ford, 'Video Through the Internet – A Primer', *TVB Europe*, September 1999, p. 80.

[14] Press release, 'Keynote Webcast Set New Broadband Content Record', 25 July 2000, www.applelinks.com/articles/2000/07/2000725100328.shtml.

In reality, we see almost no change in this area. The number of screens worldwide showing movies on film is 108,000. The number of screens showing movies in digital format is forty, less than 0.04%.[15] There is no apparent growth in the number of digital-format screens over the past five years. One obstacle is the large capital investment required for conversion. Additionally, the digital method (at least under the current organisational structure of the industry) has higher operating costs; specifically, labour costs rise by a factor of 2–4 for digital versus film. Film projection requires minimal technical expertise while digital methods demand higher-level engineering and technical skills.

Most cinematographers still prefer film to digital. The current norm is to rely entirely on film for capture of images, convert the film to digital for special effects and editing, then print the results onto film stock for display. This hybrid of optical-mechanical and digital technology is how the vast majority of films are made today.

Conclusion: convergence, trade and audio-visual services

In considering the future of trade liberalisation and the rationales for trade protectionism in audio-visual services, it is best to keep the long view in mind. Digitisation is reducing the costs of production, making every university, corporation and individual a potential producer of tradable 'content'. The quantity of audio-visual services supplied will grow enormously as the production costs decline, and as this happens new media forms with market structures and business models quite different from the norms of broadcasting and cinema will evolve. Chat, portals, instant messaging, interactive gaming, application service providers and various forms of distributed collaboration are just a few hints of the things in store for us. The policy and market battles over dominance of instant messaging in the US is a good example of the issues one can expect as convergence proceeds. It is a new battleground in which new-economy entities (Microsoft, AOL) are trying to position themselves, not a 'takeover' or 'coming together' of two established arenas.

Trade barriers will become increasingly irrelevant to the buying and selling of recorded audio-visual goods. Think of a motion picture as little more than an unusually large e-mail, or as something that can be downloaded instantly from a website. The line between 'product' and 'service' will erode. This is already happening in sound broadcasting and music.

[15] Robert Whipple, Kodak Corporation, interview, December 2001.

The Internet permits downloading of MP3 files or simultaneous playback. An extensive sharing economy among younger consumers allows word of popular or exciting new forms of digitised content to spread quickly.

Eventually, new forms of cinematic distribution will develop. Private networks could be used to simulcast all-digital motion pictures to high-tech digital display arenas, complete with the latest in digital sound. Rather than anticipating 'conversion' of the old motion-picture chains to digital equipment, it might be more reasonable to be on the lookout for new business models that are a theatrical equivalent of Amazon.com and McDonald's, using centralised administration of networking and equipment procurement to develop a geographically widespread franchise.

Both traditional broadcasting and theatrical release of films will persist for some time. Both will continue to be economically viable methods of distributing movies and scheduled news, entertainment and sports programs. It would be wrong, however, for national regulators to assume that, because these distribution channels will not be replaced by the Internet in the medium term, they can accomplish parochial policy objectives by promoting a cultural rationale for protectionism in audio-visual services.

As digital convergence progresses, broadcasting and cinema will be forced to operate in an entertainment and culture economy in which the Internet and other new distribution channels account for an ever-larger share of the relevant markets and play an increasingly prominent role in defining the content choices of the public. Broadcasting authorities who believe that they can impose cultural norms on audiences or force-feed them a diet of prescribed diversity may only succeed in wasting money and valuable airtime. Subsidised programming and national origin quotas will affect only a diminishing slice of the average household's content alternatives. If the officially promoted cultural line does not match the increasingly cosmopolitan tastes of the consumer, national regulators will only succeed in hastening the public's migration to newer media forms.

Diversity of content is not much of a policy issue in the digital economy, any more than it is in printed publications. If anything, there is an overwhelming glut of information products available, and the real need is for indexing, search and retrieval services that allow people to conveniently explore what is available and identify quality products. True, we may not approve of the choices of the masses of consumers, who prefer Britney Spears to Bach. But the diversity is there, available to those who choose to take advantage of it.

12

Whither convergence: legal, regulatory and trade opportunism in telecommunications

ROB FRIEDEN

Introduction

Technological and marketplace convergence supports the development of an integrated information communications and entertainment (ICE) marketplace.[1] Yet, for various ICE market segments to function without trade barriers and competitive distortions, the legal, regulatory and trade policy regimes involved must adapt to changed circumstances. Of key importance is the need to assess whether to change basic definitions and assumptions that worked in a pre-convergent environment, but which provide opportunities for regulatory arbitrage, i.e. opportunities to tilt the competitive playing field to one's advantage by exploiting differences in classifications and qualifying for a status with less regulatory obligations and comparatively fewer market access opportunities for competitors.

[1] The ICE marketplace also includes goods and services fitting within the broad classification of intellectual property and electronic commerce. For an assessment of whether and how trade policy forums can handle intellectual property rights issues, see Frederick M. Abbott, 'The Future of the Multilateral Trading System in the Context of the TRIPS', *Hastings International and Comparative Law Review* 20 (1997): 661; Frederick M. Abbott, 'TRIPS in Seattle: The Not-So-Surprising Failure and the Future of the TRIPS Agenda', *Berkeley Journal of International Law* 18 (2000): 165; and John H. Barton, 'The Economics of TRIPS: International Trade in Information-Intensive Products', *George Washington International Law Review* 33 (2000): 473. For an assessment of whether and how trade policy forums can handle e-commerce issues, see Stewart A. Baker, Peter Lichtenbaum, Maury D. Shenk and Matthew S. Yeo, 'E-Products and the WTO' International Lawyer 35 (2001): 5 see also Ministerial Declaration on Global Electronic Commerce, WTO Doc. WT/MIN(98) DEC/2 (25 May 1998), www.wto.org/english/tratop_e/ecom_e/mindec1_e.htm; Ludger Schuknecht and Rosa Pérez-Esteve, 'A Quantitative Assessment of Electronic Commerce', ERAD-99-01 (WTO Economic Research and Analysis Division September 1999), www.wto.org/english/res_e/reser_e/ae9901_e.htm.

Many workable, semantic dichotomies break down in the convergent ICE environment, because technological innovations promote greater service flexibility and markets become more penetrable absent countervailing regulations and trade policies. For example, ventures operating in a digital environment can easily bridge pre-existing legal and regulatory distinctions between content creator and conduit. Similarly, many types of Internet venture use digitisation to eliminate pre-existing regulatory dichotomies between basic and value-added services and between different trade policies and market access commitments made for goods versus services.

Convergence challenges many baseline assumptions legislators, regulators, jurists and trade policy-makers have made about ICE. Information services typically qualify for little, if any, regulatory oversight based on assumptions that they enhance and add value to regulated basic telecommunications. But, what happens to this assumption when an unregulated Internet venture provides services functionally equivalent to what often heavily regulated telecommunications common carriers provide? Heretofore, communications ventures fitted into a convenient regulatory dichotomy based on whether they created and disseminated content, e.g. broadcasting, or operated as neutral, transparent conduits for the content created by others, e.g. telecommunications service providers such as common carrier telephone companies. In the pre-convergent environment, creators of entertainment could largely avoid regulation and concentrate on the creative and business process. Marketplace convergence opportunities have made content creators into content disseminators like broadcasters, cable television operators, Internet service providers and satellite operators.

Efforts to liberalise and deregulate telecommunications have generated less success and more harm than anticipated, primarily because technological and market convergence raise new issues even as old ones do not simply evaporate through the remedy of competition. The legal, regulatory and trade policy-making apparatus has not kept pace with ICE convergence. As a result, plenty of opportunities exist for delay, exploiting uncertainty, and using superior skill in gaming and brinkmanship to thwart competition, or to tilt the competitive playing field to one's advantage. Stakeholders have resorted primarily to competing in courtrooms rather than in the marketplace, an outcome all the more frustrating because most of the litigants also helped write the legislation and negotiate the compromises necessary to enact laws and trade policies. Recent deregulatory and market access initiatives have not achieved 'an equilibrium among all parties: regulators, legislators, operators and consumers'.[2]

Depending on one's perspective, clever and unanticipated outcomes help blunt the adverse and meddlesome impact of poorly drafted legislation and trade policies, or forestall the full achievement of essential public policy objectives. Because of the opportunity for delay, litigation and dispute over the meaning of legislation and trade policies, great opportunities exist for stakeholders to exploit inconsistencies in the nature and scope of the new and revamped regulatory regime designed to foster competition.[3] Asymmetries in regulatory burdens create incentives to find ways to exploit artificial competitive advantages, and to avoid regulatory classifications that create a bias towards more pervasive and costly regulatory burdens.[4] Asymmetrical regulation has the potential to tilt the competitive playing field in favour of one category of stakeholder over others.[5]

[2] Michela Cimatoribus, Antonio De Tommaso and Paolo Neri, 'Impacts of the 1996 Telecommunications Act on the US Model of Telecommunications Policy', *Telecommunications Policy* 22 (1998): 493 at 509.

[3] Appellate courts have often rejected the FCC's interpretation of a legislative mandate, or an FCC unilateral rule-making initiative. For example, on several occasions the FCC unsuccessfully attempted to mandate the elimination of a statutorily imposed tariff filing requirement: 'Commission efforts to move to a nontariff environment for interexchange carriers – insofar as those carriers do not exercise market power – have not had an easy time with this court and the Supreme Court. For over six decades a tariff regime was mandated by the Communications Act of 1934, which requires the FCC to review telecommunications carriers' tariffs to ensure their reasonableness. The Act requires carriers to file their tariffs with the FCC, and they are prohibited from charging consumers except as provided in the tariffs. Starting in the early 1980s, the Commission tried to prohibit tariff-filing by nondominant carriers – in essence, those other than AT&T – but that effort was successfully challenged in this court in *MCI Telecommunications Corp.* v. *FCC*... where we struck down "mandatory detariffing" as inconsistent with the 1934 Act.' *MCI WorldCom Inc.* v. *FCC*, 209 F. 3d 760 at 761–2, 341 US App. DC 132 at 133–4 (DC Cir. 2000) (citations omitted).

[4] '[A]ll forms of asymmetric regulation contain an intrinsic bias toward some firms or technologies.' Mark Schankerman, 'Symmetric Regulation for Competitive Telecommunications', *Information Economics and Policy* 8 (1996): 55.

[5] 'There is a wide range of possible asymmetric regulation. Whereas, in the past, legal entry barriers protected monopolistic carriers, the regulatory pendulum now seems to swing in the opposite direction. Asymmetric regulation in favor of newcomers is motivated by the conviction that, even after the abolishment of the legal monopoly, the incumbent carrier would still possess a factual monopoly position on the network infrastructure and the normal voice telephone service. Therefore, initial support of newcomers, at least for a sufficient transition period, has been recommended recently in the national regulatory debates.' Gunter Knieps, 'Interconnection and Network Access', *Fordham International Law Journal* 23 (2000): 90 at 99.

Likewise, ambiguities in trade policy jeopardise mutually beneficial market access initiatives. The trade policy-making apparatus offers similar gaming and brinkmanship opportunities as some stakeholders seek to shoehorn new services into definitions and classifications that impose less burdensome market access commitments, or qualify for exemption from otherwise applicable requirements. For example, most nations have made far greater market access commitments for telecommunications than for audio-visual services, and more fundamentally market access commitments appear more robust and straightforward for goods than for services. Concerns about preserving national culture and sovereignty have prompted nations to shield and nurture indigenous audio-visual content ventures.

Does ICE convergence allow concerns, expressed in trade policy forums, about foreign cinema market penetration and 'cultural imperialism',[6] to support restricted market access for Internet-mediated audio and video services, like that provided through real-time 'streaming' delivery of digital packets? Do cultural exceptions, applicable to broadcasting and satellite-delivered programming, extend to Internet ventures providing functionally equivalent services? Similar issues arise in telecommunications policy and regulatory forums where decision-makers have established 'bright line' distinctions between regulated telecommunications and unregulated enhancement of leased services, or the creation of content transported by carriers.

This article will examine a number of semantic, telecommunications and trade classifications with an eye to determining whether technological convergence and regulatory opportunism defeat the possibility of establishing a multiple-track regime that distinguishes between basic and enhanced services in telecommunications and between telecommunications and audio-visual services. Additionally, the article scrutinises marketplace anomalies created by Internet-based services that do not readily fit into any existing classification. For example, Internet-mediated 'streaming' of

[6] See W. Ming Shao, 'Is There No Business Like Show Business? Free Trade and Cultural Protectionism', *Yale Journal of International Law* 20 (1995): 105; Thomas M. Murray, 'The US–French Dispute Over GATT Treatment of Audiovisual Products and the Limits of Public Choice Theory: How An Efficient Market Solution Was "Rent-Seeking", *Maryland Journal of International Law and Trade* 21 (1997): 203; Robin L. Van Harpen, 'Mamas, Don't Let Your Babies Grow Up to Be Cowboys: Reconciling Trade and Cultural Independence', *Minnesota Journal of Global Trade* 4 (1995): 165. But cf. C. Edwin Baker, 'An Economic Critique of Free Trade in Media Product', *North Carolina Law Review* 78 (2000): 1357 (challenging economic justifications for free trade in audio-visual products).

visual and audio content has characteristics akin to broadcasting, but also qualifies for a largely unregulated status in view of the fact that the service involves packet-switched, value-added data communications. Other innovations, like Internet telephony, possibly fit into more than one classification. Other technological applications erode pre-existing rules and policies like the international accounting rate division of long-distance toll revenues.

The marketplace attractiveness of some new services results, in part, from trade and regulatory classifications that can accord arbitrage opportunities by blocking market access, or by avoiding costly regulatory burdens. The article concludes with suggestions on how legislators, regulators and trade policy-makers might curb regulatory opportunism by abandoning the strategy of classifying carriers and services based on static technological or market-share assumptions.

Semantic game playing

Over the years, incumbents and newcomers alike have gamed the regulatory process to secure a competitive advantage in terms of reduced regulation or cost-savings. Deregulatory initiatives in the United States replace one regulatory regime with another.[7] With skilful manoeuvring, both incumbents and market entrants can provide unregulated services functionally equivalent to what a substantially regulated carrier offers. Other strategies involve securing a classification that exempts the operator from more burdensome regulatory duties, or qualifies the operator to tap into cost-savings or cost-avoidance opportunities.

Currently, Internet service providers (ISPs) in the United States can qualify for 'reciprocal' interconnection payments from local exchange carriers without having to generate a return flow of traffic.[8] ISPs can also

[7] 'In essence, legislatures liberalize an economic sector by "re-regulating" rather than deregulating it.' Viktor Mayer-Schonberger and Mathias Strasser, 'A Closer Look at Telecom Deregulation: The European Advantage', *Harvard Journal of Law and Technology* 12 (1999): 561 at 565.

[8] 'Each time a customer places a call to the ISP, the incumbent carrier winds up paying the competing carrier a per-minute termination fee. Consider also the nature of ISP traffic. First, such traffic is typically "one-way." That is, many customers call an ISP in order to connect to the Internet, but an ISP seldom places calls to other customers. Second, calls made to ISPs are typically much longer than the average voice call, since people often surf the Internet for hours at a time. The potential for regulatory arbitrage is obvious – a competing carrier that signs up an ISP as a customer stands to collect far more in reciprocal

offer Internet-mediated long-distance telephone services free of interconnection charges and the duty to make universal service contributions like that borne by competitors.[9] Cable television service providers can leverage their non-common carrier status to avoid having to provide open access to new Internet access services, despite the fact that they compete with telephone companies whose legacy of common carrier regulation extends to such services.[10]

Other longer standing tactics include selecting a favourable jurisdiction (federal instead of state), legal classification (private carrier instead of common carrier)[11] and cashflow status (reseller instead of facilities-based carrier). With skilful manoeuvring, both incumbents and market entrants can provide unregulated services functionally equivalent to what a substantially regulated carrier offers. This involves securing a classification that exempts the operator from more burdensome regulatory duties, or qualifies the operator to tap into cost-savings or cost-avoidance opportunities.

compensation fees than it will pay out in connection with serving that customer.' Rebecca Beynon, 'The FCC's Implementation of the 1996 Act: Agency Litigation Strategies and Delay', *Federal Communications Law Journal* 53 (2000) 27 at 39. 39 (Dec. 2000).

[9] See Federal State Joint Board on Universal Service, Seventh Report and Order and Thirteenth Order on Reconsideration in CC Docket No. 96-45, Fourth Report and Order in CC Docket No. 96-262 and Further Notice of Proposed Rulemaking, *FCC Record* 14 (1999): 8078. See also Robert M. Frieden, 'Universal Service: When Technologies Converge and Regulatory Models Diverge', *Harvard Journal of Law and Technology* 12 (2000): 395; Jamie N. Nafziger, 'Time to Pay Up: Internet Service Providers' Universal Service Obligations Under the Telecommunications Act of 1996', *Marshall Journal of Computer and Information Law* 16 (1997): 37; Dennis W. Moore Jr, 'Regulation of the Internet and Internet Telephony Through the Imposition of Access Charges', *Texas Law Review* 76 (1997): 183; Hank Intven, Mark Zohar and Jay Howard, 'Internet Telephony – The Regulatory Issues', *Hastings Communications and Entertainment Law Journal* 21 (1998): 1; Seth A. Cohen, 'Defragmenting and Interconnecting: Reconsidering Commercial Telecommunications Regulation in Relation to the Rise of Internet Telephony', *Journal of Law and Commerce* 18 (1998): 133; Henry E. Crawford, 'Internet Calling: FCC Jurisdiction Over Internet Telephony', *Communications Law Conspectus* 5 (1997) 43; Katherine Collins, 'International Accounting Rate Reform: The Role of International Organizations and Implications for Developing Countries', *Law and Policy of International Business* 31 (2000) 1077.

[10] See *AT&T Corp.* v. *City of Portland*, 43 F. Supp. 2d 1146 (D. Ore. 1999), rev'd, 216 F. 3d 871 (9th Cir. 2000).

[11] See James H. Lister, 'The Rights of Common Carriers and the Decision Whether to Be a Common Carrier or a Non-Regulated Communications Provider', *Federal Communications Law Journal* 53 (2000) 91.

A law of unintended consequences: the US Telecommunications Act of 1996

The authors of the Telecommunications Act of 1996[12] (the '1996 Act') had great expectations[13] that they could engineer competition and enhance consumer welfare simply by rewriting a law to remove regulatory barriers to competition.[14] Congress assumed that it could craft legislation that created complementary incentives.[15] For incumbent Bell operating companies, the law links access to long-distance markets with affirmative steps to open their networks to new local exchange service competitors.[16] The

[12] Telecommunications Act of 1996, 104 PL 104, 110 Stat. 56, codified at 47 USC §§ 151 *et seq.*

[13] 'In the floor discussions of the new legislation, it was commonplace to hear that a vision of "the convergence of these technologies" lay at "the heart of this reform effort" [citing 142 Cong. Rec. H1161 (daily edn, 1 February 1996) (statement of Rep. Oxley)] that it was "about time for Congress to update the law to catch up with the new convergence in video, computer and telephone technologies" [citing 141 Cong. Rec. S8464 (daily edn, 15 June 1995) (statement of Sen. Leahy)] and that the bill would "allow the cable, telephone, computer, broadcasting, and other telecommunications industries more easily to converge and transform themselves" [citing 141 Cong. Rec. S8477 (daily edn, 15 June 1995) (statement of Sen. Pressler)]. Digitalisation, among other things, had rendered modes of transmitting information interchangeable; as a result, many in Congress believed that historic divisions, artificially supported by legislative distinctions and federal and state bureaucratic arrangements, needed to be dissolved.' Monroe E. Price and John F. Duffy, 'Technological Change and Doctrinal Persistence: Telecommunications Reform in Congress and the Court', *Columbia Law Review* 97 (1997): 976 at 983. See also Joint Explanatory Statement of the Committee of Conference, HR Conf. Rep. No. 104-458 (1996), reprinted in 1996 USCCAN 124.

[14] For background on the Telecommunications Act of 1996, see Robert M. Frieden, 'The Telecommunications Act of 1996: Predicting the Winners and Losers', 20 HASTINGS COMM. & ENT. L. J., No. 1, 11–57, (Fall, 1997); Thomas G. Krattenmaker, 'The Telecommunications Act of 1996', *Connecticut Law Review* 29 (1996): 123 at 127; Michael I. Meyerson, 'Ideas of the Marketplace: A Guide to the 1996 Telecommunications Act', *Federal Communications Law Journal* 49 (1997): 251; Michael Glover and Donna Epps, 'Is the telecommunications Act of 1996 Working?', *Administrative Law Review* 52 (2000): 1013; John C. Roberts, 'The Sources of Statutory Meaning: An Archaeological Case Study of the 1996 Telecommunications Act', *SMU Law Review* 53 (2000): 143; Aimee M. Adler, 'Competition in Telephony: Perception or Reality? Current Barriers to the Telecommunications Act of 1996', *Journal of Law and Policy* 7 (1997): 571.

[15] 'There was a headiness to the rhetoric, a sense that a legislative revolution would assist, and perhaps even underwrite, a technological and organizational revolution in which past media categories would be swept away and a new era of national achievement and citizen and consumer empowerment would be achieved.' *Ibid.*, p. 982.

[16] See Bell Operating Company Entry into InterLATA Services, 47 USC § 271 (2000). This section contains a fourteen-point checklist which Bell operating companies must adhere to before being allowed into the InterLATA long-distance telephone service markets. LATA is an acronym for Local Access and Transport Area, a geographical region created in

drafters of the law also sought to motivate competitive local exchange carriers (CLECs) to construct facilities, which would stimulate demand with lower prices and new options, rather than resell the services of incumbent local exchange carriers (ILECs).[17] The law has not stimulated substantial competition in local telecommunication services, because Congress underestimated the ability of stakeholders to thwart progress through litigation[18] and to exploit ambiguous language in the 1996 Act to maintain or create a competitive advantage.[19]

Technological innovations and market convergence in telecommunications require commensurate adjustments in the legal and regulatory arena, particularly when ventures can now provide functionally

the AT&T divestiture within which the spun-off Bell operating companies can provide local and toll services. See 47 USC § 153(25)(A)–(B). The fourteen-point competitive checklist, 47 USC § 271(c)(2)(B), requires the Bell operating companies to provide: (1) full and fair interconnection with competitive local exchange carriers in accordance with the requirements of sections 251(c)(2) and 252(d)(1); (2) non-discriminatory and *á la carte* access to network elements in accordance with the requirements of sections 251(c)(3) and 252(d)(1); (3) non-discriminatory access to the poles, ducts, conduits, and rights-of-way owned or controlled by the Bell operating company at just and reasonable rates in accordance with the requirements of section 224; (4) local loop transmission from the central office to a customer's premises, unbundled from local switching or other services; (5) local transport from the trunk side of a wireline local exchange carrier's switch unbundled from switching or other services; (6) local switching unbundled from transport, local loop transmission, or other services; (7) non-discriminatory access to 911 emergency services, directory assistance services to allow the other carriers' customers to obtain telephone numbers and operator call completion services; (8) white pages directory listings for customers of other carriers' telephone exchange services; (9) non-discriminatory access to telephone numbers for assignment to the other carriers' telephone exchange service customers; (10) non-discriminatory access to databases and associated signaling necessary for call routing and completion; (11) number portability, i.e. the ability of a former Bell operating company customer to retain use of a pre-existing telephone number after having subscribed to telephone service from another carrier; (12) non-discriminatory access to such services or information as are necessary to allow requesting carriers to implement local dialling parity in accordance with the requirements of section 251(b)(3), i.e. the same number of digits dialled for either Bell operating company or alternative service; and (13) reciprocal compensation.

[17] 'Because the 1996 Act alone will not solve the regulatory convergence problem, the dilemma policymakers face is how to change the current system to alleviate the detrimental effects of asymmetrical regulation, and how to avoid the reflexive application of shopworn regulatory antecedents.' Alexandra M. Wilson, 'Harmonizing Regulation by Promoting Facilities-Based Competition', *George Mason Law Review* 8 (2000) 729 at 730.

[18] See Rebecca Beynon, 'The FCC's Implementation of the 1996 Act: Agency Litigation Strategies and Delay', *Federal Communications Law Journal* 53 (2000) 27.

[19] See Kathleen Wallman, 'A Birthday Party: The Terrible or Terrific Two's? 1996 Federal Telecommunications Act', *Federal Communications Law Journal* 51 (1998) 229.

equivalent services yet face different regulatory treatment. Legislative changes to the *status quo* occur most infrequently,[20] while 'regulatory lag'[21] becomes a more common occurrence as a significant period of time may run before regulations reflect changed technological and marketplace circumstances.[22] During such periods of delayed adjustment, the regulatory process may favour one competitor over others, particularly when marketplace conditions trigger new competitive opportunities and technological convergence eliminates barriers to market entry or market segmentation, e.g. a separate wire for telephone and video service.

Comparatively lighter regulation of market entrants may properly incubate and promote incipient competition. But, on the other hand, without recalibration, a regulatory dichotomy may distort markets and handicap incumbents who deserve similar deregulation or streamlined government oversight.[23]

The authors of the 1996 Act thought that they had performed such a rebalancing of the telecommunications regulatory regime so that more robust competition might ensue without unduly favouring entrants with preferential treatment or allowing incumbents to exploit market power and engage in anti-competitive practices. To the apparent dismay of Congress, telecommunication and information service providers have proven themselves quite adept at exploiting opportunities to capture greater profits and market share by tilting the competitive playing field

[20] 'Congress repeatedly ignored or rebuffed calls by the FCC and critics to amend and update the 1934 Act to provide guidance on emerging issues and technologies.' John C. Roberts, 'The Sources of Statutory Meaning: An Archaeological Case Study of the 1996 Telecommunications Act', *SMU Law Review* 53 (2000): 143 at 146.

[21] Regulatory lag has been defined as 'the general delay in the responses of regulators to changes in cost or market conditions'. Robert W. Crandall and J. Gregory Sidak, 'Competition and Regulatory Policies for Interactive Broadband Networks', *Southern California Law Review* 68 (1995): 1203 at 1220.

[22] 'For the transition to competition to succeed, asymmetric measures to control market power should be phased out as the incumbent's market power diminishes.' James Alleman, Paul N. Rappoport and Dennis Weller, 'Universal Service: The Poverty of Policy', *University of Colorado Law Review* 71 (2000): 849 at 850.

[23] Some critics of FCC policies requiring ILECs to share local distribution facilities allege that such 'unbundling would be a classic case of asymmetric regulation: the CLEC would pursue the more profitable, unregulated service, while the ILEC would be left providing basic local service (in many cases, below cost). Innovation would be eroded by regulations that arbitrarily favored CLECs, without regard to the adverse effect of such asymmetric regulation on the welfare of consumers.' Thomas M. Jorde, J. Gregory Sidak and David J. Teece, 'Innovation, Investment, and Unbundling', *Yale Journal on Regulation* 17 (2000): 1 at 32–3.

to their advantage.[24] While designed to achieve market access parity, the 1996 Act, like so many laws and implementing regulations before it, has become a vehicle for clever interpretation, exploitation and litigation.[25]

For example, Congress thought that it could ensure market access parity through a 'one-size-fits-all' regulatory classification, e.g. common carriage status for all types of commercial service providers.[26] However, Congress also authorised the Federal Communications Commission (FCC) to eliminate aspects of traditional common carrier responsibilities should the public interest support it.[27] The new legislative mandate to undo common carrier responsibilities, such as filing and complying with tariffs,[28] combines with previous FCC efforts selectively to streamline regulations if not deregulate entirely.[29] Collectively, these apparently

[24] See Eli M. Noam, 'The Future of Telecommunications Regulation', *Hastings Law Journal* 50 (1999): 1473.

[25] See Stanley M. Gorinson, 'Deregulation in Telecommunications: Competition or Confusion?', *Federal Lawyer* 47 (March/April 2000): 24.

[26] See Telecommunications Act of 1996, Section 3(44), 47 USC § 153(44), deeming every telecommunications carrier a 'common carrier under this Act only to the extent that it is engaged in providing telecommunications services'.

[27] The FCC may forbear from applying any regulation or any provision of the Communications Act if enforcement of such regulation or provision is not necessary to ensure that the charges, practices, classifications or regulations are just and reasonable and are not unjustly or unreasonably discriminatory, enforcement is not necessary to protect consumers and forbearance is consistent with the public interest. 47 USC § 160(a).

[28] In *MCI Telecommunications Corp.* v. *FCC*, 765 F. 2d 1186 (DC Cir. 1985), the Court of Appeals for the District of Columbia struck down 'mandatory detariffing' as inconsistent with the Communications Act of 1934. See also *American Telephone & Telegraph Co.* v. *FCC*, 978 F. 2d 727 (DC Cir. 1992), aff'd sub nom. *MCI Telecommunications Corp.* v. *American Telephone & Telegraph Co.*, 512 US 218, 114 S.Ct 2223, 129 L. Ed. 2d 182 (1994) (the FCC could not suspend (permissively or mandatorily) the tariff filing obligations for inter-exchange carriers, whether they had market power or not). See also *MCI WorldCom, Inc.* v. *FCC*, 209 F. 3d 760, 341 US App. DC 132 (DC Cir. 2000).

[29] See Policy and Rules Concerning Rates for Competitive Common Carrier Services and Facilities Therefor, Notice of Inquiry and Proposed Rulemaking, 77 FCC 2d 308 (1979); First Report and Order, 85 FCC 2d 1 (1980); Further Notice of Proposed Rulemaking, 84 FCC 2d 445 (1981); Second Report and Order, 91 FCC 2d 59 (1982), reconsideration denied, 93 FCC 2d 54 (1983); Second Further Notice of Proposed Rulemaking, 47 Fed. Reg. 17308 (1982); Third Further Notice of Proposed Rulemaking, 48 Fed. Reg. 46791 (1983); Third Report and Order, 48 Fed. Reg. 46791 (1983); Fourth Report and Order, 95 FCC 2d 554 (1983); Fourth Further Notice of Proposed Rulemaking, 49 Fed. Reg. 11856 (1984); Fifth Report and Order, 98 FCC 2d 1191 (1984); Sixth Report and Order, 99 FCC 2d 1020 (1985), rev'd and remanded sub nom. *MCI Telecommunications Corp.* v. *FCC*, 765 F. 2d 1186 (DC Cir. 1985); Competition in the Interstate Interexchange Marketplace, CC Docket No. 90-132, Report and Order, 6 FCC Rcd 5880, 58xx para. 2 (1991), on reconsideration, 7 FCC Rcd 2677 (1992), on further reconsideration, 8 FCC Rcd 2659 (1993), Second Report and Order, 8 FCC Rcd 3668 (1993), on further reconsideration 10 FCC Rcd 4562 (1995)

pro-competitive initiatives have had the impact of expanding the dichotomy between the nature and scope of regulation applied to dominant, incumbent carriers *vis-à-vis* market entrants and other carriers that qualify for streamlined regulation or none at all. They also blur the distinction between traditionally regulated common carriers and their unregulated private carrier counterparts.[30]

Some telecommunications ventures have avoided costly regulatory burdens simply on grounds that they lack market power,[31] or because they have semantically crafted services so that they qualify for little or no regulatory oversight. On the other hand, some incumbents have continued to incur such burdens despite changed circumstances and the 1996 Act requirement that all service providers, regardless of regulatory classification, should bear on a 'competitively neutral' basis the obligation of making financial contributions to support universal access to basic telecommunications.[32] For example, ISPs and other ventures providing enhancements to leased lines do not pay local exchange carrier access charges or contribute to universal service funding even when providing services that if provided by other carriers would trigger such payments.[33]

Both newcomers and subsidiaries of incumbents may secure regulatory exemptions on semantic grounds, i.e. by characterising and offering services in a way that qualifies for diminished regulation. Incumbents may

(reducing the scope of AT&T's dominant carrier status and allowing provision of service based on customised tariffs preceded by a contract for carriage), further reconsideration denied. 10 FCC Rcd 4421 (1995).

30 See Eli M. Noam, 'Will Universal Service and Common Carriage Survive the Telecommunications Act of 1996?', *Columbia Law Review* 97 (1997): 955.

31 The *MIT Dictionary of Modern Economics* defines 'market power' as the 'ability of a single, or group of buyer(s) or seller(s) to influence the price of the product or service in which it is trading. A perfectly competitive market in equilibrium ensures the complete absence of market power.' David W. Pearce, ed., *The MIT Dictionary of Modern Economics* (4th edn, Cambridge, MA: MIT Press, 1995), p. 268.

32 Every telecommunications carrier that provides interstate telecommunications services shall contribute, on an equitable and non-discriminatory basis, to the specific, predictable and sufficient mechanisms established by the FCC to preserve and advance universal service. 47 USC § 254(d) (1999). See also 47 USC § 254(h)2(A), which provides: 'The Commission shall establish competitively neutral rules – (A) to enhance, to the extent technically feasible and economically reasonable, access to advanced telecommunications and information services for all public and nonprofit elementary and secondary school classrooms, health care providers, and libraries.' See also *Texas Office of Public Utility Counsel* v. *FCC*, 183 F. 3d 393 (5th Cir. 1999) cert. granted sub nom. *GTE Service Corp.* v. *FCC*, 120 S.Ct 2214, 68 USLW 3496 (US, 5 June 2000) (No. 99-1244).

33 See Robert M. Frieden, 'Universal Service: When Technologies Converge and Regulatory Models Diverge', *Harvard Journal of Law and Technology* 13 (2000): 395.

exploit regulatory inertia that maintains regulatory safeguards and barriers to market entry based on persisting concepts of 'natural monopoly' and a strained view that only one enterprise can achieve public policy objectives such as effectively executing a universal service mission. Alternatively, incumbent carriers may create separate subsidiaries to qualify for unregulated or lightly regulated non-dominant, market entrant status.[34]

Trade forums have created similar arbitrage opportunities

Trade policies affecting telecommunications do not operate using technology-neutral definitions and assumptions. Instead, definitions and classifications establish a vertical, top-down structure, perhaps in part because the trade policy-making apparatus first applied solely to goods and was subsequently retrofitted to apply to services. The supply chain for manufacture, distribution and retail sale of goods lends itself to a vertical model. Services, particularly ICE services operating in a convergent marketplace, support a horizontal analysis that considers functional equivalents regardless of supplier or technology.

The General Agreement on Tariffs and Trade (GATT)[35] provides greater specificity and clarity of market access commitments, with less regard to specific types of goods. The General Agreement on Trade in Services (GATS)[36] offers less global coverage, instead relying on industry-specific annexes and the definitions contained in them. With a baseline goods versus service dichotomy, perhaps it becomes easier to derive additional dichotomies that help flesh out basic definitions. With this kind of construct, a trade policy-making system can separate content from conduit, and specify different levels of market access as between telecommunications and audio-visual services. Increasingly nations have made market

[34] As part of its initial deregulatory thrust in the 1980s, the FCC developed a regulatory dichotomy between dominant carriers, to be subject to conventional, but possibly streamlined, regulation, and non-dominant carriers to be subject to regulatory forbearance based on the view that carriers lacking market power should not be burdened with regulations designed to curb the potential for dominant carriers to engage in anticompetitive practices. See also Scott M. Schoenwald, 'Regulating Competition in the Interexchange Telecommunications Market: The Dominant/Nondominant Carrier Approach and the Evolution of Forbearance', *Federal Communications Law Journal* 49 (1997) 367.

[35] General Agreement on Tariffs and Trade, 30 October 1947, 61 Stat. A-11, TIAS 1700, 55 UNTS 194, amended by General Agreement on Tariffs and Trade 1994, 15 April 1994, Annex 1A, ILM 33 (1994): 1154.

[36] General Agreement on Trade in Services, 15 April 1994, Annex 1B, ILM 33 (1994): 1167.

access commitments in telecommunications – both basic and value added – even as little if any new initiatives apply to audio-visual services.

Quite legitimate concerns about sovereignty and culture warrant greater caution in the audio-visual sector. However, ICE convergence provides new opportunities to expand and leverage these concerns to shelter new services that seamlessly blend telecommunications transport with content. Indeed, the Internet offers an example of such convergence as one cannot easily distinguish and separate the content delivery function from the content alone. Accordingly, when market access initiatives are not forthcoming for Internet-mediated services, do concerns about sovereignty and culture forestall progress, or might ventures providing such services consider the lack of market access an arbitrage opportunity to extract greater financial rewards through reduced competition?

Regulatory arbitrage

Regulatory arbitrage refers to the ability of stakeholders to exploit differences in legislative and regulatory classifications with an eye to securing more favourable or less burdensome regulatory treatment that typically will accrue financial and competitive advantages.[37] Stakeholders in the United States have exploited loopholes to secure a competitive or financial windfall, for several reasons:

1. the organic legislation mandating regulatory reform contained ambiguities and relied on the FCC to determine the will of Congress and to implement the deregulatory process;
2. courts reviewing the FCC's implementation of legislation only conditionally defer to the expert regulatory agency's expertise; and
3. shared jurisdiction between the states and the FCC generate conflict, particularly when initiatives shift opportunities to receive subsidies and duties to finance subsidies.

Evading a regulatory burden can translate into cost-savings and greater nimbleness in a competitive environment. Sometimes, avoiding a regulatory requirement means that the stakeholder can save money, or even qualify for a flow of unexpected revenues. The arbitrage aspect of this brinkmanship involves the strategic targeting and qualifying to receive

[37] See A. Michael Froomkin, 'The Internet as a Source of Regulatory Arbitrage', in Brian Kahin and Charles Nesson, eds., *Borders in Cyberspace: Information Policy and the Global Information Infrastructure* (Cambridge, MA: MIT Press, 1997), p. 129.

lax or favourable regulatory treatment while at the same time retaining the ability to offer functionally equivalent services that compete with offerings of other stakeholders subject to more burdensome, costly and unfavourable regulatory treatment.

Over the years, a number of such regulatory anomalies and asymmetries have occurred. For example, the price, but not necessarily the cost, of a minute of telecommunication use has depended on such factors as:

- the perceived value of the service;[38]
- which regulatory agency has jurisdiction over cost-allocation and tariffing;[39]
- whether the service is domestic or international;[40]
- whether another carrier or end-user seeks facilities interconnection;[41]

[38] Both the FCC and state regulatory commissions have allowed carriers to price some services on the perceived value consumers accrue. For example, some local exchange telephone service rates have increased when the number of accessible subscribers reaches a benchmark. 'In most states, the Bell Operating Companies and larger independents charge higher rates in metropolitan areas than in rural areas – a pricing practice that dates back to the turn of the century and is traditionally justified in the belief that the value of the service provided is higher for subscribers with larger local calling areas.' Federal Communications Commission, 'FCC Releases Semiannual Study on Telephone Trends', 1991 FCC LEXIS 4305 at *10 (7 August 1991).

[39] Typically, an intrastate long-distance minute of use significantly exceeds the price of an interstate long-distance minute of use. Ironically, an intrastate call originated via a cellular telephone may be significantly cheaper than the corresponding rate for a call originated over wireline facilities. The rate differential results, in part, from rate-making policies, which may include cross-subsidies to local exchange service, as opposed to actual cost of service differences.

[40] International message telephone service substantially exceeds domestic rates on a per minute and mileage band basis, primarily because international carriers have negotiated toll revenue division agreements that have failed to reduce commensurately with cost reductions. For a discussion of these international accounting rates, see Rob Frieden, 'International Toll Revenue Division: Tackling the Inequities and Inefficiencies', *Telecommunications Policy* 17 (1993): 221–33; Rob Frieden, 'Accounting Rates: The Business of International Telecommunications and the Incentive to Cheat', *Federal Communications Law Journal* 43 (1991) 111–39.

[41] The Telecommunications Act of 1996 and pre-existing FCC regulations differentiate the terms and conditions for interconnection between carriers as opposed to customer-carrier interconnection. The Telecommunications Act orders favourable and potentially zero-cost interconnection between certain types of carriers. For example, section 251 requires all local exchange carriers 'to establish reciprocal compensation arrangements for the transport and termination of telecommunications'. 47 USC § 251(b)(5). End-users and inter-exchange ('long-distance') carriers must pay higher 'access charges'.

- the type of carrier[42] or enterprise[43] providing service;[44] and

[42] During a time when inter-exchange carrier competitors of AT&T received inferior access to the PSTN, the FCC authorised discounted access charges. However, the FCC never stated that the discounts were cost-based as opposed to a rough justice solution designed to reflect both inferior access and the FCC's desire that carriers like MCI acquire market share. See, e.g., Exchange Network Facilities for Interstate Access (ENFIA), CC Docket No. 78-371, Report and Order, 71 FCC 2d 440 (1979); on reconsideration, 93 FCC 2d 739 (1983), aff'd in part and remanded in part sub nom. *MCI Telecommunications Corp.* v. *FCC*, 712 F. 2d 517 (DC Cir. 1983). Currently, the FCC is considering whether wireless mobile service providers like cellular radio operators should be obliged to compensate wireline local exchange carriers for terminating calls while such wireline carriers are not obliged to compensate the wireless operators for similar call terminations. See Interconnection Between Local Exchange Carriers and Commercial Mobile Radio Service Providers, Notice of Proposed Rulemaking, CC Docket No. 95-185, 11 FCC Rcd 5020 (1996) (proposing reciprocal termination between wireline and wireless carriers, including the possibility of an interim zero termination charge between carriers); First Report and Order and Implementation of the Local Competition Provisions in the Telecommunications Act of 1996, Interconnection Between Local Exchange Carriers and Commercial Mobile Radio Service Providers, CC Docket No. 96-98, 11 FCC Rcd 15499 (1996), aff'd in part and vacated in part sub nom. *Competitive Telecommunications Association* v. *FCC*, 117 F. 3d 1068 (8th Cir. 1997), aff'd in part and vacated in part sub nom. *Iowa Utilities Board* v. *FCC*, 120 F. 3d 753 (8th Cir. 1997), aff'd in part, rev'd in part, and remanded sub nom. *AT&T Corp.* v. *Iowa Utilities Board*, 119 S.Ct 721 (1999), Order on Reconsideration, 11 FCC Rcd 13042 (1996), Second Order on Reconsideration, 11 FCC Rcd 19738 (1996), Third Order on Reconsideration and Further Notice of Proposed Rulemaking, 12 FCC Rcd 12460 (1997), appeals docketed, Second Further Notice of Proposed Rulemaking, FCC 99-70 (released 16 April 1999).

[43] 'Captive' long-distance callers from hotel rooms, and callers not familiar with 'dial around' options for avoiding price gouging for pay phone service recognise the vast price differences for long-distance telephone services.

[44] Certain types of service have qualified for exemption from regulatory burdens that impose extra costs. For example, enhanced services qualify for non-common carrier status and its users are exempt from having to pay an access charge payment otherwise applicable to basic service subscribers. A 1987 FCC initiative to eliminate the exemption generated substantial opposition by users who claimed the FCC had proposed to impose a 'modem tax'. 'In 1983 we adopted a comprehensive 'access charge' plan for the recovery by local exchange carriers (LECs) of the costs associated with the origination and termination of interstate calls [citing MTS and WATS Market Structure, Memorandum Opinion and Order, 97 FCC 2d 682 (1983)]. At that time, we concluded that the immediate application of this plan to certain providers of interstate services might unduly burden their operations and cause disruptions in provision of service to the public. Therefore, we granted temporary exemptions from payment of access charges to certain classes of exchange access users, including enhanced service providers.' Matter of Amendments of Part 69 of the Commission's Rules Relating to Enhanced Service Providers, CC Docket No. 87-215, Notice of Proposed Rulemaking, 2 FCC Rcd 4305 (1987) (proposing to impose access charges on enhanced service lines), terminated 3 FCC Rcd 2631 (1988) (proposal abandoned on the ground that, despite the apparent discrimination in charges, 'a period of change and uncertainty' besetting the enhanced services industry justified ongoing exemption from access charge payments). Currently, the FCC requires users of ISDN services to pay only one Subscriber Line Charge,

- the type of line or facility providing service[45] and whether the service can access the public switched telephone network (PSTN).[46]

Jurisdictional brinkmanship

A perennial candidate for regulatory arbitrage lies in securing favourable jurisdictional treatment. On a cost causation basis, traversing a state or international boundary should not make much difference. But how regulators and carriers allocate costs and to which services they attribute cost causation can result in substantially different cost levels depending on whether telecommunications traffic stays within a state, crosses state borders, or leaves a nation. Intrastate traffic in the United States and elsewhere typically triggers higher retail rates than interstate traffic, even for routes of equal distance. Similarly, international traffic may cost several times as much as domestic rates of equal mileage.

Given a significant gap between services, as a function of jurisdictional classification, arbitrage opportunities abound. Entrepreneurs have engaged in creative traffic routing to shoehorn services into a preferred

an access payment, despite the fact that ISDN circuits can derive more than one voice-grade equivalent channel.

[45] The FCC's access charge regime established a different pricing structure for switched and special access. The former includes regular dial-up services and requires end-users to pay a monthly flat-rated Subscriber Line Charge, currently US$3.50 for residential and small business users and US$6.00 for other business users. The latter includes leased, private line users, who certify that the line does not 'leak' into the PSTN through the use, for example, of an on-premises switch like a Private Branch Exchange, that could couple the private line with trunks that access the PSTN provided by Local Exchange Carriers ostensibly for local switched services. See MTS/WATS Market Structure (Phase I), 93 FCC 2d 241 (1983), modified on reconsideration, 97 FCC 2d 682, further modification on reconsideration, 97 FCC 2d 834, partially aff'd and partially remanded sub nom., *National Association of Regulated Utilities Commissioners* v. *FCC*, 737 F. 2d 1095 (1984), cert. denied, 105 S.Ct 1224; further modification, 99 FCC 2d 708 (1984), 100 FCC 2d 1222, further reconsideration denied 102 FCC 2d 899 (1985). See also Investigation of Access and Divestiture Related Tariffs, 101 FCC 2d 911 (1985), reconsideration denied 102 FCC 2d 503 (1985), Investigation of Access and Divestiture Related Tariffs, 101 FCC 2d 935 (1985).

[46] International private line services, which do not access the PSTN, are exempt from the accounting rate regime. Their per-minute costs are significantly lower than switched services. Undetected private line leakage has become commonplace, making it possible for resellers to provide a service functionally equivalent to international message telephone service at a fraction of the cost. See Rob Frieden, 'The Impact of Boomerang Boxes and Callback Services on the Accounting Rate Regime', in D. Wedemeyer and R. Nickelson, eds., *Proceedings of the Pacific Telecommunications Council Eighteenth Annual Conference* (Honolulu: Pacific Telecommunications Council, 1996), pp. 781–90.

jurisdiction. Traffic that originates in one location and terminates in another location within a single state may nevertheless traverse an adjacent state simply to avoid intrastate rate-making and the jurisdiction of a state public utility commission.[47] Until Canadian long-distance telephone rates dropped to US levels, carriers would transmit traffic via the US and back into Canada, thereby qualifying the traffic for lower Canada–US rates than the higher domestic charges. Similarly, callback operators import dial tone from nations with low international calling rates even for domestic calls. Arbitrageurs find and exploit price margins whether created by regulation (intrastate versus interstate rates) or different competitive conditions (high international calling versus lower calling rates).

Shared jurisdiction need not result in chaos. The European Union has achieved policy and regulatory harmonisation among the several different nations making up the Union. The balance between centralised policy-making and subsidiarity requires a 'delicate balance between, on the one hand, the necessity of general harmonization at the level of the EU and the desire for limited flexibility at the level of its Member States, and, on the other hand, the legislative framework and the implementation of that legislation at a subordinate level'.[48] Perhaps the EU generates a comparatively superior end product, because the EU Commission can provide greater specificity than the US Congress, while still deferring to individual national legislatures to customise the necessary legislation. Also, a more specific division of labour exists between the EU Commission, Council and Parliament.

[47] The FCC and reviewing courts have rejected a 'contamination theory' that if applied would subject a telecommunications service to intrastate jurisdiction if any portion of the service was offered solely within one state: 'The "contamination theory" contemplates that a service or facility used only partially for intrastate communication is not subject to Commission jurisdiction.' *United States Department of Defense* v. *General Telephone Co. of the Northwest*, FCC 72R-390, 1973 WL 29085 (FCC), 26 Rad. Reg. 2d (P&F) (1973); but cf. Petition of the New York Telephone Company for a Declaratory Ruling with Respect to the Physically Intrastate Private Line and Special Access Channels Utilized for Sales Agents to Computer New York State Lottery Communications, 5 FCC Rcd 1080 (1990) (the addition of two physically interstate private lines to a lottery network that is otherwise comprised of physically intrastate lines does not require the local exchange carrier providing the service to classify all of the lottery's special access lines as interstate); see also Chesapeake & Potomac Telephone Co., FCC 85-465 (released 16 August 1985), modified on reconsideration, 2 FCC Rcd 3528, vacated as moot sub nom. *Hecht Co.* v. *FCC*, No. 87-1396 (DC Cir. 1987); MTS and WATS Market Structure, Amendment of Part 36 of the Commission's Rules and Establishment of a Joint Board, 4 FCC Rcd 5660 (1989) (establishing definitive jurisdictional policy on lines having mixed intrastate and interstate use).

[48] Victor Mayer-Schoenberger and Mattias Strasser, 'A Closer Look at Telecom Deregulation: The European Advantage', *Harvard Journal of Law and Technology* 12 (1999) 561.

Semantic games: international accounting rate arbitrage

Because international accounting rates[49] remain at artificially high levels for many routes, carriers and their customers strategise on how to route traffic exempt from the settlement process. The vehicles for avoiding high accounting rates include the use of callback services, which provide dial tone to end-users physically situated in another country, and linking international private lines with a switch that secures access to the PSTN. These options may violate recommendations[50] and carrier tariffs of the International Telecommunications Union (ITU), because they enable end-users to secure services in a manner that the carrier did not intend providing. While such bypass may expedite reforms, it flouts uniform rules of the road. For example, the ITU recommendations on leased international private lines contemplate the consultation and agreement on the scope of service. Private lines, by definition, provide closed, intra-corporate networking capabilities, not the functional equivalent to switched public, long-distance services.

What is occurring in international telecommunications parallels the grey market in international commercial aviation where carriers look the other way, or clandestinely collaborate with ticket resellers, consolidators and brokers who offer seats at rates well below the published tariff.[51]

[49] For background on how international telecommunications carriers divide toll revenues using the accounting rate regime, see Robert M. Frieden, 'Falling Through the Cracks: International Accounting Rate Reform at the ITU and WTO', *Telecommunications Policy* 22 (1998): 963-75; Robert M. Frieden, 'The Impact of Call-Back and Arbitrage on the Accounting Rate Regime', *Telecommunications Policy* 21 (1997): 819–27; Robert M. Frieden, 'International Toll Revenue Division–Tackling the Inequities and Inefficiencies', *Telecommunications Policy* 17 (1993): 221–33; Paul W. Kenefick, 'A Step in the Right Direction: The FCC Provides Regulatory Relief in International Settlements and International Services Licensing', 8 *Communication Law Conspectus* 8 (2000) 43.

[50] Recommendation D.1, section. 7.1.1, of the ITU's International Telegraph and Telephone Consultative Committee Blue Book, vol. II, fascicle II.1, General Tariff Principles, Charging and Accounting in International Telecommunications Services, suggested that administrations can condition, consult and agree to the scope of access to public networks provided to users of international private leased circuits. To the extent that a private line reseller or end-user does not engage in such consultation and erects a system for accounting rate evasion, then the host country may deny access to the PSTN. However, in many instances, accounting rate avoidance schemes may go undetected by the carrier providing interconnection.

[51] International carriers do provide discounted rates to high-volume users, e.g. as an incentive to migrate from unmetered private lines to metered 'virtual' (software-defined) private lines using the PSTN. The carriers avoid the application of artificially high accounting rates by creating a new service category and applying a different, and lower, accounting rate. Foreign carriers typically have no obligation to justify how the new rate does not

In international telecommunications, sophisticated users and system integrators design private line networks that avoid accounting rates liability. Carriers originally offered unmetered private lines as a way to fill up excess capacity and satisfy large volume user requirements for closed, internal networks. Private branch exchanges and other customer-controlled equipment have enabled users to interconnect unmetered international private lines with local PSTNs. Such 'leakiness' enables the private line subscriber to access users outside the internal network. Expanded access to a private line network means that users, who otherwise would have to use IMTS circuits, can opt for specially configured private line access for functionally equivalent service.

Resellers can expand the reach of leaky private lines with higher capacity switches. Some carriers and their regulatory overseers do not object to this type of 'pure resale' that does not enhance leased lines. Resale stimulates overall capacity demand, and it can reduce outbound IMTS accounting rate liability, particularly where regulatory policies block or limit inbound resale. Some carriers, intent on capturing larger market shares by aggregating and routing regional traffic through a 'hub', may engineer a complex array of private lines and acquire both half-circuits on routes to handle accounting rate exempt traffic. Transiting, the routing of traffic destined for another country across domestic facilities, presents another opportunity for carriers and new international telephone entrepreneurs alike to engineer innovative new arrangements for users.[52]

Since the early 1990s, the FCC has taken a more proactive role in accounting rate oversight, with an eye to encouraging carrier and end-user 'self help', i.e. routing strategies that collectively make high accounting rates unsustainable. The FCC also adopted a 'get tough' policy with international carriers, including prescribed accounting rates,[53] because it

discriminate against users paying higher charges for existing offerings subject to accounting rates.

52 Even companies with limited budgets can enter the international telecommunications business and exploit high accounting rate and end-user charge differentials. A 'boomerang box' enables callers, in high-cost foreign locations, to place a call to the US, hang up and soon *receive* a call from the US with the intended call recipient on the line. At the micro-level, the foreign caller avoids having to pay the significantly higher charge for originating an international call, the foreign carrier loses some toll revenues and the USISC handling the international call accrues some additional toll revenues. At the macro-level, the transaction contributes to the expanding US accounting rate deficit, thereby blunting the foreign carrier's revenue losses and the USISC's revenue gains.

53 The FCC proposed to 'establish . . . determine and prescribe just and reasonable accounting rates' if USISCs and their foreign counterparts failed to negotiate rates downwards to an

had grown impatient with the pace of reform in private accounting rate negotiations. While the FCC can properly condition grants of regulatory authorisations and prescribe rates for the carriers it regulates, attempts to affect the behaviour and the financial performance of other carriers generated vocal opposition, at home and abroad, that the FCC had failed to appreciate international comity and national sovereignty.[54]

Similarly, an FCC proposal to impose reporting requirements and other means for overseeing the extent of participation in the US telecommunications market by foreign-owned firms[55] generated arguments that it would violate the commitment to 'national treatment' of foreign enterprises, i.e. applying identical regulatory rights, responsibilities and opportunities for foreign-owned carriers as for domestic carriers. The FCC subsequently decided to calibrate the scope of regulatory oversight of foreign carriers to the degree of market access accorded US carriers, particularly the extent to which US service providers may use leased international private lines to access the PSTN in foreign locales.[56] This mechanism provides strong leverage for achieving market access parity, by linking the scope

FCC-determined benchmark range. Regulation of International Accounting Rates, Notice of Proposed Rulemaking, 5 FCC Rcd 4950.

[54] When the FCC attempted to influence the timetable for construction and activation of the TAT-7 overseas cable through direct negotiations with foreign governments, foreign carriers deemed such activism intrusive of national sovereignty, and the US Court of Appeals for the District of Columbia deemed it a violation of the Government in the Sunshine Act. ITT World Communications, Inc., 77 FCC 2d 877 (1980) (order denying petition for rulemaking on permissible scope of FCC contacts with foreign administrations to negotiate delayed deployment of a trans-Atlantic submarine communications cable), *reversed*, *ITT World Communications* v. *FCC*, 699 F. 2d 1219 (DC Cir. 1983), *reversed on other grounds*, 466 US 463 (1984).

[55] Regulatory Policies and International Telecommunications, CC Docket No. 86-494, Notice of Inquiry, 2 FCC Rcd 1022 (1987), Report and Order and Supplemental Notice of Inquiry, 4 FCC Rcd 7387 (1988), *order on reconsideration*, 4 FCC Rcd 323 (1989). The FCC has modified its policies that impose more extensive oversight of foreign-owned carriers providing international services from the US. See Regulation of International Common Carrier Services, CC Docket No. 91-360, Notice of Proposed Rulemaking, 7 FCC Rcd 577 (1992), Report and Order, FCC 92-463 (released 6 November 1992) (retaining more burdensome 'dominant carrier' oversight only when the foreign affiliate of a USISC has the ability to discriminate against unaffiliated carriers through control of bottleneck services and facilities in the foreign market).

[56] See John J. Alissi, 'Revolutionizing the Telephone Industry: The World Trade Organization Agreement on Basic Telecommunications and the Federal Communications Commission Order', *Connecticut Journal of International Law* 13 (1999): 485 Paula Barnes Sours, 'The Impact of US Regulatory Activity on Prospects for Implementation of the WTO Agreement on Basic Telecommunications', *North Carolina Journal of International Law and Commercial Regulation* 23 (1998): 465; Kevin C. Kennedy, 'Market Openings in the Telecommunication Goods and Service Sectors', *International Lawyer* 33 (1999): 27.

of inbound US market access with reciprocal opportunities for outbound traffic.[57]

Reliance on proliferating private line resale redirected the FCC from direct confrontation with foreign carriers over their sovereign right to negotiate accounting rates, to 'procedural reforms that remove any US regulatory impediments to lower, more economically efficient, cost-based accounting rates'.[58] The FCC assumed that, if resale were available on an equivalent basis, inbound and outbound, then the incumbent facilities-based carriers would perceive new incentives to negotiate lower accounting rates to dissuade customers from migrating to private line and resale options. Facilities-based US International Service Carries (USISCs) facing competition from resellers,[59] unencumbered by accounting rate liability, may view high accounting rates as imposing a floor on how low they can price end-user rates 'to prevent diversion of . . . customers to a reseller'.[60] Presumably, resellers providing outbound services from the United States will acquire market share, thereby reducing the number of IMTS (Instructional Media and Technology Services) outbound minutes subject to accounting rate settlements. A facilities-based carrier, refusing to negotiate accounting rates closer to cost, would 'receive fewer revenues from its IMTS customers and, thus, would wind up with fewer revenues overall'.[61]

[57] See Cable & Wireless, Inc. DA-1344, Tele. Div. (released 8 December 1994); Cable & Wireless, Inc. 8 FCC Rcd 1664 (Com. Car. Bur. 1993); Fonorola Corp. and EMI Corp., 7 FCC Rcd 7312 (1992), *on reconsideration*, 9 FCC Rcd 4066 (1994) (authorising UK and Canadian resellers to provide international service upon finding that the foreign country on the other end of the circuit provides equivalent opportunities to US carriers to resell interconnected private lines).

[58] Regulation of International Accounting Rates, CC Docket No. 90-337, Phase I, 6 FCC Rcd 3552 (1991).

[59] 'Resale [of leased private lines] would bypass the accounting rate mechanism – a major cost to the traditional carrier mode of operation – and increase the feasibility of creating unidirectional traffic channels.' K. Cheong and M. Mullins, 'International Telephone Service Imbalances', Telecommunications Policy 15 (1991): 107 at 116. If resale remains unidirectional, US facilities-based carriers and consumers will not benefit. Resale occurring only in the inbound US direction, would increase the US accounting rate deficit. Resale must be bidirectional to have the effect of 'expos[ing] the differential between tariffs and accounting rates and ultimately force traditional carriers to renegotiate accounting rates closer to service costs'. *Ibid.*, pp. 116–17.

[60] Accounting Rate Phase II First Report and Order, 7 FCC Rcd 560. 'To the extent that the accounting rate is above cost, the underlying carrier will face a constraint on how much of a reduction in its revenues it can tolerate.' *Ibid.*, para. 561.

[61] *Ibid.*

The Internet as a medium for arbitrage

Absent network congestion, the cost to carry or process an additional minute of Internet traffic approaches zero, because the incremental cost is near zero.[62] This pricing system enhances consumer welfare, stimulates usage and revenue generation and accrues positive networking externalities.[63] The Internet adds thousands of new sites and users daily with such expanded access opportunities accruing greater utility for all users. As long as ample capacity remains available along with moderate transport and content costs, ISPs need not meter traffic and can offer service on an 'All You Can Eat' (AYCE) usage-insensitive basis.

ISPs can offer AYCE service, because they have been able to recover high fixed costs and incur relatively low incremental costs absent network congestion. They can represent that their network extends globally even though few, outside of a small group of Tier-1 backbone network operators, actually have built or leased such an extensive array of facilities. Until recently, ISPs have incurred little additional expense in providing their customers opportunities to access the Internet networks of networks via incumbent telecommunication carriers' facilities.[64] Accordingly, ISPs have had opportunities to tap into the same financial- and distance-insensitive service opportunities as those available when telecommunication entrepreneurs exploit the porousness of telecommunication networks and the relative ease in accessing the PSTN. One can consider Internet-mediated telephony[65] in the same context as other

[62] This pricing scenario presupposes that an ISP does not incur usage-sensitive prices for any major element of service. For many Asia-Pacific routes, the need to access network access points in far away locations, e.g. the US, does impose significant costs. To offset the charges of facilities-based telecommunications carriers, ISPs may charge end-users on a usage-sensitive basis, e.g. an hourly surcharge after an initial allocation of access time.

[63] A positive network externality exists when the cost incurred by a user of the Internet does not fully reflect the benefit derived with the addition of new users and points of communications. See John Farrell and Garth Saloner, 'Standardization, Compatibility and Innovation', *Rand Journal of Economics* 16 (1985): 70; Michael L. Katz and Carl Shapiro, 'Network Externalities, Competition and Compatibility', *American Economics Review* 75 (1985) 424; see also Mark A. Lemley and David McGowan, 'Legal Implications of Network Economic Effects', *California Law Review* 86 (1998): 479.

[64] The author acknowledges that 'free rider' opportunities via other ISPs are becoming scarcer as the Internet becomes more hierarchical and larger ISPs demand and receive payments for providing transit services to ISPs with fewer customers, less bandwidth and limited sources of desirable content. See Rob Frieden, 'Last Days of the Free Ride? The Consequences of Settlement-Based Interconnection for the Internet', *Info* 1 (1999): 225–38.

[65] See Robert Frieden, 'Dialing for Dollars: Will the FCC Regulate Internet Telephony?', *Rutgers Computer and Technology Law Journal* 23 (1997): 47.

technological innovations such as callback,[66] switched hubbing,[67] refile,[68] and international simple resale[69] that provide new, lower priced alternatives to the 'retail' rate for toll telephone services.

Internet telephony shifts the balance of market power from carriers, which traditionally have set prices on a cost-plus basis, to consumers who may emphasise price and consider telephony a commodity business. If telephony minutes of use become fungible, with voice traffic subordinate

[66] '"Callback" is a technology used to provide international telecommunications service from a foreign country through a . . . switch [in the US or other nation with low collection charges and options for private line resale and routing options that reduce or eliminate accounting rate liability].' *Philippine Long Distance Telephone Co.* v. *International Telecom Ltd.*, D/B/A Kallback Direct, File No. E-95-29, Memorandum Opinion and Order, FCC 97-233, p. 2, n. 10 (released 18 July 1997). See also Rob Frieden, 'Falling Through the Cracks: International Accounting Rate Reform at the ITU and WTO', *Telecommunications Policy* 22 (1998): 963–75; Rob Frieden, 'Without Public Peer: The Potential Regulatory and Universal Service Consequences of Internet Balkanization', *Virginia Journal of Law and Technology* 3 (1998): 8, available at http://vjolt.student.virginia.edu; Rob Frieden, 'The Impact of Call-Back and Arbitrage on the Accounting Rate Regime', *Telecommunications Policy* 21 (1997): 819–27; Organization for Economic Cooperation and Development, Committee for Information, Computer and Communications Policy, Refile and Alternative Calling Procedures: Their Impact on Accounting Rates and Collection Charges, OECD/GD(95)19 (Paris: OECD, 1995); Organisation for Economic Cooperation and Development, Committee for Information, Computer and Communications Policy, New Technologies and Their Impact on the Accounting Rate System, OECD/GD(97)14 (Paris: OECD, 1997).

[67] The FCC defined switched hubbing as 'the routing of US switched traffic over US international private lines, whether resold or facilities-based, that terminate in equivalent countries and then forwarding that traffic to a third, non-equivalent country by taking at published rates and reselling the international service of a carrier in the equivalent country.' Policy Statement on International Accounting Rate Reform, 11 FCC Rcd 3146 (1996), citing Market Entry and Regulation of Foreign-Affiliated Entities, Report and Order, IB Docket No. 95-22, 11 FCC Rcd 3873 (1995).

[68] 'Refile or the hubbing of traffic is using one country to collect traffic and switch this traffic to other countries . . . For example, the price of a call from Denmark–Finland–Australia is cheaper than a direct call from Denmark to Australia . . . US$0.46 + US$1.03 compared to US$2.01. In this case a third country calling service [using conventional switched services] would be viable having a margin of US$0.52 per minute.' 1995 OECD Refile and Call-back Report, note 66 above, p. 11.

[69] International simple resale (ISR) involves the use of a private line by more than one customer with access to the PSTN at one or both ends. ISR presents both profit-enhancing opportunities and bypass threats to facilities-based carriers providing the capacity. On the one hand, '[f]acility providers today find that it is more profitable to provide excess capacity to resellers and allow them to find customers and market this capacity rather than marketing this capacity themselves. Resale allows more segmented and flexible marketing including more market oriented prices'. 1997 OECD Accounting Rate Study, note 66 above, p. 36. On the other hand, 'ISR service provision by-passes the international charging and settlements system, and therefore places significant [downward] pressure on accounting rates'. *Ibid.*, p. 38.

to an increasing volume of data, then service providers will have limited, if any, ability to saddle users with rates significantly above cost, despite the fact that carriers do plough back a large percentage of any financial surplus to achieve universal service and infrastructure development objectives.

The onset of Internet-mediated telephony has the potential for bringing to a head the long-simmering debate over the propriety of pricing telecommunication services above cost, in part to promote a universal service mission. It also may trigger closer examination of what constitutes the actual cost a carrier incurs to route a minute of telecommunication traffic:

> a polarisation [exists] between a group of countries with relatively competitive prices and low accounting rates, and a second group of countries with prices significantly above cost . . . The danger is real, especially between OECD countries and a number of non-OECD countries who have difficulty in envisaging the benefits which they can attain from competitive telecommunication markets.[70]

Internet telephony threatens the status quo

Currently, international accounting rates for most routes substantially exceed the total cost incurred by two or more 'foreign correspondents' to switch and route a call from originator to recipient.[71] The onset of higher capacity submarine cables and satellites coupled with digital signal processing and switching and circuit multiplication technologies have significantly reduced per-mile and per-call costs,[72] although the cost

[70] *Ibid.*, p. 32.

[71] Carrier correspondents 'match' half-circuits to erect a complete link from call originator to call recipient. The half-circuit concept operates on the presumption that carrier correspondents achieve a 'whole circuit' by linking two half-circuits at the theoretical midpoint of a submarine cable, or at the satellite providing the transmission link. In the submarine cable scenario, each carrier has responsibility to secure access to circuits linking transmission facilities on its territory to the location where the cable makes its landfall (referred to as the cablehead), possibly located in a different nation, and onward to the midpoint. For more background on international telecommunications operations and policy, see Rob Frieden, *Managing Internet-Driven Change in International Telecommunications*, (Norwood, MA: Artech, 2001); and Rob Frieden, *International Telecommunications Handbook* (Norwood, MA: Artech, 1996).

[72] See International Telecommunication Union, Informal Expert Group on International Settlements, 'The Cost of International Telephone Calls', www.itu.ch/intset/dot/dot.htm (reporting that the per minute cost for routing an international telephone call via an INTELSAT satellite including operating expenses is US$0.02 and that factoring all switching, routing, interconnection and administrative costs, including licence fees, advertising and taxes, 'the average per minute cost of an international call is probably around $0.25'.

savings may not be the same for nations lacking the traffic volumes and funds available to support new technologies having lower per-unit costs. However, absent competitive or regulatory pressure to reduce accounting rates and retail collection charges to levels commensurate with such lower costs, carriers that terminate more calls than they originate want to maintain the *status quo*. Accordingly, accounting rates continue to overstate cost and overcompensate some operators:

> The pace in introducing competition in international telecommunication markets and the reform of these markets is slow, and there is an apparent reluctance in many cases by governments to accelerate reform in this area. It therefore cannot be expected that significant changes in prices (collection charges) and accounting rates will take place given present attitudes and policy frameworks.[73]

In the absence of competitive necessity, an aggressive campaign by regulators in sufficient numbers, or widespread use of Internet telephony and other arbitrage tactics, many carriers continue to benefit from traffic retardation strategies that reduce outbound calling and expand asymmetry between inbound and outbound traffic volumes.[74] For some nations,

Using a total service long-run incremental cost methodology, which factors in a reasonable contribution to common costs, the FCC established 'upper end settlement rate benchmarks of 15.4 cents for carriers in upper income nations; 19.1 cents for carriers in middle income nations; and 23.4 cents for carriers is lower income countries. See 1996 International Settlement Policy Rulemaking para. 47. The FCC proposed a 9–22 cents upper range for benchmark settlement rates for carriers in upper income nations; 12–26 cents for carriers in middle income nations; and 13–33 cents for carriers in lower income nations. *Ibid.*, 48 para. In its 1997 International Settlement Policy Order, the FCC responded to foreign carrier and government opposition to its proposed timetable by creating a fourth income category and by extending the transition period. The FCC established the following benchmarks and timetables for compliance: US-licensed carriers operating on routes to upper income countries have one year from the effective date of the Order (i.e. until 1 January 1999) to reach the applicable benchmark rate of 15 cents with carriers in upper income countries. US-licensed carriers have two years, (i.e. until 1 January 2000) to reach the applicable rate of 19 cents with upper middle income countries, and three years (i.e. until 1 January 2001) to reach the same rate with lower middle income countries. They have four years (i.e. until 1 January 2002) to reach the applicable 23 cents rate with low income countries, and an additional year (i.e. until 1 January 2003) to do so with countries with a telephone line penetration rate (teledensity) of less than one.

73 1997 OECD Accounting Rate Study, note 66 above, p. 6.

74 Many international carriers have objected to the FCC's campaign to reduce international accounting rate tactics on fairness and jurisdictional grounds. However, an appellate court has ruled that the FCC's settlement rate prescription did not violate domestic or international law, nor did it impose its jurisdiction extraterritorially. See *Cable and Wireless plc* v. *FCC*, 166 F. 3d 1224 (DC Cir. 1999).

purposefully high accounting rates and commensurately high collection charges accrue financial dividends by reducing the volume of outbound traffic that otherwise would offset at least a portion of the settlement surplus. Even as they may reduce some high-profit operator-assisted outbound international calls, callback and other call-reorigination services[75] increase the volume of inbound calls, at least some of which trigger an accounting rate settlement.[76] For nations requiring carriers to route return traffic proportionate with what they received inbound,[77] carriers from other nations with more outbound traffic than inbound traffic face the potential for expanding settlement deficits if outbound calling continues to grow even as demographic characteristics or regulatory policies elsewhere continue to dampen demand for inbound calling. Carriers with inbound traffic surpluses typically operate in small and developing countries, but others operate in nations that appear to have a strategy of deliberately maintaining high accounting and collection rates.[78]

Outbound international call retardation strategies create pent-up demand and stimulate accounting rate and collection arbitrage opportunities and incentives by users and entrepreneurial carriers[79] to find ways to route traffic that reverse the accounting rate settlement, or avoid

[75] '[C]ountry direct benefits US [and other] consumers but inflates the settlements deficit by converting foreign-originated traffic into US-billed calls.' Accounting Rate Policy Statement, para. 2.

[76] 'The traditional settlement rate system assumes that a customer's physical location determines the place of origin of an international call, with the carrier in the originating country paying a settlement rate to the carrier in the terminating country. However, service innovations such as call-back allow customers to change the originating country for settlement purposes. The result is that many more calls are originated for settlement purposes from countries like the United States with vigorous retail and wholesale markets than in monopoly markets that lack similar competition. These traffic routing patterns will only be exacerbated as countries implement their market access commitments under the WTO Basic Telecom Agreement.' 1997 Accounting Rate Report and Order, para. 12. Callback operators look for opportunities to reduce accounting rate exposure, through refile, and to avoid them entirely by routing traffic via private lines that 'leak' into the PSTN.

[77] For nations with large populations, high gross domestic products, large expatriate and immigrant communities and multiple facilities-based carriers, e.g. the US, operators may have collection rates at levels below one-half of the accounting rate. Such carriers expect to recoup outbound traffic losses with inbound traffic subject to an accounting rate settlement that would overcompensate the carrier for terminating the call.

[78] A thriving international 'dial-a-porn' industry has developed in such diverse and unpredicted places as Guyana, Russia and Tuvalu in part because operators can tap into a share of comparatively higher accounting rates well above the FCC's settlement rate prescription.

[79] Many facilities-based carriers offer services with lower per minute charges than conventional, International Direct Distance dialing. While such carriers do not want to cannibalise high-margin services, they recognise the need to compete with callback operators.

triggering one entirely. A settlement surplus generates a source of hard currency for telecommunications infrastructure development, and such transfer payments from users in developed nations to carriers in developing ones that can enhance consumer welfare and promote networking externalities. On the other hand, no guarantees exist that only developing countries will pursue an outbound call-retardation strategy, or that beneficiaries of settlement surpluses will use the funds for infrastructure development as opposed to funding the general treasury or stock dividends. Likewise, reduced outbound international calling may retard trade and industry and the integration of a nation regionally and globally.

The Internet has evolved into a vibrant medium for communications, entertainment, education and commerce. One of the primary drivers for the growing consumer reliance on Internet-mediation involves the ability of the Internet to offer instant 'real time' delivery of digital packets in addition to the store-and-forward, non-real-time delivery of packets in applications like electronic mail. Real-time 'streaming' of information packets means that the Internet can serve as a medium for audio and video programming and also for telephone services.

In the accelerated pace of product and service life cycles common to the Internet, telephone type services have quickly evolved from an awkward personal-computer-mediated curiosity to a commercial service available not just from computers, but from conventional telephones as well. Internet telephony has the potential to serve as a major threat to the international accounting rate regime and possibly as well to how telecommunication carriers price retail long-distance services for two primary reasons:

1. the Internet architecture provides for efficient facilities loading including the ability of telecommunications networks dedicated to data services to handle voice traffic at near zero cost, absent congestion; and
2. regulatory policies throughout the world largely exempt providers of Internet services from having to subject their traffic to accounting rate settlements and from having to pay the interconnection charges and contributions to universal telecommunications service funding imposed on telecommunications carriers.

Internet telephony constitutes a formidable vehicle for compressing telecommunication carrier margins on telephone services. ISPs can easily add telephony traffic onto their data lines, and technological innovations provide ways to inject Internet voice traffic into the PSTN for the 'last mile' delivery to call recipients. Given the large difference between the costs incurred by ISPs in providing Internet telephony and the retail charges for conventional telephone services, especially international rates, ISPs can profit handsomely by pricing services well below the pre-existing retail toll charge. This exploitation of a wide pricing differential constitutes a type of arbitrage as the ISP can make a business case for delivering services to consumers at significantly lower costs. ISPs have plenty of margin with which to work, i.e. the difference between its actual costs and the imputed cost established by route-specific accounting rates based on conventional telephony.

Technology provides arbitrage opportunities

Internet telephony uses the digital, packet-switched nature of the Internet along with its routing and addressing standards to provide real-time audio conferencing.[80] Internet switching and routing technology manages the transmission and processing of text, graphics, data, audio and video. The Internet's TCP/IP protocol[81] provides a standard vehicle for subdividing content, e.g. a voice conversation, into a stream of packets that are routed via any available path between the sender and intended call recipient. Each packet has space reserved for destination information so that intermediary routing facilities can read 'header' data to determine how and where to send the packets onward towards their intended destination. Headers include a sequence of digits that correspond to an Internet address, much like the numbering sequence in direct distance dialing via telephone.

Packet switching efficiently uses available switching and routing capacity. Likewise, it can operate despite outages, blockages and busy

[80] For a helpful, non-technical introduction to Internet telephony, see The Internet Telephony Consortium, 'Frequently Asked Questions: How Can I Use the Internet as a Telephone?', available at: http://itel.mit.edu/voice_faq.html.

[81] 'The common denominator for e-mail communications is the use of a standard programming protocol, TCP/IP – transmission Control Protocol/Internet Protocol – upon which inter-computer communications are based. The TCP protocol divides messages into packets which are marked with a sequence number and the address of the recipient. TCP also inserts error control information. The packets are then sent over the network to the addressee. The routing of the individual packets varies, with IP controlling the transport of the packets to the remote host computer. At the remote host, TCP receives the packets and checks for errors. When an error occurs, TCP asks for the particular packet to be resent. Once all the packets have been received, TCP will then use the sequence number to reconstruct the original message. It is the job of IP to get the packets from one place to another; it is the job of TCP to manage the flow and ensure that the data are correct.' Richard Allan Horning, 'Has Hal Signed a Contract: The Statute of Frauds in Cyberspace', *Santa Clara Computer and High Technology Law Journal* 12 (1996): 253 at 258.

conditions, because the Internet Protocol addressing scheme makes it possible to make multiple efforts to route traffic onward in the event that initial efforts fail. Resending misdelivered or unreceived packets and routing them via different and possibly circuitous links requires software processing to reassemble the packets in their proper order. For traffic and services that do not require immediate, real-time delivery, e.g. electronic mail, possible delays and reassembly present little problem. However, Internet telephony requires immediate, real-time delivery of the packets in their proper order. Any delay, loss or improper sequencing of packets will result in distortion, or the temporary loss of the audio stream.

Heretofore, Internet telephony has lacked the quality, reliability and security to be considered comparable to conventional telephone services. Traditional telephone services use circuit switching that sets up a dedicated link between call originator and call recipient. This technology provides high-quality service and reliability, because of the existence of a dedicated pathway, as opposed to the virtual, 'on the fly' links provided via the Internet. A dedicated pathway may be technologically wasteful in the sense that switching, routing and transmission capacity lies dormant during pauses in a conversation. Packet switching technology efficiently fills in gaps with other traffic so that traffic may traverse different routes and arrive at different times in getting to the same destination. In circuit switching all parts of a traffic stream traverse the same pathway, providing greater quality assurance.

What Internet telephony lacks in quality of service and reliability it makes up for in lower costs and the ability to narrow the gap between carriers' costs and retail charges. However, some users may care more about reliability of service and less about savings. Currently, Internet traffic cannot be easily classified by priority of service or by type of application. Best efforts routing of traffic may not provide the security, safety and reliability a user may require. For those willing to take the qualitative risk, the financial savings are significant. However Internet telephony consumers have to incur some initial, upfront costs. Unlike conventional telephone service, the cheapest types of Internet-mediated telephony require a significant initial capital outlay of about US$2,000 for a personal computer, modem, sound card, speakers, microphone, software and Internet access. Conventional telephone services use an inexpensive, 'dumb' terminal, the telephone handset, but users incur per-minute charges that can exceed US$1.00 per minute for many international destinations. Internet telephony provided on a conventional dial-up basis, e.g. a toll-free access number, requires an ISP to install devices that can convert circuit switched telephone traffic into packets and *vice versa*. Additionally, these devices must provide a routing function, using the Internet Protocol to bring traffic to a facility, commonly referred to as a point of presence, in the vicinity of the call recipient.

Financial and regulatory arbitrage and the potential impact on telecommunications pricing

Internet telephony provides profitable opportunities for incumbents and newcomers alike to offer services functionally equivalent to conventional telephony, but treated in a manner that subjects the service to little or no regulation and accrues lower operational costs. Entrepreneurs savour the opportunity to exploit financial and regulatory anomalies and asymmetries in telecommunications, e.g. the ability to lease private lines, link them with the PSTN and offer a long-distance telephone service to individual consumers who otherwise would not qualify for the bulk discounts offered previously only to high-volume private line users.

Internet telephony has the potential to migrate traffic from conventional telecommunications networks. Incumbent carriers surely do not want to encourage such a migration as it will create downward pressure on all telephone toll rates and cannibalise retail rates. On the other hand, incumbent carriers will probably determine that they are financially better off providing the transmission capacity for Internet telephony, albeit at lower margins, than if they lose customers' traffic entirely. The massive increase in domestic and international broadband telecommunication capacity reflects the view that carriers can make up in volume what they will lose in margin.

The problems in regulatory asymmetry

Any regulatory regime applied exclusively to Internet applications runs the risk of creating a dichotomy in regulatory rights and responsibilities between providers of functionally equivalent services. Many of the services available via the Internet provide a faster, better, cheaper and smarter evolution of pre-existing services. The Internet provides a convenient, user-friendly medium for acquiring news and entertainment and for engaging in all sorts of commercial transactions. A bias or intention not to regulate, or to regulate lightly such activities may contrast significantly with a pre-existing and more intrusive regulatory model. Governments should not automatically extend the application of legacy regulatory regimes[82] to Internet-mediated equivalent services. Nor should governments deregulate incumbent services simply because Internet options have become available, and governments have opted to apply a different and probably less burdensome regulatory regime to Internet services.

The onset of Internet-mediated services does present a regulatory challenge to governments, particularly those disinclined to treat Internet-mediated services as equivalents to services transmitted and delivered via traditional media. The juxtaposition of different regulatory regimes typically also creates an asymmetry that has the potential for tilting the competitive playing field in favour of the less regulated service. To the extent regulation can impose financial and operational burdens, the service provider subject to greater regulation typically suffers a competitive disadvantage *vis-à-vis* the less regulated operator. Governments should generate compelling justifications for establishing different regulatory regimes in view of the potential for such asymmetry to impact the marketplace attractiveness of one service *vis-à-vis* others.

Regulatory dichotomies work best when technological categories remain discrete and absolute. But they surely do not work when technological convergence results in porous service categories and diversification by operators. When cable telephone and ISPs offer telephone services functionally similar to that available from telephone companies, regulators may not be able to maintain pre-existing dichotomies. Heretofore, government regulators have assumed that incumbent telephone service providers have dominant market shares, should operate as common carriers, and should offer the best technologies and wherewithal to achieve universal service goals. Government regulators typically assume that market entrants like ISPs, other enhanced service providers and resellers of basic transmission capacity do not have the potential to acquire a dominant market share, or that they offer ancillary, non-common carrier services. While incumbent telephone companies incur significant financial duties to serve costly remote areas, the newcomers enjoy exemptions from having to pay charges for accessing the PSTN and from contributing to

[82] 'New technologies, while perhaps similar in appearance or in functionality, should not be stuffed into what may be ill-fitting regulatory categories in the name of regulation. Rather, the Commission should continue the approach of studying new technologies and only stepping in where the purpose for which the Commission was created, protecting the public interest, demands it.' Jason Oxman, 'The FCC and the Unregulation of the Internet', Federal Communications Commission, Office of Plans and Policies, OPP Working Paper No. 31, (1999) pp. 24–5, available at www.fcc.gov/opp/workingp.html.

universal service funding. These ventures qualified for such exemptions on the grounds that they did not offer a telephone service even though their offerings might require access to the PSTN.

When ISPs offer consumers telephone service equivalents, which link PSTN access with Internet-mediated telephony, pre-existing regulatory exemptions tilt the competitive playing field to their advantage. Should significant telephony traffic volumes migrate to routings exempt from a universal service contribution requirement, the sum of funds available to achieve the universal service mission will decline. The potential for declining universal service funds occurs just as many governments have articulated a broader and more ambitious universal service mission for all citizens to have access to both basic telephone service *and* advanced Internet services.

Conclusion

Most national regulators have prudently refrained from extending 'legacy' regulation to new technologies and services that may resemble something offered by incumbents. Certainly, regulation can drag and thwart marketplace development, and conversely regulatory forbearance can incubate and nature new technologies and services. However, at some point, newcomers may develop market share and services functionally equivalent to what incumbents offer, but without incurring anything like the regulatory burdens incumbents bear. At this point, regulatory asymmetry provides for less marketplace incubation and more marketplace distortion.

The private carrier, enhanced service provider, and interstate service classification each provided exemptions from more costly and intrusive regulatory classifications in the United States. But regulatory arbitrageurs came to understand that qualifying for these classifications provided 'back door' opportunities to acquire market share and profits. It appears that the FCC has emphasised the potential, but no guarantee that private carriers, CLEC affiliates of ISPs, callback operators and Internet telephony providers will provide both service diversity and financial savings to consumers. Yet the FCC does not assess whether these operators might have generated more consumer welfare enhancements if they had been forced to comply with legacy regulations and been motivated to join with incumbents to streamline or reduce them.

Conferring too comfortable an unregulated niche or financial windfall eliminates the incentive for ventures to innovate, become facilities-based operators and diversify. Unless and until an arbitrage opportunity closes, resellers, callback operators and Internet telephony vendors can possibly do better by conserving capital and not investing heavily in facilities and by not developing other indicia of similarity with incumbents lest they lose a regulatory-conferred competitive advantage.

Likewise, the trade policy-making apparatus appears to have conferred regulatory arbitrage opportunities for Internet ventures. Ventures can provide cable television or Internet-mediated audio-visual services without triggering the market access limitations applicable to broadcasters, satellite carriers and cinema operators. Similarly, ventures which can offer limited basic services but characterise them as value-added services which typically have greater market access opportunities.

At some point, national regulators and international trade policy-making forums unwittingly tilt the competitive playing field in favour of players clever enough to craft a service definition that permits aggressive competition with incumbent services, but which qualifies the clever player for a host of arbitrary and anomalous loopholes that exempt or reduce the cost and inconvenience in regulatory compliance, or market access limitations. Incumbents may suffer simply because of the legacy regulations that continue to apply rather than because they have greater market share, and the real or perceived ability to exploit a bottleneck or handicap market entrants with price squeezes.[83]

Both telecommunications and trade policy-making forums have to confront the consequences of ICE convergence. They cannot rely on service definitions based on static or historical assumptions about what technology can do. They must devise technology-neutral classifications and recognise that technological and marketplace convergence integrates content and conduit. Technology neutrality examines the nature of the service without regard to the medium or mode of delivery.

[83] In a price-squeeze situation, a vertically integrated firm with market power over an essential upstream input raises the price of this input to rivals competing in downstream retail markets. The increased cost of this essential input forces downstream rivals to raise their retail prices. The vertically integrated firm is then in a position to undercut the downstream rivals in retail markets and thereby increase market share and profits. See Michael Kende, 'The Digital Handshake: Connecting Internet Backbones', FCC, Office of Plans and Policy, Working Paper No. 32, 2000, p. 23, www.fcc.gov/opp/workingp.html. See also *United States* v. *Aluminum Co. of America*, 148 F. 2d 416 at 437–8 (2nd Cir. 1945) (articulating a four-part test for price squeeze: (1) a firm has monopoly power with respect to one product; (2) its price for that product is higher than a 'fair price'; (3) that product is required to compete in a second market where the monopolist itself competes; and (4) the monopolist's price in the second market is so low that competitor's cannot match it and still earn a 'living profit').

This model has the potential for expanding the reach of regulation, but offers greater consistency and rationality. Regulatory expansion might occur if cultural concerns led nations to expand audio-visual restrictions to cable television and Internet-mediated services. But greater consistency and rationality occurs when regulators concentrate on the effect and impact on consumers and the scope of competition without regard to the medium or technology used to access consumers and penetrate markets.

The European Union has embraced a technology-neutral, horizontal approach to telecommunications regulation in response to technological and marketplace convergence:

> Regulation needs to be transparent, clear and proportional and distinguish between transport (transmission of signals) and content. This implies a more horizontal approach to regulation with a homogeneous treatment of all transport network infrastructure and associated services, irrespective of the nature of the services carried. A balanced solution as to how public broadcasting can be best integrated into the new environment is needed.[84]

[84] European Commission, Results of the Public Consultation on the Green Paper on the Convergence of the Telecommunications, Media and Information Technology Sectors, Press Release, IP/99/164 (released 10 March 1999), http://europa.eu.int/ISPO/convergencegp/ip164en.html; see also Communication to the European Parliament, the Council, the Economic and Social Committee and the Committee of the Regions, The Convergence of the Telecommunications, Media and Information Technology Sectors, and the Implications for Regulation, Results of the Public Consultation on the Green Paper [COM(97)623], COM(1999)108 final (10 March 1999), http://europa.eu.int/ISPO/convergencegp/com(99)108/com(99)108enfinal.html; Green Paper on the Convergence of the Telecommunications, Media and Information Technology Sectors, and the Implications for Regulation. Towards an Information Society Approach, IP/97/1073 (released 3 December 1997).

13

Audio-visual and telecommunications services: a review of definitions under WTO law

P. L. G. NIHOUL

Introduction

This paper aims at reviewing the definitions given to the concept of telecommunications and audio-visual services in WTO instruments. In a first section, I will identify the instruments which contain useful information to address the issue. I will then analyse the content of the definitions (second section). In the third section, I will attempt to confront these definitions with developments in the markets. The issue is indeed to determine whether the definitions that may be found do correspond with the trend that is currently unfolding, and lead to a new information society industry where boundaries between traditional sectors (telecom, audio-visual, information) fade away.

Audio-visual and telecommunications services

Why make a distinction?

The first question to be asked is probably why a distinction should be made, on a legal basis, between audio-visual and telecommunications. Does the distinction really matter or is it purely theoretical with relevance for academics only? The answer should be straightforward. Dividing services into audio-visual and telecommunications is essential as it determines the legal regime that will apply to the activities.

Both activities are admittedly submitted to the General Agreement on Trade in Services (GATS). However, the GATS does not have as a consequence that all markets for services are suddenly and automatically open to world trade without any restriction. In practice, Members are invited to draft commitments, i.e. designate which markets they wish to open to foreign competition. They also have the possibility to put forward demands for exemptions that allow them to maintain some control on how and to what extent borders will effectively be opened.

Telecommunications is one of the sectors that WTO Members have agreed to open to world trade. States have agreed that the markets relating to these activities should be liberalised. Commitments have been taken by these states in the course of WTO negotiations, in order to dismantle trade barriers in that sector.[1]

A different scenario has unfolded in the audio-visual sector.[2] The idea of opening national borders to world trade in the audio-visual sector was already the subject of much debate at the beginning of the twentieth century. At that time, a number of countries wished to protect their audio-visual industry, and possibly their culture as a whole, against foreign influences. To that effect they imposed high tariffs on audio-visual imports. They also resorted to quotas, and decided that only a limited portion of the existing market could be served by foreign businesses. The question was addressed in the Havana Charter for an International Trade Organization, where it was admitted that ITO Members would be permitted to reserve a fixed share of airtime on domestic screens for domestically produced films. Other forms of discrimination were to disappear.

That attitude was maintained in the negotiations that led to the General Agreement on Tariffs and Trade (GATT) (1947). Some participants insisted that motion pictures should be exempted from the national treatment obligation that constituted a pillar of the GATT. As a result of this demand, a clause was inserted in Article IV of the GATT, whereby the establishment and maintenance of film screen quotas were specifically permitted. The purpose was to guarantee that a minimum percentage of total screen time would be allotted to films of national origin.[3]

The United States has never been happy with that situation. First, the United States has a strong audio-visual sector and would like to

[1] As of November 1998, sixty-nine WTO Members had included telecommunications services in their Schedules of commitments. The number has since increased, as more states completed the process of accession to the WTO.

[2] 'Audio-visual' and 'broadcasting' are often used as synonyms. We will see, however, that different meanings have to be given to these expressions.

[3] This exception is also recognised in Article III:10 of the GATT, which concerns the national treatment obligation.

see this industry develop further by selling its productions abroad. The entertainment industry constitutes an important mechanism for economic growth in general, particularly in the United States. Secondly, audio-visual services often provide a useful 'advertising' mechanism. I am not referring here to 'commercials' that are transmitted during television programmes. References are often made to specific goods, products or brands as part of audio-visual productions. Cars, for instance, are displayed in films. This can be considered a form of commercial communication. To that extent, for a country like the United States, selling audio-visual programmes abroad can be a powerful means to promote national products and services. Thirdly, audio-visual services do not only have a commercial impact: they also have a cultural and, to some extent, political value. They convey values and messages about the way of life in that country. Given the influence images and sound can have on people, audio-visual services appear in that respect to provide an interesting channel to disseminate a national way of life around the world.

It therefore comes as no surprise that the United States consistently asked that the audio-visual sector be treated like other sectors. However, this demand faced continuous resistance from other GATT Members, including the European Union. The result was that, at the end of the Uruguay Round, only thirteen countries adopted commitments in the audio-visual sector. As a result of accessions, the number of Members making commitments in this sector has risen to nineteen – but this still remains far below the level of market opening that has been reached in other parts of the economy.

Conclusion: a difference in legal regimes

A substantial difference therefore exists between audio-visual and telecommunications services under the WTO agreements. Many countries have agreed to include telecommunications in the sectors they wish to open to foreign competition. By contrast, only a few have agreed to do the same with respect to audio-visual or broadcasting services. The consequences of this divergence are wide-ranging for businesses. Telecom operators are generally allowed to perform services on other countries' territories. The same is rarely true for undertakings engaged in audio-visual activities. Such undertakings may be prohibited entry to foreign territory, and have no remedy other than those available at national level.

Definition given to telecommunications services

Generic definition

On the basis of these various instruments, how can we define telecommunications services? Telecommunications are generically defined in the Annex on Telecommunications. Pursuant to that instrument, the term refers to the transmission of signals. The transmission must occur electronically.

> For the purposes of this Annex . . . '[t]elecommunications' means the transmission and reception of signals by any electromagnetic means.[4]

Additional information may be found in the same Annex in a discussion concerning the notion of 'public telecommunications transport service'. Telecommunications are there described as:

> typically involving the real-time transmission of customer-supplied information between two or more points without any end-to-end change in the form or content of the customer's information.[5]

Basic and value-added telecommunications[6]

Information useful for a definition is also provided in the distinction between basic telecommunications and value-added telecommunications that appears in these instruments.

[4] Annex on Telecommunications, para. 3(a).
[5] *Ibid.*, para. 3(b).
[6] The definitions are operational: they serve as tools which Members agree upon without going into much detail. The aim was to identify the markets for which Members would submit Schedules of commitments. The breakdown in two categories (basic versus value-added) does not reflect any specific national practice. It corresponds to a certain period in the history of telecom liberalisation: the distinction was useful as basic telecommunications were reserved to national monopolies while value-added services were already opened to competition. The distinction provided a useful criterion to determine what activities were subject to limited liberalisation. In the meantime, monopolies have been progressively dismantled in many countries. As a result, the distinction has lost some of its relevance. This trend will continue, as audio-visual, broadcasting and telecommunications converge. That aspect will be examined below.

Basic telecommunications[7] are defined in the Ministerial Decision on Negotiations on Basic Telecommunications (hereinafter 'Ministerial Decision') as 'telecommunications transport networks and services'.[8] In that expression, the notion of 'transport' plays an essential role. As defined in that expression, basic telecommunications transmits information. In principle, there is no contribution whatsoever, in that process, in the production, nor the transformation of such information. From that perspective, telecommunication is a purely mechanical device. Information is transported from one point to another, without modification of its content.[9]

By contrast, value-added telecommunications encompass all activities whereby an additional service is provided to the client. Suppliers do not limit their service to the transmission of information. They provide additional assistance, e.g. by enhancing form or content or by providing storage and retrieval facilities. Specific examples of value-added telecommunications will be provided later in the course of this paper.

Basic telecommunications were provided in most Members on a public monopoly basis at the time of the Uruguay Round. As a result, Members were reluctant to open up these activities to foreign competition. To do so would have resulted in a loss of revenue, as public monopolies are seldom competing on favourable terms with rivals. The appearance and development of competitors would also have implied a loss of control Members formerly exercised over an important sector of the economy. That situation led Members to view with disfavour the inclusion of basic telecommunications in the commitments put forward during the Uruguay Round. Negotiations were continued after the Uruguay Round, and eventually Members came to the conclusion that a liberalisation process would

7 These services were, and still are, to a certain extent, provided on the territory of Members by monopolies. For that reason, and also for reasons relating to the strategic importance of telecommunications, Members were reluctant to open their markets to foreign competition. Given these difficulties, special negotiations have taken place, the aim of which was to tackle this issue separately, and to see how far Members would accept liberalising their markets. As a result of these negotiations, commitments were signed by a majority of the Members. They were gathered in the Fourth Protocol to the GATS.

8 Para. 1. This definition has a legal force, as the Ministerial Decision is referred to in the Fourth Protocol. The latter introduces the agreement reached by the signatories, 'having carried out negotiations under the terms of the Ministerial Decision'.

9 The definition is reflected in several other WTO informal documents. For instance, a definition in similar terms may be found on the WTO website. Pursuant to that definition, telecommunications '*involve end-to-end transmission of customer supplied information*'. They '*simply relay voice or data from the sender to the receiver*'.

Table 13.1 *Comparison of the elements of the definitions of 'basic' and 'value-added' telecommunications*

Basic telecommunications	Value-added telecommunications
End-to-end transmission of customer-supplied information.	Services in which suppliers do more than convey information. Value is added, e.g., by enhancing the content or the form of information. Other facilities may also be provided, such as storage and retrieval.
As they were reserved to public monopolies, Members were reluctant to include them in the Uruguay Round.	These services provided from the outset by private firms in a competitive environment. There was thus little difficulty in including them in the commitments laid down during the Uruguay Round.
Subsequent specific negotiations were carried out; they resulted in the adoption of the Fourth Protocol to the GATS.	Already included in the commitments as a result of the Uruguay Round and the accession of new WTO Members.

result in better and cheaper services for everybody in the basic telecommunications markets.

By contrast, value-added telecommunications were provided from the outset by private undertakings operating in a competitive environment. Value-added services encompass services based on new technologies requiring high investments. As they lacked the necessary resources and expertise, public monopolies were not in a position to enter these markets. In addition, value-added services were not considered by Members as fundamental to society. They were not therefore included in the tasks entrusted to the public monopolies. As a result, it was easier for Members to accept from the start that these value-added services should be opened up to competition. For that reason, such services were included from the start of negotiations in the Schedules of commitments drafted by numerous Members. These commitments were annexed to the GATS at the end of the Uruguay Round.[10]

[10] The division of telecommunications in these two categories is particularly important in the US context, in order to establish the authority of the Federal Communications Commission (FCC). It has less relevance in other parts of the world, including Europe.

Types of telecommunications services

Classification of services

What kinds of activity are covered by the concept of 'telecommunications service'? A 'Services Sectoral Classification List' (hereinafter 'Classification List') was elaborated by the WTO, in application of the GATS.[11] Information can be gathered on telecom services by scrutinising what activities fall under 'communications'. The Classification List contains twelve categories, with communications coming in second position:

1. Business services
2. Communications services
3. Construction and related engineering services
4. Distribution services
5. Educational services
6. Environmental services
7. Financial services
8. Health-related and social services
9. Tourism and travel-related services
10. Recreational, cultural and sporting services
11. Transport services
12. Other services not included elsewhere

Services falling under 'communications'

The category 'Communications Services' is in turn divided into fifteen sections. These sections are enumerated and examined in the following paragraphs. Among them, seven correspond to basic telecommunications, and the remaining eight are associated with value-added telecommunications.[12]

Basic telecommunications

(a) voice telephone services
(b) packet-switched data transmission services

[11] MTN.GNS/W/120. See Note by the Secretariat, Services Sectoral Classification List, 10 July 1991. The document is available at www.wto.org/english/tratop_e/serv_e/22-specm_e.htm.

[12] The breakdown into these two categories does not appear in the official classification. As noted earlier, it is an operational definition that has been introduced by Members as a tool for further negotiation on basic services.

(c) circuit-switched data transmission services
(d) telex services
(e) telegraph services
(f) facsimile services
(g) private leased circuit services

Value-added telecommunications

(h) electronic mail
(i) voice mail
(j) online information and database retrieval
(k) electronic data interchange
(l) enhanced/value-added facsimile services, including store and forward, store and retrieve
(m) code and protocol conversion
(n) online information and/or data processing (including transaction processing)
(o) other

How to interpret these notions?

These fifteen subdivisions are examined in the following paragraphs, in an attempt to identify what services qualify as telecommunications. Unfortunately, the terms appearing in the Classification List are not defined anywhere in official WTO instruments. In the absence of an official definition, we must resort to other tools in order to interpret them, such as WTO documents,[13] United Nations Provisional Central Product Classification

[13] Apart from legally binding instruments, the WTO organs produce documents that are not signed by Members but circulate within the Secretariat. Legally, these documents do not have a binding force. However, they express positions or interpretations that are presented as a common understanding by the WTO's administration. One can assume that this understanding is accepted by Members, or at least by a majority of them. Absent acceptance, such Members would demand that formulations be taken away where these were not acceptable to them. This reasoning is particularly true for notes made available on the WTO website, www.wto.org. These notes can be freely downloaded. They thus form an intellectual background on the basis of which people may understand WTO instruments and positions.

(UNCPC),[14] documents produced by delegations,[15] US and European positions[16] and private sources.[17]

[14] The United Nations drafted a classification of products and services (Statistical Papers, Series M, No. 77, 1991). This classification is used for various purposes, for instance determining what markets are affected by negotiations. It was not used, however, as a definitive classification during trade negotiations on telecommunications. Instead, the classification annexed to the GATS was used as the main reference document, as far as services were concerned. The correspondence between both classifications is indeed far from perfect. For example, the GATS subsector 2.C.a, 'Voice telephone services', is cross-referenced to UNCPC item 7521 which refers to 'public telephone services'. The GATS category thus covers public and non-public telephony, whereas only public telephony is included in the UN classification. For other critiques, see Council for Trade in Services, Telecommunications Services, Background Note by the Secretariat, S/C/W/74, 8 December 1998, p. 3, para. 7.

[15] In the absence of an official collective interpretation, it may be useful to return to the statements made by national delegations. Most of them provide explanations when they present their offer (Schedule of commitments and/or List of exemptions). Communications made by delegations during the negotiations on basic telecommunications are included on the WTO website at www.wto.org/english/tratop_e/serv_e/telecom_e/telecom_e.html. These communications sometimes contain useful information as to how a concept should be defined. Examples will be given below.

[16] In theory, communications presented by delegations have equal value irrespective of the identity of the country issuing them. These are merely positions adopted by one or several parties and do not bind any other Member. In practice, however, some delegations are in a position to influence the emergence of a collective interpretation. These delegations are often those whose legal concepts have been developed to designate and regulate services in the telecom and audio-visual sectors. As these concepts already exist, and a legal doctrine has been built around them, these delegations have the necessary background to impose their positions or interpretations on other Members. These delegations are those which have developed the greatest expertise in international negotiations. They often have considerable resources to train and inform their diplomats. As a result, they are in a position to build up convincing arguments. Among them are the delegations of the United States and the European Union. The US and Europe have legal systems in which new technologies have been carefully defined, and their legal implications worked out. For Europe, definitions may be found in various directives adopted by the Commission, the Council and the Parliament. These directives may be found at www.europa.eu.int/information_society/topics/telecoms/index_en.htm. For the United States, definitions may be found in various Acts, including the Telecommunications Act of 1996, the Communications Act of 1934 (as amended) as well as Title 47 of the Code of Federal Regulation.

[17] Academic literature may also be used in order to interpret notions appearing in the Classification List. Private definitions of course lack political force or dimension. They cannot be forced on any party during a dispute. No one is obliged to accept a definition given by a private body. In that sense, the definitions provided by such bodies do not have the same weight as those attached to formulations found in WTO documents or in proposals made by delegations. Private sources, however, provide useful tools. They mirror the understanding on which the technical community is based. They also shape knowledge within society. Finally, they can be resorted to as a neutral (i.e. not politically tainted, or strategy-biased) source, to provide a common ground for negotiation or dispute settlement.

Voice-related services

Voice-related services are given an important place in the Classification List. Voice telephone services are presented as the first item in the list of basic telecommunications. Theses services consist in the transmission of conversation between people.[18] Voice mail – another service related to voice telephony – appears in the second place in the list for value-added telecommunications.[19]

Text transmission services

Another group of services relate to text transmissions. Telex services consist in the transmission of text from a sender to a receiver. They require special equipment for both participants. Telegraphy implies the transmission of written messages, in the form of sounds. The message is composed of written signs (letters). These letters are given a code, in the form of a succession of sounds. The coding and decoding activities require human intervention.[20] As with telegraphy, facsimile services imply the transmission of written messages to a receiver. The code is, however, not made up of a succession of short and long sounds as in telegraphy. A more complex technology is used, thereby making it possible to transmit images in addition to text.[21]

These various text transmission services are bound to progressively disappear. Their functions have been progressively taken over by other services, which have become more widely available. A vast number of

[18] The definition given above corresponds with those given in European Union law (Voice telephony). They also correspond with US definitions (telephony) 'A form of telecommunication set up for the transmission of speech or, in some cases, other sounds' (47 Code of Federal Regulations 2.1, 21.2).

[19] The qualification as value-added, rather than basic, is not important for our discussion. It refers to the fact that the service cannot be reduced to a mere transmission of conversation. The service implies recording a voice message left by a correspondent, storing it and reacting to it.

[20] US law provides: 'A form of telecommunication which is concerned in any process providing transmission and reproduction at a distance of documentary matter, such as written or printed matters or fixed images, or the reproduction at a distance of any kind of information in such a form. For the purposes of the [International] Radio Regulations, unless otherwise specified therein, telegraphy shall mean a form of telecommunication for the transmission of written matter by the use of a signal code' (47 CFR 2.1).

[21] US law provides: 'A form of telegraphy for the transmission of fixed images, with or without half-tones, with a view to their reproduction in a permanent form' (47 CFR 2.1). A telephone facsimile machine is defined as: 'Equipment which has the capacity (A) to transcribe text or images, or both, from paper into an electronic signal and to transmit that signal over a regular telephone line, or (B) to transcribe text or images (or both) from an electronic signal received over a regular telephone line onto paper' (47 USC § 227).

people are now equipped with computers and have access to data transmission networks. This equipment is polyvalent. For instance, it makes it possible to transmit documents electronically. There is no longer any need to resort to dedicated and expensive equipment (a telex, a telegraph or a fax machine).

Data transmission services

Data transmission is referred to in several places in the Classification List. As used in the Classification List, the expression refers to activities consisting of the transmission of signs that are not made of voice, nor images. 'Data' is used to designate what is being transmitted, before it is encoded for transmission. In fact, the expression refers to electronic transmissions of documents.

As we will see, convergence causes a second meaning to be given to the expression. With digitisation, images, texts and sounds can be expressed using the same code. In that context, 'data transmission' plainly refers to all digital transmissions whatever the content (whether images, sounds or texts). I do not think that this second meaning is used in the Classification List. Data transmission would otherwise encompass all telecommunications, even broadcasting services.

Packet- and circuit-switched technology services

A distinction is made between packet- and circuit-switched transmissions (subdivisions (a) and (b) in the Classification List). The distinction refers to the technology that is used to ensure transmission. In the packet-based technology, data are divided into units that are sent separately to their destination. They will then be reconstituted by a decoder.[22] This technology allows for the use of the same circuit for several transmissions at the same time. The content of each transmission is sent in turn by packets on the circuit. The solution is very economical and allows for the efficient use of network resources. The circuit-based technology is more traditional. Here, data are sent to their destination as they are produced. A whole circuit must be reserved for each transmission, for the entire period of the transmission.

[22] 'A data communications service in which a data stream is divided into units called packets that are separately routed to a destination where the original message is then reconstituted' (see the glossary of terms at www.wto.org/english/tratop e/serve/telecom e/tel12 e.htm).

Purpose of the transmission

Other subdivisions of the Classification List refer to activities that can best be described in terms of function, or purpose. They do not refer merely to the nature of what is being conveyed. They in fact designate what the user intends to do with the network, the equipment and the software that are made available to them. These functions are more than mere transmissions. They require special software and equipment to allow applications to perform the intended services. These activities are as follows.

- electronic mail: sending messages comparable to letters one would traditionally send by post;
- electronic data interchange: allows for the easy exchange of data in a given community;
- code and protocol conversion: transferring data between various networks possibly resorting to different technologies and thereby making it necessary to convert signals from one technology to another;
- online information: allows for access to information through computers that are linked to a network. The classical online information service is the World Wide Web. This application allows computer users to view data made available by correspondents through the networks;
- data processing: using data for a specific purpose, for instance organising a transaction between a buyer and a seller.

Circuit leasing

Circuit leasing ordinarily refers to the situation of an infrastructure operator that rents to clients part of the network under its control. The part of the network in question may be licensed to firms that will make use of it available to the public, for example when the lessee provides electronic services to the public via the rented network. The may also be allocated to a private use. Many large undertakings ask network operators to use part of their infrastructure in order to constitute an intranet,[23] i.e. a network to be reserved for communications between designated

[23] The definition on the WTO website (note 22 above) provides: 'The service of providing permanent transmission connection between two customer premises for the exclusive use by a customer. This service may be provided over facilities owned or operated by an operator or over transmission capacity sold or leased by a non-facilities-based telecommunications provider, or reseller, and may use terrestrial or satellite facilities. It generally does not involve central office switching operations. They are also called privately leased lines.'

correspondents (most of the time the firm itself). Via such a contract, the client uses part of the public infrastructure for its own purposes.[24]

In fact, all network operators and service providers rent part of the infrastructure. Any firm, providing data, image or sound transmission provides clients with the possibility to use infrastructure for a limited period and for given uses.[25] The issue is to determine how the rental activity takes place – is it a wholesale or a retail activity? A further issue is to determine exactly what services are provided to the client: is it rental of pure capacity or are additional functions being made available to the client?[26]

Residual subdivision

The Classification List contains a residual subdivision designated as 'other'. It is difficult to determine what the content of that subdivision is exactly. No detail may be found on that point in WTO instruments. Some indications are, however, provided on the WTO Internet site. For instance, the site mentions 'paging' services.[27] That activity consists in the transmission of a signal to portable equipment. The purpose is to alert the person holding the equipment and ask her to contact the signal sender.[28]

[24] In that case, the portion of the rented infrastructure is securitised.

[25] For instance, two persons calling each other basically rent a portion of the network capacity, to which have been added software program and technical equipment to ensure the interactive communication of voice messages.

[26] In some cases, the network owner may simply rent circuits. These circuits will be equipped with material and software owned by the client renting the capacity. In other circumstances, equipment and software will be provided by the network owner. That is often the case where intranets ('networks meant for uses internal to the organisation') are made available for major clients. Alternatively, the rented capacity will be partly equipped by the network owner and partly by the service provider.

[27] The WTO website (note 22 above) defines this as: 'A service that allows transmitting a signal, usually only an alarm tone, via radio from any telephone . . . to a personal, portable receiving device in a defined operating area. More sophisticated systems provide audible or visual display messages.' US law provides: 'A one-way communications service from a base station to mobile or fixed receivers that provides signaling or information transfer by such means as tone, tone-voice, tactile, optical readout, etc.' (46 CFR 90.7). A pager is defined in the same regulation as: 'A small radio receiver designed to be carried by a person and to give an aural, visual or tactile indication when activated by the reception of a radio signal containing its specific code. It may also reproduce sounds and/or display messages that were also transmitted. Some pagers also transmit a radio signal acknowledging that a message has been received' (47 CFR 22.99).

[28] See the service mentioned as equivalent to facsimile services in the annex to the Background Note by the Secretariat, 'Telecommunications Services', Council for Trade in Services, S/C/W/74, 8 December 1998.

Distinctions based on geographical coverage, technology and the intended market

All services mentioned in the previous sections are to be considered as telecom services, without any distinction based on geographical coverage. No differentiation is made among services, be they local, long distance or international.

This is also the case with respect to technology. No differentiation is made among services based on their technology.[29] Services may be wire or radio-based.[30] Transmissions may occur with analogue or digital technology. Mobile services are now cellular.[31] The transmissions are covered whether or not they make use of satellites.

The nature of the intended usage (public or private) does not affect the analysis. Activities qualify as telecom services, whether they are meant for public or private use. Thus, the intended market does not provide any useful criterion to distinguish among activities.

[29] That is not the case in the whole classification. We have seen that a distinction was introduced in transmission services, depending on technology (packet- or circuit-switched). While examining this distinction, we have noted that no distinction should be introduced between services on the basis of the process used to ensure the transmission. The distinction would have more coherence if it was based on what was transmitted (data, images, voice) as well as on the modalities for content production. We will, however, see that these criteria tend to vanish with the development of convergence.

[30] Wire-based services are activities carried out using wires and cables. Radio-based services are activities provided without recourse to wires. They are based on the transmission of signals on frequencies. Mobile services are defined by the WTO as: 'radio communications services between ships, aircraft, road vehicles, or hand-held terminal stations for use while in motion or between such stations and fixed points on land' (WTO website (www.wto.org/english/tratop_e/serv_e/telecom_e/telecom_coverage_e.html), examples of basic telecommunications subject to the negotiations). Personal communications services are defined by the WTO as: 'A service that enables access to telecommunications services by allowing personal mobility. It enables each user to participate in a user-defined set of subscribed services as well as to initiate and receive calls on the basis of a unique, personal, network-independent number. It can be used across multiple networks at any fixed, movable, or mobile terminal regardless of geographical location.' See the glossary of terms noted in note 22 above.

[31] Cellular services are defined by the WTO as: 'A terrestrial radio-based service providing two-way communications by dividing the serving area into a regular pattern of sub-areas or cells, each with a base station having a low-power transmitter and receiver. Although cellular radio is primarily a means of providing mobile telephone services, it is also used to provide data services and private voice services, and as an alternative to fixed wired telephone service where this is scarce, such as in developing countries' (WTO website, (www.wto.org/english/tratop_e/serv_e/telecom_e/telecom_coverage_e.html), examples of basic telecommunications subject to the negotiations).

What does 'audio-visual' encompass?

Audio-visual services

This paper seeks to highlight the various types of audio-visual or broadcasting services in existence, and to analyse the important technological developments affecting them. Four types of service are of particular relevance here: TV, radio, digital TV and digital cinema.

TV and digital TV

Some view TV and digital TV as two distinct services. Yet, these expressions in fact designate the same activity. In traditional TV, as well as in digital TV, images and sound are broadcast to recipients. The distinction does not lie in the nature of the activity, but in the technology used. Digital TV (DTV) consists in a digital transmission of sound and images. Sounds and images are encoded. Each unit is expressed in the form of a succession of electromagnetic pulses or transmissions (bits). Traditional TV, by contrast, generally refers to analogue television (ATV). In this form of communication, analogue technology is used to transmit data.

Cinema and television

Cinema and TV do not really differ as to what is shown to viewers. The best proof is probably that films are displayed on television after having been seen in the cinemas. The difference lies primarily in the location where films are viewed. Cinemas are public places. By contrast, television viewing is normally a private activity,[32] reserved to household members and guests. The screen on which the film is displayed also differs as between cinema and TV. The presence of many viewers allows cinema owners to invest in wide screens. Cinema owners are obliged to make such investments, as sufficient numbers of viewers will otherwise not be able to see the film. Television screens are much smaller. The size will often depend on the affluence of the household and its readiness to invest in this type of equipment.[33]

[32] Films can also be seen in public places such as bars and cafes.

[33] 'Digital' cinema refers to the technology used to distribute films. As has been done for decades, these can be sent in a roll. The development of digital technology and the availability of broadband networks now make it possible to send films directly in an electronic form to cinemas. They can be sent ahead of the performance. They will then be stored, to be displayed in due course. An alternative is to send the films at the time of each performance. This is true digital cinema as the performance takes place instantaneously on the basis of signals sent electronically.

Developments in digital television

Digital television has not really affected the content of television programmes. Admittedly, there are more thematic channels reserved to sport, music or films. The main change has, however, affected the packaging,[34] marketing[35] and financial[36] practices.

Other services provided via TV equipment

Digitisation has also made it possible to develop new services that have little in common with traditional television. The new services existed beforehand. They were, however, provided without resorting to television or digital technology. Using television techniques, businesses can contact consumers and partners electronically without the need to gather physically. To that extent, there is no limit to the use of television. All services implying a physical presence can now be provided electronically using television screens and digital technology. Television may also be used as a computer screen. All functions previously attached to these screen may be provided by television.

There follow a few examples of the kinds of activity that may be carried out using television as a means to 'meet' electronically or to view information necessary in a transaction.

[34] DTV has also made it possible to package programmes differently, for example by offering different rates for basic and premium channels; by packaging weaker brand channels with one or two stronger brand channels in order to increase the perceived value of the package; and by creating the perception of choice with the use of multiple mini-packages while splitting channels in such a way that the subscribers have to buy several packages in order to receive all the most popular TV channels.

[35] The use of digital technology has made it possible to market television differently. The classic example is pay-TV, where broadcasters have allocated a substantial proportion of their budget to promoting digital platforms.

[36] Broadcasters have had to use innovative methods to finance the high investment required by the application of digital technology to television. One way is to require viewers to pay for the programmes they watch (pay-TV). It differs from traditional broadcasting where programmes and transmission are paid for with revenue from advertising. As at 2000, pay-TV amounts to 95 per cent of digital television activities. In general, one may distinguish three steps in the development of audio-visual services within the European Union. First, at the outset, television was paid for by public authorities. This investment was financed by a special tax imposed on viewers as well as by general tax revenue. Secondly, as television progressively attracted viewers, broadcasters were able to finance activities through advertising revenues. Thirdly, this method was no longer sufficient, as new investment needed to be made in order to finance digital television. Authorities were unwilling to step in, as they lacked the resources needed to invest in new technologies. Viewers will therefore have to pay directly.

- Electronic programme guide: the viewer may consult a list of programmes or channels, which appears on the screen of his television.
- E-commerce: firms do business with partners or clients using the television to view the objects being sold or the face of the interlocutor.
- TV banking: the client has access to his or her bank account via television. He or she may also get in touch with a bank employee who will help him or her with the transaction.
- Information and news: all types of information are provided online on television channels. The user may via a handset keyboard select the information that appear interesting to him.
- Interactive games, including games and software downloading channels.
- E-mail functions and high-speed internet access via the TV set.

A note of caution

We have noted that the possibilities offered by television and the use of digital technology are expanding. That does not mean that the new services are commonly provided by all firms or that they are ordinarily used by everybody in society. We are here talking about *possibilities* and these possibilities will have to materialise in order for us to be able to speak of real change.

The GATS services classification

A final word should also be said about where audio-visual services stand in the service Classification List elaborated under the GATS. We have seen that telecommunications appeared under 'Communications' in that Classification List. The same is true for 'Audio-visual services'.[37] The latter contains six subdivisions:

(a) motion picture and videotape production services
(b) motion picture projection services
(c) radio and television services
(d) radio and television transmission services
(e) sound recording
(f) other.

[37] The category of 'communications' is in fact subdivided into five categories: postal services, courier services, telecommunications services, audio-visual services and other.

These subdivisions refer to services that do not really differ from those that have been examined earlier. The list in fact dissociates industries whether they concern production or distribution. 'Radio and television services' refers to the production of programmes meant to be broadcast on radio or televisions. Similarly, 'motion picture and videotape production' refers to the activity consisting of making films or programmes to be displayed in cinemas. These industries are also listed according to their transmission (letter (b), motion picture projection; letter (d), radio and television transmission). No distinction is made between sound recording and record distribution, although it would have been logical to follow suit for that industry as well.

How to distinguish audio-visual, broadcasting and telecommunications

Absence of a WTO definition

As we have seen, the WTO Classification List refers to the concepts of audio-visual and telecommunications services. The duality is potentially important as, for reasons explained above, some Members wish to maintain a distinction between the two sectors.[38] The difficulty, however, lies in the absence of an official criterion for distinguishing between the two. As a WTO document, the Classification List clearly has an international character. Yet, strangely enough, Members use their national systems in order to interpret the various categories appearing in such Classification List.

This often leads to confusion. An example emerged in post-Uruguay negotiations on basic telecommunications. Delegations were negotiating on how far they would liberalise these services. In the course of negotiation, the United States asked for an exemption for one-way satellite transmission of direct-to-home (DTH) television, Direct broadcast satellite (DBS) television and digital audio services. Several delegations expressed their concern, 'in the light of the absence of a consensus on the definition of the distinction between basic telecommunications and broadcasting services'.[39]

[38] As mentioned in a report drafted by the Group on Basic Telecommunications, 'some delegations specified that broadcasting services were excluded from their draft (telecom) offers'. Report of the meeting of 14 February 1997.

[39] *Ibid.*

The following day, the US delegation justified its position, which position was in fact dictated by the interpretation given to broadcasting and telecommunications under US law. In the US, satellite services are considered as telecommunications not as broadcasting or audio-visual activities. For that reason, these services were not covered in the commitments made by the US on radio and television during the Uruguay Round. It thus appeared legitimate, to the US, to discuss the status of these services in the course of negotiation on telecommunications. A different analysis was, however, shared by most of the other Members negotiating with the US. For these Members, satellite services were indeed broadcasting activities. They were therefore already covered by commitments made by the US for radio and television markets.

During the discussion, the US emphasised that it was not bound by definitions derived from the WTO Classification List. For the US delegation, the negotiating parties may interpret the Classification List pursuant to their national system. National norms may thus be used to interpret terms appearing in international instruments.

> The United States explained that their . . . [demand for] exemption referred to three types of satellite services, which were treated as telecommunications services in the United States and not as broadcasting services. For this reason, they were not included in the United States Uruguay Round commitments regarding radio and television transmission services. The delegation of the United States also noted that the GATS does not operate under a single nomenclature of sector classification and that countries are free to select their own if they so choose. GATS commitments should be read in the light of each system, and this was particularly true for those countries, like the United States, which had never relied on the [Classification List] for scheduling in the audiovisual or basic telecommunications sectors.[40]

European law (the 1998 regulatory framework)

The attitude adopted by the European Union is not entirely clear. Telecommunications appear to be defined broadly so as to embrace all types of electronic transmission. However, exceptions are made for radio and TV broadcasting. These exceptions make it clear that specific rules will continue to be applied to broadcasting. Furthermore, the definition refers to telecommunications as transmissions between defined transmission

[40] Report of the meeting of 15 February 1997.

points. Yet, as we will see, broadcasting is made up of transmissions where the termination points cannot be identified in advance. Signals are sent through wires (cable) or are emitted in the direction of a region (antenna, satellite). They are then received by end-users who have set up their receivers for that purpose.

Exception made for radio and TV broadcasting

> Here, Council Directive 90/388/EEC states that the Directive 'shall be without prejudice to specific rules adopted by the Member States in accordance with Community law, governing the distribution of audiovisual programmes intended for the general public and the content of such programmes'.[41]

Broadcasting is excluded from the definition

Council Directive 90/388/EEC provides the following two definitions:

> 'Telecommunications services' means services whose provision consists wholly or partly in the transmission and/or routing of signals on telecommunications networks.
>
> 'Public telecommunications network' means the public telecommunications infrastructure which permits the conveyance of signals between defined termination points by wire, by microwave, by optical means or by other electromagnetic means.[42]

Council Directive 90/387/EEC provides the following two definitions:

> 'Telecommunications services' shall mean services the provision of which consists wholly or partly in the transmission and routing of signals on telecommunications networks, with the exception of radio and television broadcasting.

[41] Commission Directive 90/388/EEC of 28 June 1990 on competition in the markets for telecommunications services, OJ L192, 24 July 1990, p. 10, Article 1, para. 1, as amended. The consolidated version of the Directive can be found at www.europa.eu.int/eur-lex/en/consleg/pdf/1990/en_1990L0388_do_001.pdf.

[42] Commission Directive 90/388/EEC of 28 June 1990 on competition in the markets for telecommunications services, OJ L192, 24 July 1990, p. 10, Article 1(1), as amended. The consolidated version of the Directive can be found at www.europa.eu.int/eurlex/en/consleg/pdf/1990/en_1990L0388_do_001.pdf.

> 'Telecommunications network' shall mean transmission systems and, where applicable, switching equipment and other resources which permit the conveyance of signals between defined termination points by wire, by radio, by optical or by other electromagnetic means.[43]

Ambiguity of the approach

This approach is not entirely clear. The definitions themselves refer to the concept of 'defined termination points'. This suggestion is, however, very technical. It is not clear that it can be understood easily. The real case for a distinction appears at the stage of the determination of the applicable legislation. The approach adopted by the European Commission is interesting in that regard. The Commission does not clearly distinguish between broadcasting and telecommunications in the definition. However, it mentions that both kinds of activity should be submitted to different legal regimes – which suggests that they form a whole that cannot be divided otherwise than by stating arbitrarily that the regimes will be different.

This two-step approach indicates the unease of the European authorities, as they try to distinguish both concepts in order to determine the scope of their rules. The ambiguity also appears in the offers made by the EU delegation during the negotiations on basic telecommunications. The European delegation wanted to exclude broadcasting from the scope of the liberalisation initiatives. However, they found it difficult to express in a clear manner the distinction to be made between broadcasting and telecommunications. To achieve their goal, they introduced a complex distinction between the 'provision of content' and the 'transport of content'. For the Commission, the latter activity can be considered as a telecommunications service. By contrast, the former should be considered as a broadcasting service.

> Telecommunications services are the transport of electro-magnetic signals – sound, data, image and any combinations thereof, excluding broadcasting. Therefore, commitments in this offer do not cover the economic activity

[43] Council Directive 90/387/EEC of 28 June 1990 on the establishment of the internal market for telecommunications services through the implementation of open network provision. OJ L192, 24 July 1990, Article 2, point 3, as amended by European Parliament and Council Directive 97/51/EC of 6 October 1997 amending Council Directives 90/387/EEC and 92/44/EEC for the purpose of adaptation to a competitive environment in telecommunications OJ L295, 29 October 1997 p. 23.

> consisting of content provision which require telecommunications services for its transport. The provision of that content, transported via a telecommunications service, is subject to the specific commitments undertaken by the European Communities and their Member States in other relevant sectors.[44]

Television versus telephony

The distinction made between audio-visual and telecommunications services in fact goes back to the difference between television and telephony. These two activities have been the most important services for decades in the electronic communications sectors. Television was, and still is, to a large extent, the main channel for distribution of audio-visual programmes, although cinemas are also an important source of revenues. Telephony was a part of telecommunications. Other services were included in that sector,[45] but they never achieved the same degree of technical perfection and commercial success.

The distinction between both activities gave rise to distinct industries. The first – telephony – consists in the transmission of voice messages. The second – television – implies the transmission of programmes where images and sound are combined. These industries can be differentiated with three, or perhaps four, criteria.

Presence of images

The presence of images is the key criterion, as reflected in the name given to these sectors ('-phony' as opposed to '-vision'). Images are essential in TV programmes, but are absent in voice telephony.

Nature of transmission

The nature of the transmission is a second key factor in distinguishing the two activities. Telephony is interactive, as it implies the transmission of

[44] Communication from the European Communities and their Member States, Schedule on Basic Telecommunications, 15 February 1997, repeated in the Communication from the European Communities and their Member States, GATS 2000: Telecommunications, S/CSS/W/35, 22 December 2000. In that definition, the European delegation apparently thinks that a distinction can be made between the 'provision of content' and the 'transport' of content. In my opinion, both concepts refer to a single activity – the transport or the provision of content. The distinction should rather be made between content production and distribution.

[45] Telegraphy, telex and later facsimile: transmission of a copy of a document through wires.

Table 13.2 *Differentiation factors between the two main sectors in electronic communication*

Telephony	Television
Voice	Images and sound
Interaction	Unilateral diffusion
Point to point	Point to multipoint
Local production, by interlocutors	Content may be produced by third parties outside of the transmission

conversation. Audio-visual is by contrast unilateral. The viewer watches what is sent to him, without interacting with it.

Transmission modality

A third criterion can be found in the transmission modality. Conversation – and as a result telephony – is sent by one participant to another (point to point). Audio-visual programmes are sent by one emitter to multiple viewers and listeners.

Message content

The last criterion relates to the content of the message. We have spoken here about the nature of the object to be conveyed – voice or a combination of sound and images. However, we have not examined by whom the content was produced or the circumstances under which the content was produced. In voice telephony, the content – a conversation – is produced locally by persons speaking to each other. Content is rarely produced by third parties and when the interlocutors barely repeat what they have heard, they still locally produce the sound that will be necessary for the conversation to take place. By contrast, television often implies content made by third parties. Producers manufacture television programmes that are channelled thereafter by distributors through networks. The producers and distributors are in some instances the same, or at least belong to same undertaking. However, it need not to be so. In many instances, the programmes will be made and disseminated by different parties.

Radio broadcasting

A third service, standing between telephony and television, must be introduced. It consists of the transmission of sound. In that regard, it is

Table 13.3 *Criteria to determine whether an activity is audio-visual or broadcasting*

Audio-visual	Broadcasting
Object (combination of sounds and images)	Production (how the object has been produced: commercial production by third parties) Carriage (how the object is transmitted: one to a multitude, and unidirectional)

similar to telephony. However, in radio, sound is communicated in a unilateral transmission from one point to multiple destinations. Factor (1) above therefore implicitly associates radio broadcasting with telephony. However, factors (2), (3) and (4) imply a classification with television.

Distinguishing audio-visual and broadcasting

Thus, we see that 'audio-visual' cannot be equated with 'broadcasting'. 'Audio-visual' refers to factor (1) – what is being conveyed. As the term 'audio-visual' literally means, the object being transmitted is made of sound ('audio') and images ('visual'). By contrast, 'broadcasting' refers to factors (2) and (3) – how information is conveyed. It designates a process whereby the same message is sent to multiple users. In such a form of transmission, the transmission is one-way. The production modalities also appear to be related to 'broadcasting'. Distributors are transmitting in bulk messages that have been produced by third parties.

Telecommunications as distinct from broadcasting

A line may also be drawn between 'telecommunications' and 'broadcasting'. This line has nothing to do with *what* is transmitted (object of the transmission: sounds, images or a combination of them). It is related rather to *how* this object is transmitted. As we have seen, broadcasting implies a unilateral transmission by one sender to several recipients of information generally produced by third parties.[46] By contrast,

[46] Can a commercial criterion be used to distinguish broadcasting from telecommunications? For example, content production often takes place on a commercial basis prior to a broadcasting activity. The persons who produce the content receive remuneration for the work they perform. The transmission of content also gives the right to a financial claim.

Table 13.4 *Criteria to distinguish broadcasting from telecommunications*

Criteria	Broadcasting	Telecommunications
Direction of the transmission	The transmission is unilateral. Information is sent by the emitter to the recipients. No answer is normally expected.	The transmission takes the form of an exchange, where interaction plays a crucial role.
Number of participants	The communication goes from one point of emission to a multitude of reception points.	Information is sent by one participant to the other one(s), who then react by sending information in return.
Production of information	Information is produced outside of the transmission. In many cases, it is produced by third parties.	Information is produced in common and interactively by the participants.

telecommunications implies an exchange between participants. Participants exchange information they produce during an interaction. This exchange occurs at a distance. Therefore, the electronic form is resorted to.

Convergence and the challenge for regulators

The process of convergence

A convergence has recently emerged between these various industries that were up till now distinguished on the basis of the above-mentioned criteria. These industries had developed different products and technologies. At a certain time, it become apparent to market participants that,

Recipients pay for what they receive. This pattern seems different from what happens in telecommunications. Here, people normally exchange conversations without payment for the production of content, not the communication of it. What is being paid for is the use of a given network capacity and the associated equipment and software necessary for this exchange to take place. One should, however, note that content formulated in a telephone or teleconference is always free. Agents are paid for the information they provide to clients using telecommunications devices. One should not consider that telecommunications are only used for private purposes – although some private communications also have commercial or financial aspects. Think of a conversation between a consumer and a placement agent about shares to be bought on a stock exchange.

with technological development, they were in a position to start providing services in adjacent markets. Thus, telephony providers considered broadcasting audio-visual programmes, and broadcasting firms considered entering the telephony and telecom markets.[47]

Convergence is continuing, and is influenced by various factors, as set out below.

Technological developments

Telecommunications and television were formerly based on analogue transmission. This technology allowed for limited transmission performance, as far as speed and volume are concerned. With the development of digital technology, it has become possible to transmit all data (voice, images, text) in the same form. It has also become possible to have such data processed by computers,[48] which has increased performance.

Business development

Digitisation has then been applied to business behaviour. The use of the same, digital language makes it possible to transmit all data via all networks. Telecom businesses can now think of transporting images on their network, provided these networks are duly adapted. As a result, telecom providers can provide services that were formerly reserved to audio-visual businesses. Conversely, the audio-visual industry can use its networks to transport sound. Broadcasting infrastructure can thus be adjusted to allow the transmission of conversations.

Market structure

As is often the case, undertakings establish links with participants on markets they want to enter. Their aim is to acquire expertise in these new

[47] It is difficult, if not impossible, to date with accuracy the beginning of such a development. For example, facsimile services have always been considered a part of the telecommunications industry. The reason is that messages were conveyed in facsimile services through the wires used to provide telephony. Facsimile services were therefore provided by telephone operators. Yet, if one uses the criteria provided above, facsimile services should probably be considered as part of the audio-visual industry rather than the telecommunications sector. A facsimile is a transmission not of voice, but rather of text. Yet, text is closer to an image (page filled with signs) than to a voice message. Moreover, a fax transmission is one-way: there is no interaction; the receiver does not send any signal to the sender. Thus it could be compared with television rather than telecommunications.

[48] Computer functioning is based on digital technology.

markets, as well as access to consumers.[49] Following that pattern, one has seen telecom operators invest in audio-visual businesses. Conversely, audio-visual businesses have started investing in telecom operators and infrastructure.

Services

Finally, services are being designed that overlap the traditional boundary between the formerly separate sectors. Undertakings have acquired expertise and access to consumers. They start merging their activities after merging their structures. We are currently at that stage. The composition of communications presenting mixed aspects – multimedia services – is under way.[50]

Impossibility of maintaining traditional criteria

As sectors are converging, all criteria that were previously used to distinguish broadcasting and telecommunications are vanishing.

Voice versus images and sound

Audio-visual content was specific to television. The distinction between audio-visual and broadcasting was already made difficult by the existence of radio broadcasting, which implies the mere transmission of voice or sound independently of images. It has now become impossible to distinguish the sectors on the basis of the thing transmitted, as telecommunications allows the transmission of images. New services have appeared in which a combination of voice and images are sent in a conversation through telecommunications networks whereas this sort of content was previously reserved to broadcasting.

Interaction versus unilateral transmission

Telephony (telecommunications) was previously associated with interaction, whereas broadcasting and audio-visual were associated with

[49] Collaboration often takes the form of mergers, or takeovers. Parties do not have the time or energy to work out complex cooperation agreements. They want to proceed swiftly. The best way to achieve quick results is to acquire authority over a participant in the market which is targeted. The hope is that this participant will carry out the strategy desired by the acquirer.

[50] This, again, is facilitated by the common digital language. Through computers, it is possible, and increasingly easy, to mix data corresponding to voice and images. Such services can no longer be assigned either to broadcasting or to telecommunications.

unilateral transmissions (absence of interaction). Yet, this distinction progressively vanishes with the development of mixed services. Television programmes are progressively being developed in which the content depends on choices made by the end-user. Audio-visual games, for instance, are made available by broadcasters and allow end-users to determine how things develop. Conversely, telecommunications – including telephony – make increasing use of non-interactive techniques. An example is when callers receive a telephone number where they can call to hear a pre-recorded message that will deliver information to end-users.

One-to-one versus one-to-multitude

Particular conversations were instances of telecommunications, whereas collective diffusion was common in broadcasting and audio-visual. Yet, video-on-demand now allows broadcasters to adapt their programmes to the specific needs of end-users. Software companies, such as Microsoft, intend to provide software services and intelligence on demand through networks. By contrast, standard messages are transmitted via the telephone from one point to a multitude. That is the case, for instance, when end-users call a message centre where they receive a choice between options provided by a computer and through which they can access information useful to them.

Local versus third-party content

Telecommunications were useful for people to exchange locally made messages. It becomes possible for participants to exchange via telecommunications services data that were prepared by third parties. That is the case in video-conferences, where for example business colleagues in various locations can discuss over the phone documents displayed during the conversation, via the same network, on their computers.

A challenge for regulators

The difficulty, in that context, for regulators is to provide a framework where converging activities will successfully develop. Things are changing fast, and regulators must attempt to foresee what the future will look like, in order to establish today a suitable framework for activities to develop tomorrow.[51] This difficulty was raised by the WTO Secretariat in the context of the work of the Council for Trade in Services. In a Background Note, the Secretariat emphasised how useful it was, for the good order of negotiations, to divide the concept of 'telecommunications' into various parts. As a result of that vision, industries were segmented vertically and Members were able to determine what segments they wished to open to world trade.[52]

The elimination of borders is a source of concern in negotiations that have so far been designed on a vertical basis. Until now, economic activities have been vertically divided into sectors and subsectors, and Members were encouraged to open their borders to world trade for some or all of these vertical economic categories. What will Members do if they lose the possibility to refer to vertical sectors in their commitments – which seems to be the effect of convergence as far as the telecommunications sector is concerned? In that regard, technology and world markets are clearly posing a serious challenge to regulators and lawyers. They are leaving aside vertical divisions. Should we not do the same and adapt our mental categories to the new directions that are explored by technology and business?

A new division among rules

Significant progress has been made on those lines by the European Union authorities. They have adopted a new regulatory framework that appears

[51] Law consists of definitions. It provides a tool to analyse activities in categories and submit each category to rules that seem appropriate. This task is very difficult at a time when existing categories are disappearing or converging.

[52] In that Note, the Secretariat regretted that no distinction of that nature was made between broadcasting and telecommunications. Making such an analysis would have been essential, at a time when the distinction is increasingly vanishing yet both sectors remain submitted to different rules. 'The development of the categories, and the fundamental understanding on how to use them, did much to clarify the intended nature and scope of the commitments made on Basic Telecommunications . . . The primary shortcoming of the approach is that critical information on the scope, as well as on the exact services covered by a given commitment, is often implicit. A degree of uncertainty that may sometimes result, therefore, could be compounded in the future, as convergence of broadcast, telecommunications, and computer technologies and services continue to take hold. For example, many traditional and non-traditional telecommunications operators are now conducting the technological and market research to begin offering video on demand over internet. It will be particularly important to be clear in specifying the coverage of new commitments in these areas.' Telecommunication Services – Background Note by the Secretariat, WTO, S/C/W/74, 8 December 1998, p. 4.

compatible with convergence-related technological and economic developments. In this regulatory framework, all forms of transmission are treated alike whatever the sector (the vertical part of the industry) they are related to (broadcasting or telecommunications). The distinction between broadcasting (or audio-visual) and telecommunications is abandoned. Transmissions are all considered part of the telecommunications industry or – as it is better described in the new EU terminology – of the 'electronic communication' business.[53]

Pursuant to the European approach, there is no need to divide the rules according to the sector they relate to. The rules should rather be associated with the type of relationship that is to be addressed by the regulator – and thus the type of issue that is likely to be raised. I would classify these issues into three categories, depending on whether they are related to business-to-business relations, business-to-consumer relations or the realisation of other objectives.

Business to business

According to the new measures (which continue with the former position in this respect), the relationships between businesses, as well as the legal issues raised in these relationships, should in principle be governed by competition. A competitive marketplace should ensure that market participants choose as partners the firms that provide the best quality for the cheapest price. Where market mechanisms do not allow that result to be achieved, competition as well as sector-specific regulators must intervene to restore rivalry. Competition rules are used to that effect, as well as competition-related sector-specific regulation.

As far as relations among businesses are concerned, it is apparent that convergence is fully realised in the new regulatory framework. All activities carried out in the (as they were formerly called) telecom and audio-visual sectors are now subject to similar rules – the market mechanisms as

[53] 'Content' is treated separately. By that expression, the European authorities are refering to two kinds of meaning. On the one hand, it refers to the radio or audio-visual object that is transmitted. Member States want to retain a right to regulate these productions. The EU appears ready to accept such a right if it is exercised in conformity with other EU provisions. On the other hand, it refers to the function that is performed through the transmission. Suppose the transmission aims at selling financial services at a distance. The message that is sent to end-users is made of sound and images, for instance an advertising spot sent to their computers via the Internet. Such a transmission will be considered an electronic communications service. It will be submitted to specific rules, in that it serves a special purpose – selling at a distance to a consumer – and raises as a result specific concerns.

complemented by rules meant to restore competition where it is impaired. In that context, there is no longer any need to distinguish between what previously corresponded with telecommunications and what was previously considered as audio-visual. To apply the rules of competition, and those that complement them,[54] it is not necessary to categorise activities according to the industry to which they are supposed to belong. These rules call for an analysis of activities in markets. Competition has to exist in each market, the latter being defined (in substance) as a whole made by all products or services considered as interchangeable by clients. Activities are no longer defined in respect of industries distinguished by legislators as a result of the specific objectives they seek to achieve in each of them. Rather, they are analysed with, as point of departure, the position of business partners (in particular, that of the client).

Business to consumer

Other rules are introduced with respect to the relationship between firms and consumers. For instance, financial services are not, and could not be, regulated by mere competition rules. Consumers represent the weaker participants on the markets. Therefore, they must be protected. This necessity for protection has always been very high on the agenda of regulators. Regulators have therefore been at the root of many legislative initiatives in the past decades, and continue to call on legislators to act.[55]

For consumer issues, there is no need to define clearly audio-visual and telecommunications. Issues relating to consumers are horizontal. They occur regardless of the field concerned – audio-visual or telecommunications.[56] As a consequence, a horizontal approach may be adopted here as well. Similar rules may be established for all sectors. Such rules will apply to all activities, absent circumstance requiring specific treatment.

Other (political) objectives

We have been talking so far about rules concerning the functioning of the markets, as well as about rules concerning consumers. A third category

[54] Sector-specific regulation.

[55] For some issues, all consumers need to be protected. For instance, they have to be provided with relevant information before entering into contracts with telecommunications operators. For other issues, the protection should only be granted to some of the consumers. For instance, consumers with social difficulties may qualify for a special tariff. Similarly, consumers with physical disabilities may qualify for special equipment.

[56] For instance, one issue is that customers should receive what they are paying for, be it in the audio-visual or the telecom sector. Another issue is the protection of privacy.

should be mentioned. Some Member States of the European Union think that additional objectives should be fulfilled. These objectives depend on the activity, and therefore the service, under consideration. These objectives are grounded on political considerations, independently of a smooth market functioning based on competition among businesses and respect for consumers.

For instance, the European Parliament thinks it essential that citizens should not receive audio-visual messages based only on one culture. A diversity and plurality should be broadcast to viewers. For the European parliament, this is a prerequisite for citizens to be aware that several currents co-exist in society and that democracy implies some sort of co-existence between these differing currents.

Similarly, the European Parliament as well as a handful of national regulators considers it necessary that all citizens have access to a telephony line. This view is not based on the need for a proper functioning of the market. Rather, they feel society should provide certain fundamental services to each citizen, even when we are not in a position to pay for the service we receive. As a result, they have decided that a minimum service should be guaranteed to all citizens independently of their ability to pay.

So far, these political objectives have been envisaged in connection with a specific industry. Yet, this must change in light of the convergence that is taking place. Pluralism, for instance, was associated with radio and television. These objectives remain, insofar as these services still exist in world shaped by convergence. But they can – and should probably – be extended to types of audio-visual and telecommunications services, that may have an impact on diversity and pluralism. We can no longer consider that the audio-visual sector is the only sector affected by these concerns. Again, these objectives, and the rules that are associated with them, have a horizontal application. They apply to all activities, whatever the sector involved, as soon as the activity has any relevance for the objective which is sought by the authorities. Think of the Internet. If a government wants to ensure diversity, it must ensure that existing websites correspond, in one way or another, to that imperative. If it is to continue to proclaim its faith in pluralism, the European Parliament should not accept the situation in which all available websites, or at any rate an overwhelming majority of them, convey images of a society that do not correspond to European values.[57]

[57] The same observation can be made with respect to a minimum telecom service. This concept has so far been associated with telephony. However, bearing in mind what is

Towards a new regulatory approach

The European approach signals a fundamental change in the way regulation is being designed for the sectors pertaining to the information society. Previously, regulation was tailored to specific industries. There existed sets of rules applicable to the various industries involved. The legal order was structured alongside the division in economic sectors. Telecommunications – in particular telephony – were submitted to telecom rules, and different rules were tailored for audio-visual activities. Under this approach, a vertical division predominated. Industries coexisted, with clear dividing lines that were visible in economic activities as well as in legal rules.

This vertical separation is vanishing with convergence. As we have seen, the boundaries that existed between the two industries are progressively disappearing. This observation not only relates to economic sectors, it also relates to the legal categories. Rules are no longer applied to one industry without being simultaneously applied to the other. A horizontal approach is thus progressively developed. It is not based on a division according to sector, but rather follows an issue-based methodology. The rules are aimed at solving issues, and they apply to all activities where these issues may arise, whatever the sector concerned. That is the case for competition rules, which apply to activities, whatever the sector or the category in which these activities may be classified (audio-visual, telecom, mixed). The same goes for consumer protection rules. They apply to all issues where there is a need to protect consumers, whatever the sector. A similar analysis may be made for rules relating to other (political) objectives.

This has a consequence for future negotiations. In the aftermath of convergence, we have to abandon our habit of vertically dividing activities and replace this division with a horizontal approach. This is not just a regulatory change, but rather a change in mindset. Business and technology evolution are showing the way ahead. Our approach must become issue-rather than sector-based. There is much to be taken into account, for future negotiation, in that respect.

considered nowadays to be an essential service, minimum access to the Internet may be considered as a fundamental service, as it is a condition for people to remain 'connected' to the world.

14

Dealing with convergence at the international level

PIERRE LAROUCHE

Introduction

Like many other buzzwords of the 1990s, 'convergence' is no longer a very fashionable term. Actually, it fell out of favour some time before the telecom and Internet bubble burst in 2000 and 2001. It might accordingly seem odd to devote a contribution to an outdated fad, yet, as will be seen, the convergence phenomenon has legal implications (discussed in the second section of this paper). A number of domestic law-makers and regulators sought to respond to it, including the EC and the US, whose respective approaches on a number of key points will be surveyed in the third and fourth part of this paper. The WTO has yet to deal with the issue, and this paper will end by outlining, in line with the EC and US approaches, problems which are likely to arise at the WTO level.

The convergence phenomenon and its legal implications

'Convergence'[1] refers to the coming together of what were previously thought of as separate sectors, namely, telecommunications, information

[1] The following explanation of convergence is drawn from the European Commission's Green Paper on the Convergence of the Telecommunications, Media and Information Technology Sectors, and the Implications for Regulation, COM(97)623 (3 December 1997), pp. 1–8. Among other studies of the phenomenon, see T. F. Baldwin, D. S. McVoy and C. Steinfield, *Convergence: Integrating Media, Information and Communication* (London: Sage, 1996); C. Cowie and C. Marsden, 'Convergence, Competition and Regulation', IJCLP Web-Doc. 6-1-1998, available at www.digital-law.net/IJCLP/index.html; KPMG, *Public Policy Issues Arising from Telecommunications and Audio-visual Convergence* (KPMG, 1996); M. Latzer, *Mediamatik – Die Konvergenz von Telekommunikation, Computer und Rundfunk* (Opladen: Westdeutscher Verlag, 1997); and the special issue of *Telecommunications Policy* 22 (1998): 161, with articles by C. Blackman, J. van Cuilenburg and P. Verhoest, Y. Benkler, B. Clements, P. Nihoul, P. Larouche, C. Scott and L.-L. Christians.

technology (IT)[2] and media, as a result of technological developments[3] that enabled pent-up customer demand to be satisfied. Convergence is taking place at a number of different levels. First, it can already be seen at the level of terminal equipment and networks. Nowadays, computers can be used not just for computing, but also for telecommunication and the reception of audio-visual media, telephones now have limited computing and media abilities and TV sets are following the trend. Similarly, networks originally conceived for telecommunications or broadcasting of audio-visual media (cable TV networks) can now be used for the other purpose, as well as for computing purposes (access to the Internet, etc.). Secondly, convergence is taking place at the service level, with the introduction, albeit later than foreseen, of new services which combine elements of telecommunications and media, for instance pay-per-view or video-on-demand. Thirdly, the industry itself is converging through alliances and cross-sectoral mergers (the epitome being the AOL/TimeWarner merger).

The common wisdom of the 1990s, as sketched above, was based upon a vision of the evolution of the various sectors which did not materialise, or at least did not materialise quite according to plan. That vision foresaw major players in the telecommunications and media sectors upgrading their networks and equipment to bring the requisite amount of bandwidth and computing power down to customers, after which these players would begin to offer converged services on these networks. Reality did not unfold as predicted. The costs turned out to be much higher than originally forecasted, and the first trials showed that customer demand was not as high as was thought. Accordingly, that vision is not yet realised, and it may never be.

At the same time, convergence did occur on a smaller, more incremental scale and in a way that was not foreseen at all. The Internet is a converged network within the meaning of that vision, using the most converged terminal equipment (the computer) to deliver services that closely resemble the converged services which were forecast.[4] Yet, the Internet was originally narrowband, and it was not the result of single-handed efforts by large vertically-integrated firms along proprietary lines, but rather of the collective and co-operative work of small start-ups in an open standard

[2] Telecommunications and IT have been converging since the 1980s (albeit mostly at the level of larger customers).

[3] Including digitalisation and compression techniques, the introduction of optical fibre and the advent of packet switching.

[4] For instance, streaming audio and video allow for the kind of on-demand media services that were supposed to appear with convergence.

environment. A few of those start-ups became large firms in their own right or were integrated into larger firms, so that they survived the downturn in the sector. It could be that future developments will come closer to the vision expounded in the 1990s, albeit with actors that grew out of or with the Internet wave. In any event, one cannot help thinking that the rise of the Internet might have had a very positive impact, among others, in providing a welcome reality check on the forecasts of industry gurus and avoiding that the existing industry structure be perpetuated.

Irrespective of how convergence may play out as far as services and industry structure are concerned, however, it is undeniable that major changes have occurred at the level of underlying technology (networks, equipment). Even though it has become hard to make any prediction on the future of the converging sectors, it seems reasonable to assume that some form of convergence is already taking place and will pick up speed in the coming years, albeit not according to the grandiose scenarios of the 1990s.

In the face of so much buzz around convergence in industry circles during the past decade, the law had to keep pace with developments. First, convergence, real or apprehended, challenged the traditional closely guarded realms of telecommunications and media, as well as the absence of regulation of the computer industry. In each of them, the law rests on a number of technical assumptions, which have been translated into basic concepts and definitions:

- Telecommunications is seen as a network-based activity, conducted in real time on the basis of two-way, point-to-point networks.
- Media is seen also as a network-based activity conducted in real time, but functioning according to different parameters. Here the network is one-way (only from the emitter to the receiver, with no feedback) and point-to-multipoint.
- Information technology (IT) and computing were not originally seen as network-based activities, but rather as localised activities, conducted in one place.

Whole regulatory constructions were then built on these models, with the aim of addressing specific policy concerns arising in each case (with the exception of IT, where no such concerns were deemed to arise). Any change in these models therefore requires a reassessment and rethinking of the law, all the more when the change takes the form of a breakdown in the hitherto hermetic separation between them, coupled with the apparition of new mixed models.

In addition, the evolution of the converging sectors in recent times brought to the forefront a second and no less impressive challenge for law and regulation. Convergence appears to be taking place, or at least bound to take place, yet not according to the original scenarios. There is therefore a fair amount of uncertainty as to the future, beyond the basic recognition that it will not be like the past. Accordingly, the law itself must be in a position to deal with uncertainty as to the evolution of the sector. In essence, it must be framed in such a way that its policy objectives would, on the one hand, be fulfilled irrespective of how the future unfolds and, on the other hand, come under constant review to ensure that they are still appropriate in the light of changed circumstances, whatever they may be.

These two challenges (the breakdown in underlying technological models and the uncertainty regarding the future) did not vanish with the bursting of the technology bubble in 2000. Hence, a paper dedicated to a critical examination of the legal response to convergence remains very relevant still.

The EC response to convergence

The EC took a relatively proactive approach to convergence. Already by the mid-1990s, the Commission had decided to address the regulatory implications of convergence. The first round of reflection and consultation resulted in the Convergence Green Paper of 1997.[5] The results of the discussions around that document were fed into the so-called 1999 Review[6] and the subsequent legislative process (which is discussed below). They are reflected in a number of elements of the new regulatory framework concerning electronic communications.

Structural and definitional issues: the separation of content and networks

In the wake of the consultations following the Convergence Green Paper, the Commission proposed a large, across-the-board regulatory

5 Note 1 above.

6 Towards a New Framework for Electronic Communications Infrastructure and Associated Services – The 1999 Communications Review, COM(1999)539 (10 November 1999).

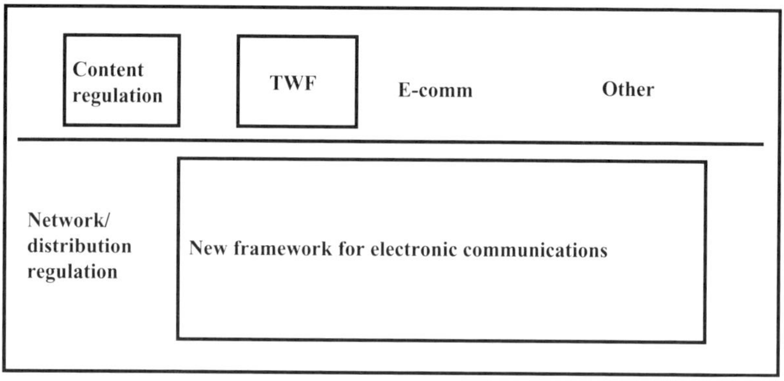

Figure 14.1

framework concerning all sorts of networks, with a number of more specific regulations concerning certain aspects of content, as shown in Figure 14.1.[7] In terms of mass, network regulation would be the main component and presumably the main focus of attention as well. Content regulation would be more fragmented. This network/content distinction is now implemented in the Framework Directive.[8]

The regulatory distinction between content and network/distribution has obvious practical advantages: it allows some order to be brought in the overall regulatory scheme and enables policy review processes to tackle each branch of the distinction one at a time.[9] At the same time, the network/content divide shows the hallmarks of distinctions which are borne out of convenience. First, it is too simple for the reality of the sectors in question: while a number of actors indeed busy themselves with content

[7] The Convergence of the Telecommunications, Media and Information Technology Sectors, and the Implications for Regulation – Results of the Public Consultation on the Green Paper, COM(1999)108 (10 March 1999).

[8] See Directive 2002/21/EC of 7 March 2002 on a common regulatory framework for electronic communications networks and services (the 'Framework Directive'), 2002 OJ L108/33, Articles 1(2), 2(a) and 2(c) and Rec. 5. The distinction between content and networks is discussed in greater detail in P. Larouche,' Communications Convergence and Public Broadcasting', in B. de Witte, ed., *Public Service Broadcasting and European Law* (Oxford: Hart Publishing, 2003).

[9] In addition, the distinction separates the respective turfs of the Commission: Information Society (concerned with networks) and Culture (concerned with content) Directorates-General. The Competition Directorate-General is less concerned with the distinction and makes its influence felt on both sides of the regulatory divide.

production or with the operation of distribution/communication networks, an impressive number of players straddle the divide, or at least do not quite fit the ideal picture underlying the regulatory distinction. It suffices here to mention content resellers and repackagers, operators of conditional access networks, etc. In fact, there are a number of other ways in which a distinction could have been drawn. Secondly, while the network/content divide may have some meaning against the backdrop of the traditional telecommunications and media sectors, it becomes more difficult to apply in newer sectors where communications networks are infused with non-audio-visual content. This is the case in particular for the various forms of e-commerce which have emerged in recent years. In the case of electronic banking, for instance, the banking transaction would constitute the content being carried out using electronic communications networks and services. While this may make sense from a formal perspective, at the same time it is difficult to see why the content and network elements of e-commerce should be put under separate regulatory frameworks, given that they raise similar policy issues (standardisation, privacy, etc.). Directive 2000/31/EC on e-commerce illustrates this very well when it relies on a definition of a 'Information Society' services which does not appear to distinguish very strongly between content and networks.[10]

Technological neutrality

The telecommunications regulatory framework put in place in the run-up to liberalisation relied extensively on technological concepts such as voice telephony[11] or fixed and mobile telecommunications.[12] These concepts cannot evolve very well with time, when technological changes lead to

[10] Directive 2000/31/EC of 8 June 2000 on electronic commerce, 2000 OJ L178/1, rests on the definition of Information Society service given in Directive 98/34/EC of 22 June 1998 laying down a procedure for the provision of information in the field of technical standards and regulations and of rules on information society services, 1998 OJ L204/37, Article 1(2), as amended by Directive 98/48/EC of 20 July 1998, 1998 OJ L217/18, i.e. any service normally provided for remuneration, at a distance, by electronic means and at the request of a recipient of services. That definition does not incorporate a distinction between content and transmission, as is reinforced by the explanations given at Recital (18) of Directive 2000/31/EC.

[11] See Directive 98/10/EC of 26 February 1998, 1998 OJ L101/24, Article 2(2)(e); and Directive 90/388/EC of 28 June 1990, 1990 OJ L192/10, Article 1(1).

[12] Both Directive 90/388/EC, ibid. and Directive 97/33/EC of 30 June 1997, 1997 OJ L199/32, relied extensively on the distinction between fixed and mobile telecommunications.

shifts in the underlying policy concerns.[13] In addition, they are not well suited to a climate of uncertainty about the future development of the sector.

Accordingly, the new electronic communications framework is meant to be technology-neutral. According to the 1999 Review, '[t]echnological neutrality means that legislation should define the objectives to be achieved, and should neither impose, nor discriminate in favour of, the use of a particular type of technology to achieve those objectives'.[14] From that principle, interested parties have derived a number of sometimes contradictory propositions.[15] Nevertheless, it is beyond debate that the regulatory framework must avoid being trapped in a technological strait-jacket, through the use of non-evolutive concepts which are linked to one specific technological model. This becomes all the more necessary when the uncertainty surrounding the evolution of the sector is factored in.

Taking technological neutrality as a starting point, a number of options are available for the proper design of the regulatory framework. For instance, it is possible to seek to replace technological definitions with functional or economic ones, which are suited to a number of different technological environments.

Another available option would be to move away from the specificities of the communications sector altogether and use the concepts of general economic regulation, i.e. competition law. This option was chosen in the EC.

The relationship with competition law

Early on, in the 1999 Review, the Commission stated that 'it will be appropriate for sector-specific regulation to make more use of competition law concepts like dominant position found in Article 82 of the Treaty'.[16] In the

[13] See, for instance, the two Commission Communications on the status of voice communications on Internet under Community law and, in particular, pursuant to Directive 90/388/EC, 1998 OJ C6/4 and 2000 OJ C369/3, where the Commission is caught up in its famous 'public voice telephony' definition and has difficulties escaping superficial formalism in its discussion.

[14] 1999 Review, note 6 above, p. 13.

[15] For instance, it has been sustained by some that technological neutrality implied that the regulatory framework applicable to fixed-line communications should be extended to mobile communications as well, while others were arguing the contrary, on the basis that fixed-line regulation stems from problems specific to that technology, which cannot therefore be assumed to exist in other technologies.

[16] 1999 Review, note 6 above, p. 9.

Framework Directive, the key concepts of the new regulatory framework are given an unmistakable competition law flavour. For one, the concept of 'significant market power' (SMP) is used, as before, as a definitional trigger for the imposition of heavier regulatory obligations relating among others to transparency, non-discrimination, accounting, access to facilities and price control.[17] The SMP regime rests on a three-step assessment procedure to be repeated regularly by each national regulatory authority (NRA), under Commission supervision.[18] First, the Commission sets out in a Recommendation the relevant product and service markets to be considered by each NRA in the course of its assessment. On that basis, the NRA then determines the relevant product/service markets, as well as the relevant geographic markets. In a second step, the NRA is to analyse those markets to see if they are effectively competitive. If so, then no regulatory obligations shall be imposed, and existing ones shall be removed. If not, then firm(s) holding SMP shall be identified. SMP is defined as a position equivalent to dominance.[19] In a third step, as the case may be, the NRA shall impose or maintain appropriate obligations, among those listed above, upon the firm(s) holding SMP. The decisions of NRAs at every step of the process are scrutinised at Community level, with deviant relevant product/service market definitions as well as SMP findings being subject to a Commission veto.[20]

Furthermore, it is the very design of this SMP regime to limit the use of sector-specific regulation to those areas where competition law would not suffice to ensure a proper functioning of the market, as stated in the Framework Directive.[21]

The heart of the new regulatory framework therefore beats to a competition law rhythm. At the same time, it is open to discussion whether the use of competition law concepts was optimal and whether those

17 These obligations are set out at Articles 9–13 of Directive 2002/19/EC of 7 March 2002, 2002 OJ L108/7 (the 'Access Directive') as well as Article 17 of Directive 2002/22/EC of 7 March 2002, 2002 OJ L108/51 (the 'Universal Service Directive').

18 See Framework Directive, note 8 above, Articles 15–16.

19 *Ibid.*, Article 14(2).

20 See *Ibid.*, Article 7. That provision was intensely debated during the legislative process.

21 See *Ibid.*, Recital 27. This recital is somewhat ambiguous, since it does not clearly indicate whether the sufficiency of competition law is to be assessed at the outset (i.e. in the selection of markets to be examined by the NRA) or at the end of the process (i.e. in the course of selecting appropriate remedies). The Commission appears to favour the former option: see the draft Recommendation on relevant product and service markets (17 June 2002) and the explanatory memorandum attached thereto.

concepts are truly taken over in the regulatory framework or simply paid lip-service.[22] Space constraints do not allow for a discussion of that point in the present paper.

With such a substantive alignment, the dividing line between sector-specific regulation and competition law becomes very thin. It had already become blurred as a result of the expansion of competition law in matters which one would intuitively associate more with the regulatory realm.[23] On the following points, EC competition law evolved throughout the 1990s in such a way that it can now be used to deal with many regulatory matters, such as access and interconnection disputes between market players:

- The rise of the essential facilities doctrine (EFD) provided a basis to address access issues, even in the absence of any dealings between firms. A given facility can therefore be singled out and carved out of a firm, so that the firm can be obliged to give access to it under terms to be specified.[24]
- The principle of non-discrimination has been given a new meaning, involving a comparison not only between the terms and conditions offered by a firm to various third-parties, but also with the terms and conditions offered internally to that firm's own operations within the same market.[25]
- The scrutiny of pricing is no longer marginal (no excessive or predatory pricing), and increasingly rests on a principle of cost-oriented pricing, which requires much more intensive enquiry into costing and accounting.[26]

In addition, given this substantive overlap, competition law has been applied in such a way as to complement, strengthen or foreshadow as the case may be regulatory developments. Such was the case, for instance, with the decisions concerning the so-called telecommunications alliances

[22] On these points, see P. Larouche, 'A Closer Look at Some Assumptions Underlying EC Regulation of Electronic Communications', *Journal of Network Industries* 3 (2002): 129.

[23] These matters were discussed in greater detail in P. Larouche, *Competition Law and Regulation in European Telecommunications* (Oxford: Hart Publishing, 2000).

[24] *Ibid.*, pp. 165–217.

[25] *Ibid.*, pp. 218–31.

[26] *Ibid.*, pp. 231–59.

of the mid-1990s[27] or with the Notice on Access Agreements of 1998.[28] As concerns convergence, the same phenomenon could be observed in two Commission Decisions of 2000, concerning two well-publicised transactions, *AOL/Time Warner*[29] and *Vivendi/Canal/Seagram.*[30] It can be seen that, in both cases, the Commission's analysis rests on the assumption that the market will be structured along the lines of a series of content providers and a number of network operators.[31] What is more, those two decisions, through the remedial conditions attached thereto, contribute to realising that assumption. The Commission is keen to ensure that the entities resulting from those mergers are not in a position to use an alleged dominant position concerning content (either music or movies) to favour their operations on relevant markets at the distribution stage (including online music sales, pay-TV and Internet portals). The remedies tend to remove dominance at the content stage (through divestiture or severance of contractual links)[32] and open up access to content to competing operators at the distribution stage.[33]

Universal service

Despite intense debate on the point, it was decided not to change the scope of the Universal Service Obligations (USOs) defined at EC level comprising narrowband access to the fixed network, directory services, public

[27] See in particular Decision 96/546 of 17 July 1996, *Atlas*, 1996 OJ L239/23, Decision 96/547 of 17 July 1996, *Phoenix/GlobalOne*, 1996 OJ L239/57, Decision 97/815 of 14 May 1997, Case IV/M.856, *BT/MCI II*, 1997 OJ L336/1, Decision 97/780 of 29 October 1997, *Unisource*, 1997 OJ L318/1, Decision 97/781 of 29 October 1997, *Uniworld*, 1997 OJ L381/24, Decision of 30 March 1999, Case IV/JV.15, *BT/AT&T*, CELEX No. 399J0015 and Decision 2001/98 of 13 October 1999, Case IV/M.1439, *Telia/Telenor*, 2001 OJ L40/1.

[28] Notice on the application of the competition rules to access agreements in the telecommunications sector, 1998 OJ C265/2.

[29] Decision of 11 October 2000, Case COMP/M.1845, *AOL/TimeWarner*, 2001 OJ L268/28.

[30] Decision of 13 October 2000, Case COMP/M.2050, *Vivendi/Canal/Seagram*, 2000 OJ C311/3, CELEX No. 32000M2050.

[31] The Commission's analysis is open to criticism, however: see Larouche, 'Communications Convergence and Public Broadcasting', note 8 above.

[32] AOL/Time Warner was forced to abandon a proposed merger with EMI and to sever links with Bertelsmann. Vivendi/Canal+/Seagram was forced to divest its stake in Fox (BSkyB).

[33] Vivendi/Canal+/Seagram was obliged, for a limited period, to limit Canal's intake of movie rights to 50 per cent of Universal's output and to make PolyGram's music available to all distribution channels on a non-discriminatory basis. No such conditions were imposed by the European Commission in the case of AOL/TimeWarner.

phones and measures for disabled users[34] so as to include broadband services within them.[35] Of course, the EC-level USO is not exhaustive: Member States may still decide to impose USOs as concerns broadband services on their own account. Yet, should they choose to do so, EC law constrains their policy options as regards financing mechanisms to compensate for possible extra costs linked to USOs. For USOs outside the scope of the basket defined at EC level, only direct compensation from public funds is available, to the exclusion of any industry-wide sharing mechanisms, such as a universal service fund.[36]

Content regulation

In the EC, contrary to the regulation of electronic communications, content regulation has not kept up with the pace of evolution of the sector. Directive 89/552/EEC[37] remains the mainstay of content regulation, but it concerns only television broadcasting. A good argument can be made that its main provisions, dealing with European content requirements, advertising rules and the protection of minors, are closely linked to a technical model where a limited number of broadcasters prepare programmes and distribute them to the general public.[38] In a context of convergence, should these provisions be maintained as they are, they will probably not be applicable to a number of actors who compete directly with broadcasters, thus jeopardising the achievement of the public policy objectives which underpin them and potentially putting traditional broadcasters at a competitive disadvantage. If on the other hand it appears desirable to adapt these provisions, one might find it impossible to design equivalent legal devices in a broader sector where classical broadcasting is but one technical formula competing with a number of others.

[34] Now to be found in the Universal Service Directive, note 17 above, Articles 3–7.

[35] That issue is to be revisited in 2005: Universal Service Directive, note 17 above, Article 15.

[36] This follows from the Universal Service Directive, note 17 above, Article 13(1) and (2).

[37] Directive 89/552/EEC of 3 October 1989 ('Television Without Frontiers'), 1989 OJ L298/23.

[38] For instance, Article 4 of Directive 89/552/EEC, *ibid.*, states that broadcasters are to reserve 'a majority proportion of their transmission time' to European works. Similarly, Articles 10 (general rules on advertising), 11 (placements of advertising) and 18 (amount of advertising) all rest upon concepts such as 'programme' and 'transmission time'. Article 22 on the protection of minors similarly relies on a traditional view of broadcasting.

The Commission had at first given priority to the review of telecommunications legislation, indicating that it intended to conduct a thorough revision of content regulation at the end of 2003.[39]

Institutional dimensions

In parallel to these substantive changes, the institutional framework must also be rethought against the background of convergence. There are two dimensions to this exercise. On the one hand, the *horizontal* institutional organisation includes questions such as (i) whether, and if so which, specific authorities might be created or left in place, and (ii) as the case may be, their relationship with general regulatory authorities, in particular competition authorities.[40] On the other hand, the *vertical* division of competences between authorities at national and supranational level also becomes an issue.

In the EC, the new regulatory framework proves a disappointment in regards to both dimensions. With respect to the horizontal dimension, the Framework Directive does not even require Member States to entrust all the regulatory tasks to one and the same authority.[41] Similarly, it is silent on the relationship between the NRA and the authority in charge of media/broadcasting regulation: some Member States have brought the two together,[42] while others are likely to keep them separate.[43]

Furthermore, Member States must provide for a consultation and co-operation mechanism (including the exchange of information) between

[39] The revision is provided for by Directive 89/552/EEC, *ibid.*, Article 26. See the Communication, 'Principles and Guidelines for the Community's Audio-visual Policy in the Digital Age', COM(1999)657 (14 December 1999). A timetable for the revision of Directive 89/552/EEC is set in the fourth report from the Commission to the Council, the European Parliament, the European Economic and Social Committee and the Committee of the Regions on the application of the Directive 89/552/EEC 'Television Without Frontiers', COM(2002)778 final (6 January 2003).

[40] In the EC, these authorities are usually referred to as national regulatory authorities (NRAs) and national competition authorities (NCAs).

[41] This is implicit from the Framework Directive, note 8 above, Article 3(4) and (6). Member States are only bound to ensure that the respective tasks of the authorities are clearly set out and published.

[42] See for instance the UK with its new Ofcom (Office of Communications Act 2002, c. 11) or Italy, with the *Autorità per le garanzie nelle comunicazioni* (Act of 31 July 1997, GU 177, 31 July 1997).

[43] In Germany, the regulation of telecommunications falls under the jurisdiction of the federal government, while the regulation of broadcasting and media falls under the jurisdiction of the *Länder*, thereby making it difficult to bring the various authorities together.

the NRA and the NCA (national competition authority), but nothing more.[44] Accordingly, within these limited constraints, Member States are free to organise their national institutions as they see fit. Some Member States have chosen to allow the NRA to apply competition law in the telecommunications sector,[45] while others are contemplating the opposite, i.e. integrating the NRA into the NCA.[46] Yet others will probably leave the NRA and NCA as separate entities, as is the case in most Member States now. While such diversity may be in keeping with the principles of subsidiarity and national procedural autonomy, it makes for quite a patchwork of institutions when seen from a pan-European perspective.

As regards the vertical dimension, it was agreed at the outset of the review process leading to the new EC framework that no European Regulatory Authority should be put in place, and that the implementation of EC law and policy should remain in the hands of the Member States. At the same time, it was felt that pan-European co-ordination had to be improved, to avoid NRAs going in all directions. After intense discussion during the legislative process, the Framework Directive was adorned with a co-ordination mechanism which, as a rule, gives the Commission a consultative role when NRAs take important decisions, while leaving it with a veto right over a limited number of key decisions from NRAs.[47] In parallel, the Commission keeps its power to guide and even discipline NRAs through the application of EC competition law, as stated in the 1998 Notice on Access Agreements.[48]

The US response to convergence

In comparison with the EC, the US response to convergence was far more subdued. In general, US authorities, first and foremost the Federal Communications Commission (FCC), have been less proactive than EC authorities. Only in recent times has the FCC's begun to conduct in-depth reflection on the regulation of the converged sector, in a series of

[44] Framework Directive, note 8 above, Article 3(4) and (5).

[45] See the UK Telecommunications Act 1984, c. 12, s. 50.

[46] See the intention of the Dutch government, as set out in *Kamerstukken II*, 2000–2001, 21693, No. 56.

[47] See the Framework Directive, note 8 above, Article 7. The Commission can veto a proposed NRA decision which would stray from the recommended product market definitions or which determines whether to designate certain firms as having SMP.

[48] Note 28 above, para. 30.

proceedings concerning what is presented as 'broadband policy'.[49] The same regulatory principles underlie the FCC's approach in all of these proceedings:

- first, the regulatory authorities must seek to promote the ubiquitous availability of broadband-capable infrastructure to all Americans;
- secondly, broadband includes any platform where communications and computing converge to provide content requiring broadband capacity (i.e. not just cable modem or ADSL technologies);
- thirdly, the regulatory environment must foster investment and innovation; and
- fourthly, regulation should be rationalised so that harmonised rights and obligations are applied to similarly situated services across different technological platforms.

It is already apparent that, while the FCC pushes US regulatory policy in a similar direction to that of the EC, some differences remain. In the following paragraphs, a brief survey will be made of US policy as regards the various elements examined above in relation to the EC.

Structural and definitional issues: regulated and unregulated fields

Whereas the EC struggled with its overall approach, finally opting for separate horizontal layers of regulation concerning content and networks, the main structural and definitional issues in the US were rather more practical. They stemmed from the need to evolve within an already quite complex system of regulatory pigeonholes whose foundations were laid by Congress in the Communications Act and elaborated by the FCC.

The US regulatory framework tends to be articulated around definitions which are often based on technological features. A specific set of rights or obligations is then attached to each definition. Firms whose offerings fall within the definition in question will then be subject to those

[49] These are: (i) FCC, 'Cable Modems', GN Docket 00-185, Declaratory Ruling and NPRM, FCC 02-77 (14 March 2002) (concerning the regulatory treatment of high-speed Internet access over cable); (ii) FCC, 'Incumbent LEC Broadband Telecommunications Services', CC Docket 01-337, NPRM, FCC 01-360 (20 December 2001) (concerning the regulatory treatment of broadband services offered by incumbents); (iii) FCC, 'Triennal Review of LEC Unbundling Obligations', CC Docket 01-338, NPRM, FCC 01-361 (20 December 2001) (concerning unbundling obligations relating to broadband services); and (iv) FCC, 'High-Speed Broadband Internet Access Services', CC Docket 02-33, NPRM, FCC 02-42 (14 February 2002) (concerning more general policy issues relating to broadband services).

rights and obligations. For instance, at a very general level, the Communications Act makes a distinction between common carriers (dealt with in Title II) and users of the radio spectrum (covered by Title III). Accordingly, a large amount of time and energy can be spent on assessing where a given service fits within the various definitions. To continue with the example, telecommunications services have traditionally been found to fall under Title II, whereas wireless broadcasting services have usually been assigned to Title III.

In addition, the FCC has a tendency to fence off new service offerings within regulatory definitions (usually based on technical considerations), even if only for the purposes of determining within which of the broader statutory definitions those service offerings would figure. Accordingly, in the most recent proceedings mentioned before, distinctions are made between wireline broadband Internet access services, cable modem services and similar services provided over other platforms (satellite, terrestrial wireless, power line, etc.).[50]

It will therefore come as no surprise that the proper classification of services in the convergence era is one of the key questions taken up in these proceedings. Historically, in the so-called *Computer* proceedings, the FCC has found that so-called 'enhanced services' fell outside of the scope of its jurisdiction under Title II of the Communications Act.[51] Hence these services are not subject to the extensive sector-specific regulation concerning telecommunications, save for some anti-competitive safeguards.[52] The FCC approach was endorsed by Congress in the Telecommunications Act of 1996.[53] The latter introduced into the Communications Act of 1934 a notion of information services, whose definition and function come very close to 'enhanced services'. Information services consist in 'the offering of a capability for generating, acquiring, storing, transforming, processing, retrieving, utilizing, or making available information via telecommunications'.[54]

[50] See, for instance, the 'High-Speed Broadband Internet Access Services' proceeding, note 50 above, para. 1.

[51] See among other decisions in these proceedings, FCC, 'Computer II', Docket 20828, Final Decision, FCC 80-189, 77 FCC 2d 384 (7 April 1980), 'Computer III', CC Docket 85-229, Report and Order, FCC 86-252, 104 FCC 2d 958 (15 May 1986).

[52] See 'High-Speed Broadband Internet Access Services', note 50 above, paras. 33ff.

[53] Pub. L. No. 104-104, 110 Stat. 56.

[54] 47 USC 153 (20).

So far, the FCC has been inclined to classify newer services based on broadband technology as information services,[55] and thus to place them under a lighter regulatory framework.

Technological neutrality

It is apparent from the regulatory principles mentioned above that the FCC intends to use its powers to make the US regulatory framework technology-neutral. At the same time, the pigeonhole approach described above is difficult to abandon after so many decades. To a certain extent, such an approach is mandated by the Communications Act itself, which as noted above enshrines separate treatment according to specific technological models, as reflected in its main titles, dealing with telecommunications, radio networks and cable systems.

Accordingly, if technological neutrality is achieved, it is more likely to result from an effort by the FCC to tie together those various strands at the implementation level, so that the different technology-based regimes reach similar outcomes, rather than from the deliberate design of the regulatory framework.

The relationship with competition law

In the US framework, the relationship between sector-specific regulation and competition law is not so explicitly articulated as is now the case in the EC. The two legal frameworks compete with one another in a certain way, with antitrust law sometimes stepping in to shake up cosy regulatory relationships, as was the case with the AT&T break-up in 1982.

The US Communications Act (as amended by the Telecommunications Act 1996) is geared towards the forbearance from, or removal of, sector-specific regulation when it is not necessary to ensure that markets are competitive and deliver the anticipated benefits to customers. For instance, the FCC has the general power to refrain from applying the Act or regulations adopted thereunder[56] and must review its regulations every other year.[57] The logical consequence is that the markets where the

[55] The FCC reached that conclusion for broadband services delivered over cable networks in 'Cable Modems', note 50 above, paras. 34–59, and proposed to do the same for delivery over telecommunications networks in 'High-Speed Broadband Internet Access Services', note 50 above, paras. 17–29.

[56] See 47 USC 160.

[57] See 47 USC 161.

FCC chooses to refrain from exerting its jurisdiction or to remove its regulations are then left to be policed by competition law.

Perhaps unsurprisingly, the FCC has then sought both to increase its competence to carry out economic analysis and to show that its work involves more than the kind of assessment conducted under competition law. In recent times, the FCC has sought to assert jurisdiction to conduct a form of merger review, on the basis of its powers under various provisions of the Communications Act.[58] Such a merger review is very much informed by competition law considerations,[59] even though another agency (the Department of Justice or the Federal Trade Commission (FTC)) will normally be responsible for merger review under the Sherman Act in any event.[60] While the FCC responds that it is applying a 'public interest' standard which differs from the examination conducted by the antitrust authorities, in practice this creates questionable duplication. For instance, in *AOL/TimeWarner*, the FCC re-examined the transaction after both the European Commission[61] and the FTC[62] had already cleared it after substantial commitments from the parties. The FCC inquiry did not oblige the parties to wait too long, but they did have to agree to conditions which both the European Commission and the FTC had examined but ultimately declined to impose.[63]

In the end, US law also envisages the phasing-out of sector-specific regulation. In the meantime, while the relationship between competition law and sector-specific regulation in the US is not as articulated as it is in the EC, it seems undeniable that, as in the EC but perhaps less

[58] Starting with *Bell Atlantic/NYNEX*, NSD-L-96-10, Memorandum Opinion and Order, FCC 97-286 (14 August 1997), where the FCC laid out its framework for analysis. It has been applied ever since, despite strong criticism, even amongst the FCC Commissioners. The basis for this merger review process is supposed to lie in the jurisdiction of the FCC, pursuant to sections 214(a) and 310(d) of the Communications Act (47 USC §§ 214(a) and 310(d) respectively), to review the transfer of control of licences, which unavoidably occurs with a merger.

[59] The FCC explains the interplay between its review and antitrust law in, among others, *Worldcom/MCI*, CC Docket 97-211, Memorandum Opinion and Order, FCC 98-225 (14 September 1998) at paras. 8–14.

[60] Pursuant to sections 7 and 11 of the Clayton Act (15 USC §§ 7 and 11). It should be noted that the FCC itself has jurisdiction to apply those provisions (see 15 USC § 21(a)), but that it has preferred to rest its merger review powers on the Communications Act instead.

[61] Decision of 11 October 2000, Case COMP/M.1845, *AOL/TimeWarner*, 2001 OJ L268/28.

[62] FTC, Docket C-3989, *AOL/TimeWarner* (17 April 2001), available at www.ftc.gov. The decision was based on an agreement (consent order) reached in December 2000.

[63] FCC, *AOL/TimeWarner*, CS Docket 00-30, Memorandum Opinion and Order, FCC 01-12 (11 January 2001). See note 89 below.

consciously, the substance of regulation is being infused with ever more elements derived or taken from competition law.

Universal service considerations

From the principles set out above, it can be seen that universal service considerations are central to the FCC approach to broadband (converged) services, in contrast to the position in the EC, where as mentioned previously the new regulatory framework tends to be agnostic on this point.

Nevertheless, the inclusion of such broadband services within the scope of the universal service schemes is still some time away. The FCC monitors the deployment and availability of so-called 'advanced telecommunications capability',[64] but so far it has concluded that progress is adequate, alleviating the need for intervention through broad-based universal service measures.[65]

Content regulation

US law also contains some content regulation, yet of a far less controversial nature than on the European side, dealing with matters such as obscenity and indecency, programming directed at children, fairness in advertising, etc. There is no equivalent to European content requirements or advertising limits.

At the same time, the US rules, like those of the EC, are often premised on the traditional broadcasting model, with reference to programmes or channels. They are therefore equally at risk of being undercut, and their policy objectives undermined, by newer services competing with broadcasting while not following the traditional technical model associated with broadcasting. There is no indication so far that any concrete action has been taken to address that problem.

Institutional dimensions

In the US as well, difficulties arise with respect to both the horizontal and vertical dimensions. As regards the former, the overlap between the

[64] Section 706 of the Telecommunications Act of 1996, note 54 above, mandates the FCC to do so. See most recently FCC, 'Inquiry on Deployment of Advanced Telecommunications Capability', CC Docket 98-146, Third Report, FCC 02-33 (6 February 2002).

[65] See the Third Report, *ibid.*, paras. 133 and 139–40.

FCC and the antitrust enforcement agencies (the Department of Justice and the FTC) was noted earlier, with *AOL/TimeWarner* as an example of questionable duplication of work. A similar situation is likely to be found at state level, between the state Public Utilities Commission (PUC) and the Attorney General (or other person in charge of antitrust enforcement). At this point in time, there is no indication that guidelines of some sort would be adopted to improve the coordination between these organisations.

At the very least, regulatory supervision over the telecommunications and broadcasting sectors at federal level has been entrusted to one and the same agency, the FCC. A recent internal overhaul has improved the coordination between what were previously separate divisions of the FCC dealing with these respective sectors.[66]

While horizontal overlaps have so far resulted mostly in inefficiencies due to delays and duplication, vertical tensions have proved more harmful. The Telecommunications Act of 1996 envisaged a high degree of cooperation between the FCC and its state counterparts, each acting within the limits of the respective constitutional powers of its level of government.[67] Nonetheless, the Act did not settle all matters so conclusively. The first major court battle fought around the Telecommunications Act of 1996 involved a vertical dimension, with a number of state PUCs challenging a series of provisions in the FCC's Local Competition Order,[68] arguing that the FCC had overstepped its jurisdiction and curtailed the freedom of PUCs. The Supreme Court upheld the FCC's jurisdiction in 1999,[69] thereby putting an end to two years of delay in the implementation of the Act.

[66] See www.fcc.gov for more information.

[67] See, for instance, § 254 (47 USC § 254) concerning universal service, which provides for the creation of a Federal-State Joint Board on Universal Service to establish a universal service framework.

[68] FCC, 'Implementation of the Local Competition Provisions in the Telecommunications Act of 1996', CC Docket 96-98, First Report and Order, 11 FCC Rcd 15499 (1996).

[69] *AT&T Corp.* v. *Iowa Utilities Board*, 525 US 366 (1999). In that decision, the Supreme Court invalidated other aspects of the Local Competition Order concerning the unbundling of network elements. Furthermore, in light of the Supreme Court's finding on the jurisdictional issue (reversing the Court of Appeals on that point), the case was remanded to the Court of Appeals for consideration of whether the costing method chosen by the FCC for interconnection pricing (total element long-run incremental cost, or TELRIC) was valid. The Court of Appeals subsequently found that TELRIC was not a valid choice, but on that point the Supreme Court reversed and upheld once more the position of the FCC in its recent decision *Verizon Communications Inc.* v. *FCC* (13 May 2002).

Relevance and significance of EU and US experience at the international level

Developments at the international level are lagging behind those at the domestic or regional level, as described above. The main event in recent years in international telecommunications regulation was the conclusion of the WTO Telecommunications Agreement, the Fourth Protocol to the GATS, in 1997.[70] The WTO thereby made its entry as a central player in international telecommunications regulation, challenging the position of the ITU. Nevertheless, the Fourth Protocol was very much in line with the liberalisation trend of the 1990s, and accordingly it concerned telecommunications in the classical sense, i.e. without anticipating the convergence with neighbouring sectors.

Since then, no major new initiative has been taken. In 2000, the WTO launched a new round of negotiations on services,[71] which was strengthened when the WTO at its ministerial meeting in Doha decided to launch a new comprehensive round of negotiations.[72] As regards telecommunications and broadcasting, convergence is likely to figure as a central theme of the new negotiations. Accordingly, it is interesting to try to draw some conclusions from the EU and US experience, as it was sketched above, for the benefit of the upcoming round of negotiations.

Structural and definitional issues

Looking at the US and the EU approaches to convergence, two different options appear:

1. On the one hand, a more horizontal approach was chosen in the EC, relying on more general concepts and definitions and attempting to avoid the pitfalls of regulatory constructions based on technological definitions. It must be said, however, that some dividing lines are still needed (if only to mark the limits of sector-specific regulation), and the example of the content/network distinction in the new EC regulatory framework shows that they remain difficult to draw.

[70] The Fourth Protocol, as well as other parts of the WTO Agreement that are of particular relevance for telecommunications, are discussed in M. C. E. J. Bronckers and P. Larouche, 'The WTO Regime for Telecommunications Services', in P. Macrory and A. Appleton, eds., *The Kluwer Companion to the WTO* (forthcoming).

[71] The so-called 'built-in agenda', i.e. the subsequent negotiations provided for at Article XIX of the GATS.

[72] See the ministerial declaration, WT/MIN(01)/DEC/1 (20 November 2001).

2. On the other hand, a more vertical or segmented approach is still followed in the US, where individual services are defined separately, often by reference to technological features, and subjected to a specific regulatory framework. This approach entails a considerable risk that gaps or inequities would arise because the evolution of regulation would be lagging behind that of the sector.

In the WTO context, the very structure of the GATS constrains the range of available choices. Indeed, besides a few general commitments (MFN and transparency), the substance of the GATS is to be found in a series of specific commitments made by WTO Members in their respective schedules. In order to structure these schedules, a classification list was issued in the course of the Uruguay Round.[73] It must be underlined that this list is not very precise and left Members the opportunity to define and refine further the various terms included therein.

In that list, converged services figure under a number of headings, including 'telecommunications services' (2.B), 'audio-visual services' (2.C) and 'computer and related services' (1.B). The classification list therefore naturally leads to a distinction between these various service headings, which has only been reinforced through the tensions between the US and the EU as regards the so-called 'cultural exception'.[74] In addition, it cannot be excluded that, due to definitional shortcomings, a gap would arise when it comes to new services which do not fall within the understanding or definition of either of these broad headings: a service like video-on-demand, for instance (either as it was originally conceived or in an Internet-based fashion), might very well fall outside of all of these headings and therefore be subject to no commitments at all.

What is more, these broad headings have sub-headings, for instance no less than fifteen different ones under 'telecommunications services' (2.B.a to 2.B.o), defined essentially along technological lines. In the case of telecommunications, the sub-headings were used in the course of negotiations to introduce a distinction between so-called 'enhanced' or 'value-added' services and 'basic' services, which proved convenient for negotiation purposes.[75] However, this distinction should have been dropped

[73] Services Sectoral Classification List, MTN.GNS/W/120 (10 July 1991).

[74] See notes 97–9 below and the accompanying text.

[75] Essentially, sub-headings 2.C.h to 2.C.n were deemed to constitute 'enhanced' or 'value-added' services, and the other sub-headings (2.C.a to 2.C.g and 2.C.o), basic services. Negotiations on the former were concluded in time for the conclusion of the WTO Agreement in 1994, while the latter remained on the negotiating table until the conclusion of the Fourth Protocol to GATS in 1997.

afterwards. It is taken over from US law, and it has no equivalent purpose in the WTO context.[76] It remains, nonetheless, and it seems set to weather the next round of negotiations.[77]

The WTO Members have generally followed the classification list in scheduling their commitments, but they have used the room left to their discretion in fairly different ways. The EU has decided to rest its commitments on a general definition of telecommunications services, of which the sub-headings would only constitute illustrations.[78] The US has rather chosen to include a general definition of enhanced services,[79] but to leave basic services to be defined by reference to the list of sub-headings, without any overarching concept.[80]

In the light of the preceding paragraphs, it will have become apparent that the very structure of GATS scheduling can create an obstacle to the proper treatment of convergence under the WTO. With its numerous headings and their further sub-divisions, the GATS scheduling model is more likely to lead to finely distinguished than to broader commitments. There is much to be said for the more global approach of the EU in its telecommunications schedule, but it is doubtful whether it can be replicated at a higher level by fusing the telecommunications and audiovisual commitments into a coherent whole. Given the inertia acquired by the classification list, major changes seem unlikely, all the more since they might open the door to indirect modifications of existing commitments.

Technological neutrality

As was mentioned above, the principle of technological neutrality remains somewhat vague, but most will agree that the regulatory framework should seek to avoid being caught in a technological trap.

Should the principle of technological neutrality be taken up in the WTO context, a number of issues would arise.

[76] See Bronckers and Larouche, 'The WTO Regime', note 71 above.

[77] See *ibid.* The US appears to be insisting on the distinction between basic and value-added services in its proposals for the next round of negotiations: Communication from the United States, Market Access in Telecommunications and Complementary Services, S/CSS/W/30 (18 December 2000).

[78] See the third supplement to the EC Schedule of Specific Commitments, GATS/SC/31/Suppl.3 (14 April 1997).

[79] See the US Schedule of Specific Commitments, GATS/SC/90 (15 April 1994).

[80] See the second supplement to the US Schedule of Specific Commitments, GATS/SC/90/Suppl.2 (11 April 1997).

First, the very structure of the GATS schedules is not conducive to technological neutrality, as was noted above. Despite official invitations to the contrary,[81] for instance, a number of members, including the EU and the US,[82] still saw fit to schedule their commitments concerning mobile communications separately from those concerning fixed telecommunications. Fortunately, at least in the case of the EU and the US, the commitments concerning fixed and mobile services are identical in substance, so that a separate listing does not create any technological barriers.

Secondly and perhaps more significantly, the precise manner in which a principle of technological neutrality would be translated into the GATS framework remains uncertain. Broadly speaking, in the telecommunications sector, such a regulatory principle could have an impact in three different ways:

1. It could help to identify regulatory measures that create a restriction on access or national treatment, within the meaning of the criteria set out in Articles XVI (market access) and XVII (national treatment) of the GATS. These measures would then have to be listed in the schedules of specific commitments, otherwise they would be in breach of the GATS.
2. It could rank as part of the regulatory disciplines imposed through Article VI of the GATS. These disciplines concern regulatory measures that do not fall under Articles XVI and XVII of the GATS, but nonetheless affect the position of suppliers of services. In that sense, Article VI of the GATS imposes limits on what a state can do once it decides (in its discretion) to intervene.
3. It could also be part of the regulatory measures that are necessary to give meaning to the specific commitments regarding market access (Article XVI of the GATS) and national treatment (Article XVII of the GATS), such as are listed in the Reference Paper attached as an additional commitment (pursuant to Article XVIII of the GATS) by most signatories to the Fourth Protocol. For example, the obligations listed in the Reference Paper concerning competitive safeguards, interconnection and the independence of the regulatory authority go much beyond regulatory disciplines, and actually create a positive obligation on the part of the signatories to put in place certain regulatory provisions which are

[81] See the Note by the Chairman of the Group on Basic Telecommunications, S/GBT/W/2/Rev.1 (16 January 1997).

[82] See their respective revised Schedules of Commitments, notes 79 and 81 above.

seen as essential to ensuring that market access and national treatment commitments are not frustrated by private action.[83]

At this point in time, technological neutrality has not reached such a significance that departures from it would breach Articles XVI or XVII of the GATS. It does not fall within any of the items on the black list of Article XVI on market access. As for Article XVII on national treatment, it would come into play if measures were to depart from technological neutrality in such a way that they would favour local suppliers to the detriment of suppliers from other WTO Members, or distort competition so as to reach that result.[84] While this could happen in individual cases, measures with a technological slant generally affect local and foreign suppliers alike. Furthermore, in order to justify a mention in the specific commitments of a WTO Member, departures from technological neutrality in breach of Article XVII would have to reach a systemic level.

Rather, it might be more appropriate to introduce technological neutrality as a regulatory discipline within the meaning of Article VI of the GATS. In that sense, it would be a consequence of the general principles listed in that Article and currently elaborated within the GATS, such as objectivity, necessity, proportionality and non-discrimination. Under that interpretation, WTO Members would then have to ensure that whatever domestic regulation they choose to put in place complies with technological neutrality, i.e. treats the various technological avenues and solutions on the same footing. While this could be seen as a desirable development, some room should be left for departures which are necessary to achieve other public policy goals, such as the establishment of effective competition,[85] universal service, access to certain cultural and/or public affairs content, etc.[86]

Beyond that, technological neutrality could also be a candidate for inclusion in a complementary or revised Reference Paper containing additional commitments. The Members undertaking such commitments would then be positively obliged to take measures to ensure technological

[83] Essentially, action on the part of 'major suppliers', i.e. in practice the incumbent.

[84] See Article XVII(1) and (3) of the GATS.

[85] Which may be hindered by the presence of dominant players under one technological option but not another, as is still often the case with fixed and mobile telephony.

[86] In this respect, Article VI(4)(b) of the GATS already seems to allow some flexibility when it allows requirements which are 'not more burdensome than necessary to ensure the quality of the service'. However, arguably, quality of service is too narrow a concept to encompass the kind of objectives listed in the main text.

neutrality. At this point in time, this would appear to exaggerate the significance of that principle.

Thirdly, in practical terms, including technological neutrality within the GATS framework concerning telecommunications and media could have considerable implications for standardisation and frequency allocation. With respect to the former, any standardisation decision would be very closely scrutinised, since they almost always imply a choice of one technology over the available alternatives. Not only would the actual choices be open to challenge, as is already envisaged,[87] but the very necessity of standardisation could be questioned. In other words, one could argue that technological neutrality should dictate that a WTO Member does not standardise unless that Member can show that it was necessary to do so.[88] While such a spinoff of technological neutrality could be detrimental if it deterred standardisation activity below an optimal level, at the same time it underscores the need for international co-operation in standardisation, as already occurs through numerous bodies. Given the softer nature of international standards in telecommunications and media[89] and the inherent difficulty of agreeing standards at international level, the risk of over-standardisation would appear lower. As regards frequency allocation, it has so far been conducted overwhelmingly with a specific technological bias. Before they are assigned to individual firms, frequency bands are first allocated to specific services: a band reserved for TV cannot be used for mobile communications. A technologically neutral approach to frequency allocation would seek rather to distribute the

[87] Under Article VI of the GATS, disciplines to be negotiated within the WTO framework are meant to apply to the choice of standards (Article VI(4)). Until such disciplines are adopted, the Members are already subject to the minimal constraints of Article VI(5) of the GATS.

[88] For example, in the course of the competition law proceedings concerning AOL/TimeWarner, discussed notes 62–4 above and the accompanying text, a number of intervening parties petitioned the various authorities for AOL/TimeWarner to be forced to open up its Instant Messenger (IM) services to messages coming from or going to competing third-party services. In practice, this would have led to some form of standardisation of those services. Both the European Commission and the US Federal Trade Commission refused to do so, finding that this was not necessary, at least from a competition perspective. The FCC, on the other hand, ordered AOL/TimeWarner to open up its IM services. One could then argue that the FCC decision breached the principle of technological neutrality.

[89] For instance, the ITU merely issues recommendations, albeit with a strong persuasive force. More recent standardisation fora, like those concerning the Internet (IETF, etc.), also tend to work more in a consensual and non-binding fashion. Accordingly, a 'bad' standard, either unnecessary or sub-optimal from a technological perspective, is likely to be ignored or sidestepped.

rights to use the frequency spectrum without regard to the purpose for which it would be used.[90] Such an approach is still considered innovative, if not revolutionary. Accordingly, it is probably much too early to seek to mandate that approach using the principle of technological neutrality, but one should not forget the link between the two.

Finally, it was seen above that, in the EU at least, the principle of technological neutrality was used to support the alignment of sector-specific regulation with competition law.

The relationship with competition law

At the international level, the conditions for an alignment of telecommunications regulation with competition law principles are simply not present at the current time, nor will they be realised in the foreseeable future: to wit, there are no established competition law principles at the international level to which regulation could turn for inspiration. Recently, the Doha ministerial conference endorsed the idea of negotiations on a multilateral competition law framework, but starting only in 2005.[91] In any event, the resulting declaration foresees that the substance of such a multilateral framework would be centred around so-called hard-core cartels,[92] without necessarily touching upon those parts of competition law which are more germane to telecommunications and media regulation, namely, the policing of dominant positions. In any event, international competition law principles are unlikely ever to go as far as EC competition law in areas such as access to facilities (including the Essential Facilities Doctrine), non-discrimination or cross-subsidisation and cost-oriented pricing.[93] As outlined above, it is in no small part because of this recent expansion that EC competition law can double as an alternative for sector-specific regulation.

Accordingly, at the WTO level, further developments concerning telecommunications and media will have to make do without a competition law framework to fall back upon. Incidentally, this means that some tensions might arise between WTO law and the laws of those Members whose sector-specific regulation, purposely or not, are being aligned with competition law. The new EC regulatory framework, for one,

[90] This could conceivably be done on a first-come, first-served basis or through auctions.
[91] Note 73 above, paras. 23–5.
[92] *Ibid.*
[93] See notes 23–6 above and the accompanying text.

explicitly makes room for cases where the NRA would have to intervene in order to comply with the EU's obligations under the WTO, even though the new regulatory framework would not justify intervention (or at least intervention of a lesser intensity).[94]

The absence of an international competition law framework does not mean that competition law will not play a role in the evolution of the international regulation of telecommunications and media in the convergence era. Rather, as *AOL/TimeWarner* and other similar cases show, the impetus is more likely to come from the cooperation between domestic competition authorities applying their respective competition laws.

In the end, it would seem that the Reference Paper, and the underlying approach based on sector-specific commitments, are here to stay. It will be interesting to see then if and how the Reference Paper will be further developed to incorporate the experience gathered through the application of the current regulatory framework and of competition law to the telecommunications and media sectors. In this respect, the Reference Paper could provide a useful platform for an alternative to a competition-law-based regulatory framework. Like other first-generation post-liberalisation regulation, the Reference Paper is fairly prescriptive. In order to have more flexibility, and given the unavailability of competition law principles agreed upon at the international level, one could seek to improve it by outlining broad conditions for regulatory intervention, relying on the economic and functional characteristics of the sector instead of competition law concepts. For instance, policy concerns can arise as a result of well-known phenomena such as (i) the control of the means of access to the customer, with high switching barriers for the customer (whether because of costs or technology), or (ii) network effects. Both could then provide a solid foundation to explain and justify regulatory action, without being linked to a specific technology.[95]

[94] See the Access Directive, note 17 above, Article 8(3). This provision covers cases where a firm would qualify as a 'major supplier' within the meaning of the Reference Paper, without having SMP within the meaning of the new regulatory framework (Framework Directive, note 8 above, Articles 14–16). In addition, it is not impossible that WTO obligations would constrain an NRA in the exercise of its discretion as to the appropriate remedies: for instance, the Reference Paper obliges WTO Members to ensure that major suppliers grant interconnection at cost-oriented rates (point 2.2(b)), whereas under the new EC regulatory framework, NRAs have discretion as to whether they will impose such an obligation on SMP operators (Access Directive, Article 8(2)).

[95] On this point, with reference to the new EC regulatory framework, see Larouche, 'A Closer Look', note 22 above.

Universal service

It was seen above that both the USA and the EU are reluctant to change universal service regimes in the light of convergence, for reasons having to do both with subsidiarity (US state or EU Member State authorities have a large role to play in the running of universal service) and with doubts as to the necessity to extend universal service regimes to new converged services (broadband Internet access, etc.).

The universal service provisions of the Reference Paper are very minimal in any event, essentially leaving it to each WTO Member to operate its own universal service regime if it so wishes, subject to regulatory disciplines (transparency, non-discrimination, proportionality, etc.). Accordingly, it is fairly unlikely that discussions would take place on whether and how universal service should evolve in the light of convergence. At the same time, should an important WTO Member, such as the US, the EU or Japan, decide to go ahead with an extension of universal service to broadband Internet access, that Member would very likely complement that decision with a sizeable influx of public financing for the rollout of improved access networks. As a result, the conditions of competition would probably be affected worldwide, which might prompt international discussions on the scope of universal service.

Content regulation

At the international level, content regulation has so far remained off the negotiating table, in great part due to the EU's insistence on the so-called 'cultural exception', which in the area of telecommunications and media services seems far less grandiose in practice than the official rhetoric would sometimes have one believe. In real terms, the EC made no specific commitments regarding audio-visual services.[96] In addition, the EC made an explicit reservation in its telecommunications commitments to the effect that telecommunications does not extend to broadcasting, namely, 'the uninterrupted chain of transmission required for the distribution of TV and radio programme signals to the general public'. Furthermore, the EC expressly noted that its commitments do not cover 'content provision which require[s] telecommunications services for its transport'.[97] This reservation was apparently accepted by other signatories to the Fourth Protocol, although it leaves certain services, for instance the distribution

[96] See the EC Schedule of Specific Commitments, GATS/SC/31 (15 April 1994).

[97] See the third supplement to the EC Schedule of Specific Commitments, note 79 above.

of audio or video files via the Internet, in a grey zone. In contrast, the US entered broad-ranging commitments regarding 'audio-visual services'[98] and made no equivalent reservation on its telecommunications commitments.

As is the case at the domestic level, the current position (leaving content regulation to the WTO Members in practice, for lack of a critical mass of commitments in the area) might be difficult to maintain in a converged world, irrespective of the political situation. First, content regulation designed for the traditional broadcasting environment is hardly applicable to new competing services which do not rely on technical notions such as programmes, broadcasts, etc.; at the same time, leaving current regulation to apply only to traditional broadcasting might lead to undesirable distortions of competition. Secondly, new competing services, such as distributing content over the Internet, video-on-demand, etc., potentially involve a much greater number of sources of content, when compared to the limited and finite number of broadcasters now in existence. Content regulation applied at the source might then become unenforceable without closer international co-operation.

Furthermore, it can be noted that now that the EU, as explained above, decided to introduce internally a single regulatory framework for telecommunications and broadcasting networks and services, doing away with the vertical distinction between telecommunications and broadcasting and replacing it with a horizontal division between content and networks. Against that background, it will be increasingly difficult for the EU to argue for separate treatment of telecommunications and broadcasting/media at the WTO level. The scope of the cultural exception is therefore likely to be questioned.

In part against that background, the US has already indicated that it would like to include the audio-visual sector in the next round of negotiations.[99] The controversy over content regulation in the audio-visual sector is therefore likely to flare up again. This time around, in light of the preceding paragraphs, it seems difficult to envisage an agreement to disagree once more.

Fundamentally, convergence forces a reassessment of the rationale underpinning content regulation. It is submitted that the various content

[98] See the US Schedule of Specific Commitments, note 80 above.

[99] See Communication from the United States, Audiovisual and Related Services, S/CSS/W/21 (18 December 2000).

regulation measures each pertain more to one or the other of the following rationales:

1. On the one hand, content regulation can reflect a concern with the content itself. Such is the case with regulation concerning the protection of minors, of good morals, consumer protection against false or misleading advertising, etc.
2. On the other hand, content regulation could be a response to the specific impact of the means of distribution of the content. Regulation relating to plurality or cultural identity would rather proceed from this rationale. In short, the policy concern here is that the concurrent dispatching of that content to the entire population shapes how that population perceives itself and its surroundings. Hence one might need to ensure that the population is exposed to certain types of content, lest its identity is shaped by the most widely available content items.

The first rationale is hardly affected by convergence. The efficacy of regulation falling under that rationale, however, can be seriously undermined by the increase in the number of sources, hence the need for stronger international cooperation.[100] As for the second rationale, the situation is much different. One of the consequences of convergence is an ever greater fragmentation[101] of the audience, which means that the particular societal impact of broadcasting becomes more rarely felt. Hence one might be led to question the appropriateness of the items of content regulation currently falling under the second rationale, which does not mean that they should be removed altogether, but perhaps that they should be replaced by other means of ensuring the presence and availability of certain content.

For the WTO, a number of consequences can be predicted. First, should there be meaningful discussions regarding content regulation? One will have to agree on how to treat such regulation, i.e. how to classify measures such as prohibitions on certain offensive content, content requirements (or quotas), must-carry rules, etc. As outlined above, three outcomes are possible: (i) an outright incompatibility with market access and national treatment obligations, in which case these measures must be included in schedules of specific commitments; (ii) the inclusion within the broad class of domestic regulation subject to the regulatory disciplines developed under Article VI of the GATS; or (iii) an agreement on positive obligations

[100] Which can already be seen as regards the most grievous cases, such as child pornography.
[101] Beyond that which is already observed with the multiplication of broadcasting programmes and their increased specialisation.

concerning certain content regulation measures, which could then take the form of a supplementary or separate 'Reference Paper'.

Beyond that, on the assumption that the current content regulation measures will have to be replaced, or at least reoriented, in light of convergence, some new issues could find their way to the WTO negotiating table. For instance, should content regulation measures falling under the second rationale be recast in the form of support programmes, how are they to be treated? Can they be reserved to local producers? By the same token, should measures falling under the first rationale migrate away from domestic law towards more self-regulatory instruments, how are these to be dealt with under the GATS framework?

Institutional dimensions

It was seen earlier that, when compared to the developments on the substantive side, neither the EU nor the US has made any significant progress in addressing the institutional dimensions of convergence, namely, the horizontal (coordination among the work of the various authorities involved, be they NRAs, NCAs or media authorities) and vertical ones (co-ordination between central and local authorities). It is unlikely that the situation will be better at the international level.

With respect to the horizontal dimension, the WTO is not in a position to cast itself as either a competition or a regulatory authority, concerned as it is with trade matters first and foremost. The Fourth Protocol and its Reference Paper already threw the WTO on the international regulatory scene, and created some tensions with the ITU. The two institutions now seem to have found a *modus vivendi*. They have concluded a co-operation agreement to formalise their relationship and ensure the co-ordination of their respective activities.[102] It is likely that they will become partners in the management of international telecommunications regulation, with the WTO perhaps focusing on general issues of economic regulation, as well as enforcement, and the ITU taking care of more technical issues, including frequency allocation and standardisation. Similarly, some relationship must be established with other actors on the international regulatory scene, such as the ISO and the various bodies taking care of Internet regulation,[103] as well as regional bodies dealing with broadcasting or media regulation. With respect to competition law, in the absence of

[102] To be found as WTO document S/C/9/Rev.1 (15 June 2000).

[103] Such as the Internet Engineering Task Force (IETF), the various registrars, etc.

an international authority, the WTO will have to ensure some liaison with the most influential domestic authorities (perhaps through the OECD).

As far as the vertical dimension is concerned, it is unlikely that the WTO can go much beyond the general provisions of Article VI of the GATS,[104] together with the content of the Reference Paper, which stipulated that domestic regulatory bodies must be independent and impartial.[105] More precise obligations, including for instance provisions on the jurisdiction of the regulatory authority or coordination mechanisms at international level, appear difficult to envisage. Here, more than is already the case within the EU or the USA, diverging and conflicting interpretations and implementations at the domestic level present a serious threat to the effectiveness of the substantive commitments undertaken at the higher level. The WTO dispute settlement mechanism, while it marks a significant improvement over the previous situation and constitutes one of the greatest achievement of the WTO Agreement, appears ill-suited to the resolution of conflicts in the fast-moving telecommunications and media sectors.

Conclusion

Even though convergence never materialised as planned and the telecommunications and media sectors were shattered in the current economic downturn, it remains likely that convergence will occur, perhaps sooner rather than later. Accordingly, it is quite appropriate to continue reflecting on how law should seek to respond to it adequately.

Convergence challenges legal thinking by doing away with the hermetic technological models which enabled telecommunications and media law to exist as separate and self-contained domains. In addition, it introduces an element of dynamism and uncertainty which the law had not been used to cope with.

This paper discussed a number of central themes surrounding the impact of convergence on law and regulation:

1. the general approach, as it is reflected in the structure of law and regulation and the main concepts used therein;
2. the notion of technological neutrality;

[104] Members must administer regulation reasonably, objectively and impartially (Article VI(1)). They must provide for judicial, arbitral or administrative review of administrative decisions (Article VI(2)). They must ensure that administrative decisions are taken within a reasonable time and communicated to the applicant (Article VI(3)).

[105] See Reference Paper, point 5.'The WTO Regime'.

3. the relationship between competition law and sector-specific regulation;
4. universal service;
5. the future of content regulation; and
6. the institutional dimensions (horizontal and vertical).

An examination of the domestic EU and US response on each of these points showed that these two major WTO Members did not find any simple solutions, to the extent they found any. In particular, the EU sought to be proactive and consistent, and yet its new regulatory framework leaves most issues either open or unsatisfactorily settled. In addition, the EU and US responses are not always consistent with one another.

For the WTO, which has not yet seriously tried to address the convergence issue, this does not bode well. Furthermore, the WTO remains first and foremost a trade law framework. Its structure, including the scheduling classification, creates additional difficulties over and above those already registered at domestic level. It can be seen already in the treatment of telecommunications services in the GATS and its Fourth Protocol that the WTO was being taken outside of its traditional realm and into new areas.[106] Dealing with convergence will only exacerbate that trend.

At the same time, the convergence phenomenon only reinforces the need for stronger international coordination with telecommunications and media regulation. The WTO appears as the natural starting point for such an attempt, but it is unlikely that only the WTO will be involved in the end.

[106] See Bronckers and Larouche, note 71 above.

15

Overcoming the three digital divides

ELI NOAM

Introduction

We find ourselves today at one of those great divides of economic history, where we can either go forward into the unknown, or go back, with a sigh of relief, to familiar territory. The new economy – dot-coms, new-style telecom entrants, new media companies, e-commerce sites etc. – has become an old-style bust. The adults are back in charge. Legacy is in. Balance sheets are in. Blue chips are in. We need not listen anymore to the purveyors of hype, about how bits play by different business rules than atoms, how the silicon economy is different from the carbon one, and how a P/E ratio need not have any E that stands for earnings, as long as that e- stands instead for electronic.

Yet, it would be tragic if we let the pendulum swing too far, or use this breathing space for smug self-satisfaction rather than regrouping, retooling and re-planning. The black ships challenging the old economy may have retreated over the horizon, but they will be back. No temporary slow-down should obscure the fact that we have just gone through something very fundamental.

With Internet connectivity progressing at a dizzying rate, the focus of attention has shifted to those left behind. The short-hand word for this concern is the 'digital divide'. Underlying virtually every discussion about this digital divide in Internet connectivity is the implicit assumption that such a divide is a bad thing, requiring us to 'do something'. But maybe we should first pause for a moment and understand the implications of ending this divide. If we do that, we might end up changing our perspective on Internet policy in an important way: away from a focus on *Internet connectivity*, and towards the creation of *e-commerce*.

For a number of years US administrations have been talking prominently about the digital divide. However, if one looks at the US government's own numbers, one can reach a more hopeful conclusion. With present trends continuing, in a few years Internet connectivity will be near universal in rich countries, like electricity or television. A major reason is that the access mechanisms to the Internet will have changed and become user-friendly or user-independent. The Internet will soon be liberated from the complex gateway bottleneck of the personal computer, arguably the least friendly consumer mass product ever made. There will be many other gateways to the Internet, such as regular phones or TV sets. Therefore, for the rich world the universality of narrowband Internet connectivity will not be an issue.

It is most likely that an Internet differentiation will emerge along dimensions of *quality*. High-speed broadband Internet access requires an upgrade of the infrastructure – whether telecom, cable or wireless – which must be recovered through higher prices. Income, location and demand will be factors for bandwidth consumption. Broadband will therefore be the digital divide issue for wealthy countries. Yet, one cannot expect that high-speed Internet access (most likely used by consumers primarily for video applications) would command the same societal priority as the basic type of Internet service.

But the transformation in rich countries of the divide into a gentle slope does not mean that the issue will not last and persist for the poor countries of the developing world. And in an interdependent world this becomes a problem not just for the South, but also for the North, because such a gap will inevitably lead to international conflict.

In talking about the Internet for poor countries, it is easy to feel like a modern-day Marie Antoinette. Let them eat laptops. Of course the Internet is important. But is it really a priority? The answer is yes, because tomorrow's problems originate in today's actions and omissions. There is no luxury to solve other problems first. The world does not stand still and wait.

Spain and Portugal, the first European colonisers of the New World, were the world's leaders in shipping, which was the primary communications technology in the sixteenth and seventeenth centuries. They had the best vessels, navigation equipment, maps, seafaring skills and weapons. This combination catapulted the Iberian region to prosperity. And yet, by the eighteenth century, these countries had fallen behind England in industrial hardware and scientific software. They missed the next revolution, and centuries later have yet to catch up.

Today we are at the beginning of another revolution, driven by the Internet, and the question is: what is the cost of falling behind this time?

It is important to distinguish between three kinds of gap. The first gap is that of *telecommunications connectivity*. This gap is being closed by investment in infrastructure and by liberalising policy reform. In consequence, the telephone penetration of the developing countries has been improving. Governments have been making telecom connectivity a priority. Overcoming this gap is therefore something that engineers, investors and governments now know how to do. But progress in telecom connectivity, difficult as it may be, will prove to be the easy part.

The second type of gap is that of *Internet access*. In 2000, only 3% of Internet computer hosts were domiciled in non-OECD countries. Telecom and Internet are related, of course. Internet usage is much more expensive in developing countries, both relative to income and in absolute terms. For an ISP in Argentina, to lease a T-1 equivalent capacity (~1.5 Mbps) line from a phone company cost, in 1999, fifty times as much as it did in the US. Of course, progress is being made in Internet connectivity, too. For Latin America, growth exceeds 50% annually. But closing this gap, too, will prove to be, relatively speaking, an easy task. In fact, it is easier to overcome this gap than the one in telecom infrastructure. Once telephone lines exist, it is not very difficult to connect a computer or a simple Internet device to them. Specific policies to encourage Internet usage include to establish flat-rate telecom pricing on local calls; to accept widespread use of IP telephony; to create public Internet access points such as kiosks at public places, government departments or post office; and to use e-mail for some government business with citizens.

Internet connectivity does not take care of the third and critical gap, which is that of *e-commerce*. In fact, progress in overcoming the first and second gaps may exacerbate the third gap. Today, developing countries account for only 5% of world commercial websites and receive only 2.4% of world Internet commerce revenues. In contrast, twelve countries will account for almost 85 percent of e-commerce and eight countries will account for 80% of e-content.

To understand why this is so, let us make three observations about the global dynamics of e-transactions:

1. the price of international transmission is dropping rapidly;
2. domestic internet penetration is increasing rapidly; and
3. most e-commerce applications have strong economies of scale.

Low-cost global transmission leads to a large rise in electronic transactions with consequences for business. Of course, traditional ways of doing business will not disappear, just as the mom-and-pop store did not vanish when supermarkets emerged. But the energy and dynamism will be in electronic modes of commerce. And here, US firms will be the most successful. They will be technologically at the leading edge, with risk capital at their disposal, with the advantage of being an early entrant and having a large home market. Once a firm establishes a successful model for the US market, invests the fixed costs, and secures nearly non-existent transmission prices, there is no reason to stop at the border.

The implications are that e-commerce will be dominated by firms from the US and other electronically advanced countries. Closing the first two gaps therefore exacerbates the third gap by creating the highways and instrumentalities for rich countries to sell in poor countries.

Of course, it is not purely a one-way street. The Internet also provides poor countries with opportunities to participate and share information. We have all heard stories about how a local craftsman in a remote village can now access the world market for his woodcarvings. True, for certain types of product marketing becomes easier. But for most mass products, the complexities of sophisticated e-commerce sites are great. These complexities are greater still for information products and services and will be even greater in a broadband internet environment where the production costs of attractive e-sites are high.

What counts is not absolute but relative cost reductions, relative advantage of e-commerce go to advanced countries. One lesson we have learned the hard way is that it is expensive to do e-commerce well. E-commerce operations are difficult. They are vastly more involved than running a website and a shopping cart. Many systems need to be in place and integrated. Some elements needed are supply chain EDI (electronic data interchange), payment systems, integration with financial institutions, fulfilment systems, customer data mining, production, customisation, community creation and the creation of consumer lock-in by additional features. Intermediaries need to be reshaped. Processes are accelerated domestically and internationally, at lightning speed, great reliability, easy scalability, and flexibility of configuration.

What are some of the implications?

Instead of being that frictionless competitive capitalism rhapsodised about by many people, many parts of the new economy will actually be a fortress of market power. Economies of scale are returning. On the supply side, the fixed costs of e-commerce operations tend to be high, but the variable cost of spreading the service to the entire world is relatively low – the classic attributes of a 'natural' monopoly. On the demand side, there are 'positive network externalities' of having large user communities. Put these three things together – high fixed costs, low marginal costs and network externalities – and there are real advantages to being large.

All of this is still true for the emerging broadband Internet. The costs for consumer e-commerce sites will rise considerably. Text and still images will not be sufficient in a competitive environment and expensive video and multimedia will be required.

This low share has been disturbing. For several centuries, culture flowed largely in one direction: out of Europe, and to the colonies and the rest of the world. Then, after World War I, the flow reversed direction for the young medium of film. Around the world, audiences flocked to Hollywood movies. European cultural elites, shocked at the loss of control over their publics, led a counter-charge. They promoted protectionism to support centuries-old national cultures against a few vaudeville theatre promoters who had pitched their tents in Hollywood. But, despite seven decades of effort, this challenge remains.

And now, a new medium is knocking – television over the internet – and the question is what will enter when the door is opened. Will it be a multicultural richness of many national sources or will it be more Hollywood?

The knee-jerk response to this question is to invoke Internet platitudes. Anybody can enter, you can't tell a dog on the Internet, a bit is a bit, silicon economics are different from carbon economics, Internet penetration is higher in Finland than in the US, etc. It is as if the Internet community, staunchly internationalist and multicultural by outlook and background, does not want to face the very question of whether it contributes to the further ascendancy of US mass culture.

For electronic media, transmission technology is destiny: it affects format, content and economics. It used to be expensive to move information; now it is cheap. We can do old things in new ways, new things in old ways, and new things in new ways.

So now we are in the midst of an historic move: from the *kilobit* stages of individualised communications to the *megabit* stage, and within the foreseeable future, to the *gigabit* stage. The implications of this transition are as great as the change from a horse-and-cart system and railroads to automobiles and airplanes had been in the twentieth century.

Let us analyse the relative costs of audio-visual media. Each form of delivery has its specific cost characteristics, which have implications. These calculations will be order-of-magnitude only.

Internet TV

The cost of Internet TV content is hard to estimate. It includes a lot of low-budget, experimental, volunteer TV programmes. There is a significant need to keep costs down, especially in the early stages. At the same time, the whole point of Internet TV is to be more than standard, linear TV. The whole point is interactivity, multimedia and new creation. The interactivity and multimedia aspects of the medium require additional features beyond straight video. And, after an initial amateur period, competition will soon be fierce for audiences, and commercial providers of Internet TV will have to offer quality content. Therefore, once broadband Internet is available to most households and once people will consider it nightly among their entertainment options, it cannot possibly be produced cheaply.

Hence, the programme cost of original content that is not merely the replay or retransmission of traditional video will be no lower than that of linear cable TV, and will more likely be higher. Distribution costs are 1.85 m¢ per second and user.[1] This is forty times higher than the distribution cost per cable channel. The reason is that individualisation requires significantly larger transmission resources. A similar disadvantage exists in another synchronous mass-audience medium, broadcast TV, where the ratio is 1:27. Hence, Internet TV can function economically only as a premium medium or a specialised medium. This defines several types of application.

The use of the Internet purely as a distribution medium

Internet TV for video-on-demand (VOD)

Delivery of films, at the very top of the distribution chain, occurs immediately after cinema distribution and maybe even ahead of it (there is probably no better way to generate a worldwide buzz for a movie than distribution of it through the Internet). It is more expensive to distribute than cable and TV, but viewers can be charged more, in a more differentiated way.

[1] Based on US $40/mo for a 1 Mbps internet channel.

Specialised programmes

Thin and specialised audiences that would not be served by synchronous TV would be amenable to specialised programmes. For example, those desiring to watch TV programmes in Hungarian, or soccer matches of their home team in Stockholm while they are vacationing in Spain, or on specialised topics would be well served by Internet TV.

Office viewing

Perhaps the most popular use of Internet TV might be by office workers who cannot watch broadcast or cable TV. The economics of all three types of such content delivery depends on the size and willingness-to-pay of such audiences. Content would often be already produced – e.g. Hungarian soccer on TV – and would reach wider audiences. Only if such audiences become a significant factor are they likely to affect the content itself and its production budget.

The use of the Internet as a storage medium : archived programmes

Old video and film become accessible by viewers as they link to servers that store them. The content costs for such programmes have already been incurred. Archive access would benefit, in particular, documentaries, because they tend to depreciate more slowly than most entertainment programmes.

Use of the Internet as an interactive medium

Interactive content supplementary to one-way distribution

Here, a two-way channel is added to a one-way broadcast programme, enabling the viewer to obtain additional information about the main programme, or, more likely, to engage in commercial transactions.

Interactivity and multimedia applications

This includes using the medium in ways that cannot be done over regular, one-way TV. This content type is the main innovative aspect of Internet TV, and should be our main focus. It enables new genres of programmes rather than merely a more flexible access to traditional programmes. It is, however, also by far the most expensive content to produce, both because it cannot fall back on existing content, and because it requires complex designs and software programming.

Furthermore, it is the major form of content that can prevail economically due to its uniqueness, against established and upgraded channels such as those of cable TV. This will be developed further now.

Basic economics drives applications

Our previous analysis showed that the cost advantages of cable-style distribution over Internet-style distribution are significant, by a factor of about forty. The increased efficiency and declining cost of fibre does not mean that all pipes will become individualised. This is a common mistake made by people who argue that transmission is becoming cheap. It drops just as much for cable TV distribution. The relative cost of shared (synchronous) transmission is still much lower than that of non-shared, asynchronous transmission. At best, the two will coexist, with the individualised Internet channels providing the premium offerings. At worst, Internet TV will never become competitive enough to be a mass medium and will remain a niche offering.

What the drop in cost means, however, is that the impact of distance becomes much less and that both synchronous and asynchronous networks can be designed for national and global distribution rather than for local distribution. This means that terrestrial TV loses the protection of distance, and that satellite and cable TV lose the protection of limited spectrum on licensing.

From the numbers it is quite clear that one would not want to use Internet TV for regular video content distribution. For that purpose, cable TV and its fibre digital variants will be much cheaper. Internet TV's market is for applications that go beyond regular TV: distant, specialised, archived, interactive, asynchronous, linked, multimedia.

To produce such interactive content is expensive. It requires creativity, lots of programmers, and significant alpha and beta testing, and many new versions. It might be a bit like *Dungeons and Dragons* meets *Baywatch* meets *Survivor*. It also exhibits strong economies of scale on the content production side, and network externalities on the demand side. Both favour content providers that can come up with big budgets, diversify risk, distribute also over other multiple platforms, create product tie-ins, and establish global user communities.

Even for non-premium programme, such as creative small productions, or sex-shows and games – where the absolute production costs are lower, the economic advantages of a large user base still apply.

And these requirements will favour US companies when Internet TV emerges as a serious offering. The US has a large Internet community, significant hardware and software entrepreneurial energy barely contained by the recent economic downturn, a financial system that provides risk capital, big content-producing companies with worldwide distribution and with experience in reaching popular audiences, talent in content creativity and technology from all over the world, efficient geographic clusters in production and technology, the cultural prowess of the world's superpower, language, a diverse culture, and a university system that generates technology and entrepreneurship. These factors are also available elsewhere, but probably nowhere else in such a combination. On the other hand, the US lacks the supportive mechanism of public TV that exists in Europe and Japan.

Thus, the medium of Internet TV combines the strengths of the US economy and society in entertainment content, Internet, and e-transactions. Add to that economies of scale, and there is nothing on the horizon that can match it. And, therefore, Internet TV will be strongly American. Participants from other countries will also be players, but most likely either domestically without much global reach, or global players who will offer basically American-style content to the world, like sitcoms and the Italian 'spaghetti westerns' of the past.

The Internet is a revolution, and it is a characteristic of revolutions that they create many losers – banks will be threatened by electronic global financial institutions; universities will find their students migrating to distance education; TV broadcasters will be bypassed by global Hollywood video servers; etc. Most institutions will be losing the protection of distance, and will be exposed to world markets.

It is characteristic of losers, especially if they are domestically still large and powerful, to seek protection through the political sphere. And, therefore, there will be an inevitable global political backlash against e-commerce. This is likely to take the form of restrictions, by countries on the wrong side of the e-commerce gap. And there will be a strong likelihood for international cyber-trade wars.

Centuries ago, in Spain, the powers resisting the industrial revolution and its reshaping of domestic power were the Church, the State, and agricultural economic interests. They won out, and Spain was slowed on the road to industrialisation. A similar scenario will play itself out as we enter the digital economy, and as the losers begin to organise themselves.

The main alternative to future conflicts over cyber-trade and the best remedy for the gap in e-commerce is for developing countries to create progress in e-commerce that makes the electronic highways into two-way routes. But what can a developing country do, concretely? This is much more difficult than catching up with telecom densities, because it is a question of general societal modernisation, not just of an infrastructure construction programme.

There is no single strategy, no silver bullet. But here are several suggested elements.

1. Telecom policy of entry and investment based on market forces and competition.
2. Use the government as the lead user, to help create domestic critical mass and experts. The US military had been successful in getting the Internet started initially. Government operations such as procurement should move to the web. This would create transparency, reduce procurement costs, and force domestic suppliers to move to electronic marketing. Governments could also provide some services electronically, such as the filing of forms and applications, or information on subjects such as health, education, taxes and agriculture.
3. Be prepared to ignore domestic consumer markets. It takes too much time to develop them. The focus should instead be on the global market, mostly business-to-business. The domestic consumer market is relatively small, but the global internet market is huge and open. The creation of free trade zones for e-commerce is one concrete step in that direction.
4. Develop niche markets. Leverage cultural proximity. Examples could include:
   - regional hub: Tunisia for North Africa;
   - language: Brazil for Portuguese speakers;
   - religion: Saudi Arabia for Moslems; and
   - economics: Bahrain for the oil industry.
5. Reform the legal system to make e-transactions possible. The recognition of digital signatures is an example. Adapt commercial codes to online environments and update rules applying to liability, contract, privacy and security issues. Examples include the UNCITRAL Model Law (1996), and the ITU EC-DC project. It is also essential to combat

the fraud, illegal operations and piracy that undercut the emergence of a domestic industry.

6. Strengthen the physical delivery infrastructure and investments in it. One cannot sell abroad if one cannot ship quickly. This is one of the secrets of Singapore's success. This includes the physical delivery infrastructure of harbours, airports and export facilities.
7. Strengthen the investment climate. Provide tax incentives for e-commerce and e-exports, offer low international telecom rates, support micro-credit institutions, encourage local entrepreneurship and cooperatives, and support the venture capital industry and incubators.
8. Support technological education. Investments are important, but not as important as IT skills and a new economy mindset. There are 3.8 R&D scientists and technicians per 1,000 people in developed countries and only 0.4% per 1,000 in developing countries.
9. Create wealth incentives. Permit e-commerce entrepreneurs to become rich through the Internet, thereby fuelling the emergence of local start-ups.
10. Encourage foreign investments.
11. Provide back-office functions to major e-commerce sites as a way to establish experience. India and Jamaica are examples.

Most well-informed people understand the importance of e-commerce. But they often do not have a sense of urgency. Right now, the foundations are being laid for a great new economic system and for a new generation of business empires. Even if less developed countries cannot be expected to be among the leaders, there are enough emerging countries and striving firms that could be suppliers and not only buyers. India, for example, may be a poor country by most measures, yet it could become an e-commerce participant beyond its growing Internet technology role.

Success in e-commerce means participation in modernisation, but also participation in the disruptions brought about by modernisation. The Internet will lead to less stability, more fragmentation and less consensus. But the alternative is much less palatable. Failure to participate in global e-commerce means fundamental long-term economic stagnation.

Different countries are affected differently, depending on, among other things, their economic mix. The US had a troubled industrial sector, and the new economy was one way to resume growth. US society is also capable of change, being perhaps strongest in situations of accelerating change – 'second derivative' situations. In contrast, Europe and Japan had stronger old economies, and are stronger in managing steady growth – 'first derivative' economies. And less developed countries had, for a multitude of reasons, the greatest difficulties in changing to new economy activities, primarily because these require substantial societal modernisation and infrastructure investments.

This is then the challenge to developing countries. To get moving, to move beyond the first gap, that of telecommunications, by overcoming the traditional policy squabbles about the rights of entrants and the privileges of incumbents – issues that will seem in a few years quite trivial – and to close the second gap, that of the Internet. They should also deal aggressively with the closing of the e-commerce gap, because it is the real, critical and fundamental threat – as well as a major opportunity – to them and a way to improve economic relations around the world.

INDEX